Combat Trauma and the Ancient Greeks

The New Antiquity

Edited by Matthew S. Santirocco

Over the past two decades, our understanding of the ancient world has been dramatically transformed as classicists and other scholars of antiquity have moved beyond traditional geographical, chronological, and methodological boundaries to focus on new topics and different questions. By providing a major venue for further cutting-edge scholarship, *The New Antiquity* will reflect, shape, and participate in this transformation. The series will focus on the literature, history, thought, and material culture of not only ancient Europe, but also Egypt, the Middle East, and the Far East. With an emphasis also on the reception of the ancient world into later periods, *The New Antiquity* will reveal how present concerns can be brilliantly illuminated by this new understanding of the past.

MATTHEW S. SANTIROCCO is Senior Vice Provost for Undergraduate Academic Affairs at New York University, where he is Professor of Classics and Angelo J. Ranieri Director of Ancient Studies, and he served for many years as Seryl Kushner Dean of the College of Arts and Science. He taught previously at the University of Pennsylvania, Columbia, Brown, Emory, and Pittsburgh. He is the former editor of the American Philological Association Monograph Series, *American Classical Studies* and the journal *Classical World*. His publications include a book on Horace, as well as several edited volumes and many articles. In 2009, he was elected a Fellow of the American Academy of Arts and Sciences and is currently Assistant Secretary of the Academy for Humanities and Social Sciences.

Published by Palgrave Macmillan:

Horace and Housman by Richard Gaskin
Combat Trauma and the Ancient Greeks edited by Peter Meineck and David Konstan

Selected Previous Publications

Peter Meineck
The Electra Plays with Paul Woodruff, Celia Eaton Luschnig, and Justina Gregory (2010)
Sophocles: Four Tragedies with Paul Woodruff (2007)
Sophocles: The Theban Plays with Paul Woodruff (2003)
Aeschylus: Oresteia (1998)
Aristophanes 1: Clouds, Wasps, Birds (1998)

David Konstan

Before Forgiveness (2010)
The Emotions of the Ancient Greeks (2006)
Pity Transformed (2001)
Friendship in the Classical World (1997)

Combat Trauma and the Ancient Greeks

Edited by
Peter Meineck
and
David Konstan

First published in 2014 by
PALGRAVE MACMILLAN®
in the United States—a division of St. Martin's Press LLC,
175 Fifth Avenue, New York, NY 10010.

Where this book is distributed in the UK, Europe and the rest of the world, this is by Palgrave Macmillan, a division of Macmillan Publishers Limited, registered in England, company number 785998, of Houndmills, Basingstoke, Hampshire RG21 6XS.

Palgrave Macmillan is the global academic imprint of the above companies and has companies and representatives throughout the world.

Palgrave® and Macmillan® are registered trademarks in the United States, the United Kingdom, Europe and other countries.

ISBN: 978–1–137–39885–7

Library of Congress Cataloging-in-Publication Data

    Combat trauma and the ancient Greeks / edited by Peter Meineck and David Konstan.
       pages cm—(New antiquity)
    Includes bibliographical references and index.
    ISBN 978–1–137–39885–7 (hardback : alk. paper)
      1. Greek literature—History and criticism. 2. Post-traumatic stress disorder in literature. I. Meineck, Peter, 1967– II. Konstan, David. III. Series: New antiquity.

PA3015.P67C66 2014
880.9′3581—dc23   2014011518

A catalogue record of the book is available from the British Library.

Design by Newgen Knowledge Works (P) Ltd., Chennai, India.

First edition: September 2014

10 9 8 7 6 5 4 3 2 1

Not even sleep can relieve the painful memories
That fall upon the heart, drop by drop

Aeschylus, *Agamemnon* 179–80

CONTENTS

FIGURES

PREFACE

This volume of essays grew from a conference entitled *Combat Trauma and the Ancient Stage* held at New York University in April 2011. This two-day event was part of a national public program led by Aquila Theatre, in partnership with the Center for Ancient Studies at New York University, the American Philological Association, and the Urban Libraries Council, that received a Chairman's Special Award grant from the National Endowment for the Humanities, called *Ancient Greeks/Modern Lives*. This program visited one hundred communities across the United States and used staged readings by professional actors of ancient Greek tragedy and Epic, moderated by scholars and followed by open "town-hall" style meetings to bring together members of the American veteran community with the public to explore issues related to war and society. *Ancient Greeks/Modern Lives* also staged hundreds of public talks, drama workshops, and reading groups at public libraries, arts centers, museums, community centers, and military bases and placed new sets of books of translations of Greek drama and Epic in one hundred American public libraries. In 2012, the program was invited to represent the National Endowment for the Humanities at a special performance at the White House, where a combined group of American veterans and actors read scenes from Aeschylus' *Agamemnon*, Sophocles' *Ajax,* Euripides' *Herakles,* and Homer's *Odyssey*.

We were struck at how modern American veterans and their families that came to *Ancient Greeks/Modern Lives* programming frequently responded to hearing these ancient stories told again—as if the classic works conveyed an acknowledgment of the kind of extremes faced by many men, women, and children who have experienced the devastation of combat and war (Meineck 2010; Buxton and Painter 2010). Many of the scholars who participated in the program also noted the effectiveness of ancient material, albeit in translation, to inspire the frank and honest discussion of very difficult subjects, as men and women told their own stories of war, sometimes for the very first time in public. Subsequently these observations led to a series of scholarly questions that formed the basis for our conference and this book: Do these ancient works reflect the issues of warfare and its aftereffects? If so, were the ancient Greeks aware of what we now call "Combat Trauma," but has also been variously termed, "Combat Stress Reaction" (Iraq and Afghanistan); "Post Traumatic Stress Disorder" (Vietnam); "Battle

Fatigue" (World War II); "Shell Shock" (World War I); and "Soldier's Heart" (American Civil War)? Can we detect responses to Combat Trauma in ancient Greek culture?

The Veterans' Administration psychiatrist Jonathan Shay was among the first to foreground the relationship between Greek literature and the experiences of the modern combat soldier in his 1994 book, *Achilles in Vietnam: Combat Trauma and the Undoing of Character* (New York: Scribner), which examined the behavior of Achilles in the Iliad as a mythic parable of Combat Trauma. In his 2002 book, *Odysseus in America*, which tested a similar thesis on Homer's Odyssey, Shay described Athenian classical drama as "a theater of combat veterans, by combat veterans to and for combat veterans" and suggested that it may have offered a form of "cultural therapy" for an audience traumatized by the effects of war (Shay 2002, 153). Greek drama, along with Epic, spread across the Hellenistic world from Athens, developing from a variety of performance forms such as epic, choral song, and ritual enactments and probably not as a specific response to combat trauma. However, tragedy, in particular always reflected social, political, and cultural stresses and we can certainly detect this Greek art form responding to the realities of ancient warfare in the fifth century—every surviving Greek play from this period deals with the effects of combat and violence on families and societies (Meineck 2013, 20, note 1.). Beyond Athens and the genre of drama, in the wider literary and iconographic traditions of the Greeks, the effects of combat trauma are well described: the trials of Odysseus; the rage of Achilles; the madness of Herakles; the loss of Andromache; the suicide of Ajax; the isolation of Philoctetes; the fate of the women of Troy, to name just a few famous stories of trauma that are found throughout Greek poetry and iconography.

In this volume several scholars, each with expertise of different areas of Greek culture, were asked to respond to and explore these basic questions. We deliberately sought to reflect both a multiplicity of differing viewpoints and to ask our contributors to respond to each other's work to create a vibrant thread of dialogue throughout the chapters. We also hope that both specialists and nonspecialists will find value in this collection. All Greek references have been translated and although we have assumed our readers will have basic familiarity with most of the works described, we also feel it is entirely possible to read these chapters with little or no knowledge of the ancient material and to then be inspired to seek them out. With this in mind, it is our hope that in addition to scholars and students of the Classics, members of the veteran community, their families, and people interested in this important subject will find value in this collection.

I would like to thank Matthew Santirrocco at New York University, for facilitating the original conference and encouraging us to publish the proceedings and seek other contributors to add their respective viewpoints. My colleagues in Classics at NYU have always been supportive of my outreach work and understand its value. Adam Blistein, Executive Director of the American Philological Association, helped us select over 50 scholars to send out into libraries, museums, arts centers, and military bases to make *Ancient Greeks/Modern Lives* work so well. Kimberly Donato and Masha Carey at Aquila Theatre proved invaluable in organizing the conference, which included a staged reading event and a post-performance talk on trauma and Pirandello after Desiree Sanchez's exceptional performance of *Six Characters in Search of an Author* at the Skirball Center in New York City.

David Konstan, who gave the fine keynote address at the conference and then graciously agreed to lend his considerable experience and coedit this volume with me, provided expert guidance and incredible support to all the contributors. I would also like to thank the more than 50 professors of Classics, Theater, and English who acted as "local scholars" at over one hundred sites, who moderated staged readings, gave public talks, and led readings groups for thousands of people all over the United States. Many actors also traveled many miles to bring these ancient works to life. I want to remember one in particular, John Buxton, who passed away in 2013 after battling cancer. John was a long-standing member of Aquila Theatre and loved participating in *the Ancient Greeks/Modern Lives* readings. John died at the age of 35, but in his short life he brought a plethora of classical characters to vivid life for thousands of people, whether reducing them to tears of laughter with his brilliant portrayal of both Antipholus twins in Shakespeare's *Comedy of Errors,* or pulling them to the edge of their seats with his powerful performance of Achilles in Aquila's *Iliad: Book One.*

I thank my wife Desiree, who has been so supportive and strong from this program's inception, through its execution, and on into its next incarnation called *YouStories: Poetry, Drama, Dialogue,* which adds a social media component to the programming to preserve veteran's stories with the Library of Congress. I could not have done any of this without her. Finally, I wish to thank the members of the veteran community and their families who came to the events of *Ancient Greeks/Modern Lives* and shared their deeply personal stories. One Vietnam Veteran, Brian Delate, who went on to join Aquila as a member of the acting company, described the program as "helping to make American's literate about the cost of war." Another, John Meyer, a US Ranger who served in Iraq and Afghanistan and who read the role of Ajax at the White House performance, used Sophocles' words to articulate how he felt to the members of the high command, who were either in attendance or whose offices lined the corridors of the Executive Administration Building and the White House, where he came to speak those ancient lines. Several of the veterans who attended the program were invited to participate in a dramatic project staged at the Brooklyn Academy of Music in New York in March 2013. Here Euripides' *Herakles* was staged with a chorus of film clips of male and female American veterans from World War II to Afghanistan. Their contribution to this project, which closed the *Ancient Greeks/Modern Lives* program, along with several scholars who led talk-backs with the audience who completely filled all the performances, was much appreciated.

Whatever conclusions one might draw from reading this volume about Combat Trauma in ancient Greece, one thing we can be sure of: Greek drama, poetry, and art still retain the power to move people today and remain a vital force in modern American culture. Plato (*Phaedrus* 245a, *Laws* 665c), Aristotle (*Poetics* 1450a 33), and Isocrates (*Evagoras* 9.10), all wrote that poetry had the power "to move the soul"—this book asks if the Greeks also used their art to help it heal.

PETER MEINECK
New York, December 2013

Works Cited

Buxton, John, and Jay Painter. 2010. "'Page and Stage': The Actor's Perspective." *Classical World* 103.2: 251–55.

Meineck, Peter. 2009. "These Are Men Whose Minds the Dead Have Ravished." *Arion* 17.1: 173–91.

Meineck, Peter. 2013. "Combat Trauma and the Tragic Stage: 'Restoration' by Cultural Catharsis." *Intertexts* 16.1: 7–24.

Shay, Jonathan. 2002. *Odysseus in America: Combat Trauma and the Trials of Homecoming.* New York: Scribner.

INTRODUCTION

Combat Trauma: The Missing Diagnosis in Ancient Greece?

DAVID KONSTAN

I was not quite five years old when World War II came to an end with the surrender of Japan on August 15, 1945. At the time, we were staying in a rooming house in the foothills of the Catskill Mountains, where many families—that is to say, mothers and their children—spent summers to avoid the heat and the danger of contagious polio (as it was imagined) in New York City; the husbands worked in the city and drove out to join their families on weekends. I still recall vividly the response to the announcement of the end of hostilities. The women collected pots and pans—which had a symbolic value, since metal was recycled and scarce during the war—and marched around the central building, clashing them like cymbals or banging on them with spoons and ladles. This wasn't ancient Greece: there was no image of a god to lead the procession, much less a giant phallus, like the one that Dicaeopolis carries after he negotiates a private truce with the Spartans in Aristophanes' comedy, *The Acharnians*. But the spirit of joy was not so very different, I imagine.

It was shortly after this that the son of one of the other couples arrived, right at the end of the summer. He was about 20, and seemed old to me, not only because he was a grown-up, but because he was very withdrawn, barely speaking to other people; he seemed to spend the greater part of the day throwing a bowie knife at the ground, which invariably landed blade down despite the twirl he gave it. I asked my mother at one point why he was so strange, and she explained that he had been in the war and seen things he couldn't talk about. I think I intuitively understood what she meant; in any case, the episode has stayed with me until today.

This was my first experience, indirect as it was, of what is today called combat trauma, but was then, I think, still known as shell shock. Years later, after an aborted career plan as an astronaut and a professional degree in classics, I found myself studying up close two cultures—ancient Greece and Rome—in which war was a permanent condition of life, and virtually no citizen escaped the duty of military service. Like most of my peers, I was impressed by the depth and beauty of classical literature and philosophy, and didn't wonder at the connection this might have with the unrelenting violence they experienced at firsthand. I had read, for example, the passage in Plato's *Republic*, in which he recognizes how difficult it will be to train the guardians of his ideal state to be aggressive toward strangers and yet mild toward their own people. Socrates asks his interlocutor Glaucon, who in real life was one of Plato's brothers, how people who have such fierce characters will "not be savage toward each other and their fellow citizens?" "It won't be easy," Glaucon replies. "And yet," Socrates says, "they must be gentle toward their own, but rough toward their enemies. Otherwise, they won't wait for others to destroy them but will do it first themselves" (*Republic* 2, 375B5–C6). Plato's answer is to adduce the example of guard dogs, which can be trained to protect their own but attack anyone they don't recognize. It never occurred to me, or, it seems, to Plato, to wonder whether war itself might brutalize these guardians—a nicely sanitized word for what was in fact a military caste—and increase the danger that they might turn their belligerence against their own families upon returning home.

It is remarkable, and has indeed been remarked, that the Greeks and Romans seem never to have identified the pathology of combat trauma explicitly.[1] Not that they were alone in having this blind spot: it was really only with World War I that such effects of battle began to be observed and identified as a disorder, and more recently still that post-traumatic stress in general has been classified as a medical condition. When I first read the *Iliad* and *Odyssey* in Greek, in graduate school, it was during the heyday of the New Criticism, and we were attuned to finding deep meanings in the texts we admired. No longer did we view Homer as a primitive poet; his epics touched on grand themes of fate and freedom, collective identity versus individualism. We—or some of us—interpreted Achilles' refusal to fight after he had been insulted by Agamemnon, and his declaration that his honor came not from the king but from Zeus, as a sign of a new conception of personal autonomy, an internalization of values that was the harbinger of a modern sense of morality and responsibility. We puzzled over how characters could assign to Zeus' scales the outcome of a battle between warriors, and wondered whether this was merely a metaphor or an indication of a pre-moral fatalism. Even then, I recall thinking that a tendency to see the hand of destiny behind life-and-death events was not foreign even today, and that in time of war men and women seeking to brace themselves for battle often say things like "if that bullet has my name on it," or imagine that there is a day appointed for their death and there's no avoiding it when it comes, but till then they are safe. But these thoughts were marginal to my appreciation of the poem as an exploration of ethics and human consciousness.

Then I encountered Jonathan Shay's remarkable book, *Achilles in Vietnam*.[2] I confess it was a student who urged me to read it, since I might have put off examining a volume with such a title. Shay, a psychiatrist who had worked with traumatized veterans of the war in Vietnam, saw a deep similarity between the experiences of his patients and that of Achilles, as narrated in the poem. Very summarily, Shay found there were two conditions that, in combination, were catalysts for combat trauma: first, a loss of faith in the commanding officer or other representative of the system, and hence in the justification for the war; and second, the death in battle of an especially close friend, invariably described as gentle or loving, however murderous he might have been on the battlefield. When Agamemnon humiliates Achilles by taking his war prize, the captured girl Briseis, he loses Achilles' respect not only for his authority but also for the motive of the entire war, which was the theft, as the Greeks saw it, of Menelaus' bride Helen. If Agamemnon, Menelaus' brother and the leader of the expedition to recover Helen, can take away Achilles' girl with impunity, why should Achilles risk his life to rescue his tramp of a sister-in-law? Then, as a result of Achilles' abstention, his dearest friend Patroclus enters the battle in his stead, and is slain. The consequence of such a double whammy, Shay explained, is often a period of manic battle frenzy, in which the person feels unusually powerful and invulnerable, or at any event indifferent to death, and wreaks havoc upon the enemy, just as Achilles does, until he slays Hector, the man responsible for his comrade's death. If he survives, he may then experience a range of post-traumatic symptoms, including flashbacks, trouble sleeping, and a generalized rage or hostility that may express itself in unmotivated aggression against others.

Of course, there is no indication that Achilles suffers from such a syndrome at the end of the *Iliad*. True, he senselessly abuses the body of Hector, but he eventually agrees to return it to Hector's father for a whopping ransom; he remains his violent self, at one point threatening old Priam, but he is not represented as mentally disturbed in the aftermath. Shay was aware of this and suggested that the elaborate rituals by which Achilles honored his friend and committed his corpse to the pyre might have helped him to recover his sanity. In Vietnam, when a soldier was killed his body was often whisked away as quickly as possible and his mates were urged to get over their grief, and so found no healthy means of working it through. This is, I think, a weak point in Shay's argument, for reasons I will indicate in a moment. But what I most took away from Shay's book—and this changed my whole view of the epic—was the sense that Homer knew what war was about, and was writing for an audience who did as well. The *Iliad* is first and foremost a brilliant study in how people behave under the stress of battle. It is not a mere repository of traditional motifs, organized so as to tell a great story or to illustrate timeless ethical issues, though it is those things too, of course. But it is, above all, a poem of war.

Now, Achilles is not the only hero to go on a rampage. It happens all the time in the *Iliad*, and even has a technical name in Greek: it is an *aristeia*, deriving from the Greek word meaning "best." Heroes, like

athletes, have their sudden moments of perfect coordination and exhilara-
tion, and for a while they are invincible. From the ancient Greek point
of view, these episodes of elation are not signs of mental disorder, but the
highest manifestation of a fighter's excellence. All the heroes can't all be
suffering from combat trauma—or can they? Might it be that the Greeks
and Romans did not isolate such a syndrome in their soldiers precisely
because it was so common, so practically universal, that it didn't stand out?
Can we speak of a culture of trauma?

Let me offer another example of a soldier who put his life at risk in
what might seem an act of desperation. During the famous battle at
Thermopylae, in which 300 Spartans perished defending a narrow pass
against the invading Persians, a certain Aristodemus, Herodotus tells us
(7.229–231), missed the fighting because of eye trouble. Upon returning alive to Sparta, he was the object of "reproach and dishonor" (*onei-
dos, atimiê*) and was dubbed "he who trembled" (*ho tresas*, 231); indeed,
another Spartan who also sat out the conflict for the same reason escaped
such slander by committing suicide. Aristodemus, however, sought to
remove the stigma by distinguishing himself subsequently at the battle
of Plataea, where, Herodotus says (9.71), he proved himself to be far and
away the bravest of all, and clearly the best candidate for the customary award for courage. The Spartans, however, declined to grant him
this honor, because "he clearly desired to die on account of the censure
that attached to him, and only by raging madly and leaving the battle
formation did he demonstrate great deeds; Posidonius, however, was a
commendable man although he did not wish to die, and precisely to this
extent he was the better." Now, Aristodemus is not described as having
suffered from combat trauma; indeed, he was out of action at the time
of his ostensible disgrace. It was just this chance occurrence that led to
his foolhardy bravado in battle, in order to annul any suspicion that he
had been shirking. Here is a man with a death wish, traumatized—if it
is a trauma—by the shame attaching to his having missed the fatal skir-
mish. His motive is to restore his honor—falsely impugned—as a warrior
in the eyes of his comrades, not doubts about the justice of the war or
agony over the loss of a personal friend. His behavior is deliberate and
oriented toward a goal. It does not seem in principle different from that
of Achilles.

What happened when these battle-hardened fighters returned home,
and had now to adjust to peacetime life amidst their families? Were they
able to make the transition easily, trained, like Plato's guardians, to behave
mildly toward their fellow citizens and relatives, despite their ferocity
toward the enemy, or did they carry over some of the violence they exhibited on the battlefield into the domestic setting? There is one play in particular that would seem to constitute a reflection on this question. At the
beginning of Euripides' *Heracles*, Amphitryon, Heracles' father, explains
that he, his daughter-in-law Megara, and the children she has had with
Heracles are to be killed by Lycus, the tyrant who has usurped power in

Thebes. Lycus' motive is to destroy all the relatives of the former king so as to eliminate potential rivals for the throne. Heracles cannot help his family, since he has gone to Hades to capture Cerberus, the hound of hell. Just when the situation seems hopeless, Heracles appears, and when Lycus returns to kill his family, he slays Lycus instead. At this juncture, Iris, the messenger of the gods, and Lyssa, that is, "Madness" personified, descend and announce that, at Hera's orders, they are going to drive Heracles mad. Heracles immediately begins foaming at the mouth and imagines that he has driven in a chariot to Argos, where he will take vengeance on Eurystheus, the king at whose orders he undertook his labors. Amphitryon asks in alarm: "My son, what is happening to you…? Is the slaughter of the corpses whom you just now killed making you frenzied?" (965–7). Under the impression, however, that he is in Eurystheus' palace and that his father and children are those of Eurystheus, he kills his three sons and Megara as well, collapsing just before he manages to add Amphitryon to the carnage. When Heracles awakens and becomes aware of what he has done, he contemplates committing suicide, but at this point Theseus, whom Heracles had rescued from Hades, arrives with troops from Athens, for the purpose of driving out the tyrant Lycus. Heracles accepts Theseus' offer of asylum and departs with him for Athens.

In his deluded condition, Heracles, the greatest mortal champion in Greek mythology, returns from his adventures and ends up slaughtering his own family—the very people he hoped to save from Lycus' vengeance. Ever since Wilamowitz, the great German scholar who produced a three-volume edition of this tragedy, some have seen Heracles' madness as a consequence of his own nature or actions. Most recently, for example, Robert Emmet Meagher states, "Lyssa is merely a prop, an empty mask, as it were. Herakles' madness neither required then nor requires now any elaborate explanation for those who have taken part in the insane rampage of war"; his domestic violence is simply an extension of his martial savagery, and he is best understood as a "trauma victim."[3] Kathleen Riley, after surveying earlier views, arrives at exactly the opposite conclusion: "There is nothing in Euripides' portrait of the sane hero to suggest that killing is attractive to him or that his normal use of violence is excessive,"[4] and she takes the cause of his madness to be wholly external, that is, induced by Lyssa at Hera's behest. On this view, brutality in the home and violence at war are neatly quarantined, with no suggestion that the two might be connected. But Riley also notes that "The madness of Herakles…is dramatized, paradoxically, in an extremely well-reasoned and orderly manner," and that "Herakles' hallucinatory exploits, which appear to the bystanders as crazed and haphazard, are, in his mind, one continuous and logical sequence of events." Now, this kind of reason within madness is not foreign to the traumatized state: the sufferer imagines a threat and reacts accordingly. The disorder manifests itself not necessarily in a lack of calculation, but in mistaking friends for foes. Once we accept the misidentification, the rest of the behavior may be perfectly rational.

Are we, then, to see Heracles as an example—rare in classical literature—of combat trauma? He is certainly hallucinating: this is what Madness has done to him. He is not directing his violence consciously against his own family but against genuine enemies. Is his delusion, which in the play is ascribed to Hera's hostility but is not otherwise motivated, best understood as a consequence of his ferocious campaigns? His father, after all, suggests that the sight of the corpses of Lycus and his men may be the cause: not war, precisely, but an analogous kind of violence. Has he lost the ability to distinguish between those dear to him and his adversaries, as Plato feared might happen to a poorly trained dog or guardian?

Such an interpretation is possible, but I should like to step back, for a moment, from Heracles' manifest delirium and consider what he imagines he is accomplishing. His intention is to slay not just Eurystheus, the tyrannical and jealous king who sent Heracles on his all but impossible missions, but his entire family, wife and children included. Is this plan also a function of his frenzy, or are the effects of Lyssa's intervention limited to the confusion of identities between Eurystheus' family and his own? If his altered mental condition is responsible for his entire action, not just his delusion but also his desire to wipe out Eurystheus' family, then we might conclude that, under normal circumstances, Heracles does not massacre women and children; he is a warrior, yes, but not a butcher, and we must attribute his extraordinary brutality to his madness— his combat trauma, if you like. But what if we are meant to see his attack, as he imagines it, against Eurytheus' family as a perfectly sane thing to do? The problem here is that such an act does not seem to be different, in principle, from what the tyrant Lycus was planning for Heracles' own family. With this, the moral distinction between Heracles and Lycus—whose name, let us recall, is Greek for "wolf"—is blurred if not altogether eradicated. Shall we say, then, that this kind of barbaric behavior is consistent with Greek ideas of vengeance, or rather that both Heracles and Lycus manifest symptoms of a kind of war madness? The tragedy itself does not call attention to the analogy between Heracles' and Lycus' intentions, but that may reinforce the point: good guys and bad guys alike are prone to extreme acts of retribution, and in a world beset by war and civil strife, it may be hard to tell who is crazy and who is not. Everyone bears scars.

Now, you may be thinking I am in danger of reading too much into a tragedy that is really about how we human beings are playthings in the hands of the gods—"they kill us for their sport," as Gloucester says in *King Lear*—and not about war trauma at all; after all, Heracles was most recently in Hades, not on the battlefield, and what do we know about Lycus' activities? Recently, I came across the following words of caution:

> If there is anything pleasant in life, it is doing what we aren't meant to do. If there is anything pleasant in criticism, it is finding out what we aren't meant to find out. It is the method by which we treat as significant what the author did not mean to be significant, by which

we single out as essential what the author regarded as incidental. Thus, if one brings out a book on turnips, the modern scholar tries to discover from it whether the author was on good terms with his wife; if a poet writes on buttercups, every word he says may be used as evidence against him at an inquest of his views on a future existence. On this fascinating principle, we delight to extort economic evidence from Aristophanes, because Aristophanes knew nothing of economics.

Though this sounds like a critique of postmodern over subtlety, it actually dates to the year 1911, when Monsignor Ronald A. Knox opened in this way his lecture on "Studies in the Literature of Sherlock Holmes," delivered before the Gryphon Club at Trinity College, Oxford (published in *The Blue Book Magazine* 1912, and again *Essays in Satire* in 1928). The lecture was a send-up of hyper-ingenious criticism, like that which argued that there were really two Dr. Watsons, not just one (this idea too was, of course, an invention of Monsignor Knox). But let us take the Monsignor's reference to Aristophanes as a reminder that this poet, at least, was most certainly on the side of peace, and wrote three comedies in its favor: *Acharnians*, which I mentioned above; *Peace*, in celebration of a truce with Sparta; and the unforgettable *Lysistrata*, in which the women organize a sex strike to induce their husbands to terminate the war. Surely this testifies to an opposition to warfare and is a sign that not everyone in Athens was traumatized.

But let us take a closer look. In Aristophanes' *Acharnians*, Dicaeopolis seeks to persuade charcoal sellers from the deme of Acharnae, who form the chorus of the play, that the war with Sparta is a blunder (497–556). As he explains it, Aspasia, a former courtesan from Miletus who was now Pericles' concubine, pushed Pericles into declaring an embargo against the nearby town of Megara. It all began, he says, when some drunken Athenian youngsters carried off a whore named Simaetha from Megara. In return, the Megarians stole two of Aspasia's own girls. The Megarians, reduced to starvation, appealed to Sparta for help, and so the war began.[5] Now, this is a pretty silly reason for initiating a major war, which went on to last almost 30 years, but Dicaeopolis does not leave it at that. He argues rather that the Megarian reaction is understandable, since if a Spartan had stolen so much as a puppy from one of their own allies, the Athenians would have sent a fleet of 300 ships to avenge it (541–556). In other words, it is not just Pericles' fault: the Athenians as a whole are hotheads, which is why they are in favor of continuing the war. If they feel they have been slighted, never mind how trivial the offense, they rise to the occasion, and to do otherwise would violate their sense of manliness. A disposition to anger or indignation was conceived of as the hallmark of free citizens, who did not take insults lying down.[6] A quick temper, in particular, was characteristic of the great fighters at Marathon, who repelled the Persian invasion and were ready to fight at a moment's notice.[7] It is not an accident that Dicaeopolis puts his head on a chopping block before offering his arguments. These men have a sting in their tails—indeed, the chorus in another of Aristophanes' comedies are dressed as wasps; if you wish to reason with people who carry a chip on their shoulders, you had best assume a humble posture.

It is one thing to be hot-tempered and to think this is a virtue, another thing to be traumatized by the horrors that one has witnessed, and even committed, in battle. I do not mean for a moment to minimize or trivialize the psychological problems that have afflicted veterans of modern wars. I am trying to explain rather why ancient Greeks and Romans, who fought almost continually in vicious hand-to-hand engagements, seem not to have recognized such a syndrome. The cause, I think, may lie in a valorization of irascibility, or a disposition to pugnaciousness, which was nourished by combat experience and which in turn inclined them to fight whenever they thought their honor had been challenged. Of course, some men emerged from battle more scarred than others, less able to function in civil society. But rather than label such people as damaged, one might prize them as fierce warriors and send them back to the front. In Aristophanes' *Birds*, two Athenians establish a utopian empire among the birds. At one point, a young sociopath turns up, inspired by the birds' own declaration earlier in the play (757–758) that in their new city boys will be allowed to beat their fathers—the worst offense against the family that an ordinary Greek could imagine. It turns out that the laws in Birdland will in fact require him to tend his father in old age. But Peisthetaerus, who is now the leader of state, tells the boy: "Don't beat your father" (1363–1364), then dresses him up as a fighting cock and urges him to find employment as a soldier: "Since you are so warlike (*makhimos*), fly off to Thrace and fight there" (1368–1369).

My object in these introductory remarks has been to call attention to a problem—the apparent absence of a concern with combat trauma among people almost continually at war—not to provide a definite answer or set of answers. Much more might be said, and is said in the chapters that follow, in relation both to the evidence for combat trauma in antiquity, which is by no means exhausted in my brief survey, and to the reasons why it was so rarely singled out as a consequence of war. Perhaps the most basic cause of this blind spot was the pervasive glorification of militarism, and the idea that it was a necessary condition for survival in a world where enemies might always attack and defeat might well mean annihilation. Under such conditions, any acknowledgment of the negative consequences of war was repressed beneath the dominant celebration of valor and duty.

In the first chapter, Kurt Raaflaub provides a chillingly comprehensive overview of the nature of war in archaic and classical Greece and its impact on civil society, including such matters as care for the dead, treatment of the injured, and the effects of war on the noncombatant population. Following this, William Race offers an original interpretation of the reception of Odysseus in the land of the Phaeacians, showing how carefully and sensitively King Alcinous guides Odysseus in the process of facing the horrors of the war in Troy, thereby enabling him to overcome his crippling relation to the past and prepare himself for the trials that face him at home—where he will have to act again with uncompromising brutality. Corinne Pache, in turn, argues that women's experience of war is also in evidence in Homer's *Odyssey*: it is no accident that Penelope, Odysseus' long-suffering wife, is compared to a lioness, an analogy usually reserved for male warriors. Pache examines the connection with the experiences of a troop of women who saw action in Iraq, and who were called, not without subtle ironies, Team Lioness. Each moment of women's endurance illuminates the other and helps bring the role of gender in war into sharp focus.

Lawrence Tritle brings to his discussion of ancient combat stress his personal experience of war in Vietnam, with which he, like Shay, sees clear analogies. He argues forcefully that post-traumatic stress disorder can be clearly recognized in the reports of ancient warfare that come down to us. Jason Crowley, in turn, places more emphasis on the relative lack of testimony to such trauma in our sources, and explains it as a consequence of the differences between ancient and modern warfare—a little like the way Shay accounted for the reintegration of Achilles into the Greek community as a result of the ritual burial of his slain friend. Crowley argues that the communal support for warfare as a source of glory, and the conditions of direct combat, which offered the chance to react immediately to threats (not to mention that periods of service were relatively brief), contributed to diminishing the risk of the kind of trauma experienced by troops today. We may see something of this ready transition from war to peace in Sara Monoson's account of Socrates' war experience, as recorded by Plato; Socrates, like his fellows, seems to have moved effortlessly between the battlefield and civilian life. And yet Socrates is also characterized as exceptional in this regard, which casts indirect light on the experiences of more ordinary soldiers. But technical factors too might have affected the way war was seen—or not seen. Juan Sebastian de Vivo argues that the chaos of battle may well have been exacerbated by the construction of the military helmet, which imposed a severe limitation on vision, and that one function of the victory monument or "trophy" that was set up after a battle was to impose some shape or order on the indescribable and terrifying experience of war.

Nancy Rabinowitz examines how Greek tragedy represented the effect of war on women—women as victims now, not Team Lioness fighters (though they were victims, too). Women, as she observes, suffered their own kind of combat trauma, thanks to the madness of men, and they too can act in monstrous ways, when sufficiently tormented and oppressed. The plays are not "antiwar," but rather revelatory of what war does, to combatants and noncombatants alike.

Nancy Sherman takes up the problem of trust under conditions of war, particularly in connection with a betrayal or abuse on the part of those in command—one of the two causes that Shay identified as leading to post-traumatic stress disorder. War invites suspicion, whether of comrades who fail to fulfill their end of the bargain or of those back home, who may seem smug when they speak from their position of relative safety to returning veterans who have experienced unutterable things. How does one learn to have confidence in others, after a loss of faith? Sherman offers an analysis of trust as an emotion and shows how an ancient Greek tragedy, Sophocles' *Philoctetes*, reveals how trust can be restored.

Alan Sommerstein looks rather at comedy and shows that the horrors of war are systematically avoided. Generals may be mentioned and sometimes appear on stage, but they are figures of fun and ridicule; scenes of slaughter may be described, but there is a dispassionate quality about the accounts. Even Aristophanes' *Lysistrata* limits the effects of war to what we might call discomfort—there are no men to sleep with—rather than truly traumatic experiences; death is kept at arm's length. We see that, even in the so-called antiwar comedies, war was in some way sanitized in the genre. Sharon James, however, focuses on one of the comedies of Menander (who wrote a century or so after Aristophanes) and treats his play, "The Shield" (*Aspis*, in Greek), as a kind of cathartic experience, in which survivor's guilt, family trauma, and combat stress are constantly on exhibit but resolved through a fantasy of rescue and reunion. The indirection, the ellipses, and avoidances that Sommerstein documents have a function, for they allow grief to give way to healing, and comedy wins out.

Thomas Palaima contrasts the unsentimental acceptance of war, in classical antiquity, as the natural condition of mankind, with the idealistic (which is not to say thoughtless) optimism of some modern politicians and intellectuals who have expected to see an end to war for all time. It is not that the ancients liked war, or at least no more than moderns do (some do, after all), but because they described accurately its horrors, its traumas we might say, their poems and plays still speak to soldiers and veterans. Some of our contemporaries capture war in this way—Palaima cites songs by Johnny Cash and by Bruce Springsteen, among others—but it takes a special talent: Homer had it, as did Euripides. Finally, Paul Woodruff looks at the representation, also by Sophocles, of a woman—Electra—who cannot forget or forgive; but this is theater, and theater, he explains, offers possibilities of safe identification and closure. Finally, Woodruff offers in illustration a play of his own, written on his return from Vietnam, drawing inspiration from Homer's *Odyssey*. The moving scene in which Odysseus and Penelope, here in modern and much altered guise, are reunited concludes his essay and this volume.

Reviewing the contents of this work, it seems to me that the greatest danger that traumatized veterans pose to civil society lies, perhaps, in the area of domestic violence, the effects of trauma precisely on the noncombatants, and so, by reflex, on the damaged soldiers themselves. I may be permitted, then, to conclude this introduction with a rather chilling passage from a later time and another society, but a world not wholly different, perhaps, from classical Athens. St. Augustine, in his *Confessions*, describes his sainted mother Monica, whom he adored throughout his life, as follows:

> When she reached marriageable age, she was given to a man and served him as her master (*domino*)...She bore with his infidelities and never had any quarrel with her husband on this account...He was, moreover, as exceptional for his quick temper (*ira fervidus*) as for his kindness. She knew that an angry (*irato*) husband should not be opposed, not merely by anything she did, but even by a word. Once she saw that he had become calm and quiet, and that the occasion was opportune, she would explain the reason for her action, in case perhaps he had reacted without sufficient consideration. Indeed, many wives married to gentler (*mansuetiores*) husbands bore the marks of blows and suffered disfigurement to their faces. In conversation together they used to complain about their husbands' behavior. Monica, speaking as if in jest but offering serious advice, used to blame their tongues. She would say that since the day when they heard the so-called matrimonial contract read out to them, they should reckon them to be legally binding documents by which they had become slaves (*ancillae*). She thought they should remember their condition and not proudly withstand their masters (*dominos*). The wives were astounded, knowing what a violent (*ferocem*) husband she had to put up with. Yet it was unheard of, nor was there ever a mark to show, that Patricius [Monica's husband] had beaten his wife or that a domestic quarrel had caused dissension between them for even a single day.[8]

St. Augustine is extolling his mother's forbearance and perhaps exaggerating the brutality of other husbands. I am deeply conscious of the hazards of drawing conclusions about real life behavior from literary texts, however devout and self-revealing. But suppose that such household cruelty was not uncommon in the classical world—and I have not mentioned the beating of slaves, which, as Augustine goes on to say, even Monica approved of as a way of discouraging them from causing friction by their gossip between herself and her domineering mother-in-law. Of course, some people were more volatile than others, more troubled and tense, more given to sudden rages; the Greeks recognized that such temperaments were unbalanced, and Aristotle defined virtue as the mean between extremes of excess and deficiency. But in a society where the average level violence may have been more like that in a frontier town than in a modern city (though I wouldn't want to underestimate the incidence of aggression there), and where there was a premium on channeling animosity into militarism rather than disarming it entirely, the dividing line between irritability and pathology may have been blurrier than it is today, even to the point of disappearing altogether.

Notes

1. For a similar absence of what we regard as a clinical condition, see John T. Fitzgerald, "Paul, Wine in the Ancient Mediterranean World, and the Problem of Intoxication" (Paper delivered on 18 July 2013 at the 62nd annual conference of the Colloquium Biblicum Lovaniense; cited by permission of the author): "although ancient writers did not operate with the modern conception of alcoholism, some were well aware of the difference between someone who was drunk on a particular occasion and someone who was habitually intoxicated. Seneca, for instance, says, 'You will surely agree that there is a big difference between a person who is drunk (*ebrius*) and a drunkard (*ebriosus*). He who is actually drunk may be in this state for the first time and may not have the habit, while the drunkard is often free from drunkenness' (*Ep.* 83.11). In a similar way Posidonius argued that the word 'drunk' (*ebrius*) was used in two different ways: 'In the one case it is used of a man who is loaded with wine and has no control over himself (that is, "drunk"); in the other it refers to a man who is accustomed to get drunk, and is a slave to drink (that is, a "drunkard")' (*apud* Seneca, *Ep.* 83.10)." Fitzgerald cites the medical historian Jacques Jouanna: "It is striking to note that the medical writings of the Hippocratic Corpus never condemn intoxication" (*Greek Medicine from Hippocrates to Galen: Selected Papers*, trans. Neil Allies [Leiden: E.J. Brill, 2012] p. 176). Fitzgerald notes further: "The basic medical premise, as Plato has the physician Eryximachus say in the *Symposium*, is simply that 'drunkenness is harmful to man'" (176c–d), namely, by causing sickness (cf. Jouanna 2012: 177).
2. Shay (1995).
3. Meagher (2006, 48, 50).
4. Riley (2008, 34, 37).
5. MacDowell (1995, 65–6) notes that Thucydides assigns the Megarian Decree some role in bringing on hostilities and argues (66) that "Dikaiopolis' account…is not inconsistent with the account given by Thucydides; it is not illogical or incredible; and I see no reason why it should not be essentially true."
6. On anger (*orgê*) as a mark of citizen independence and spirit, cf. Lenz (1980); Konstan (1995, 18–19); Allen (1999); Allen (2000); and Konstan (2006, 75–6).
7. Cf. *Acharnians* 696–7, *Knights* 781, 1334, *Clouds* 985–6, and *Wasps* 711; cf. *Lysistrata* 1254–61 for the comparable pride of the Spartans for their role at Thermopylae.
8. Augustine *Confessions* = Augustine (1991, 168–9), modified. I am indebted to Fitzgerald (2009), a path-breaking paper on a topic all too rarely touched on.

Bibliography

Allen, Danielle. 1999. "Democratic Dis-Ease: Of Anger and the Troubling Nature of Punishment." In *The Passions of Law*, edited by Susan A. Bandes, 191–214. New York: New York University Press.

———. 2000. *The World of Prometheus: The Politics of Punishing in Democratic Athens*. Princeton, NJ: Princeton University Press.

Augustine. 1991. *Confessions*. Translated by Henry Chadwick. New York: Oxford University Press.

Fitzgerald, John T. 2009. "Domestic Violence in the Ancient World: Preliminary Considerations and the Problem of Wife-Beating." In *Animosity, the Bible, and Us: Some European, North American, and South African Perspectives*, edited by J. T. Fitzgerald, H. F. van Rooy, and F. J. van Rensburg, 101–21. Atlanta, GA: Society of Biblical Literature.

———. 2013. "Paul, Wine in the Ancient Mediterranean World, and the Problem of Intoxication." Paper presented at the 62nd annual conference of the Colloquium Biblicum Lovaniense, Leuven, Belgium, July 18, 2013.

Jouanna, Jacques. 2012. *Greek Medicine from Hippocrates to Galen: Selected Papers*. Translated by Neil Allies. Leiden: E.J. Brill.

Konstan, David. 1995. *Greek Comedy and Ideology*. New York: Oxford University Press.

———. 2006. *The Emotions of the Ancient Greeks: Studies in Aristotle and Classical Literature*. Toronto, ON: University of Toronto Press.

Lenz, Lutz. 1980. "Komik und Kritik in Aristophanes' 'Wespen'" *Hermes* 108: 15–44.

MacDowell, Douglas, M. 1995. *Aristophanes and Athens: An Introduction to the Plays*. Oxford: Oxford University Press.

Meagher, Robert Emmet. 2006. *Herakes Gone Mad: Rethinking Heroism in an Age of Endless War*. Northampton, MA: Olive Branch Press.

Riley, Kathleen. 2008. *The Reception and Performance of Euripides' Herakles: Reasoning Madness*. Oxford: Oxford University Press.

Shay, Jonathan. 1995. *Achilles in Vietnam: Combat Trauma and the Undoing of Character*. New York: Simon and Schuster.

CHAPTER ONE

War and the City: The Brutality of War and Its Impact on the Community

KURT A. RAAFLAUB

Introduction

Almost all Greek authors, from Homer to Plato and beyond, deal with war and its impact, some more intensely and directly than others, but war seems an ever-present reality.[1] Homer's *Iliad* is an epic about war and how it affects those who fight it. Tyrtaeus, the mid-seventh-century elegist, composed songs that became "hits," celebrating the hero's beautiful death and urging the Spartans to fight bravely to protect their families and community. The Athenian sage and lawgiver Solon recognizes in civil strife and war and the deaths of young men the inevitable consequence of elite abuse of power. The early philosopher Heraclitus sees in war one of the natural forces that produces contrast and never-ending transformation. In the early fifth century, Simonides was in high demand to write poems celebrating the achievements of the Persian War heroes. In *Persians* Aeschylus dramatized and mythologized a recent war, showing the loser's misery and warning against overstepping god-set limits. Sophocles' *Ajax* confronts us with a hero whose mind cracks under the intense emotional experience of war. Euripides' Trojan War plays stage the human consequences of Athens' power and war policies and the price even the victors have to pay for martial glory. Herodotus' and Thucydides' invention of large-scale prose history, stimulated by extraordinary wars, focuses on war as an agent that drives history and challenges humans to excel in great deeds. Prompted by excesses of warfare in their time, the sophists think seriously and even theoretically about possibilities to avoid war and secure peace. Plato and Aristotle try to find a place for a responsible use of war in their designs of ideal states and analyses of politics.

By the late fifth century, war pervaded the lives and thoughts especially of the Athenian citizens: they experienced it on sea and land almost every year; saw it dramatized in tragedy and comedy; competed in war-related disciplines at their Panathenaic festival; talked about it in their shops, tavernas, and assemblies; and saw it represented in statues, reliefs, monuments, and paintings in their public buildings and sanctuaries. From the Piraeus to the Acropolis, in streets and public spaces, they were constantly confronted with reminders of their community's awesome victories, its imperial might, and its unprecedented power, greatness, and liberty. Their ancestors had achieved all this through their labor and sacrifice, and they were expected to emulate them through their own commitment to power gained by war and maintained by imperial control.[2]

Despite the prominence of war in archaic poetry, its role in Greek life had not always been that intense. Hesiod, author of didactic epics, lists War and Strife as children of Night in his genealogy of gods and divine forces that influence human life, and ranks Peace together with Justice and Good Order very high among the factors that make prosperous communal life possible, but otherwise war is conspicuously absent in his poems. For a few lyric poets (Sappho foremost among them), war is a marginal aspect of life, ranking far behind others like love, elite rivalries, or justice. Whatever the reality underlying the *Iliad*, in archaic Greece (c. 750–480 BCE) war was intermittent, always a possibility but rarely a fact, and it was mostly fought among neighboring communities about booty and contested land, not to subject others permanently to one's rule. During this period in large parts of Greece and along much of the Mediterranean and Black Sea coastline, a world of micro-citizen-states (*poleis*, sg. *polis*) emerged, communities with their own territory, customs, laws, and cults, governed in some form or other collectively by their citizens: the citizens were the polis. This world of poleis was immensely competitive but allowed for alliances and other means to balance the potential power of a few exceptionally large communities that had grown by incorporating conquered rivals into their own polis, not by treating them as subject entities, and even such growth soon found its limits. Another method to increase one's influence was the hegemonial alliance, as Sparta demonstrated successfully with the "Peloponnesian League" (a modern term).[3]

Indeed, well into the fifth century Sparta, with its peculiar social structure and educational system that aimed at producing nothing but excellent soldiers, and with its outstanding record of victories and leadership, was considered the preeminent military power in Greece. But it was increasingly hampered by an alarming decline in citizen numbers and worries about maintaining the rule of its small citizen body over a large servile population (the helots) and numerous dependent communities (the *perioikoi*: those "living around"); hence Sparta used its military power reluctantly and mostly aimed at maintaining the status quo.[4]

All this changed with the Persian Wars, when an alliance of Greek poleis (the "Hellenic League" consisting mostly of Sparta, Athens, and their allies) repelled invasions by two Persian armies in 490 and 480–479.

In the latter, the Persians attacked with both a land force and a naval force; Sparta's strength on land was unsurpassed but the Athenians proved the saviors on sea. In the mid–480s, they decided in assembly to use the revenue from a newly discovered silver mine for the construction of a large war fleet rather than distributing it among all citizens, and to bank their defense against the Persians on this fleet, evacuating their population to safer places and sacrificing their city. In this dire emergency, all able-bodied men, whether rich or poor, citizen or noncitizen, free or slave, manned this fleet that, supported by some allies, won overwhelming victories at Salamis (480) and Mycale (479).[5] When the Spartans and their allies lost interest in continuing the war, the Athenians and a number of Greek poleis that had rebelled against Persia founded a new alliance, centered in Apollo's sanctuary on Delos (hence we call it the "Delian League"). Its purpose was to liberate the Greeks still under Persian rule, prevent another Persian attack, and seek compensation for the devastations caused by the Persians by looting Persian territory. The League met these goals with great success but in the process changed its composition and nature. Within a generation, Athens transformed the League into an increasingly centralized naval empire and eventually moved its seat to Athens, disregarding the allied synod and using its own citizen assembly to decide and legislate for the League.[6]

Athens' naval and imperial policies assigned to the fleet unprecedented responsibility for the security, power, and prosperity of the polis. Apart from increasing numbers of resident aliens (metics), mercenaries, and slaves, the crews consisted of lower-class citizens. The same citizens probably also provided the bulk of the huge labor force employed in the shipyards. Moving from the back country to the harbor area, thousands of them now lived close to the political center and made their voices and wishes heard. All this facilitated a major political change: the breakthrough of democracy in reforms enacted in 462/1 and subsequent years to 451/0. Essentially, these changes increased the power of those institutions that directly represented the citizen body: the assembly, democratic council, and law courts. The citizens in assembly now controlled the entire political process, from electing and controlling most officeholders to devising policies and supervising their execution. The demos now truly ruled.[7]

This democracy pursued an aggressive foreign policy, increasing and tightening the empire. Despite initial successes in wars against the Peloponnesian League and the Persians, Athens was not able to sustain such efforts on multiple fronts; by about 450, an agreement ended the war with Persia, and in 446 a treaty ended the war with Sparta. After 15 years of prosperity under Pericles' leadership, tensions between Athens and some of Sparta's allies rose to a level that forced Sparta to intervene. In 431 a war broke out that turned increasingly bitter and devastating and, barely interrupted by an official peace period from 421 to 415, ended in 404 with Athens' total defeat: it survived as a community but lost its walls, fleet, and empire.[8]

In the course of these conflicts, war changed its character. Traditional battles between heavily armed infantry forces (called "hoplites") continued but cavalry and light-armed troops, now organized in special units, played an increasingly important role. Naval warfare made it possible to transport troops rapidly over great distances but required a coastal support network and large funds; hence, Athenian naval power, imperial revenue, and imperial control of the coasts depended on one another.[9] Traditional hoplite warfare had been short, usually decided after one battle. Wars based on navies could last weeks, months, or even years (as Athenian expeditions to Egypt or Sicily showed). War thus became ubiquitous and permanent: between the Persian and Peloponnesian Wars, Athens fought some kind of war in two out of every three years and the latter lasted 27 years. Wars became increasingly brutal, often ending with the execution of the male fighters, the sale into slavery of women and children, and the destruction or annexation of the victims' territory and settlement. And wars became total, involving every sphere of life, including the economy—for example, in the notorious Athenian embargo against neighboring Megara. They often prompted as a corollary civil strife with excesses of cruelty and affected large areas and communities that might not have wanted to be involved.[10] Hence, losses skyrocketed; poleis had to deal with large numbers of wounded and maimed warriors, war widows, and orphans; refugees became a common plight and undisciplined crowds of mercenaries a pest.

The impact of war on both those who fought it and the noncombatant population is thus an important and multifaceted topic. It was part of daily life and thus rarely commented upon in extant literature; accordingly, it too often escapes the attention of modern scholarship. Still, if we throw our net widely and look at all the extant evidence, the resulting picture is rich—and depressing—enough. I shall begin with three case studies, then discuss the relevant issues in a more systematic survey, focusing here on the human and social dimension of war and leaving political, religious, and ideological issues to be treated in a companion piece elsewhere.[11] Even so, I cannot even try to be complete in listing either ancient evidence or modern comments.

Three Case Studies

In 427, severe civil strife broke out on the island of Corcyra between supporters of an alliance with Athens, who claimed to be democrats and their oligarchic opponents. When five wealthy citizens were brought to trial by a leading "democrat" and convicted to pay exorbitant fines, "they joined up with the rest of their party and, armed with daggers, suddenly broke in on the Council and killed [their accuser] and some sixty others, members of the Council and private individuals." Violence soon escalated beyond control on both sides. At some point, under the protection of an Athenian fleet that prevented the Spartans from supporting the oligarchs, the "democratic party" "seized upon all their enemies whom they could find and put them to death." They then killed supporters of the opposing party who had manned ships for an anticipated battle, as they landed (Thucydides 3.81).

> Next they went to the temple of Hera and persuaded about fifty of the suppliants there to submit to a trial. They then condemned every one of them to death. Seeing what was happening most of the other suppliants, who had refused to be tried, killed each other there in the temple; some hanged themselves on the trees, and others found various other means of committing suicide. [During the seven days that the Athenian fleet stayed there,] the Corcyraeans continued to massacre those of their own citizens whom they considered to be their enemies. Their victims were accused of conspiring to overthrow the democracy, but in fact men were often killed on grounds of personal hatred or else by their debtors because of the money that they owed. There was death in every shape and form. And, as usually happens in such situations, people went to every extreme and beyond it. There were fathers who killed their sons; men were dragged from the temples or butchered on the very altars; some were actually walled up in the temple of Dionysus and died there. (Thucydides 3.81)

This was the first case of *stasis* in the war; Thucydides thus describes it in great detail and adds at the end three chapters of penetrating political analysis, establishing a typology or pathology of civil war that the reader can apply to other cases as they occur during the war.[12]

In 415, Euripides put on stage *Trojan Women*, a play that throws a harsh light on the human cost exacted by Athens' war policies. A few weeks earlier, the tiny island of Melos that refused to yield to Athenian pressure had capitulated after heroic resistance; the victors eradicated the population and sent colonists to settle the island. A few weeks later, a huge Athenian armada was going to depart to Sicily, with orders to conquer the island, perhaps with similar consequences for resisting city populations. In this play, Troy has been taken and destroyed, the men are dead, and the surviving women are rounded up, to be distributed as slaves among the victorious Achaeans. Further atrocities happen during the play: the princess Polyxena is sacrificed at the tomb of Achilles; Apollo's prophetess, Cassandra, is designated as Agamemnon's concubine; and Hector's little son, Astyanax, is cruelly murdered. Deprived of everything but not broken, the Trojan women put things in perspective: the fate of the Trojans is preferable to that of the Achaeans because "for one woman's sake" they "threw thousands of lives away" (366–9; trans. R. Lattimore). "They died day after day, though none sought to wrench

their land from them nor their own towering cities." Those who fell
were not buried by their families' loving hands. But the Trojans "have
that glory which is loveliest: they died for their own country," became
heroes, and were brought home after battle, to be cared for by their
loved ones (374–402). Achaeans, says Hecuba, after they have thrown
Astyanax from the wall, "all your strength is in your spears, not in your
minds!" The little son of a mighty hero must be killed because they
fear him as a symbol of future resurgence. What will be written on the
child's funeral stone? "Here lies a little child the Argives killed, because
they were afraid of him! A horrible inscription for Hellas!" (1158–91).
We cannot but think of Melos (or any other polis that suffered its fate):
here lies a little town the Athenians destroyed because they feared it as
a symbol of independence! More than that: the victors will pay a huge
price for the atrocities they committed: Athena turns from friend to
foe to avenge the desecration of her sanctuary in Troy, and their return
home will end in disaster. Of their own city, the women say: "I see the
work of gods who pile tower-high the pride of those who are nothing and dash present grandeur down!" (612–13). Noble becomes slave.
A great city (*megalopolis*) becomes a non-city (*apolis*), and Troy is gone
(1291–2). This is one of the leitmotifs in Herodotus' *Histories*, and it can
be applied to Athens as well: this greatest of all cities too may one day
be crushed into a pile of smoking rubble. When its citizenry had to face
defeat, the historian Xenophon writes, "they could see no future for
themselves except to suffer what they had made others suffer, people of
small states, whom they had injured not in retaliation for anything they
had done but out of the arrogance of power" (*Hellenica* 2.2.10). They
escaped this fate by a hair![13]

In 411, Aristophanes performed the third and deepest of his peace
comedies, *Lysistrata*. On one level, this play is an indictment of Athens'
civic ideology that is inseparably tied to its war ideology. On another,
it illuminates the plight of the Athenian women, whose families suffer
because their men serve in the war for months and years on end.[14] To
break the men's stubborn war mania—that is opposed by women from all
over Greece—and cut off its financial support, the women engage in a sex
strike and occupy the treasury on the Acropolis. Although comedy generally avoids specific allusions to the war's death toll, one scene gets very
close to doing just that. An official attacks the women, challenging their
right to take on public issues; after all, they "have no share in the war"
(588). While he means, "You are not fighting in the war," the women
understand, "The war is none of your business," a phrase men had used
since Homer to put their womenfolk in place. Here Lysistrata objects:
women bear children and then send them out as soldiers; they therefore
carry more than double the burden of the war (588–90). Angrily, the official interjects: "Be silent! Don't bring up bad memories!" (590). He might
be referring to the Sicilian disaster or simply to the fact that war causes
many sons not to return home, but the poet here at least hints at the losses

it causes. Instead, Lysistrata goes on to describe the sad fate of so many women whose lives are transformed by the loss of their men (see below).

All these documents represent indictments of the war based on its excessively cruel impact on the noncombatant population, and all three are exemplary in throwing light on the human dimension of war that narratives of war, usually focusing on battles and generals, mostly ignore.

War's Impact on the Fighting Men

War's Brutality

In an age of air strikes, laser bombs, and assaults of tank formations, it is difficult to imagine an infantry battle with close-up fighting between man and man, killing to avoid being killed. Even the well-documented battles of the American Civil War and First World War contain a decisive element that is alien to ancient warfare: the fire power of individual weapons, machine guns, and artillery. Thucydides describes the first battle in the Sicilian expedition, between the Athenians and their allies, drawn up 8 lines deep, and the Syracusans 16 lines deep. Ideally, hoplites were uniformly armed with bronze protective armor (helmet, cuirass, and greaves), a large round shield carried on the left arm, and spear and sword, and lined up in a compact formation.

> First the stone-throwers, slingers, and archers on both sides engaged each other in front of the main lines of battle.... Then soothsayers brought forward the usual victims for sacrifice and trumpeters sounded the charge to the hoplites. So they went into action.... The armies now came to close quarters, and for some time no ground was yielded on either side.... It was the Argives who first forced the Syracusan left wing back, and then the Athenians broke through the troops in front of them. The Syracusan army was now cut in two and took to flight. The Athenians did not pursue them far. They were prevented from doing so by the numbers of still undefeated Syracusan cavalry.... Nevertheless they followed up the enemy as far as it was safe to do so in compact bodies, and then returned to their own lines and put up a trophy.... They collected their dead, put them on a pyre, and camped there for the night. Next day they gave the Syracusans back their dead under an armistice. (Thucydides 6.67–71)

What this sober report does not convey is that hoplite battles were a terrifying experience, at least in the "killing zone" and for those who did not flee before they even met the enemy.[15] Even if Homer describes at best "proto-hoplites" in battle, his narrative offers a vivid impression and helps fill gaps left by later less-detailed reports. Still, classical authors give a few explicit insights. Xenophon, a mercenary leader himself, writes about the battle at Coronea in 395. As the armies converged,

> A deep silence fell on both sides for a while, but when about [200 meters] separated them the Thebans raised the war cry and charged into the attack. When the gap was down to [c. 100 meters] a counter-charge was launched from Agesilaus' lines....They were just a spear's thrust from the enemy when the lines facing them gave way. And the Argives did not even wait for Agesilaus and his men, but turned and ran for Helicon....[A little later, Agesilaus' troops] smashed head-on into the Thebans. So with shield thrust against shield they pushed, fought, killed, died. The air was not filled with cries, but it was not silent either: there were the typical sounds made by men in the heat of battle fury. In the end some of the Thebans did break through to Helicon, but many of them retreated and were killed....With the fighting over, the battlefield presented a vision of bloodstained earth, corpses of friends and foes lying intermingled, shattered shields, splintered spears and daggers bare of their sheaths—some on the ground, some sticking out of bodies, some still clasped in hands. (*Agesilaus* 2.10–14)

No doubt, as Everett Wheeler says, "The ferocity of the 'killing zone,' where opposing hoplites stood toe-to-toe, shield-to-shield, stabbing and struggling in a confined space, defies description."[16] Still, as Larry Tritle demands, we need to get beyond such general statements, trying to place ourselves "inside the hoplite agony": "The sights and sounds of this fight—like any battle, ancient or modern—are nearly beyond the comprehension of the inexperienced. The battleground itself would have become...littered with bodies of the wounded, dying, and dead, making it difficult to walk and fight at the same time. Blood and viscera would have made the ground slippery and the air foul. The noise and confusion would have been bewildering and disorienting all at once."

Even if hoplites, hampered by their heavy equipment, usually did not pursue the enemy very far, the heaviest losses often occurred in the phase of flight and pursuit. Xenophon describes an especially appalling scene in fighting about Corinth in 393 BCE:

> When the Argives heard that the Spartans were in their rear, they turned round again and rushed out of the stockade at the double. Those of them who were on their extreme right were killed by the Spartans, who could thrust and strike at their unprotected sides, but those who were close to the wall fell back towards the city in a dense throng and with no sort of order. However, when they met the Corinthian exiles and discovered that they were enemies, they turned back again. Some of them now climbed up the steps to the ramparts, leapt down from the wall and were killed; others were

herded together by the enemy and struck down at the foot of the steps; others were trodden under the feet of their own people and were suffocated. As for the Spartans, they were at no loss about whom to kill next.... Here was a great mass of their enemies delivered over to them in a state of utter panic, offering their unprotected sides, with no one making the least effort to fight and everyone doing everything possible to ensure his own destruction: what can one call this except an instance of divine intervention? Certainly on this occasion so many fell in such a short time that the dead bodies seemed to be heaped together like heaps of corn or piles of wood or stones. (*Hellenica* 4.4.11–12)

"The typical sounds made by men in the heat of battle fury": all men knew about this; hence, there was no need to go into details. Isocrates makes a similar remark about the noises typical of naval battles, and Lysias imaginatively reconstructs the mental state of the sailors on the fleet at Salamis, giving us a good impression of why such scenes soon became topoi that could be reproduced without much relation to the reality of the situation described.[17]

Despite extreme cases like that at Corinth quoted above, or Marathon in 490, where supposedly 6,400 Persians died but only 192 Athenians,[18] losses in hoplite battles often were surprisingly small, even on the losing side. Yet the exceptions stuck in historical memory. At Delium in 424, both sides had about 7,000 hoplites and some cavalry, the Boeotians in addition a large number of light-armed troops. Registers were kept only of the hoplites (and cavalry). Hence, Thucydides' statement is typical: "Nearly 500 Boeotians fell in the battle, and nearly 1,000 Athenians, among whom was Hippocrates, the general; also a great number of light troops and baggage carriers": 7 percent of the hoplites on the Boeotian, 14 percent on the Athenian side. At Chaeronea in 338 the 1,000 Athenian dead and 2,000 captured represented at least 10 percent of the adult male citizen body—but in this case, unlike, for example, after the battle of Aigospotamoi in 405, those captured were not permanently lost.[19]

Casualty figures in naval battles could be much higher, given the large numbers of sailors involved (up to 200 per trireme), but we have no exact figures. What made losses disastrous were aggravating circumstances (such as a storm preventing the rescue of shipwrecked crews after the Athenian victory at the Arginusae in 406) or the failure of entire naval expeditions, such as that to Egypt in the 450s, where the Athenians lost an estimated 8,000 citizens, or that to Sicily in 415–413 (at least 10,000). The Egyptian figure, if correct, would amount to roughly one out of seven or eight adult male citizens. Inscribed Athenian casualty lists allow similar conclusions: that of 460 lists 177 dead of one of the ten tribes (civic subdivisions) alone (about 3.5–4.5 percent of its adult men). By the end of the Peloponnesian War, the citizen body had shrunk to less than half its prewar level.[20]

As Peter Hunt observes, if prorated the Athenian losses at Chaeronea are comparable to the losses of the main combatants in the entire First World War.[21] The total figures of the Peloponnesian War, again prorated, dwarf anything that is known from modern warfare.

On the other hand, we have good reason to think that between the Persian and Peloponnesian Wars the citizen and overall population of the Athenian polis increased enormously, perhaps by 100 percent, not least as the direct or indirect result of war and empire. It is hard to overestimate the impact on the community of such dramatic shifts in the size of the population.[22]

Care for the Dead

In continuation of his report on the battle of Coronea, Xenophon writes:

> By now it was late in the afternoon, so once they had dragged the bodies of the enemy dead inside their lines, [the Spartans] ate and bedded down for the night. Early the next day Agesilaus gave Gylis the polemarch his orders: he was to deploy the men at battle stations and set up a trophy, all the men were to wear garlands in honour of [Apollo], and all the pipe-players were to play their pipes. While they were busy carrying out these orders, the Thebans sent a herald to ask for a truce to bury their dead. (*Agesilaus* 2.15–16)

The trophy, a heap of enemy weapons and equipment piled up around a tree trunk or pole, the garlands, and the music—by the *aulos*-players who also gave the rhythm during the Spartans' quiet and disciplined march into battle—were an expression of thanks to the gods for their support in gaining victory. The erection of a trophy and possession of the enemy dead also demonstrated control of the battlefield and thus victory. When the enemy officially asked for a truce to rescue their dead, they admitted defeat.[23] The truce agreed upon to retrieve and burn the dead was part of an age-old ritual; it is described in the *Iliad*, including the detail that the companions of the dead will gather the ashes and keep them, eventually to bring them home to their families.[24] Sometimes a mound was erected to cover the pyre; that of Marathon (the *soros*) still stands today and was a tourist attraction in antiquity. There, the names of the fallen were inscribed on stelae, and sacrifices were offered on the anniversary of the battle.[25]

Soon after the Persian Wars, the Athenians changed the burial custom. They now brought the ashes of the war dead home and buried them in the "public cemetery" in a solemn public ceremony. This innovation probably was, like others, motivated by the dramatic changes in the Athenians' experience of war: its greater frequency and, especially, the involvement of much larger segments of the citizen population in campaigns that were driven by communal policies. Thucydides writes:

> Two days before the ceremony the bones of the fallen are brought and put in a tent which has been erected, and people make whatever offerings they wish to their own dead. Then there is a funeral procession in which coffins of cypress wood are carried on wagons. There is one coffin for each tribe, which contains the bones of members of that tribe. One empty bier is decorated and carried in the procession: this is for the missing, whose bodies could not be recovered. Everyone who wishes to . . . can join in the procession, and the women who are related to the dead are there to make their laments at the tomb. The bones are laid in the public burial-place. (2.34)

Traditionally, the families buried their dead. In claiming this function for the war dead, the democratic state here interfered with age-old family prerogatives, and it is quite possible that the conflicts about the burial of heroes that Sophocles dramatized in *Ajax* and *Antigone* were at least partly prompted by this tension.[26] The fallen of each year were buried in a common tomb that was covered by a tumulus and crowned with a stele that recorded their names. The stele of the state burial of 447/6 is well preserved.[27] The title line ("In the Chersonese of the Athenians these men died") is followed by the name of the leader ("Epiteles the general") and the names of all the other war dead, ordered by tribe ("of the tribe Erechtheïs: Pythodoros, Aristodikos, Telephos, Pythodoros; of the tribe Aigeïs: Epichares, Mnesiphilos, Phaidimides, Laches, Nikophilos"). Other lists concern men who died in Byzantium, and yet others those who fell "in the other campaigns." An honorary epigram eternalizes the glory of the heroes:

> These men lost their flowering youth at the Hellespont,
> fighting, and they brought glory upon their fatherland,
> while the enemies groaned as they carried away the harvest of war,
> but for themselves these men set up an eternal memorial of bravery.

This tomb stood among many others along the street that led from the Dipylon Gate to the shrine of the hero Academus (later the place of Plato's Academy), forming a panorama of civic glory.

Continuing the public ceremony, a speaker chosen for his outstanding reputation (Pericles and Demosthenes among them) delivered the annual "funeral oration," which quickly developed into a distinct type of oration with its own range of traditional topoi, emphasizing the achievements of the dead heroes against a long list of remarkable victories of previous generations. Its purpose clearly was to emphasize shared pride in communal glory in order to overcome grief and loss and condition the citizens for further ordeals.[28]

Care for the Wounded

Lack of information on this crucial issue is most disturbing, even if, as scholars estimate, about 80 percent of the seriously wounded died on the day of the battle and about a third of the rest after returning home. Half of those who survived their wounds probably incurred permanent disabilities.[29] The difficulties begin in knowing how wounded warriors got safely out of the battle at all. Xenophon writes of a battle between Spartan hoplites and Athenian light-armed troops at Lechaeum near Corinth in 390 BCE that consisted of a series of attacks, flights, and pursuits. Early in the battle, the Spartan commander ordered the shield bearers to evacuate the bodies of the dead and wounded to Lechaeum; this could presumably be done because the fight had moved beyond the place where they were lying.[30] Homer is helpful again: in the *Iliad* leaders get rescued out of battle and survive, cared for by doctors and healers who enjoy high prestige; comrades protect their wounded friends with their shields; vase paintings show one soldier bandaging the wound of another. Most importantly, the rescue of Patroclus' body illustrates that it took hard work by four men to achieve this: two to carry the body and two to protect the carriers; the poet compares the effort involved with the sweat and exertion of two mules who pull a heavy beam over a rocky mountain path. In the classical period, generals were wounded and survived; so did Philip II of Macedon and Alexander the Great, even numerous times. In his portrait of the coward, Theophrastus describes a soldier who wrongly claims to have rescued a fellow soldier singlehandedly.[31]

The wounded who had the best chance to be rescued from the battle and receive proper care probably were officers or, at any rate, those on the winning side; wounded enemies presumably were killed or left to die.[32] We should expect that in a polis that was involved in such frequent and intense warfare as Athens was, invalids were a common sight in the streets. Tritle suggests that "the plight of the wounded in an era without painkillers must have been horrific". "In the warring towns of Greece, people lived close to one another. The cries of the war-wounded, their hobbling about town, would have been commonplace sounds and sights." In Sophocles' play, Philoctetes is cast out by his community because of his miserable cries and the stench of his never-healing wound; he must have reminded the audience of extreme cases of veteran invalids.[33] The sanctuary of the healing god Asclepius in Epidauros attracted those whom human doctors could not help; inscriptions recording miracles that happened there mention men who carried spear- and arrowheads in their bodies and suffered from other permanent damage.[34] I give two examples:

[A 12] Euhippos bore a spearhead in his jaw for six years. While he was sleeping here, the god drew the spearhead from him and gave it to him in his hands. When day came, he walked out well, having the spearhead in his hands.

[B 12 (32)] Anticrates of Cnidus, eyes. This man had been struck with a spear through both eyes in some battle, and he became blind and carried around the spearhead with him, inside his face. Sleeping here, he saw a vision. It seemed to him the god pulled out the dart and fitted the so-called girls (i.e., pupils) back into his eyelids. When day came he left well.

We know very little about how society dealt with the challenge posed by war invalids, except that invalids—of all kinds, not only those afflicted by war—received a small state pension (one-third or two-thirds of the minimal wage for workers) if they were incapable of working and owned only minimal property.[35]

Herodotus tells a story that was apparently well known in Athens at his time:

Epizelus, the son of Cuphagoras, an Athenian soldier, was fighting bravely when he suddenly lost the sight of both eyes, though nothing had touched him anywhere—neither sword, spear, nor missile. From that moment he continued blind as long as he lived. I have heard that in speaking about what happened to him he used to say that he thought he was opposed by a man of great stature in heavy armour, whose beard overshadowed his shield; but the phantom passed him by, and killed the man at his side. (6.117)

This is the first attested case of "hysterical blindness." The sophist Gorgias explains the impact of visual experiences in overpowering the mind:

Whatever we see has a nature, not the one we wish, but whatever each happens to have. And by seeing the mind is molded even in its character. As soon as men in war arm their bodies against the enemy with armor of bronze and iron—some for defense, some for attack—if the sight sees this, it is shaken and shakes the mind, so that men often flee in panic from danger that lies in the future.... Some indeed, who have seen fearful things, have lost their present purpose in the present moment, so thoroughly does fear extinguish and expel thought; and many have fallen into useless labors, terrible diseases, and incurable madness, so thoroughly does sight engrave on the mind images of things that are seen. (*Encomium of Helen* 1517; trans. Gagarin and Woodruff 1995, 194)[36]

Again, we do not know how society dealt with men who had gone mad because their mind could not master the fear induced by the experience of battle. That such cases were all but rare has been confirmed by the observation of symptoms resembling posttraumatic stress disorder (PTSD) in Greek poetry from Homer—Achilles' reaction to Patroclus' death (his mutilation of Hector's body and his going berserk in the final battle) and

Odysseus' excessive violence in reclaiming his home from the suitors of his wife after returning from a long war—to tragedy (Sophocles' *Ajax*, Euripides' *Heracles* and *Orestes*) and beyond (Alexander's killing of Cleitus the Black).[37]

Prisoners of War

Peter Krentz quotes Xenophon's formulation of the basic rule of war: "It is a custom established for all time among all people that when a city is captured in war, the persons and the property of the inhabitants belong to the captors. It will be no injustice for you to keep what you have, but if you let them keep anything, it will be only out of generosity that you do not take it away" (*Cyropaedia* 7.5.73).[38] Hence, the decision about the fate of the population of a captured city was entirely the victor's, and this decision was usually driven by pragmatic and economic, not humanitarian, considerations. There was no Geneva Convention, and no facilities existed to keep or employ large numbers of prisoners. The easiest solution thus was to kill the surviving men in fighting age. Estimates are that this happened in 20–25 percent of known instances and that in a slightly larger percentage of cases they were sold into slavery. If men were spared either fate, this usually was because they served as bargaining chips in an expected political deal—as happened most spectacularly to the more than 100 Spartiates the Athenians captured on the island of Sphacteria in 425—or were to be exchanged for ransom at a higher price than slaves would yield—an issue frequently mentioned already in the *Iliad*.[39] Plutarch's story about what Cimon, the architect of the Athenian empire, considered the cleverest thing he had done is informative: the Athenians and their allies had captured a great number of barbarian prisoners, and Cimon was in charge of distributing them. He

> placed the prisoners on one side and all their clothes and ornaments on the other. The allies then blamed him for distributing the shares unfairly, but he told them to make their own choice first and the Athenians would be content with whatever share they left.... The allies took the ornaments and left the prisoners to the Athenians. At the time Cimon was regarded as having made a fool of himself and come away with the worst of the bargain, since the allies could go about with gold anklets, bracelets, collars, jackets, and robes of purple, while the Athenians had gained nothing but a lot of naked bodies of men who were not even trained to work. But a little while after, the friends and relatives of the prisoners came down from Phrygia and Lydia and ransomed every one of them at a high price, so that Cimon received the equivalent of four months' maintenance for his fleet and still had a large sum of gold from these ransoms left over for the city. (*Cimon* 9)

War's Impact on the Noncombatant Population

Refugees

In 1922, after the failure of a Greek attempt to conquer territories settled by Greeks on the northern and eastern coasts of the Aegean, the Greeks and Turks agreed in the Treaty of Lausanne on a massive population exchange: over 1 million orthodox Greeks who had lived in the Ottoman Empire were moved to Greece and about half a million Muslims from Greek territories to Turkey. Hundreds of thousands became refugees.[40] Almost two-and-a-half millennia earlier, a similar proposal was made in ancient Greece. In 479 BCE, after they had defeated the Persians at Plataea and Mycale, the Greeks debated about what to do with the Greek poleis that had been ruled by the Persians and had rebelled against them. Herodotus writes:

> The idea was to remove the Ionians and resettle them in some part of Greece which was under their own control, and to abandon Ionia itself to the Persians. They did not think it was possible to be forever on the watch in order to protect Ionia, and at the same time there was little hope, failing such perpetual vigilance, of the Ionians escaping Persian vengeance for their revolt. It was accordingly proposed by the Peloponnesian leaders to turn out the Greeks who had supported Persia and settle the Ionians in their commercial centers; the Athenians, however, strongly disapproved. (Herodotus, 9.106)

Since the Greek polis was primarily a community of citizens, the idea to move a polis by resettling the citizens and their families in a new place was less horrendous than it sounds to us. Some Greek poleis did so to escape the wrath of the conquering Persians.[41] Even earlier, Pausanias writes,

> When the Spartans...invaded Argolis with an army, the Asinaeans joined in the invasion, and with them ravaged the land of the Argives. When the Spartan expedition departed home, the Argives...attacked Asine. For a time the Asinaeans defended themselves from their wall....But when the wall was lost, the citizens put their wives and children on board their vessels and abandoned their own country. (Pausanias 2.36.45)

Still, the decision to deprive the "medizing" Greeks, who had collaborated with the invading Persians, of their homes and to distribute these among the Ionians would have created an unprecedented mass of dislocated persons and unimaginable misery. The project did not materialize because the Athenians had their own good reasons to prevent it. But the wars of the fifth century still produced armies of refugees.

The small but prosperous island of Aegina offers a good example. It had been a rival and thorn in Athens' side for decades, and relations had often turned violent. In addition, Aegina's sympathies lay with Sparta, although in the late 450s Athens had forced it to join the Delian League. Its complaints to Sparta about Athens' oppressive leadership had helped rouse Sparta to war, and in the summer of the first year of the war (431) the Athenians took drastic action: they "expelled the Aeginetans with their wives and children from Aegina, accusing them of having been largely responsible for the war." To protect the island, they settled their own colonists there. "The exiles from Aegina received from Sparta the town of Thyrea to live in, with land to cultivate.... While some of the Aeginetans settled there, others were scattered about throughout the rest of Hellas" (Thucydides 2.27). This lasted until 424, when the Athenians raided the Spartan coast of Laconia and attacked Thyrea. Abandoned by a nearby Spartan garrison, the Aeginetans were killed or taken prisoner and brought to Athens where they were put to death "because of the inveterate hatred between the two peoples" (4.56–57). Only after the war's end did some of the survivors return to their island.

Similar cases occurred elsewhere. To end their revolt, the Spartans in the 460s allowed the Messenians to leave their stronghold on Mt. Ithome under the condition that they emigrated from the Peloponnese and never returned; the Athenians settled them in Naupactus on the Gulf of Corinth. When Potidaea capitulated after a long Athenian siege, the Athenians allowed the survivors to leave essentially with the clothes they were wearing and a minimal sum of money. The same happened to the inhabitants of Samos when Sparta took their city. Their fate is unknown.[42] In the early fourth century streams of refugees crowded the Greek countryside, and many Athenian citizens, or at least their womenfolk and children, expelled from the properties they had acquired in the territory of subject cities, returned to Athens and increased the misery there. Xenophon throws a stray light on the latter problem in a conversation of his Socrates, and Isocrates makes a few general statements on this problem, blaming it on the callous rule of Greece's new overlord, Sparta: as the result of wars and civil strife, many "are wandering with their women and children in strange lands." Generally, though, this aspect of the war's impact is sadly underrepresented in both sources and modern scholarship.[43]

The Plague of Mercenaries

In the passage quoted above, Isocrates juxtaposes the plight of the refugees with that of mercenaries: "Many, compelled through lack of the necessities of life to enlist in foreign armies, are being slain, fighting for their foes against their friends" (*Panegyric* 168). Some 40 years later, in his *Address to Philip* (king of Macedon), Isocrates comments that, under the conditions prevailing at the time (after decades of almost constant wars among

Greeks), "it is easier to get together a greater and stronger army from among those who wander in exile than from those who live under their own polities" (96). "Wandering from place to place," they commit "outrages upon whomsoever they encounter" (120). In a *Letter to Archidamus* (king of Sparta), Isocrates is more specific: the roving bands of mercenaries form armed contingents more numerous and powerful than the citizen forces of the communities in the area. "Every Hellenic city they enter they utterly destroy, killing some, driving others into exile, and robbing still others of their possessions; furthermore, they treat with indignity children and women" (910).

All this may be rhetorically exaggerated, but it is clear that mercenaries, although used all over the eastern Mediterranean since the late eighth century, were employed in increasing numbers during the Peloponnesian War and in the continuing wars of the early fourth century.[44] Each time their employment ended, or when their employers ran out of funds, they had to fend for themselves and posed a threat to the communities and civilian population of the area. A fourth-century manual on how to manage a city under siege illuminates these aspects:

> If allied forces have been brought into the city they should never be quartered all together but split up.... Likewise with paid mercenaries: the citizens who call them in to do something must always be superior to them in numbers and strength, or else both they and the state will be at the foreigners' mercy...; to be in power of foreigners and dominated by mercenaries is not safe. What happened to the men of Herakleia on the Black Sea illustrates this. By calling in more mercenaries than they should they were able in the short run to destroy the opposition faction but subsequently brought themselves and their state to ruin—under the tyranny of the man who led the mercenaries in. (Aeneas Tacticus, *How to Survive under Siege* 12.25; trans. Whitehead 1990)

Just as the tiny island of Melos attests to the dark side of imperialism, so too the tiny town of Mycalessus in Boeotia attests to the threat posed by mercenaries. In 413, the Athenians sent large reinforcements to Sicily to reinvigorate the stalled attack on Syracuse. A troop of Thracian mercenaries had arrived too late to join the expedition and was sent back with instructions to the commander "to use them in doing whatever damage he could to the enemy on their voyage along the coast." They raided one town in Boeotia and then attacked another, Mycalessus, farther inland. At daybreak they assaulted and took the town, which was hardly defended because nobody expected an attack.

> The Thracians burst into Mycalessus, sacked the houses and temples, and butchered the inhabitants, sparing neither the young nor the old, but methodically killing everyone they met, women and

children alike, and even the farm animals and every living thing they saw.... [T]here was confusion on all sides and death in every shape and form. Among other things, they broke into a boys' school, the largest in the place, into which the children had just entered, and killed every one of them....Mycalessus lost a considerable part of its population. It was a small city, but in the disaster just described its people suffered calamities as pitiable as any which took place during the war. (Thucydides 7.29–30)

These were Thracians, "barbarians" whom Thucydides describes as "always particularly bloodthirsty when everything is going their own way." But they were acting on Athenian instructions and under an Athenian commander.

War's Impact on Women and Families

War, like politics, was men's business, and women were supposed to be silent and invisible, simply accepting what their men decided and did.[45] It is only in comedy that women, fed up with the men's irresponsible decisions, take over; unrealistic though these stories are, what they reveal about what was going on inside the house walls may contain more than a kernel of truth. Thus, for example, Lysistrata complains:

All along, being proper women, we used to suffer
in silence no matter what you men did, because you wouldn't let us
make a sound. But you weren't exactly all we could ask for. No,
we knew only too well what you were up to, and too many times we'd hear
in our homes about a bad decision you'd made on some great issue of
state. Then, masking the pain in our hearts, we'd put on a smile and
ask you, "How did the Assembly go today? Any decision about a rider
to the peace treaty?" And my husband would say, "What's that to you?
Shut up!" And I'd shut up ...
            Later on, we began to hear
about even worse decisions you'd made, and then we would ask,
"Husband, how come you're handling this so stupidly?" And right away
he'd glare at me and tell me to get back to my sewing if I didn't want
major damage to my head. Quote: War shall be the business of
menfolk, unquote!
            (Aristophanes, *Lysistrata* 522–38; trans. Henderson 1996, 60)

Naturally, with the exception of the mythical Amazons and other legendary female tribes, women were not expected to participate in actual fighting. But in situations of dire emergency, they did, supplying food and missiles to the male fighters or even occupying the walls or house roofs and pelting the enemy with tiles and other missiles, in some cases actually turning the battle around. In Corcyra in 427 BCE, "the people won, as they had the advantage in the strength of their position as well as in numbers. The women also boldly took part with them in the fight, hurling tiles from the houses and enduring the uproar with a courage beyond their sex" (Thucydides 3.74.1). Interestingly, Plato thinks that women should be trained in military matters so that, like men, they would be able to defend their community, and Plutarch's essay *On the Bravery of Women* contains several stories that show to what extent they were capable of doing so.[46] For example,

> of all the deeds performed by women for the community, none is more famous than the struggle against Cleomenes for Argos, which the women carried out at the instigation of Telesilla the poetess.... When Cleomenes king of the Spartans, having slain many Argives... proceeded against the city, an impulsive daring, divinely inspired, came to the younger women to try, for their country's sake, to hold off the enemy. Under the lead of Telesilla they took up arms, and taking their stand by the battlements, manned the walls all round, so that the enemy were amazed. The result was that Cleomenes they repulsed with great loss, and the other king, Demaratus, who managed to get inside... they drove out. In this way the city was saved. The women who fell in the battle they buried close by the Argive Road, and to the survivors they granted the privilege of erecting a statue of Ares as a memorial of their surpassing valor.... On the anniversary [of this day] they celebrate... the "Festival of Impudence," at which they clothe the women in men's shirts and cloaks, and the men in women's robes and veils. (Plutarch *Moralia* 245c–f)

These clearly were rare exceptions. Usually women experienced war as wives and mothers of warriors, as widows—and as victims (see below). It is again Lysistrata who in her confrontation with an official draws attention to this aspect:

> *Lysistrata:* Then, when we ought to be having fun and enjoying our bloom of youth, we sleep alone because of the campaigns. And to say no more about *our* case, it pains me to think of the maidens growing old in their rooms [because the war kills their prospective husbands].
> *Official:* Men grow old too, don't they?
> *Lysistrata:* That's quite a different story. When a man comes home he can quickly find a girl to marry, even if he's a greybeard. But a woman's prime is brief; if she doesn't seize it no one wants to marry her, and she sits at home looking for good omens.
>
> (*Lysistrata* 620–628)

Exceptionally, Thucydides lets Pericles in the Funeral Oration tackle the sensitive issue of women's suffering in war. Trying to comfort the parents of the fallen, he encourages them to think of the good fortune involved:

> for men to end their lives with honor, as these have done, and for you honorably to lament them. . . . I know that it is difficult to convince you of this. When you see other people happy you will often be reminded of what used to make you happy too. . . . All the same, those of you who are of the right age must bear up and take comfort in the thought of having more children. In your own homes these new children will prevent you from brooding over those who are no more, and they will be a help to the city, too, both in filling the empty places, and in assuring her security. As for those of you who are now too old to have children, I would ask you to count as gain the greater part of your life, in which you have been happy. (Thucydides 2.44)

Remarkably, Pericles does not encourage the widows (as opposed to mothers) in the same way. What did the community do for them and the war orphans? In the same oration, Pericles states: "The city will undertake the upbringing of their children (*paides*) until they grow up, thus conferring a valuable crown on them. . . . Where the prizes for valour are the greatest, there the men will be the best citizens" (2.46.1; trans Rhodes).[47] State support for orphans, though minimal, is well attested: it was probably introduced in the 460s or 450s, when communal warfare intensified, losses increased due to the predominance of naval warfare, especially among lower-class men whose families could not rely on the security net available to farmers, and perhaps a big disaster drew public attention to the plight of those affected. Support lasted until the orphans reached adulthood and were discharged to their families during a public ceremony on the first day of the Great Dionysia: their and their fathers' names were proclaimed and they received spear and shield, thus qualifying for military service.[48]

Much else is unclear. What about female war orphans? After all, the words used (*paides* and *orphanoi*) can apply to boys and girls. We know that in other places state maintenance was provided to parents and daughters of war heroes, and the daughters received a dowry as well. In Athens, daughters perhaps were given a food allowance, parents moral and legal support. It is astonishing that we know nothing about material support for war widows. Nor, apparently, were any provisions made for the families of the thousands of resident aliens (metics) who were not only a crucial part of the Athenian workforce but fought and died alongside the Athenian citizens. Social measures in this sphere, as Pericles suggests, were primarily intended to raise future citizen soldiers and strengthen the fighting citizens' morale: if they knew that their families would be cared for, they were likely to fight with greater determination.[49]

The most obvious impact of war on women was the sexual violence and enslavement they suffered when they fell into the hands of conquering troops. Homer illustrates this aspect with multiple examples, from enslaved princesses and heroes' wives like Briseis and Andromache to anonymous women; Euripides puts it on stage in his war plays (*Trojan Women, Hecuba, Andromache*); in Hesiod, in peace "women bear children who resemble their fathers" (in war, this often is not the case). Like so much else, everybody knew about all this, and other sources, especially the historians, rarely mention it.[50] In our own time, it is all too familiar not least from news reports about abuses and atrocities committed by combatants in local African wars or the debates about recognition of forced prostitution imposed on women in areas conquered by Japanese troops before and during World War II.

Dependence on Slaves

The ancient Greek poleis were slave societies; their relationship to slaves was ambivalent. They treated them with contempt as foreigners and unfree but integrated them into their households and businesses. Especially in Athens and Sparta, the community also came to depend on them both economically and militarily. This prompted changes in treatment of slaves and attitudes toward them, and caused disconcerting contradictions between economic or military role and legal status that affected the entire community. The discomfort the Greeks felt especially about the slaves' military role seems to be reflected in the historians' efforts to ignore or obfuscate their contribution.[51]

The Spartan citizens (Spartiates) depended doubly on their exceptionally large population of helots. On the one hand, the helots cultivated the citizens' farms and thus enabled them to live their privileged life of professional citizen-soldiers.[52] On the other hand, given that the Spartiates' number was small and declining, the helots (and the second-class citizens living in the "perioikic" communities) were also indispensable to complement the ranks of the Spartiate hoplite army. At the battle of Plataea, supposedly seven helots accompanied every single Spartiate, for a total of 35,000, mostly serving as light-armed troops and probably filling the hind ranks of the phalanx—certainly an exceptional number. It is quite possible that, just as the participation of large numbers of African soldiers in the British armies of World War II accelerated decolonization, so too the helot veterans of Plataea upon returning home played a crucial role in fomenting the massive helot revolt of the 460s. Helots were also used in large numbers for campaigns far away from home (such as those of Brasidas in the northern Aegean in the late 420s). The survivors were often freed and settled in marginal areas. Most importantly, Thucydides offers reports

that illustrate the extraordinary measures the Spartiates took, in addition
to their usual oppressive methods of controlling and terrorizing the helots, to neutralize the potential sociopolitical impact of the helots' military
service.[53] In one case, he says, the Spartiates

> were so frightened of [the helots'] unyielding character and of their
> numbers that they had had recourse to the following plan.... They
> made a proclamation to the effect that the helots should choose out
> of their own number those who claimed to have done the best ser-
> vice to Sparta on the battlefield, implying that they would be given
> their freedom. This was, however, a test conducted in the belief that
> the ones who showed most spirit and came forward first to claim
> their freedom would be the ones most likely to turn against Sparta.
> So about 2,000 were selected, who put garlands on their heads and
> went round the temples under the impression that they were being
> made free men. Soon afterwards, however, the Spartans did away
> with them, and no one ever knew exactly how each one of them was
> killed. (Thucydides 4.80.34)

Moreover, there are good reasons to think that the "helot problem" had
a deep impact on the Spartans' foreign policy, forcing them to abandon
their expansionist drive and focus on maintaining the status quo.[54]

In many ways, Sparta was an exception. But in Athens too slave labor
was a crucial condition for making an unusual political system—imperial
democracy—possible. Here too this happened in two major ways. On the
one hand, slaves contributed to their city's military achievements. They
are attested in the Athenian land army at Marathon and probably served
more often, if not regularly; they certainly rowed the warships side by side
with their masters. Large numbers were enlisted in times of emergency,
especially during the Peloponnesian War.[55] A rare light falls on this in
a letter of the Athenian commander in Sicily, Nicias, who noted that,
since the war was not going well, the slaves began running away. Often
they were freed before going into action. Very exceptionally, those fighting in the Arginusae battle were enfranchised collectively (yet remained
second-class citizens without the active citizen capacities typical of full
citizens).[56]

The pamphlet of an opponent of democracy, preserved among
Xenophon's works, illustrates how the Athenian community's dependence
on its slaves affected their treatment and actual (though not legal) status.
He observes that in Athens one must not strike slaves because in appearance and clothing they are indistinguishable from metics, freedmen, and
even lower-class citizens.

> If someone is surprised at this, that [the Athenians] allow their slaves
> to live in the lap of luxury, and some of them indeed to live a life of

real magnificence, this too is something that they can be seen to do with good reason. For where power is based on the navy, because of the need for money there is no choice but to end up enslaved to slaves, so that we can take a share of their earnings, and to let them go free.... This is why in the matter of freedom of speech we have put slaves on equal terms with free men, and metics with citizens, for the city needs metics because of all its skilled activities and because of the fleet. (Pseudo-Xenophon, *Constitution of the Athenians* 1.10–12; trans. Osborne 2004)

Sarcasm and exaggeration should not obscure the very real causal connection the author establishes here between increased freedom of movement and enterprise on the part of slaves, the monetary needs of an imperial power based on a large fleet, and the extraordinary commitment to the public sphere that democracy demanded of its citizens. The formulation that the citizens are enslaved to the slaves is extraordinary. Of course, there were enormous differences, but in the urban and domestic spheres Athenian slaves were freer than elsewhere.[57]

The City under Siege

From the end of the Peloponnesian War to the Macedonian victory at Chaeronea that led to the imposition of peace and outside control, large parts of Greece were almost constantly at war or under the threat of war. This period witnessed the professionalization of warfare and the emergence of manuals with instructions for various aspects of warfare. One of these, written in the mid-fourth century by one Aeneas called "the Tactician," is entitled "How to Survive under Siege."[58] It deals with the responsibility of those in charge of a city's security to be constantly alert and prepared for expected or unexpected attacks. One of the most interesting aspects of this treatise is its frequent warning to be aware of the danger of betrayal from among the citizens.[59] Thus, for example, the troops selected to defend and patrol the city

must be men who are both loyal and satisfied with the status quo: the existence of such a unified body is important, to stand citadel-like against the plots of traitors and intimidate the opposition within the state.... [Gatekeepers] ought to be well-to-do individuals with something at stake in the community—children and a wife, I mean—and not men whom poverty, or the pressure of obligations, or desperation of some other kind might leave open to being persuaded to join a revolution.... As for the mass of the citizens, it is of the utmost importance...to foster unanimity, winning them over by such means as lessening the burdens on debtors by reducing or completely cancelling interest payments. At times of extreme danger, even the capital sums owed may be partially or, if necessary, wholly cancelled.... Provide the basic amenities of life for the needy, too...(*How to Survive Under Siege* 1.6; 5.1; 14.1)

Apart from strictly military measures, issues discussed include censorship of incoming and outgoing letters (10.6); caution during competitions or festivals held outside the city to prevent opponents from exploiting such moments of vulnerability (17); methods to send secret messages (31); and ways to prevent panic and deal with it (27).

Of course, a city enclosed in wartime, whether by a siege or by choice, was likely to suffer other calamities too. I mention only two Athenian examples. At the beginning of the Peloponnesian War, when the Athenians accepted Pericles' war plan to sacrifice their country-side, evacuate the rural population inside the Long Walls, focus on the defense of the impregnable fortress Athens-Piraeus, and use their control of the seas to bring in the necessary supplies, they could indeed not be harmed by Spartan war efforts but they fell victims to a terrible epidemic that raged through the population crowded into shantytowns and killed tens of thousands.[60] In the final stage of the war, when Athens had lost its sea power and was no longer able to import food, scores of people died of starvation.[61] Finally, it was presumably more because of Sparta's pragmatic decision to use a severely weakened Athenian ally to balance Theban and Corinthian aspirations than in recognition of Athens' merits in the Persian Wars that after its capitulation it was spared the fate it had imposed on many defeated communities and that many Spartan allies demanded now: wholesale erasure of the community (by destroying the city, killing the men, and selling women and children into slavery).[62]

Conclusion

I have discussed war's impact on those fighting (the brutal face of war, care for the dead, care for the wounded, and the fate of prisoners of war) and on the noncombatant population (refugees, suffering caused by mercenaries, war's impact on women and families and on the role and treatment of slaves, and the fate of cities under siege). Despite its length, this survey has only scratched the surface. Much more could (and eventually should) be said, not only in adding further details but also in engaging in deeper analysis and expanding the study to other areas, such as the impact of war on political and religious life and ideological conflicts. The latter aspects will be discussed at least briefly elsewhere.[63] As is evident from my notes and bibliography, scholars have analyzed many relevant aspects thoroughly in individual studies. What has been missing is a comprehensive, systematic, and coherent analysis of the entire range of issues, preferably covering a longer period of time. Despite the reticence of our sources, enough material survives to justify such an attempt. It will enormously enrich our understanding of the social dimension of ancient warfare.

Notes

1. All dates are BCE. Unless indicated otherwise, translations are taken from Penguin or Loeb Classical Library volumes.
2. See Raaflaub (2001). Military competitions at the Panathenaic Festival: Kyle (1992). Plutarch, *Nicias* 20 on the eve of the Sicilian expedition: "the young men in the wrestling-schools and the old men in the shops or the public meeting-places sat about tracing maps of Sicily or charts of the sea and the harbours and the coast–line facing Africa."
3. Hesiod, *Theogony* 211–32, 901–2. Micro-states: Davies (1997); citizen-states: Hansen (1993). The citizens are the polis: Alcaeus 112.10, 426; Campbell (1982); Thucydides 7.77.7.
4. Hodkinson (2000) and Cartledge (2001, 2002).
5. Hellenic League: Brunt (1993, ch. 3). Persian Wars: Green (1996). Athenian decisions: Herodotus 7.140–144.
6. Meiggs (1972).
7. Shipyards: Garland (1987); Democracy: Rhodes (1992); Hansen (1999); Raaflaub (2007).
8. On the Peloponnesian War, see Kagan (2003) and Tritle (2010).
9. On hoplite warfare, see n. 15 below. Cavalry: for example, Spence (1993); Gaebel (2002). Light-armed troops: Lippelt (1910); Best (1969); Anderson (1970, 111–40); Lissarrague (1990). Naval warfare: Gabrielsen (1994); Morrison et al. (2000). See also Hanson (2001) and Hunt (2007).
10. On the Megarian embargo, see Brunt (1993, ch. 1); on excesses of civil war, see the first of three case studies below.
11. Raaflaub forthcoming. Various sections in Pritchett (1971–1991) and van Wees (2004) deal with issues relevant to this study. Meier (1990) offers incisive observations on archaic and classical Greek warfare.
12. Description: Thucydides 3.69–81; typology: 82–4; see Price (2001) and, more generally, Gehrke (1984) and Fisher (2000).
13. Herodotus 1.5. On Athens' capitulation, see Bleckmann (1998) and Munn (2000: ch. 8). On *Trojan Women*, see, for example, Scodel (1980); Gregory (1991, 155–81); and Croally (1994).
14. On the play's interpretation, see Henderson (1980) and Newiger (1980). On the ideological aspects, see Raaflaub (2001, 329–34).
15. On hoplite battle, see, for example, Anderson (1970); Lazenby (1991); Mitchell (1996); Hanson (2000); Wheeler (2007); and Tritle (2009b); see also Dayton (2005). On hoplite armor, see Anderson (1991). On the agony of infantry fighting in Homer, see Raaflaub (2013).
16. Wheeler (2007, 209–10) and Tritle (2009b, 60).
17. Isocrates 4.97 and Lysias 2.37–39; see also Thucydides 7.72 on the great battle in the harbor of Syracuse. Strauss (2007, 233–4) offers further evidence.
18. Herodotus 6.117. The number of Persian dead was certainly much higher than that of the Athenians but the number cited is the result of an artificial calculation, counting 100 Persians for every 3 Athenians: Avery (1973, 756); Wyatt (1976).

19. Thucydides 4.93.3, 94.1, 101.2 (quote), Xenophon, *Hellenica* 2.1.31–32 (Aigospotamoi); Lazenby (1991, 101); and Wheeler (2007, 12–13).

20. Krentz (1985); Strauss (2007, 236; 2000); Arginusae: Xenophon, *Hellenica* 1.6.27ff.; Egypt: Thucydides 1.104, 109–10; on Athenian war losses in general, see Strauss (1986, 179–82); Hansen (1988, 14–28); and Brulé (1999). See also Hanson (1999, 208–15) on the eradication of Boetian Thespiae as the result of repeated war losses.

21. Hunt (2010, 11).

22. See Akrigg (2014).

23. For discussion, see Vaughn (1991) and Jackson (1991).

24. *Iliad* 7.325–335, 394–6, 421–32.

25. Pausanias 1.32.4. One of the Marathon stelae has been discovered: Steinhauer (2010). On the burial of the war dead, see Pritchett (1971–1991, IV. 94–259).

26. Meier (1993, 166–203).

27. *IG* I³ 1162, ML 48, and Clairmont (1983, no. 32b).

28. On the funeral orations, see Loraux (1986).

29. Estimates of the mortality of the wounded: Wheeler (2007, 212–13); see also Jacob (1932); Hanson (2000, 210–18); and Salazar (2000).

30. *Hellenica* 4.5.14.

31. *Characters* 25.4–8. On the transport of wounded warriors, see Sternberg (1999). The Homeric evidence is discussed in Raaflaub (2013).

32. The story in Herodotus 7.181 presumably is a great exception.

33. Philoctetes: Edwards (2000); Tritle (2010: 191–3) (quote: 192).

34. Miracle inscriptions: LiDonnici (1995) (with the quotes).

35. Aristotle, *Constitution of the Athenians* 49.4 with Rhodes (1981): *ad loc.*; Lysias 24 with Roussel (1966); Edwards and Usher (1986: 200–7, 263–9); Aeschines 1.103–104; Plato, *Crito* 53a (blind, lame, and crippled persons); Thucydides 2.49.7–8 (the plague's crippling effects on the body).

36. See Tritle (2009a, 2010, 158–60).

37. Symptoms of PTSD in Homer: Shay (1994, 2000, 2002); Tritle (1997); see further Tritle (2000, 2003, 2004, 2010, 193).

38. Krentz (2007, 180–1).

39. Sphacteria: Thucydides 4.38, 41. On war captives, see Pritchett (1991, 203–312) and Ducrey (1999). On their enslavement, see Gaca (2010, 2011b). A vase painting reproduced in Krentz (2007, 181) shows men (perhaps war captives) being tortured or executed by drowning. If the former, not even "waterboarding" is a modern invention. On the fate of women, see below.

40. See Hirschon (2003) and Clark (2006); for the larger context, see Fromkin 1989.

41. See, for example, Herodotus 1.164–165 on Phocaea, 1.168 on Teos, 6.22 on Samos. On the topic of "urban relocation," see Demand (1990).

42. Thucydides 1.103.1, 2.70.3 and Xenophon, *Hellenica* 2.3.6.

43. Xenophon, *Memorabilia* 2.7 and Isocrates 4 (*Panegyric*) 168. See generally Seibert (1979).

44. On mercenaries, see Parke (1933); Bettalli (1995); Burckhardt (1996, ch. 3); and Hunt (2007, 140–4).

45. See especially Thucydides 2.46.1: "the greatest glory of a woman is to be least talked about by men, whether they are praising you or criticizing you."

46. Plato, *Laws* 813e–814c; cf. *Republic* 451e–452a, c, 466c–d and Plutarch, *Moralia* 242e–263c; see also, for example, Aeneas Tacticus 40.4–5; Diodorus 13.55.4–5, 56.6–7; and Plutarch, *Pyrrhus* 27. On the Amazons, see Blok (1995); on Scythian women warriors, see Hippocrates, *Airs, Waters, Places* 17.

47. See also Cratinus fr. 183 *PCG*.
48. State support for orphans: Aristotle, *Constitution of the Athenians* 24.3 (with other refs. in Rhodes 1981, 308–9); cf. Pseudo-Xenophon, *Constitution of the Athenians* 3.4. One obol: *Supplementum Epigraphicum Graecum* 28: 46 with Stroud (1971, 287). For discussion, see Raaflaub (1998, 30–1) with bibliog. in nn. 117–20 on pp. 353–4. Ruschenbusch (1979, 81) suggests the Egyptian disaster as an event that triggered such legislation. On the ceremony at the Dionysia, see Isocrates 8 (*Peace*), 82; Aeschines 3 (*Against Ctesiphon*), 153–4; Loraux (1986, 26–7); and Goldhill (1990, 107–14).
49. For sources and bibliography on these issues, see Raaflaub (1998, 31–2). Widows in Funeral Oration: Thucydides 2.45.2. Raising citizen soldiers: ibid. 44.3.
50. Hesiod, *Works and Days* 235 (West (1978, 215–16) misses this meaning which seems obvious in the context). See Schaps (1982) and Gaca (2008, 2011a) with bibliography. What Harvey (1985) says about women in Thucydides is instructive.
51. On slavery in general, see, for example, Garlan (1988); Cartledge (1993, ch. 6); and Bradley and Cartledge (2011). On the use of slaves in war, see Garlan (1972, 1975, 78–82) and Welwei (1974–1988). On ideology and the historians, see Hunt (1998).
52. On the helots, see Ducat (1990); Cartledge (2002, ch. 10); Luraghi and Alcock (2003); and Welwei (2006).
53. Citizen numbers: Hodkinson (1993). Helots at Plataea: Herodotus 9.10–11, 28; Hunt (1997, 1998, 31–9, 53–82). Role in revolt: Luraghi (2001, 301). Distant campaigns: for example, Thucydides 4.80.5. Oppressive measures: Cartledge (1987, 170–7).
54. See the debate between Talbert (1989) and Cartledge (1991).
55. Welwei (1974–1988, I. 96–107) and Rosivach (1985). On slavery and democracy, see Osborne (1995) and Raaflaub (1998, 26–8).
56. Thucydides 7.13.2. Enfranchisement: Hunt (2001).
57. Humphreys (1978); Osborne (1995); and Raaflaub (1998, 26–8). On Pseudo-Xenophon 1.11, see also Bechtle (1996).
58. Translation and commentary in Bettalli (1990) and Whitehead (1990). See also Lehmann (1980) and Lintott (1982).
59. We are reminded of Thucydides' account of civil strife (*stasis*) in Corcyra (3.69–84) and his observation that the frequency and intensity of *stasis* are directly connected with war (82.1). See Gehrke 1985; Price 2001.
60. Thucydides 2.47–54; see Hornblower (1991, 316–18).
61. Xenophon, *Hellenica* 2.2.11, 16, 21.
62. Xenophon, *Hellenica* 2.2.19–20.
63. Raaflaub forthcoming.

Bibliography

Akrigg, Benjamin. Forthcoming. *Population and Economy in Classical Athens*. Cambridge: University Press.

Anderson, J. K. 1970. *Military Theory and Practice in the Age of Xenophon*. Berkeley and Los Angeles: University of California Press.

———. 1991. "Hoplite Weapons and Offensive Arms." In Hanson 1991, 15–37.

Avery, Harry. 1973. "Persian Dead at Marathon." *Historia* 22: 756.

Bechtle, Gerald. 1996. "A Note on Pseudo-Xenophon, *The Constitution of the Athenians*, 1.11." *Classical Quarterly* 46: 564–6.

Best, J. G. P. 1969. *Thracian Peltasts and Their Influence on Greek Warfare*. Groningen: Wolters-Noordhoff.

Bettalli, Marco. 1990. *La difesa di una città assediata (Poliorketika). Introduzione, traduzione e commento.* Pisa: ETS Editrice.

——. 1995. *I mercenari nel mondo greco,* I: *Dalle origini alla fine del V sec. a.C.* Pisa: ETS Editrice.

Bleckmann, Bruno. 1998. *Athens Weg in die Niederlage. Die letzten Jahre des Peloponnesischen Kriegs.* Stuttgart: Teubner.

Blok, Josine. 1995. *The Early Amazons: Modern and Ancient Perspectives on a Persistent Myth.* Leiden: Brill.

Bradley, Keith, and Paul Cartledge, eds. 2011. *The Cambridge World History of Slavery,* I: *The Ancient Mediterranean World.* Cambridge: Cambridge University Press.

Brulé, P. 1999. "La mortalité de guerre en Grèce classique: L'exemple d'Athènes de 490 à 322." In *Armées et sociétés de la Grèce classique: Aspects sociaux et politiques de la guerre aux Ve et IVe s. av. J.-C.,* edited by F. Prost, 51–68. Paris: Editions Errances.

Brunt, P. A. 1993. *Studies in Greek History and Thought.* Oxford: Clarendon.

Burckhardt, Leonhard A. 1996. *Bürger und Soldaten.* Stuttgart: Steiner.

Campbell, D.A., ed., trans. 1982. *Greek Lyric,* 1. Cambridge, MA: Harvard University Press.

Cartledge, Paul. 1987. *Agesilaos and the Crisis of Sparta.* London: Duckworth.

——. 1991. "Richard Talbert's Revision of the Spartan-Helot Struggle: A Reply." *Historia* 40: 379–81.

——. 1993. *The Greeks: A Portrait of Self and Others.* Oxford: Oxford University Press.

——. 2001. *Spartan Reflections.* London: Duckworth.

——. 2002. *Sparta and Lakonia: A Regional History 1300 to 362 BC.* 2nd ed. London: Routledge.

Clairmont, Christoph W. 1983. *Patrios Nomos: Public Burial in Athens during the Fifth and Fourth Centuries B.C.* Oxford: British Archaeological Reports.

Clark, Bruce. 2006. *Twice a Stranger: The Mass Expulsions That Forged Modern Greece and Turkey.* Cambridge, MA: Harvard University Press.

Croally, N. T. 1994. *Euripidean Polemic: The Trojan Women and the Function of Tragedy.* Cambridge: Cambridge University Press.

Davies, J. K. 1997. "The 'Origins of the Greek *Polis*': Where Should We Be Looking?" In *The Development of the* polis *in Archaic Greece,* edited by L. G. Mitchell and P. J. Rhodes, 24–38. London: Routledge.

Dayton, John C. 2005. *The Athletes of War: An Evaluation of the Agonistic Elements in Greek Warfare.* Toronto: E. Kent.

Demand, Nancy H. 1990. *Urban Relocation in Archaic and Classical Greece.* Norman: University of Oklahoma Press.

Ducat, Jean. 1990. *Les hilotes.* Athens and Paris: Ecole française d'Athènes.

Ducrey, Pierre. 1999. *Le traitement des prisonniers de guerre dans la Grèce antique.* 2nd ed. Athens and Paris: Ecole française d'Athènes.

Edwards, M., and S. Usher. 1986. *Greek Orators,* I: *Antiphon & Lysias. Trans. with Comm. and Notes.* Warminster: Aris and Phillips.

Edwards, Martha. 2000. "Philoctetes in Historical Context." In *Disabled Veterans in History,* edited by David A. Gerber, 55–69. Ann Arbor: University of Michigan Press.

Fisher, Nick. 2000. "Hybris, Revenge, and Stasis in the Greek City-States." In van Wees 2000, 83–123.

Fromkin, David. 1989. *A Peace to End All Peace: Creating the Modern Middle East, 1914–1922.* New York: Avon Books.

Gabrielsen, Vincent. 1994. *Financing the Athenian Fleet: Public Taxation and Social Relations.* Baltimore, MD: Johns Hopkins University Press.

Gaca, Kathy L. 2008. "The Little Girl and Her Mother: *Iliad* 16.7–11 and Ancient Greek Warfare." *American Journal of Philology* 129: 145–71.

——. 2010. "The Andrapodizing of War Captives in Greek Historical Memory." *Transactions of the American Philological Association* 140: 117–61.

——. 2011a. "Girls, Women, and the Significance of Sexual Violence in Ancient Warfare." In *Sexual Violence in Conflict Zones,* edited by Elizabeth Heineman, 73–88. Philadelphia: University of Pennsylvania Press.

————. 2011b. "Manhandled and Kicked Around: Reinterpreting the Etymology and Significance of *andrapoda*." *Indogermanische Forschungen* 116: 110–46.

Gaebel, Robert E. 2002. *Cavalry Operations in the Ancient Greek World*. Norman: University of Oklahoma Press.

Gagarin, Michael, and Paul Woodruff, eds., trans. 1995. *Early Greek Political Thought from Homer to the Sophists*. Cambridge: Cambridge University Press.

Garlan, Yvon. 1972. "Les esclaves grecs en temps de guerre." In *Actes du colloque d'histoire sociale 1970*, 29–62. Paris: Belles Lettres.

————. 1975. *War in the Ancient World: A Social History*. Trans. Janet Lloyd. London: Chatto and Windus.

————. 1988. *Slavery in Ancient Greece*. Trans. Janet Lloyd. Rev. ed. Ithaca, NY: Cornell University Press.

Gehrke, Hans-Joachim. 1985. *Stasis. Untersuchungen zu den inneren Kriegen in den griechischen Staaten des 5. und 4. Jahrhunderts v.Chr.* Munich: Beck.

Goldhill, Simon. 1990. "The Great Dionysia and Civic Ideology." In *Nothing to Do with Dionysos? Athenian Drama in Its Social Context*, edited by J. J. Winkler and Froma Zeitlin, 97–129. Princeton, NJ: Princeton University Press.

Green, Peter. 1996. *The Greco-Persian Wars*. Berkeley and Los Angeles: University of California Press.

Gregory, Justina. 1991. *Euripides and the Instruction of the Athenians*. Ann Arbor: University of Michigan Press.

Hansen, M. H. 1988. *Three Studies in Athenian Demography*. Copenhagen: The Royal Danish Academy of Sciences and Letters.

————, ed. 1993. *The Ancient Greek City-State*. Copenhagen: The Royal Danish Academy of Sciences and Letters.

————. 1999. *The Athenian Democracy in the Age of Demosthenes*. Exp. ed. Norman: University of Oklahoma Press.

Hanson, Victor D., ed. 1991. *Hoplites: The Classical Greek Battle Experience*. London: Routledge.

————. 1999. "Hoplite Obliteration: The Case of the Town of Thespiae." In *Ancient Warfare: Archaeological Perspectives*, edited by John Carman and Anthony Harding, 203–17. Stroud, Gloucestershire: Sutton Pub.

————. 2000. *The Western Way of War*. 2nd ed. Berkeley and Los Angeles: University of California Press.

————. 2001. "Democratic Warfare, Ancient and Modern." In McCann and Strauss 2001, 3–33.

Harvey, David. 1985. "Women in Thucydides." *Arethusa* 18: 67–90.

Henderson, Jeffrey, ed. 1980a. *Aristophanes: Essays in Interpretation*. *Yale Classical Studies* 26.

————. 1980b. "Lysistrata: The Play and Its Themes." In Henderson 1980a, 153–218.

————. 1996. *Three Plays by Aristophanes Staging Women*. New York and London: Routledge.

Hirschon, Renée, ed. 2003. *Crossing the Aegean: An Appraisal of the 1923 Compulsory Population Exchange between Greece and Turkey*. New York: Berghahn Books.

Hodkinson, Stephen. 1993. "Warfare, Wealth, and the Crisis of Spartiate Society." In Rich and Shipley 1993, 146–76.

————. 2000. *Property and Wealth in Classical Sparta*. London: Duckworth, and Swansea: Classical Press of Wales.

Hornblower, Simon. 1991. *A Commentary on Thucydides*, I. Oxford: Clarendon.

Humphreys, S. C. 1978. "Economy and Society in Classical Athens." In Humphreys, *Anthropology and the Greeks*, 136–58. London: Routledge and Kegan Paul.

Hunt, Peter. 1997. "Helots at the Battle of Plataea." *Historia* 46: 129–44.

————. 1998. *Slaves, Warfare and Ideology in the Greek Historians*. Cambridge: Cambridge University Press.

————. 2001. "The Slaves and the Generals of Arginusae." *American Journal of Philology* 122: 359–80.

————. 2007. "Military Forces." In Sabin et al. 2007, 108–46.

————. 2010. *War, Peace, and Alliance in Demosthenes' Athens*. Cambridge: Cambridge University Press.

Jackson, A. H. 1991. "Hoplites and the Gods: The Dedication of Captured Arms and Armour." In Hanson 1991, 228–49.

Jacob, O. 1932. "La cité grecque et les blessés de guerre." In *Mélanges Gustave Glotz*, II, 961–81. Paris: Presses Universitaires de France.

Kagan, Donald. 2003. *The Peloponnesian War*. New York: Viking.

Krentz, Peter. 1985. "Casualties in Hoplite Battles." *Greek, Roman, and Byzantine Studies* 26: 13–21.

———. 2007. "War." In Sabin et al. 2007, I.147–85.

Kyle, Donald G. 1992. "The Panathenaic Games: Sacred and Civic Athletics." In *Goddess and Polis: The Panathenaic Festival in Ancient Athens*, edited by Jenifer Neils, 77–101. Hanover, NH: Hood Museum of Art and Princeton, NJ: Princeton University Press.

Lazenby, John. 1991. "The Killing Zone." In Hanson 1991, 87–109.

Lehmann, G. A. 1980. "Krise und innere Bedrohung der hellenischen Polis bei Aeneas Tacticus." In *Studien zur antiken Sozialgeschichte: Festschrift Friedrich Vittinghoff*, edited by Werner Eck, Hartmut Galsterer, and Hartmut Wolff, /1–86. Cologne: Böhlau.

LiDonnici, L. R. 1995. *The Epidaurian Miracle Inscriptions*. Atlanta: Scholars Press.

Lintott, Andrew. 1982. *Violence, Civil Strife and Revolution in the Classical City, 750–330 BC*. Baltimore, MD: Johns Hopkins University Press.

Lippelt, Otto. 1910. *Die griechischen Leichtbewaffneten bis auf Alexander den Grossen*. Weida, Thüringen: Thomas and Hubert.

Lissarrague, François. 1990. *L'autre guerrier: Archers, peltastes, cavaliers dans l'imagerie attique*. Paris: La Découverte.

Loraux, Nicole. 1986. *The Invention of Athens: The Funeral Oration in the Classical City*. Trans. Alan Sheridan. Cambridge, MA: Harvard University Press.

Luraghi, Nino. 2001. "Der Erdbebenaufstand und die Entstehung der messenischen Identität." In *Gab es das griechische Wunder? Griechenland zwischen dem Ende des 6. und der Mitte des 5. Jahrhunderts v.Chr.*, edited by Dietrich Papenfuss and Volker M. Strocka, 279–301. Mainz: von Zabern.

Luraghi, Nino and Susan Alcock, eds. 2003. *Helots and Their Masters in Laconia and Messenia: Histories, Ideologies, Structures*. Washington DC: Center for Hellenic Studies.

McCann, David R., and Barry S. Strauss, eds. 2001. *War and Democracy: A Comparative Study of the Korean War and the Peloponnesian War*. Armonk, NY and London: M. E. Sharpe.

Meier, Christian. 1990. "Die Rolle des Krieges im klassischen Athen." *Historische Zeitschrift* 251: 555–605.

———. 1993. *The Political Art of Greek Tragedy*. Trans. Andrew Webber. Baltimore, MD: Johns Hopkins University Press. Orig. German ed. Munich: Beck, 1988.

Meiggs, Russell. 1972. *The Athenian Empire*. Oxford: Clarendon.

Mitchell, Stephen. 1996. "Hoplite Warfare in Ancient Greece." In *Battle in Antiquity*, edited by A. B. Lloyd, 87–105. London: Duckworth, and Swansea: Classical Press of Wales.

Morrison, J. S., J. F. Coates, and N. B. Rankov. 2000. *The Athenian Trireme: The History and Reconstruction of an Ancient Greek Warship*. 2nd ed. Cambridge: Cambridge University Press.

Munn, Mark. 2000. *The School of History: Athens in the Age of Socrates*. Berkeley and Los Angeles: University of California Press.

Newiger, Hans-Joachim. 1980. "War and Peace in the Comedy of Aristphanes." In Henderson 1980a, 219–37.

Osborne, Robin. 1995. "The Economics and Politics of Slavery at Athens." In *The Greek World*, edited by Anton Powell, 27–43. London: Routledge.

———. 2004. *The Old Oligarch: Pseudo-Xenophon's Constitution of the Athenians. Introduction, Translation, and Commentary*. 2nd ed. London: LACTOR.

Parke, H. W. 1933. *Greek Mercenary Soldiers from the Earliest Times to the Battle of Ipsus*. Oxford: Clarendon. Repr. Chicago: Ares, 1981.

Price, Jonathan. 2001. *Thucydides and Internal War*. Cambridge: Cambridge University Press.

Pritchett, W. Kendrick. 1971–1991. *The Greek State at War*. 5 vols. Berkeley and Los Angeles: University of California Press.

Raaflaub, Kurt A. 1998. "The Transformation of Athens in the Fifth Century." In *Democracy, Empire, and the Arts in Fifth-Century Athens*, edited by Deborah Boedeker and Kurt A. Raaflaub, 15–41, 348–57. Cambridge, MA: Harvard University Press.

————. 2001. "Father of All—Destroyer of All: War in Late Fifth-Century Athenian Discourse and Ideology." In McCann and Strauss 2001, 307–56.

————. 2007. "The Breakthrough of *Dēmokratia* in Mid-Fifth-Century Athens." In *Origins of Democracy in Ancient Greece*, edited by Raaflaub, Josiah Ober, and Robert W. Wallace, 105–54. Berkeley and Los Angeles: University of California Press.

————. 2013. "Homer and the Agony of Hoplite Battle." *Ancient History Bulletin* 27.1–2: 1–22.

————. 2015. Our Ancient Wars: Rethinking War through the Classics, edited by Victor Caston and Silke-Maria Weineck. University of Michigan Press.

Rhodes, P. J. 1981. *A Commentary on the Aristotelian* Athenaion Politeia. Oxford: Clarendon.

————. 1992. "The Athenian Revolution." *Cambridge Ancient History* V: 62–95. 2nd ed. Cambridge: Cambridge University Press.

Rosivach, V. J. 1985. "Manning the Athenian Fleet, 433–426 B.C." *American Journal of Ancient History* 10: 41–66.

Roussel, L. 1966. *Lysias, l'Invalide*. Paris: Presses Universitaires de France.

Ruschenbusch, Eberhard. 1979. *Athenische Innenpolitik im 5. Jh. v. Chr. Ideologie oder Pragmatismus?* Bamberg: aku Fotodruck und Verlag.

Sabin, Philip, Hans van Wees, and Michael Whitby, eds. 2007. *The Cambridge History of Greek and Roman Warfare*. 2 vols. Cambridge: Cambridge University Press.

Salazar, Christine F., ed. 2000. *The Treatment of War Wounds in Graeco-Roman Antiquity*. Leiden: Brill.

Schaps, David. 1982. "The Women of Greece in Wartime." *Classical Philology* 77: 193–213.

Scodel, Ruth. 1980. *The Trojan Trilogy of Euripides*. Göttingen: Vandenhoeck und Ruprecht.

Seibert, Jakob. 1979. *Die politischen Flüchtlinge und Verbannten in der griechischen Geschichte von den Anfängen bis zur Unterwerfung durch die Römer*. 2 vols. Darmstadt: Wissenschaftliche Buchgesellschaft.

Shay, Jonathan. 1994. *Achilles in Vietnam: Combat Trauma and the Undoing of Character*. New York: Maxwell Macmillan International.

————. 2000. "Killing Rage: *physis* or *nomos*—or Both?" In van Wees 2000, 31–56.

————. 2002. *Odysseus in America: Combat Trauma and the Trials of Homecoming*. New York: Scribner.

Spence, Iain G. 1993. *The Cavalry of Classical Greece: A Social and Military History with Particular Reference to Athens*. Oxford: Clarendon.

Steinhauer, George. 2010. "The Stele of the Fallen of Marathon from the Villa of Herodes Atticus at Loukou (Cynouria)." In *Marathon: The Battle and the Ancient Deme*, edited by Kostas Buraselis and Katerina Meidani, 199–205. Athens: Institut du Livre A. Kardamitsa.

Sternberg, R. H. 1999. "The Transport of Sick and Wounded Soldiers in Classical Greece." *Phoenix* 53: 191–205.

Strauss, Barry S. 1986. *Athens after the Peloponnesian War: Class, Faction and Politics, 403–386 BC*. Ithaca, NY: Cornell University Press.

————. 2000. "Perspectives on the Death of Fifth-Century Athenian Seamen." In van Wees 2000, 261–83.

————. 2007. "Naval Battles and Sieges." In Sabin et al. 2007, 223–47.

Stroud, Ronald. 1971. "Greek Inscriptions: Theozotides and the Athenian Orphans." *Hesperia* 40: 280–301.

Talbert, Richard. 1989. "The Role of the Helots in the Class Struggle at Sparta." *Historia* 38: 22–40.

Tritle, Lawrence A. 1997. "Hector's Body: Mutilation of the Dead in Ancient Greece and Vietnam." *Ancient History Bulletin* 11: 123–36.

————. 2000. *From Melos to My Lai: War and Survival*. London: Routledge.

————. 2003. "Alexander and the Killing of Cleitus the Black." In *Crossroads of History: The Age of Alexander*, edited by Waldemar Heckel and Lawrence Tritle, 127–46. Claremont, CA: Regina Books.

————. 2004. "Xenophon's Portrait of Clearchus: A Study in Post-Traumatic Stress Disorder." In *Xenophon and His World*, edited by Christopher Tuplin, 325–39. Stuttgart: Steiner.

————. 2009a. "Gorgias, the Encomium of Helen, and the Trauma of War." *Clio's Psyche* 16.2: 195–9.

Tritle, Lawrence A. 2009b. "Inside the Hoplite Agony." *Ancient History Bulletin* 23: 50–69.

———. 2010. *A New History of the Peloponnesian War.* Malden, MA and Oxford: Wiley-Blackwell.

Vaughn, Pamela. 1991. "The Identification and Retrieval of the Hoplite Battle-Dead." In Hanson 1991, 38–62.

Wees, Hans van, ed. 2000. *War and Violence in Ancient Greece.* London: Duckworth and Swansea: Classical Press of Wales.

———. 2004. *Greek Warfare: Myths and Realities.* London: Duckworth.

Welwei, Karl-Wilhelm. 1974–1988. *Unfreie im antiken Kriegsdienst.* 3 vols. Wiesbaden: Steiner.

———. 2006. "Überlegungen zur frühen Helotie in Lakonien." In *Das Frühe Sparta,* edited by Andreas Luther, Mischa Meier, and Lukas Thommen, 29–41. Stuttgart: Steiner.

West, M. L. 1978. *Hesiod, Works and Days. Edited with Prolegomena and Commentary.* Oxford: Clarendon.

Wheeler, Everett. 2007. "Land Battles." In Sabin et al. 2007, 186–247.

Whitehead, David. 1990. *Aineias the Tactician, How to Survive under Siege. Translated with Introduction and Commentary.* Oxford: Clarendon.

Wyatt, William F. 1976. "Persian Dead at Marathon." *Historia* 25: 483–4.

CHAPTER TWO

Phaeacian Therapy in Homer's Odyssey*

WILLIAM H. RACE

Imagine a place isolated from normal society, whose inhabitants take in an exhausted, destitute veteran, give him clothes, feed and bathe him, devote their full attention to his presence, provide gifts, entertainment, and athletic recreation, watch him break down in tears when he is reminded of his past, listen intently to his personal story, even asking for more details, and send him off with a store of wealth to use when he arrives back home. What might we call such a place? A sanitarium? A rehab facility?

I wish to argue that in Books 5 through 12 of the *Odyssey* we witness the rehabilitation of Odysseus through the Phaeacians' provision of basic physical necessities, socialization, and physical and psychological therapy. In short, I will argue that the land of the Phaeacians serves as a kind of idealized halfway house where Odysseus is prepared to reenter the society from which he has been absent for so many years as a warrior and a wanderer.

It has often been observed that Odysseus' sojourn with the Phaeacians is a transitional episode from the fantasy island of Calypso to the "reality" of Ithaca, but no one, to my knowledge, has examined in any detail the actual progression of the healing that takes place there. On the whole, German scholarship has stressed Odysseus' recovery of his name and heroic status.[1] Scholarship in English, however, has been dominated by the 1969 article by Gilbert Rose, "The Unfriendly Phaeacians," which stresses the underlying hostile environment of Phaeacia.[2] Steve Reece,[3] building on Rose's article, finds that "their [the Phaeacians'] attitude toward strangers appears ambivalent, and their behavior is often inexplicable" (102); that "the Phaeacians bungle in the entertainment of their guest" (106); and that they are "socially inept" (107). Another strain of interpretation views the Phaeacians as shallow aesthetes. Thus, Sheila Murnaghan claims that the Phaeacians experience Odysseus' narrative "solely as entertainment."[4] Even Jonathan Shay, himself a noted therapist of veterans and author of an insightful study of Odysseus' psychological rehabilitation, calls the

Phaeacians "rich tourists" only capable of "entertainment."[5] I will argue that Alcinous and Odysseus conduct themselves much like therapist and patient, that far from being a bungling host as he is sometimes portrayed, Alcinous is an insightful judge of character and masterful host.

In order to chart Odysseus' rehabilitation, we must begin with his condition before he arrives on Phaeacia. He has been removed from society, in particular from any contact with males, for seven years of isolation at the end of the world on Calypso's island, where she desires to keep him forever to herself. Not only has Odysseus suffered from ten years of war and three years of wandering, but he has also endured a seven-year captivity. When we first see Odysseus, as Calypso approaches, he is in a state of deep dejection, wasting away as he sits alone on the beach, crying, and looking out helplessly over the expanse of water:

> τὸν δ' ἄρ' ἐπ' ἀκτῆς εὗρε καθήμενον· οὐδέ ποτ' ὄσσε
> δακρυόφιν τέρσοντο, κατείβετο δὲ γλυκὺς αἰὼν
> νόστον ὀδυρομένῳ, ἐπεὶ οὐκέτι ἥνδανε νύμφη.
> ἀλλ' ἦ τοι νύκτας μὲν ἰαύεσκεν καὶ ἀνάγκῃ
> ἐν σπέεσι γλαφυροῖσι παρ' οὐκ ἐθέλων ἐθελούσῃ·
> ἤματα δ' ἂμ πέτρῃσι καὶ ἠϊόνεσσι καθίζων
> δάκρυσι καὶ στοναχῇσι καὶ ἄλγεσι θυμὸν ἐρέχθων
> πόντον ἐπ' ἀτρύγετον δερκέσκετο δάκρυα λείβων.
> (*Odyssey* 5.151–158)

She found him sitting on the shore, and never were his eyes
dry of tears, for his sweet life was ebbing away
as he grieved for his return, since the nymph was no longer pleasing.
But indeed at night he slept with her out of necessity
in her hollow cave, unwillingly beside one who was willing.
But by day he would sit on the rocks and the sand
racking his heart with tears and groans and pains,
as he looked out over the barren sea shedding tears.

The extent of Odysseus' depressed state is conveyed by the unique expression "his sweet life was ebbing away" (κατείβετο δὲ γλυκὺς αἰών, 152).[6] Another indication of his state is that he no longer enjoys sex. When, however, Calypso tells him that he is free to leave and swears by Styx that she will help him prepare, through a subtle indication the narrator signals that Odysseus' spirits are revived, for they go to bed that night as usual, but this time sex is pleasurable (5.226–227): "Then the two of them went to the recess of the hollow cave and took delight in sex as they stayed beside each other" (ἐλθόντες δ' ἄρα τώ γε μυχῷ σπείους γλαφυροῖο | τερπέσθην φιλότητι παρ' ἀλλήλοισι μένοντες).[7]

Odysseus' 20-day ordeal at sea might be compared to the terrifying, lonely period of coming off a long addiction, in this case from an artificial paradise of food, drink, and sex that is no longer satisfying.[8]

He must venture into the unknown "on the misty sea" (ἐπ᾽ ἠεροειδέα πόντον, 5.164) and expose himself to retribution for his past offenses when Poseidon fulfills Polyphemus' curse. For 17 days Odysseus has smooth sailing, but then on Poseidon's intervention he is systematically stripped of every aid: his raft is shattered, he lets go of the tiller, he sheds the clothes Calypso had given him along with all vestiges of her proffered immortality (the clothes themselves being immortal, ἄμβροτα, 7.260, 265), puts all his trust in Ino's immortal veil (κρήδεμνον... ἄμβροτον, 5.346–347), and for two sleepless days and nights envisions his own death (πολλὰ δέ οἱ κραδίη προτιόσσετ᾽ ὄλεθρον, 5.389). When land is finally in sight, there is no safe place to come ashore. At last he finds an inlet, gains entrance as a suppliant in need of pity (ἀλλ᾽ ἐλέαιρε... ἱκέτης, 450), releases Ino's veil back to the sea (thereby bidding farewell to the sea and any claim to immortality), and, completely stripped of all identity, hides himself (καλύψατο, 5.491) naked and exhausted in a pile of leaves. This is his lowest point in the narrative. From here on, step by step, he regains his strength (through food, drink, and hygiene), self-confidence (through excelling at sports), and identity (through narrating his past actions that brought him to this point), in preparation for his return to his family and kingdom.

Athena, who was behind the scenes during his ordeal on the open water,[9] is much more present on the Phaeacians' island of Scheria, where she orchestrates his reception by the princess Nausicaa (who gives him clothes to wear), and wraps him in a mist to ensure "that no great-hearted Phaeacian might cross his path, verbally provoke him, and ask who he is" (μή τις Φαιήκων μεγαθύμων ἀντιβολήσας, | κερτομέοι τ᾽ ἐπέεσσι καὶ ἐξερέοιθ᾽ ὅτις εἴη, 7.16–17). She even appears to him as a young girl and guides him to the palace, also warning him not to look directly at any person, or to ask questions, because the Phaeacians do not take kindly to strangers (7.32–33). By these measures and warnings, she keeps him from being exposed to challenges—especially from males—before he reaches the safe environment of the palace.[10]

There are numerous ways in which Phaeacia resembles a halfway house. No stranger apparently settles there permanently, for the Phaeacians escort people back to their native lands, however far away those might be. Scheria is a place of stasis, where seasons do not matter (7.112–128) and all necessary provisions are available in abundance year-round (7.98–99). The fountains always flow, the trees always produce fruit, there is always light for dining (7.100–102), and servants take care of all the tasks (7.103–107). As Alcinous points out, they excel at recreational activities and transporting all wayfarers.[11]

But once Odysseus does gain entrance to the palace, there begins a game of concealment and withholding of information, as he is challenged at each step to be forthcoming about his past. A crisis is reached during the nighttime interview at the end of Book 7 when he is alone with Alcinous and his wife Arete (7.230–342). The queen asks Odysseus who he is, and who gave him these clothes (that she herself had made), when he had said that he arrived on the island after wandering on the sea.[12] He avoids the first question (his identity) and narrowly answers the second by employing a *praeteritio* of his sufferings,[13] choosing to recount only his stay at Circe's and Calypso's islands, his harrowing journey to reach Scheria, and his encounter with Nausicaa.[14]

After getting a good night's sleep, Odysseus arises at the beginning of Book 8, the pivotal book in his recovery, when for the first time in the epic he is called "city-sacking Odysseus" (πτολίπορθος Ὀδυσσεύς, 8.3).[15] This epithet programmatically indicates one traumatic part of his past that he will have to face: the Trojan War and his instrumental role that wreaked such disaster on Trojans and Achaeans alike. The second part consists of the subsequent ten years of wandering during which he lost all his companions. In modern times, with tens of thousands of veterans returning from ten-year wars involving multiple deployments, we have reason to pay particular attention to the way in which Odysseus recuperates from his harrowing experiences in war and wandering. He does this through two chief means, tears and tales: tears that are prompted by emotionally reexperiencing those many woes (κήδεα…πολλά, 7.242) and tales that put them into a narrative to share with sympathetic listeners.

In the course of this second day with the Phaeacians, Demodocus the bard sings three songs: one at the midday feast, one in the afternoon outdoors, and one at the evening banquet. His first song after the midday meal is prompted by the Muse:

αὐτὰρ ἐπεὶ πόσιος καὶ ἐδητύος ἐξ ἔρον ἔντο,
Μοῦσ᾽ ἄρ᾽ ἀοιδὸν ἀνῆκεν ἀειδέμεναι κλέα ἀνδρῶν,
οἴμης, τῆς τότ᾽ ἄρα κλέος οὐρανὸν εὐρὺν ἵκανε,
νεῖκος Ὀδυσσῆος καὶ Πηλεΐδεω Ἀχιλῆος,
ὥς ποτε δηρίσαντο θεῶν ἐν δαιτὶ θαλείῃ
ἐκπάγλοισ᾽ ἐπέεσσιν, ἄναξ δ᾽ ἀνδρῶν Ἀγαμέμνων
χαῖρε νόῳ, ὅ τ᾽ ἄριστοι Ἀχαιῶν δηριόωντο.
ὣς γάρ οἱ χρείων μυθήσατο Φοῖβος Ἀπόλλων
Πυθοῖ ἐν ἠγαθέῃ, ὅθ᾽ ὑπέρβη λάϊνον οὐδὸν
χρησόμενος. τότε γάρ ῥα κυλίνδετο πήματος ἀρχὴ
Τρωσί τε καὶ Δαναοῖσι Διὸς μεγάλου διὰ βουλάς.

(*Odyssey* 8.72–82)

And when they had put away their desire for food and drink,
then the Muse prompted the bard to sing of the famous deeds of men,
from the song whose fame had then reached broad heaven,
the quarrel of Odysseus and Peleus' son Achilles,
how they once contended during a flourishing festival of the gods
with violent words, and the king of men Agamemnon
was joyful in his mind that the best of the Achaeans were contending,
because thus had Phoebus Apollo told him in prophecy

in holy Pytho, when he had stepped over the stone threshold
to receive his oracle, for then the beginning of misery was rolling
    down
on the Trojans and Danaans through the counsels of great Zeus.

In contrast to the Phaeacian audience, who enjoy the song, Odysseus
laments:[16]

αὐτὰρ Ὀδυσσεὺς
πορφύρεον μέγα φᾶρος ἑλὼν χερσὶ στιβαρῇσι
κὰκ κεφαλῆς εἴρυσσε, κάλυψε δὲ καλὰ πρόσωπα·
αἴδετο γὰρ Φαίηκας ὑπ' ὀφρύσι δάκρυα λείβων.
ἦ τοι ὅτε λήξειεν ἀείδων θεῖος ἀοιδός,
δάκρυ' ὀμορξάμενος κεφαλῆς ἄπο φᾶρος ἕλεσκε
καὶ δέπας ἀμφικύπελλον ἑλὼν σπείσασκε θεοῖσιν·
αὐτὰρ ὅτ' ἂψ ἄρχοιτο καὶ ὀτρύνειαν ἀείδειν
Φαιήκων οἱ ἄριστοι, ἐπεὶ τέρποντ' ἐπέεσσιν,
ἂψ Ὀδυσεὺς κατὰ κρᾶτα καλυψάμενος γοάασκεν.

(*Odyssey* 8.83–92)

But Odysseus
took his great purple robe in his stout hands
and drew it over his head and hid his handsome face, for he was
ashamed to be shedding tears under his brow before the Phaeacians.
And whenever the divine bard ceased from singing,
he would wipe his tears and take his robe away from his head
and take a two-handled cup and pour libations to the gods.
But whenever he again began—and the best of the Phaeacians would
urge him to sing because they were enjoying his words—
again would Odysseus cover his head and lament.

Since the song was chosen by the Muse and the bard, Odysseus is apparently blindsided by its content, which outlines a plot stretching from an
oracle before the war to the point at which this quarrel between Odysseus
and Achilles marked the turning point, when "the beginning of misery
was rolling down on the Trojans and Danaans through the counsels of
great Zeus." The poet's song lasts long enough to have repeated intermis-
sions that give Odysseus some time to recover. The narrator notes that he
hid his tears because he was ashamed (αἴδετο, 86) to be seen crying by
his hosts, not because he was afraid of giving himself away.[17] One person,
however, Alcinous, notices Odysseus' reaction:

ἔνθ' ἄλλους μὲν πάντας ἐλάνθανε δάκρυα λείβων,
Ἀλκίνοος δέ μιν οἶος ἐπεφράσατ' ἠδ' ἐνόησεν
ἥμενος ἄγχ' αὐτοῦ, βαρὺ δὲ στενάχοντος ἄκουσεν.

(*Odyssey* 8.93–95)

Then from all the others he hid that he was shedding tears,
but Alcinous alone observed him and perceived it,
for he was sitting next to him and heard him groaning deeply.

Far from being an inattentive host, Alcinous has a perceptive awareness
of others' unspoken thoughts. Our very first impression of him (and in
the *Odyssey* first appearances are always determinative)[18] is formed in the
encounter with his daughter Nausicaa at the beginning of Book 6. She has
been dreaming of marriage, but conceals her thoughts when she asks her
father for a wagon to go wash clothes:

ὣς ἔφατ'· αἴδετο γὰρ θαλερὸν γάμον ἐξονομῆναι
πατρὶ φίλῳ· ὁ δὲ πάντα νόει καὶ ἀμείβετο μύθῳ·
"οὔτε τοι ἡμιόνων φθονέω, τέκος, οὔτε τευ ἄλλου."
(Odyssey 6.66–68)

Thus she spoke, for she was ashamed to mention her budding wedding
to her dear father. But he perceived everything and said to her:
"I do not begrudge you the mules, my child, nor anything else."

Like Odysseus, she is ashamed (αἴδετο, 6.66) to mention what is on her
mind, but her father has perceived everything (πάντα νόει, 6.67) and provided transportation. That is precisely how he handles Odysseus' hidden
thoughts: he alone perceived (ἐνόησεν, 6.94) that Odysseus was grieving.
The phrase "groaning deeply" (βαρὺ...στενάχοντος) is an expression of
deeply felt pain and grief that occurs in this form only here and after the
third song of the bard at 8.534.[19]
     Making no public acknowledgment of Odysseus' grief, Alcinous
bids the party go outside for sports, thereby buying time and relief for
Odysseus. After a display of several athletic competitions by the young
Phaeacians, the king's son Laodamas tries to provoke (cf. προκάλεσσαι,
8.142) Odysseus to participate in the athletic contests, "but come, make
trial of them and scatter the woes from your heart" (ἀλλ' ἄγε πείρησαι,
σκέδασον δ' ἀπὸ κήδεα θυμοῦ, 8.149), but Odysseus resists, saying
"woes are much more on my mind than games" (κήδεά μοι καὶ μᾶλλον
ἐνὶ φρεσὶν ἤ περ ἄεθλοι, 8.154). In psychological terms, we might say
that Odysseus is too depressed by his woes (κήδεα) to exert himself. At
this point another young Phaeacian, Euryalus, taunts him to his face
(νείκεσέ τ' ἄντην, 8.158) by saying that he looks more like a greedy
merchant than an athlete. This challenge elicits an angry response from
Odysseus ("with a glare," ὑπόδρα ἰδών, 8.165) and he calls Euryalus'
challenge a "heart-biting speech" (θυμοδακής...μῦθος, 8.185).[20] After
upbraiding Euryalus and without even bothering to take off his cloak,
Odysseus picks up a huge stone discus and hurls it far beyond any of the
throws of the Phaeacians.

This physical exertion, occasioned by this two-stage provocation, has in fact brought Odysseus out of his despondency (κήδεα) and restored his self-confidence in the public arena of the agora. He takes delight (γήθησεν, 199) in the recognition he receives from Athena (disguised as a Phaeacian) and—in a lighter vein (κουφότερον, 8.201)—chides the Phaeacians and challenges all comers. He even brags about his athletic prowess at Troy and his skill at archery.[21] Alcinous congratulates him on his willingness to display his excellence (ἀρετήν, 8.237, 239) and then defuses the tension by admitting that the Phaeacians are not all that good at the heavy contests like boxing and wrestling (the events of Laodamas and Euryalus) and by having the young Phaeacians put on an impressive exhibition of their dancing skills that earns Odysseus' compliments. Thereafter, Demodocus the bard strikes up his second song, in the style of a Homeric hymn, about the adultery of Ares and Aphrodite, the delightfully humorous tale that everyone, including Odysseus, enjoys. One might add that we too, as an audience, especially enjoy it because it is the only song of the three performed in direct speech. It serves to relax the tension of the two indoor framing songs that affect Odysseus so strongly.[22]

This pattern of quarrel and anger (νεῖκος/χόλος), arising during athletics and then being allayed through apology and gift-giving, parallels the scene at Il. 23.566–613, where anger is quelled when the young and impetuous Antilochus apologizes to the older Menelaus for having unfairly defeated him and offers him his prize. Here in Phaeacia Euryalus (also a young man) apologizes to Odysseus, his elder, and gives him a sword along with recognition of Odysseus' long suffering:

ὣς εἰπὼν ἐν χερσὶ τίθει ξίφος ἀργυρόηλον,
καί μιν φωνήσας ἔπεα πτερόεντα προσηύδα·
"χαῖρε, πάτερ ὦ ξεῖνε· ἔπος δ' εἴ περ τι βέβακται
δεινόν, ἄφαρ τὸ φέροιεν ἀναρπάξασαι ἄελλαι.
σοὶ δὲ θεοὶ ἄλοχόν τ' ἰδέειν καὶ πατρίδ' ἱκέσθαι
δοῖεν, ἐπεὶ δὴ δηθὰ φίλων ἄπο πήματα πάσχεις."

(Odyssey 8.406–411)

Thus he spoke and placed in his hands the silver-studded sword
and spoke and addressed him with winged words:
"Hail, fatherly stranger. If any word has been spoken
harshly, immediately let the storm winds seize it and bear it away.
And may the gods grant that you see your wife and reach your
    country,
since long indeed have you suffered troubles apart from your loved
    ones."

Odysseus accepts the sword, apology, and good wishes (8.415),[23] and the two pass from being strangers (ξεῖνοι) to becoming friends (φίλοι).[24]

That evening, Odysseus enjoys a warm bath—the first he has had since leaving Calypso and it constitutes "the largest 'bathing' type-scene in the *Odyssey*,"[25] an expansion that in Homeric epic often indicates the importance of the scene to come. After he is given a promise of swift conveyance home, Odysseus begins the evening feast with an extraordinary gesture: he presents the bard Demodocus with his choice portion of meat and praises his vivid depiction of the Trojan War:

Δημόδοκ', ἔξοχα δή σε βροτῶν αἰνίζομ' ἁπάντων·
ἢ σέ γε Μοῦσ' ἐδίδαξε, Διὸς πάϊς, ἢ σέ γ' Ἀπόλλων·
λίην γὰρ κατὰ κόσμον Ἀχαιῶν οἶτον ἀείδεις,
ὅσσ' ἔρξαν τ' ἔπαθόν τε καὶ ὅσσ' ἐμόγησαν Ἀχαιοί,
ὥς τέ που ἢ αὐτὸς παρεὼν ἢ ἄλλου ἀκούσας.

(Odyssey 8.487–491)

Demodocus, I compliment you beyond all other mortals:
either the Muse, daughter of Zeus, taught you or else Apollo,
for very properly do you sing of the fate of the Achaeans,
all the Achaeans did and suffered and all their toils,
as if somehow you yourself were there or heard from another who was.

In contrast to that earlier song that the Muse had chosen, Odysseus himself requests this subject:

ἀλλ' ἄγε δὴ μετάβηθι καὶ ἵππου κόσμον ἄεισον
δουρατέου, τὸν Ἐπειὸς ἐποίησεν σὺν Ἀθήνῃ,
ὅν ποτ' ἐς ἀκρόπολιν δόλον ἤγαγε δῖος Ὀδυσσεὺς
ἀνδρῶν ἐμπλήσας, οἳ Ἴλιον ἐξαλάπαξαν.

(Odyssey 8.492–495)

But come, change your theme and sing of the contrivance of the horse
of wood that Epeius made with the help of Athena,
the ruse which glorious Odysseus once led to the acropolis,
having filled it with the men who sacked Ilion.

Whereas the earlier subject was of "the beginning of misery" (πήματος ἀρχή, 81), this theme is its ending, with an account of Odysseus and "the men who sacked Ilion" (οἳ Ἴλιον ἐξαλάπαξαν, 495). Since Odysseus had chosen this precise episode, one would expect him to take delight in hearing such a talented bard give a vivid account of his actions. And, after describing the ordeal in the wooden horse, Demodocus ends his account by singling out Odysseus himself in the final hours of the sack, battling at the house of Deiphobus, who had become Helen's husband after the death of Paris:

ἄλλον δ' ἄλλῃ ἄειδε πόλιν κεραϊζέμεν αἰπήν,
αὐτὰρ Ὀδυσσῆα προτὶ δώματα Δηϊφόβοιο

βήμεναι, ἠΰτ' Ἄρηα, σὺν ἀντιθέῳ Μενελάῳ.
κεῖθι δὴ αἰνότατον πόλεμον φάτο τολμήσαντα
νικῆσαι καὶ ἔπειτα διὰ μεγάθυμον Ἀθήνην.

(8.516–520)

He sang how they were ravaging the lofty city—one here, another
   there—
but that Odysseus had gone to the house of Deiphobus,
like Ares, along with godlike Menelaus.
And there indeed he said Odysseus dared the most terrible battle
and in the end won with the aid of great-hearted Athena.

This time, Odysseus' reaction is one of the most extreme found in the
epic:

ταῦτ' ἄρ' ἀοιδὸς ἄειδε περικλυτός· αὐτὰρ Ὀδυσσεὺς
τήκετο, δάκρυ δ' ἔδευεν ὑπὸ βλεφάροισι παρειάς.
ὡς δὲ γυνὴ κλαίῃσι φίλον πόσιν ἀμφιπεσοῦσα,
ὅς τε ἑῆς πρόσθεν πόλιος λαῶν τε πέσῃσιν,
ἄστεϊ καὶ τεκέεσσιν ἀμύνων νηλεὲς ἦμαρ·
ἡ μὲν τὸν θνῄσκοντα καὶ ἀσπαίροντα ἰδοῦσα
ἀμφ' αὐτῷ χυμένη λίγα κωκύει· οἱ δέ τ' ὄπισθε
κόπτοντες δούρεσσι μετάφρενον ἠδὲ καὶ ὤμους
εἴρερον εἰσανάγουσι, πόνον τ' ἐχέμεν καὶ ὀϊζύν·
τῆς δ' ἐλεεινοτάτῳ ἄχεϊ φθινύθουσι παρειαί·
ὣς Ὀδυσεὺς ἐλεεινὸν ὑπ' ὀφρύσι δάκρυον εἶβεν.

(*Odyssey* 8.521–531)

The most famous bard was singing those things, but Odysseus
melted, and poured tears from under his eyelids onto his cheeks.
And as a woman cries who has fallen around her dear husband
who has fallen in front of his city and its people
trying to ward off the pitiless day from the town and his children,
and seeing him dying and gasping for breath,
she throws herself around him and wails loudly, while others from
   behind
beat on her back and shoulders with their spears
and lead her off as a slave to endure toil and pain,
and her cheeks are wasted with the most pitiful grief,
so did Odysseus shed pitiful tears beneath his brow.

Reverse similes are common in the *Odyssey*, but this one is startling.
Odysseus cries like the distressed female victim of his own sack of Troy.
Far from glorying in his actions, he "melted"[26] and sobbed uncontrollably. The passage is a virtual lexicon of words for grief.[27] Moreover, he has
cried throughout the very song he requested.[28] The alert host Alcinous

again perceives his guest's reaction and hears him groaning deeply (βαρὺ... στενάχοντος),[29] but this time he orders the bard to stop and announces to everyone that the guest has been sorrowing:

ἐξ οὗ δορπέομέν τε καὶ ὤρορε θεῖος ἀοιδός,
ἐκ τοῦδ' οὔ πω παύσατ' ὀϊζυροῖο γόοιο
ὁ ξεῖνος· μάλα πού μιν ἄχος φρένας ἀμφιβέβηκεν.

(Odyssey 8.539–541)

Ever since we were eating and the divine singer began,
from that time our guest has never ceased from sorrowful lamentation;
surely, it seems, grief has encompassed his mind.

Grief (ἄχος) has indeed encompassed his mind. But what precisely are the sources and cause of that grief? Scholars have offered various interpretations, many summed up by Ahl and Roisman (1996, 85):

> Scholars have struggled to account for Odysseus' tears and the curious simile. It has been variously suggested that the tears are prompted by nostalgia, a contrast between his former achievements and his present ignoble state, sorrow for his lost comrades, simple grief, or grief that paves the way for him to cross from the world of fantasy to reality, even the simple memory of past toils.[30]

A. F. Garvie (1994, 339) says: "We might expect him to take pleasure and pride in the narration of his victory. Why then does he weep? It may be because mixed with that victory is the recollection of all his sufferings that went before and after it, and of his decline from his hero status."[31] Some have even considered it a ruse on Odysseus' part to force Alcinous to ask his identity or a narrative ploy by the poet to delay recognition.[32] Neither the ancient scholia nor the twelfth-century commentator Eustathius offers any suggestions.

The work of Jonathan Shay, who has so brilliantly analyzed combat trauma and treated its effects, has revolutionized our understanding of Homer's psychological sophistication. In *Achilles in Vietnam*, he tells briefly of the value of "griefwork" and of sharing experiences with others in rehabilitation,[33] and in *Odysseus in America* he astutely observes that in his breakdown Odysseus is "ambushed by his own emotional reaction... These stories rip Odysseus' heart out,"[34] but he goes into no greater depth about the Phaeacians' role in this process. Building on Shay's insight that the Homeric epics realistically depict the emotional life of soldiers and veterans, I argue that Odysseus' tears and groans are typical of combat veterans' sudden rush of sorrow and grief at revisiting intense combat situations, even when they were the victors—or survivors. Anecdotes are, admittedly, selective evidence, but I will indulge one. A few years ago, a student in my class told how his grandfather frequently talked about his World War II experiences in Europe with great pride. One day when he was young, the student asked him to tell what it was like at Normandy. He began as usual, but then suddenly burst into tears and wept uncontrollably; needless to say, the boy was shocked. Many veterans have had that experience. It is one way that humans deal with grief and trauma; it may represent a step toward recovery.

If we locate Odysseus' pitiful tears, so understood, in the larger context of his mental and physical recuperation in Phaeacia, we may understand them as representing a key stage in the process by which he comes to terms with his war (and postwar) experiences, thus allowing him to tell his woes (κήδεα) to sympathetic listeners, to face his gruesome past, and prepare himself for his homecoming. As Alcinous concludes from hearing Odysseus' "deep groans" and "sorrowful lamentation": "surely, it seems, grief (ἄχος) has encompassed his mind."

So what emotion is expressed by Odysseus' tears and deep groans? Is it a form of posttraumatic stress disorder? Is it perhaps survivor guilt, since after all he faces the embittered souls of Achilles and Ajax in Hades? Is it the accumulated grief from all those Trojan deaths at his hands? Is it guilt for losing all the comrades under his command?[35] Ultimately, we cannot fix the particular details—Homer uses the general term ἄχος, "grief." But we do know what triggered this particular reaction: the vivid portrayal of his most intense wartime experience (cf. "the most terrible battle," αἰνότατον πόλεμον, 8.519). From this point on, he faces his past as he narrates his sorrows, which he calls "my groan-causing woes," ἐμὰ κήδεα...στονόεντα (9.12).

Alcinous reiterates his good intentions toward his revered guest (ξείνοιο...αἰδοίοιο, 544), including the promised conveyance and loving gifts, given out of friendship (πομπὴ καὶ φίλα δῶρα, τά οἱ δίδομεν φιλέοντες, 545), and even compares Odysseus to a brother (ἀντὶ κασιγνήτου, 546). After these reassurances, he asks him to answer his questions truthfully and openly: "Therefore, do not now hide what I ask you by crafty thoughts, for it is more fitting that you speak out" (τῷ νῦν μηδὲ σὺ κεῦθε νοήμασι κερδαλέοισιν | ὅττι κέ σ' εἴρωμαι· φάσθαι δέ σε κάλλιόν ἐστιν, 8.548–549).

Alcinous asks him (1) his name; (2) his city; (3) about his wanderings; and (4) why he cries and grieves upon hearing about the fate of the Argives and Troy:

εἰπὲ δ' ὅ τι κλαίεις καὶ ὀδύρεαι ἔνδοθι θυμῷ
Ἀργείων Δαναῶν ἠδ' Ἰλίου οἶτον ἀκούων.

(*Odyssey* 8.577–578)

And tell why you cry and lament in your heart
when you hear the fate of the Argive Danaans and of Ilion.[36]

Once again Odysseus avoids answering one of the questions: he does
not tell about his experiences at Troy but instead picks up from where
Demodocus had left off with the sacking of Troy and launches into his
wanderings. The importance of narrative in healing psychological trauma
is well known.[37] Odysseus is remarkably forthcoming: his narrative is full
of his own blunders.[38] He begins by saying: "Your heart is determined to
ask about my groan-causing woes, to make me lament and groan all the
more" (σοὶ δ' ἐμὰ κήδεα θυμὸς ἐπετράπετο στονόεντα | εἴρεσθ',
ὄφρ' ἔτι μᾶλλον ὀδυρόμενος στεναχίζω, 9.12–13).

   In the famous interlude in Book 11, which occurs in the midst of his
confrontation with figures from the past in his account of the underworld,
Odysseus suddenly requests to stop and go to bed, significantly before
recounting anything about Troy. After relating his conversation with his
dead mother and cataloguing other women he saw in Hades, he expresses
aporia and says that it is time for him to go to sleep:

πάσας δ' οὐκ ἂν ἐγὼ μυθήσομαι οὐδ' ὀνομήνω,
ὅσσας ἡρώων ἀλόχους ἴδον ἠδὲ θύγατρας·
πρὶν γάρ κεν καὶ νὺξ φθῖτ' ἄμβροτος. ἀλλὰ καὶ ὥρη
εὕδειν, ἢ ἐπὶ νῆα θοὴν ἐλθόντ' ἐς ἑταίρους
ἢ αὐτοῦ· πομπὴ δὲ θεοῖσ' ὑμῖν τε μελήσει.
                                        (*Odyssey* 11.328–332)

I could not tell or give the names of all
the wives of heroes or their daughters whom I saw,
for sooner would the ambrosial night end. But it is the hour for me
to sleep, either going to the swift ship and the comrades
or else here, since the conveyance will depend on the gods and on you.

But Alcinous will not let him stop and asks him to hold out until the next
day, so that he can complete his gift-giving:

ξεῖνος δὲ τλήτω, μάλα περ νόστοιο χατίζων,
ἔμπης οὖν ἐπιμεῖναι ἐς αὔριον, εἰς ὅ κε πᾶσαν
δωτίνην τελέσω.
                                        (*Odyssey* 11.350–352)

Let our guest endure—although greatly longing to return—
nevertheless to remain until tomorrow, until I can make my
entire gift complete.

The entire gift (πᾶσαν δωτίνην) is more than the material goods, as
symbolically important as they are. In the ensuing words of Alcinous,
it is apparent that his gift is in exchange for hearing the whole story of

Odysseus' painful woes (κήδεα λυγρά, 11.369). He compliments Odysseus on his expert storytelling about the woes of the Argives and his own:

σοὶ δ' ἔπι μὲν μορφὴ ἐπέων, ἔνι δὲ φρένες ἐσθλαί,
μῦθον δ' ὡς ὅτ' ἀοιδὸς ἐπισταμένως κατέλεξας,
πάντων Ἀργείων σέο τ' αὐτοῦ κήδεα λυγρά.

(Odyssey 11.367–369)

Upon you is elegance of words; within you is a good mind.
You have intelligently told your story like a bard,
about the painful woes of all the Argives and of you yourself.

He then asks him the question that Odysseus has avoided answering so far:

ἀλλ' ἄγε μοι τόδε εἰπὲ καὶ ἀτρεκέως κατάλεξον,
εἴ τινας ἀντιθέων ἑτάρων ἴδες, οἵ τοι ἅμ' αὐτῷ
Ἴλιον εἰς ἅμ' ἕποντο καὶ αὐτοῦ πότμον ἐπέσπον.
νὺξ δ' ἥδε μάλα μακρή, ἀθέσφατος, οὐδέ πω ὥρη
εὕδειν ἐν μεγάρῳ· σὺ δέ μοι λέγε θέσκελα ἔργα.
καί κεν ἐς ἠῶ δῖαν ἀνασχοίμην, ὅτε μοι σὺ
τλαίης ἐν μεγάρῳ τὰ σὰ κήδεα μυθήσασθαι.

(Odyssey 11.370–376)

But come, tell me this and relate it accurately,
whether you saw any of the godlike companions who went with you
to Troy and there met their fate.
This night is very long, wondrously so, and not yet is it the hour
to sleep in the hall. Tell me your marvelous deeds.
I could hold out even until the bright dawn, if you would
endure to tell those woes of yours in the hall.

The night is wondrously long—an expression of intimate conversation that will continue until all is revealed, until one endures (τλαίης; cf. τλήτω, 11.350) to put one's woes into a narrative (τὰ σὰ κήδεα μυθήσασθαι, 11.376).[39] By facing the fates of Agamemnon, Achilles, and Ajax, Odysseus closes out his account of the war itself, especially when he tells of the time in the Trojan horse with Neoptolemus (11.523–532).[40] Thereafter he continues the story of his own wanderings, including "the woes of my comrades" (κήδε' ἐμῶν ἑτάρων, 11.382) that brought death to them and a seven-year exile upon himself.

In Book 13, we see the salutary effect of Odysseus' therapy in the description of him on board the ship bringing him home.

ὃς πρὶν μὲν μάλα πολλὰ πάθ' ἄλγεα ὃν κατὰ θυμόν,
ἀνδρῶν τε πτολέμους ἀλεγεινά τε κύματα πείρων·

δὴ τότε γ᾽ ἀτρέμας εὗδε, λελασμένος ὅσσ᾽ ἐπεπόνθει.

(*Odyssey* 13.90–92)

[he] who had previously suffered many pains in his heart
as he passed through wars with men and grievous seas,
then at least slept calmly, having forgotten all he had suffered.

Of particular importance here is the doublet line 91, which sketches his
experiences fighting at Troy (ἀνδρῶν τε πτολέμους) and wandering at
sea (ἀλεγεινά τε κύματα):[41] his therapy on Phaeacia covers both periods
and has at last brought him restful sleep and forgetfulness of his past suffering.[42] When he does wake up on Ithaca, it is an Ithaca he does not
recognize, one with which he will have to reacquaint himself, but one
which he is psychologically prepared to face. From this point on he reac-
quaints himself with his family and friends and, in disguise, sets about
healing their despondency—for they too have suffered trauma—with the
therapeutic skills he experienced in Phaeacia.[43]

Notes

*I wish to thank Andrew Miller, Henry Spelman, and David Konstan for their many
improvements of content and style. Portions of this chapter were delivered at the
University of South Carolina, the University of Pittsburgh, and at the 2012 CAMWS
meeting in Baton Rouge. All translations are my own.

1. Cf. Mattes (1958, 104–12) and Latacz (1985, 182–5) = Holoka (1996, 145–7). Fenik
   (1974, 5–20) provides a detailed review of the positions of Hölscher (1939); Mattes
   (1958); and Beßlich (1966) on why Odysseus withholds his name for so long. De Jong
   (2001, 150) reflects German scholarship in saying, "Odysseus regains his heroic status
   and confidence, indeed his identity."
2. Rose (1969, 387–406). Cf. Most (1989, esp. 27–9); Reece (1993, 101–21); and
   Broeniman (1996, 6–12).
3. Reece (1993, 102–7). Rose (1969, 405–6) calls Alcinous "a clumsy host" with a "lax
   ineptitude."
4. Murnaghan (1987, 102). Whitman (1958, 116) similarly labels Demodocus' rendition
   "just a song for an evening's amusement."
5. In his chapter "Odysseus among the Rich Civilians," Shay (2002, 16) says, "Homer
   shows us the Phaeacians as rich tourists in the landscape of suffering." Shay's view
   of the Phaeacians may be influenced by the disdain veterans often feel for civilians
   asking to be told "war stories" only to be shocked and offended; see Shay (1994,
   xxi–xxii).
6. Calypso varies the expression in her plea: "do not let your life waste away" (μηδέ τοι
   αἰὼν | φθινέτω, 5.160–161). The narrator's inclusion of "sweet" (γλυκύς, 152) indi-
   cates that it is the pleasure of life that Odysseus is losing.
7. His enjoyment might be considered the first step in his rehabilitation, a sign that he
   is coming out of his depression. Sex plays a similar role in Achilles' recovery in the

Iliad. Thetis advises him at *Il.* 24.128–131: "My child, how long will you eat out your heart sorrowing and grieving and remembering neither food nor sex? It is good to make love to a woman" (τέκνον ἐμὸν τέο μέχρις ὀδυρόμενος καὶ ἀχεύων | σὴν ἔδεαι κραδίην μεμνημένος οὔτε τι σίτου | οὔτ' εὐνῆς; ἀγαθὸν δὲ γυναικί περ ἐν φιλότητι | μίσγεσθαι), and the very last thing we hear of him at 24.675–676 is: "And Achilles slept in the recess of his well-built shelter; and beautiful-cheeked Briseis lay beside him" (αὐτὰρ Ἀχιλλεὺς εὗδε μυχῷ κλισίης ἐϋπήκτου | τῷ δὲ Βρισηῒς παρελέξατο καλλιπάρῃος). Homer elsewhere incorporates small changes of behavior that indicate changes of psychological disposition; cf. Eumaeus' change of attitude at 14.414–417, when he calls for the best of the boars after previously complaining that the suitors only allow him and the servants to eat piglets.

8. For the addiction to (unsatisfying) sex, see the chapter "Calypso: Odysseus the Sexaholic" in Shay (2002, 113–19).

9. Cf. 5.382–387, 427, and 437.

10. Both this warning and that of Nausicaa at 6.273–285, upon which those who disparage the hospitality of the Phaeacians depend, hint at potential hostility, most prominently displayed when Euryalus chides Odysseus, but even that is diffused by the fair-minded and hospitable Phaeacians under the leadership of Alcinous. De Vries (1977, 121) suggests, perhaps correctly, that "it is his [Odysseus'] own distrust which he has to overcome, not Phaeacian unfriendliness." Here, as in all the new places to which he comes, Odysseus has learned to exercise extreme caution. This wariness may also reflect the state of high alert that returning veterans often exhibit in fear that they may suddenly be confronted and provoked to lose control.

11. Cf. 8.248–249: "We always love dining, lyre-playing, dancing, fresh clothes, warm baths, and bed" (αἰεὶ δ' ἡμῖν δαίς τε φίλη κίθαρίς τε χοροί τε | εἵματά τ' ἐξημοιβὰ λοετρά τε θερμὰ καὶ εὐναί) and 8.566 (cf. 13.174): "we are safe transporters of all men" (πομποὶ ἀπήμονές εἰμεν ἁπάντων). Cf. also 8.31–33.

12. As Fenik (1974, 128) shows, Arete's question at 7.238, "who gave you these clothes?" (τίς τοι τάδε εἵματ' ἔδωκεν;), coming suddenly after the caesura, poses the test that he must pass in order to gain her favor: "the meeting with Nausicaa, and with it the references to the Phaeacians' hostility to strangers, as well as the predictions of the queen's importance, are all directed towards the one climactic moment when Arete suddenly jolts us out of our easy confidence with her abrupt and menacing question." I would add that the formulaic question that elsewhere follows "who are you?" (τίς πόθεν εἰς ἀνδρῶν;) is "where is your city and parents?" (πόθι τοι πόλις ἠδὲ τοκῆες; at 1.170, 10.325, 14.187, 15.264, 19.105, and 24.298). Only here is it followed by the "abrupt" "Who gave you these clothes?" (τίς τοι τάδε εἵματ' ἔδωκεν;).

13. "It would be difficult, O queen, to tell of my woes all the way through, because the Heavenly gods have given me many" (ἀργαλέον, βασίλεια, διηνεκέως ἀγορεῦσαι | κήδε', ἐπεί μοι πολλὰ δόσαν θεοὶ Οὐρανίωνες, 7.241–242).

14. Hainsworth (1988, 335–6) notes: "In the usual Homeric way Odysseus takes up Arete's questions in reverse order: first how he had come ἐπὶ πόντον ἀλώμενος ['wandering over the sea']; second how he had acquired his clothing. This convention helps to gloss over the fact that Odysseus does not go on to answer her first question and reveal his identity." De Jong (2001, 184) labels this procedure "the distraction device."

15. Although the designation "sacker of cities" recalls the opening of the epic, "he sacked the holy city of Troy" (Τροίης ἱερὸν πτολίεθρον ἔπερσεν, 1.2), the only other occurrence of this epithet in the Phaeacian episode is when Odysseus recounts

his triumphant vaunt over the Cyclops at 9.504: "say that Odysseus, sacker of cities, blinded you" (φάσθαι Ὀδυσσῆα πτολιπόρθιον ἐξαλαῶσαι), which is repeated in the Cyclops' curse at 9.530, "grant that Odysseus, sacker of cities, not arrive home" (δὸς μὴ Ὀδυσσῆα πτολιπόρθιον οἴκαδ' ἱκέσθαι). De Jong (2001, 192) labels this epithet a "seed" that "prepares for Demodocus' third song."

16. A parallel is in Book 1, where Phemius' song about the sad homecomings of the Danaans entertains the suitors, "who sat listening in silence" (οἱ δὲ σιωπῇ | εἵατ' ἀκούοντες, 1.325–326) but makes Penelope cry (δακρύσασα, 1.336) by reminding her of her missing husband (μεμνημένη αἰεὶ | ἀνδρός, 1.343–344). Strong emotional memory of Odysseus, expressed in tears, characterizes all the good characters in the epic: for example, Telemachus (4.113–116); Penelope (1.336, 19.204, etc.); Eurycleia (19.361–362); Eumaeus (21.82); Philoetius (20.204–205); and Laertes (24.280).

17. A parallel situation occurs at 4.114–115, when Telemachus conceals his tears upon hearing his father mentioned: "He let fall tears from his eyes to the ground when he heard tell of his father, holding up his purple cloak before his eyes" (δάκρυ δ' ἀπὸ βλεφάρων χαμάδις βάλε πατρὸς ἀκούσας, | χλαῖναν πορφυρέην ἄντ' ὀφθαλμοῖιν ἀνασχών).

18. For first appearances as significant determiners of character, see Race (1993, esp. 93–4). Austin (1975, 194–6) provides a good appreciation of Alcinous' "intuition and discretion" (194). Before we even see him, the narrator describes Alcinous as "knowing counsels from the gods" (θεῶν ἄπο μήδεα εἰδώς, 6.12). After Odysseus passes Arete's test ("Who gave you these clothes?"), Alcinous (who knows his daughter very well) declares that Odysseus thinks the same thoughts as he does (τά τε φρονέων ἅ τ' ἐγώ περ, 7.312) and even wishes that he might become his son-in-law, a possibility that Nausicaa herself had entertained at 6.244–245. There is an indication that even the Phaeacian ships possess the ability to read people's thoughts; cf. 8.559: "but the ships themselves know the thoughts and minds of men" (ἀλλ' αὐταὶ ἴσασι νοήματα καὶ φρένας ἀνδρῶν).

19. The similar phrase βαρέα στενάχοντα occurs four times in the *Odyssey* (of Odysseus at 5.420, 10.76, and 23.317; of Agamemnon at 4.516) in situations of extreme disappointment and helplessness. For examples in the *Iliad*, see note 9.

20. Provocations of characters that elicit spontaneous reactions are frequent in the epic. An important parallel occurs when Penelope provokes Odysseus about their bed at 23.177–180 and he reacts angrily (ὀχθήσας, 182) at what he calls her "heart-paining word" (ἔπος θυμαλγές, 183). The final variation is when Odysseus tests his father with provocative words (κερτομίοισ' ἔπεσιν διαπειρηθῆναι, 24.240), but breaks down himself upon seeing his father's violent reaction.

21. For a complete list of Odysseus' dropped hints as to his identity ("stückweise Enthüllung"), see de Jong (2001, 172).

22. It also has thematic relevance to Book 8 (Braswell 1982) and to the situation on Ithaca (Alden 1997). Demodocus sings a fourth song the following day (13.27–28), but its subject is not even given and it has no relevance to Odysseus' therapy, as he is distracted by his longing for his evening departure to come (13.28–30).

23. De Jong (2001, 211) astutely observes, "For the first time in years Odysseus has a sword over his shoulder, marking the recovery of his heroic self-confidence." David Konstan *per litteras* points out that the athletic games in Book 23 of the *Iliad* also have a therapeutic effect on Achilles: "true, he presides rather than participates, but they provide a competitive context marked by cooperation rather than warlike conflict,

and prepare the way for his reintegration into the community in Book 24." A sure sign of Achilles' reintegration comes at the very end of the games (23.884–897), when he awards first prize to Agamemnon in the spear-throwing contest without even making him compete, because "we know how you surpass all others" (23.890). Thus, the book ends with Agamemnon accepting the first prize of a tripod; the deadly quarrel between the two has finally ended. I owe this observation to Henry Spelman.

24. See Konstan (1997, 35).

25. De Jong (2001, 211).

26. τήκετο describes a person's physical surrender to grief and occurs elsewhere in the *Odyssey* only of Penelope at 19.204 (cf. 19.263–264), when Odysseus in disguise describes, at her insistence, his own clothing when he set out for Troy.

27. Cf. δάκρυ (522; δάκρυον, 531; δάκρυα, 532); κλαίῃσι (523; κλαίεις, 577); κωκύει (527); ἄχεϊ (530; ἄχος, 541); στενάχοντος (534); γόοιο (540); and ὀδύρεαι (577). The comparison between the woman's "most pitiful grief" (ἐλεεινοτάτῳ ἄχεϊ, 530) and Odysseus' "pitiful tears" (ἐλεεινὸν…δάκρυον, 531) is paralleled at the reunion of Telemachus and Odysseus in Eumaeus' hut at 16.213–219:

> Τηλέμαχος δὲ
> ἀμφιχυθεὶς πατέρ᾽ ἐσθλὸν ὀδύρετο δάκρυα λείβων.
> ἀμφοτέροισι δὲ τοῖσιν ὑφ᾽ ἵμερος ὦρτο γόοιο·
> κλαῖον δὲ λιγέως, ἁδινώτερον ἤ τ᾽ οἰωνοί,
> φῆναι ἢ αἰγυπιοὶ γαμψώνυχες, οἷσί τε τέκνα
> ἀγρόται ἐξείλοντο πάρος πετεηνὰ γενέσθαι·
> ὣς ἄρα τοί γ᾽ ἐλεεινὸν ὑπ᾽ ὀφρύσι δάκρυον εἶδον.

> And Telemachus
> threw himself around his good father and wept and cried tears.
> Upon both of them came desire for lamentation
> and they cried shrilly, more forcefully than birds do,
> sea eagles or curve-clawed vultures, whose chicks
> farmers have taken from their nest before they could fly:
> so did they shed pitiful tears beneath their brows.

Here too the powerful simile reverses the situation; instead of parent and child uniting, chicks are taken from the parent bird. The parallel phrases are used only in these two places: ὣς Ὀδυσεὺς ἐλεεινὸν ὑπ᾽ ὀφρύσι δάκρυον εἶβεν (8.531) ~ ὣς ἄρα τοί γ᾽ ἐλεεινὸν ὑπ᾽ ὀφρύσι δάκρυον εἶβον (16.219). We badly need a study of the emotions that elicit tears in Homer and the effects of those tears.

28. Cf. Macleod (1983, 11): "So the song which was to glorify the hero is felt by the hero himself as a moving record of the pain and sorrow he helped to cause."

29. The emotional reaction of "groaning deeply" (βαρὺ στενάχων) results from profound grief. It occurs more often in the *Iliad*. At 1.357–364 Thetis appears to Achilles in his grief and tells him to speak out and hide nothing (ἐξαύδα, μὴ κεῦθε νόῳ, 363), and he groans deeply (βαρὺ στενάχων, 364) as he explains to her what happened. In other places in the *Iliad*, βαρὺ στενάχων expresses grief mixed with guilt. At *Il.* 4.153 Agamemnon groans deeply (βαρὺ στενάχων) when he sees Menelaus wounded, and his ensuing speech is full of self-blame for his brother's plight. At *Il.* 9.16 Agamemnon again groans deeply in despair at his failure and loss of men (ἐπεὶ πολὺν ὤλεσα λαόν, 9.22). At *Il.* 18.70–82, in an intensified doublet of the scene in Book 1, Thetis holds the head of Achilles as he groans deeply (βαρὺ στενάχοντι, 70) and tells him to speak openly and not hold back (ἐξαύδα, μὴ κεῦθε, 74). He then

groans deeply (βαρὺ στενάχων, 78) as he tells her of Patroclus' death, first in the
passive "my dear comrade died" (φίλος ὤλεθ' ἑταῖρος, 80), but then acknowledges
his own role in his friend's demise, "he whom I destroyed" (τὸν ἀπώλεσα, 82).
Likewise, Achilles' speech at *Il.* 18.323–342 (delivered βαρὺ στενάχων, 323) is full
of guilt at not fulfilling his promise to Menoetius to bring back his son Patroclus.
Finally at *Il.* 23.60 Achilles groans deeply as he again laments for Patroclus. Might
Odysseus' groans also be tinged with survivor-guilt over the men he lost? Cf. Shay
(2002, 76–85), "Among the Dead: Memory and Guilt."

30. Ahl and Roisman (1996, 85). Their own proposal (85), that Odysseus is piqued
because Demodocus must have diminished his role in the saga of the horse, is unten-
able (cf. Thalmann 1999, 298), but shows how perplexed scholars have been by
Odysseus' tears. In his commentary, Garvie (1994) gives various (and sometimes
conflicting) explanations; cf. 27, 29, 331, and 339. Benardete (1997, 58) rightly
points out that "Homer goes out of his way not to tell us the reason for Odysseus'
tears," but offers an overly pessimistic interpretation: "The simile calls into question the apparent triumph of right that the fall of Troy represents...The hollow-
ness of past and future right, when they are measured against all he has lost, makes
him experience the equivalent of Andromache's fate. He has beaten everything and
everyone, but for what?" I would reply that the answer to "for what?" is the *Odyssey*.
Di Benedetto (2010, 491) claims that the simile expresses an antiwar sentiment ("un
proposito antibellicista"). Morrison (2003, 87) briefly observes, I believe correctly:
"This third song again makes Odysseus break down in tears. We must think of how
soldiers today react when hearing about a battle or reliving it themselves in their own
minds."

31. Garvie (1994, 339). Similarly de Jong (2001, 197): "Odysseus weeps here and in
521–54 (specifically because the songs make clear painfully to him the contrast
between his heroic successes of the past and his misery of the ten years which followed)." Thalmann (1984, 165) rightly points out that "the simile expresses the
Odyssey's revaluation of the Trojan War," but goes too far in saying: "It shows that
the grief of both victors and vanquished is finally the same." There certainly is grief
on both sides, but that of the vanquished is both qualitatively and quantitatively
greater. In a similar vein Rutherford (1986, 155) claims: "[Odysseus sees] that the
profits which he gained have slipped through his fingers; and above all that his own
sufferings and his own separation from wife, child and home are not *more* important
than the sufferings of the Trojans, but mirror-images of them (as is brought out by
the marital theme in the simile)" (Italics in original). Two recent works concentrate on the aesthetic experience of Odysseus. Halliwell (2011, 77–92) offers many
insightful comments, but I cannot agree with his conclusion (87–8): "We are left to
infer that Odysseus has no need to hear a merely accurate reminder of what he has
lived through. He needs, in a way which even so threatens to overwhelm his long-
suffering mind, to hear his life transfigured into the quasi-divine beauty that he
discovers in Demodocus' singing." Peponi (2012, 33–69), after helpfully comparing and contrasting the responses of various audiences to the narratives of Phemius
(Book 1), Menelaus and Helen (Book 4), and Demodocus (Book 8), arrives at a
similar conclusion (69): "The poet of the *Odyssey* makes Odysseus cry, not over the
raw materials of his life, but over exquisitely molded poetic representations of such
materials that he explicitly appreciates as such within the poem."

32. Cf. Finkelberg (1987, 129) and Cook (1999, 159). Hexter (1993, 117–18) argues
against "Odysseus' 'spiritual rehabilitation'" as proposed by Mattes (1958, 112): "In
sum, I see nothing in Book VIII that cannot be explained as the plan of a master
rhetorician (Odysseus) and a poet who has determined to postpone as long as possible

the moment at which his hero's identity is revealed." This extends a long line of (mainly) German criticism that discounts psychological verisimilitude in the epic. As a result, Hexter has little to say about the simile of the weeping wife. Hainsworth (1988, 381) warns against exact interpretation of the simile with the general claim that "Heroic exploit is for Homer always an ἄεθλος leading to no permanent happiness, cf. in this regard the tears of Menelaus and others at iv 183, of Odysseus and the ghost of Agamemnon at xi 466, and of Achilles at *Il.* xxiv 511."

33. Cf. Shay (1994, index s.v. "griefwork" and esp. 4): "healing from trauma depends upon communalization of the trauma—being able safely to tell the story to someone who is listening and who can be trusted to retell it truthfully to others in the community."

34. Shay (2002, 15).

35. Cf. Eupeithes' taunt at 24.428: "he lost the hollow ships and destroyed the men" (ὤλεσε μὲν νῆας γλαφυράς, ἀπὸ δ' ὤλεσε λαούς).

36. The phrase ὀδύρεαι ἔνδοθι θυμῷ is unique in Homer. Eustathius *ad* 8.577 says: "The words ὀδύρεσθαι ἔνδοθι θυμῷ do not indicate mere groaning, but quite simply deep, heartfelt grief" (τὸ δὲ ὀδύρεσθαι ἔνδοθι θυμῷ, οὐ στεναγμὸν δηλοῖ μόνον ἀλλὰ καὶ ἁπλῶς λύπην βαθεῖαν ἐνδιάθετον).

37. Cf. Shay (1994, 188–93), "Why and How Does Narrative Heal?" and especially his point (192): "Narrative can transform involuntary re-experiencing of traumatic events into memory of the events, thereby reestablishing authority over memory."

38. Shay (2002, 19–119) provides a detailed indictment of Odysseus' leadership that lost some 500 men under his command.

39. Nighttime is regularly the time of intimately shared stories about the past as in Book 4 (stories about Odysseus told in Menelaus' palace), Book 15 (Eumaeus' sad story of his early life; cf. "these wondrously long nights," αἵδε δὲ νύκτες ἀθέσφατοι, 15.392), and Book 23 (Odysseus' complete account of his wanderings to Penelope, when Athena prolongs the night). For a good discussion of these poetic narratives, see Louden 1999, 56–9.

40. Odysseus' account from within the horse (11.523–532) complements Demodocus' account of the Trojans' deliberations outside the horse (8.504–513).

41. Stanford (1965, 201 ad 90–2): "These grave lines with their echo of the exordium (cp. 1, 1–4)...tenderly conclude the story of O.'s wanderings...Now O.'s destiny is to be worked out in Ithaca."

42. Contrast the restlessness of Achilles at *Iliad* 24.7–9, when he would cry at the memory of the pains (ἄλγεα, 7) he had shared with Patroclus "as he passed through wars with men and grievous seas" (ἀνδρῶν τε πτολέμους ἀλεγεινά τε κύματα πείρων, 8).

43. Odysseus' therapy is most evident in the case of Eumaeus, whom he finds "full of denial" and "distrustful" (cf. 14.149, 391), but gradually brings out of his pessimism to the point that he tells Odysseus his life story (15.403–484).

Bibliography

Ahl, F. and H. M. Roisman. 1996. *The Odyssey Re-Formed.* Ithaca, NY: Cornell University Press.

Alden, M. J. 1997. "The Resonances of the Song of Ares and Aphrodite." *Mnemosyne* 50: 513–29.

Austin, N. 1975. *Archery at the Dark of the Moon.* Berkeley: University of California Press.

Benardete, S. 1997. *The Bow and the Lyre: A Platonic Reading of the Odyssey.* Lanham, MD: Rowman.

Beßlich, S. 1966. *Schweigen—Verschweigen—Übergehen. Die Darstellung des Unausgesprochenen in der Odyssee.* Heidelberg: Carl Winter.

Braswell, B. K. 1982. "The Song of Ares and Aphrodite: Theme and Relevance to *Odyssey* 8." *Hermes* 110: 129–37.

Broeniman, C. 1996. "Demodocus, Odysseus, and the Trojan War in *Odyssey* 8." *Classical World* 90: 3–13.

Cook, E. 1999. "'Active' and 'Passive' Heroics in the *Odyssey*." *Classical World* 93: 149–67.

De Jong, I. J. F. 2001. *A Narratological Commentary on the Odyssey*. Cambridge: Cambridge University Press.

De Vries, G. J. 1977. "Phaeacian Manners." *Mnemosyne* 30: 113–21.

Di Benedeto, V. 2010. *Omero: Odissea*. Milano: Rizzoli.

Fenik, B. 1974. *Studies in the Odyssey*. Wiesbaden: F. Steiner.

Finkelberg, M. 1987. "The First Song of Demodocus." *Mnemosyne* 40: 128–32.

Garvie, A. F. 1994. *Homer: Odyssey Books VI–VIII*. Cambridge: Cambridge University Press.

Hainsworth, J. B. 1988. "A Commentary on Homer's *Odyssey*, Books V–VIII." In *A Commentary on Homer's Odyssey, Volume I*, edited by A. Heubeck, S. West, and J. B. Hainsworth. Oxford: Oxford University Press.

Halliwell, S. 2011. *Between Ecstasy and Truth: Interpretations of Greek Poetics from Homer to Longinus*. Oxford: Oxford University Press.

Hexter, R. A. 1993. *A Guide to the Odyssey*. New York: Random House.

Hölscher, U. 1939. *Untersuchungen zur Form der Odyssee: Szenenwechsel und gleichzeitige Handlungen*. Berlin: Weidmann.

———. 1960. "Das Schweigen der Arete." *Hermes* 88: 257–65.

Konstan, D. 1997. *Friendship in the Classical World*. Cambridge: Cambridge University Press.

Latacz, J. 1985. *Homer: Eine Einführung*. München und Zürich: Artemis. Translated by J. P. Holoka. 1996. *Homer: His Art and His World*. Ann Arbor: University of Michigan Press.

Louden, B. 1999. *The Odyssey: Structure, Narration, and Meaning*. Baltimore, MD: Johns Hopkins University Press.

Macleod, C. 1983. "Homer on Poetry and the Poetry of Homer." In *Collected Essays of Colin Macleod*, edited by O. Taplin, 1–15. Oxford: Oxford University Press.

Mattes, W. 1958. *Odysseus bei den Phäaken: Kritisches zur Homeranalyse*. Würzburg: K. Trilsch.

Morrison, J. 2003. *A Companion to Homer's Odyssey*. Westport, CT: Greenwood Press.

Most, G. W. 1989. "The Structure and Function of Odysseus' *Apologoi*." *Transactions of the American Philological Association* 119: 15–30.

Murnaghan, S. 1987. *Disguise and Recognition in the Odyssey*. Princeton, NJ: Princeton University Press.

Peponi, A.-E. 2012. *Frontiers of Pleasure: Models of Aesthetic Response in Archaic and Classical Greek Thought*. Oxford: Oxford University Press.

Race, W. H. 1993. "First Appearances in the *Odyssey*." *Transactions of the American Philological Association* 123: 79–107.

Reece, S. 1993. *The Stranger's Welcome: Oral Theory and the Aesthetics of the Homeric Hospitality Scene*. Ann Arbor: University of Michigan Press.

Rose, G. 1969. "The Unfriendly Phaeacians." *Transactions of the American Philological Association* 100: 387–406.

Rutherford, R. B. 1986. "The Philosophy of the *Odyssey*." *Journal of Hellenic Studies* 106: 145–62.

Shay, J. 1994. *Achilles in Vietnam: Combat Trauma and the Undoing of Character*. New York: Atheneum.

———. 2002. *Odysseus in America: Combat Trauma and the Trials of Homecoming*. New York: Scribner.

Stanford, W. B. 1965. *Homer: Odyssey, Books XIII–XXIV*. 2nd ed. Basingstoke: Macmillan.

Thalmann, W. G. 1984. *Conventions of Form and Thought in Early Greek Epic Poetry*. Baltimore, MD: Johns Hopkins University Press.

———. 1999. Review of Ahl and Roisman (1996). *Classical World* 92: 297–8.

Whitman, C. H. 1958. *Homer and the Heroic Tradition*. Cambridge, MA. Harvard University Press.

CHAPTER THREE

Women after War: Weaving Nostos in Homeric Epic and in the Twenty-First Century

CORINNE PACHE

While women play a circumscribed role in ancient epic, Homer's *Odyssey* depicts both Helen and Penelope as undergoing their own forms of home-coming, or *nostos*, after the Trojan War: Helen returns to her husband Menelaus after experiencing the war firsthand at Troy and a ten-year separation; Penelope stays home, but Odysseus' return is in many ways as much a challenge for her as it is for him and the *Odyssey* portrays her domestic ordeal as a form of heroic *nostos*. In this essay, I explore female ways of homecoming in the *Odyssey* and draw connections between Homeric heroines and members of "Team Lioness" returning home from Afghanistan and Iraq in the twenty-first century.[1] The 2008 documentary *Lioness* gives voice to some of these women, the country's first generation of female combat veterans, as they struggle to reconcile their experience of war in Iraq with their lives at home. While the ancient Greeks could not have conceived of women experiencing battle in the way the members of Team Lioness did, Helen's and Penelope's marginalized roles in the *Odyssey* open a window into the contemporary experience of women soldiers and veterans and provide ways of understanding the challenges of the trauma of war and female homecoming in the twenty-first century.

A central theme of the Homeric *Odyssey* is the connection between memory and identity. In the aftermath of the ten-year Trojan War, all the Greek heroes struggle to find their way back home, but Odysseus famously undergoes the most difficult—and the longest—of the home-comings, taking ten years to return to his family on the island of Ithaca. Odysseus' journey culminates in his reunion with his wife, Penelope, who tests his identity by appealing to their common memories of their marriage bed, a physical object that symbolizes the stability of their rela-tionship. While Penelope stays home and does not experience war first-hand, she is presented as undergoing some of the same challenges at home as Odysseus experiences abroad, and through her husband's absence and

return, Penelope in fact experiences her own *nostos*, culminating in the
restoration of her home and marriage.

A striking Homeric image links the modern warriors in Ramadi and
Penelope at home:

ἡ δ᾽ ὑπερῴῳ αὖθι περίφρων Πηνελόπεια
κεῖτ᾽ ἄρ᾽ ἄσιτος, ἄπαστος ἐδητύος ἠδὲ ποτῆτος,
ὁρμαίνουσ᾽, ἢ οἱ θάνατον φύγοι υἱὸς ἀμύμων,
ἦ ὅ γ᾽ ὑπὸ μνηστῆρσιν ὑπερφιάλοισι δαμείη.
ὅσσα δὲ μερμήριξε λέων ἀνδρῶν ἐν ὁμίλῳ
δείσας, ὁππότε μιν δόλιον περὶ κύκλον ἄγωσι,
τόσσα μιν ὁρμαίνουσαν ἐπήλυθε νήδυμος ὕπνος·
εὗδε δ᾽ ἀνακλινθεῖσα, λύθεν δέ οἱ ἅψεα πάντα.

(Odyssey 4.787–794)

But she in the upper chamber, circumspect Penelope,
lay there fasting, she had tasted no food nor drink, only
pondering whether her stately son would escape from dying
or have to go down under the hands of the insolent suitors;
and as much as a lion caught in a crowd of men turns about
in fear, when they have made a treacherous circle about him,
so she was pondering, when the painless sleep came upon her
and all her joints were relaxed so that she slept there reclining.[2]

Lion similes in Homeric poetry typically depict warriors in combat situations, and so the connection between Penelope and a trapped predator at first seems tenuous. The fearful beast of the simile is ostensibly in
great danger, but the animal's plight is left unresolved as Penelope falls
asleep. The lion simile at the end of Book 4 is the second lion simile in
that book, and in the poem, following upon the first extended simile
in the *Odyssey*, a few hundred lines earlier, where Menelaus imagines
Odysseus' eventual return home as a lion attacking a doe and the fawns
she has brought to the lion's lair (4.332–340 = 17.124–131). When the
narrator compares Penelope to a lion later in Book 4, the audience
must recall Menelaus' description and thus the leonine Odysseus and
Penelope are placed in a dialogue with each other.[3] Odysseus is in
addition compared to a lion in five other similes, culminating in the
simile of Book 22, which describes his nurse, Eurycleia, finding him
covered in blood, standing among the suitors like a lion, "a terrible
thing to look in the face," a simile that is then repeated by Eurycleia
when she in turn describes the same scene to Penelope at the beginning of Book 23.[4]

It is significant that Penelope is compared to a lion in a poem that is
framed by two similes describing Odysseus' vengeance as that of a lion.
Lionesses, real or imagined, are also predators, who, when they become
surrounded by hunters, kill to save themselves and their young. When

Homeric lions face a human opponent, moreover, they almost always prevail. Penelope may resemble a lion, but never finds herself in a position
where she has to do the fighting. While Penelope does not experience
combat, through the lion simile she is associated with Odysseus' brutal
slaughter of the suitors and by extension with the many Iliadic lion similes
depicting men in combat. The lion simile thus gives us an ancient Lioness,
a woman thrust into the "treacherous circle" of battle.

The lion simile has another important counterpart in the *Iliad*, where
Achilles, strikingly, mourns Patroclus like a lion who has lost its cubs
(18.316–322), an image that we also find in the earlier *Epic of Gilgamesh*,
where the hero mourns the death of his friend Enkidu, "like a lioness
whose cubs are in a pitfall."[5] Another Iliadic simile describes Ajax protecting the body of Patroclus as a maternal lion:[6]

Αἴας δ' ἀμφὶ Μενοιτιάδῃ σάκος εὐρὺ καλύψας
ἑστήκει ὥς τίς τε λέων περὶ οἷσι τέκεσσιν,
ᾧ ῥά τε νήπι' ἄγοντι συναντήσωνται ἐν ὕλῃ
ἄνδρες ἐπακτῆρες· ὃ δέ τε σθένεϊ βλεμεαίνει,
πᾶν δέ τ' ἐπισκύνιον κάτω ἕλκεται ὄσσε καλύπτων·

(*Iliad* 17.132–137)

Now Aias covering the son of Menoitios under his broad shield
stood fast, like a lion over his young, when the lion
is leading his little ones along, and men who are hunting
come upon them in the forest. He stands in the pride of his great
        strength
hooding his eyes under the cover of down-drawn eyelids.

While the Homeric lions are grammatically male, they seem to share
the maternal inclinations of the mother lioness in the *Epic of Gilgamesh*.
In all these examples, lions (and lioness) are always depicted in the act of
attempting to protect, or lamenting, their own blood relatives, most especially their own children.[7]

Homeric lions often appear on the battlefield via similes, but strikingly, as we have just seen, they often figure as maternal animals trying
to protect their offspring or mourning their loss. Homeric warriors are
thus imagined as mothers to one another.[8] The lion is also a symbol of
vengeance and of the predator's proverbial superiority over its human and
animal rivals. The implications of the Iliadic simile comparing mourning
Achilles to a lion are clear: nothing is more dangerous than a mourning
lion keen on revenge.

At the moment she is compared to a lion in *Odyssey* 4, Penelope is
also in a state of mourning for her presumably lost husband and absent
son. Lion similes thus evoke both war and its consequences by suggesting a kind of mourning that gives rise to wrath and desire for revenge.
Penelope the lioness does not experience battle, yet Homer's comparison

strikingly suggests just this possibility, in an image that is all the more surprising given the attitudes of ancient Greeks toward fighting women. (As an aside, the Greeks did not seem to be aware that among real lions, it is in fact the lioness who does the hunting, while the males are, as it were, the homebodies.)

While women do not experience battle firsthand in Homeric epic, war affects them in many ways, including their social position. Defined by their marital status in everyday life, women become prizes during conflict, and wives risk becoming slaves. Helen, a stolen wife, is the cause of the Trojan War and is central to the conflict, even as she stands by as an observer. She finds herself briefly on the losing side when the Greeks sack Troy, but is ultimately reunited with her husband Menelaus, instead of enslaved by the Greek victors, which is the fate of the Trojan women. For Penelope, war and her husband's long absence have also put her in a deeply ambiguous situation: she is neither wife nor widow, thus attractive as a potential bride yet unable—and certainly unwilling—to remarry. The end of the Trojan War restores both Helen's and Penelope's identities as married women, but both figures remain ambiguous because of their potential for independence. While modern attitudes toward women in war are fundamentally different, the Homeric image of Penelope the lion and the struggles of the Homeric heroines can be connected to those faced by the women of Team Lioness, the first generation of US women sent into direct ground combat in Iraq (Figure 3.1).

Because it is unacceptable in Iraqi culture for male soldiers to interact with women, in late 2003 US Army commanders started to attach teams of female support soldiers to battalions of Marines to interview and search Iraqi women during search missions. *Lioness*, directed by Meg McLagan and Daria Sommers, tells the story of five female soldiers: Shannon Morgan, Rebecca Nava, Kate Guttormsen, Ranie Ruthig, and Anastasia Breslow.[9] Through the women's own words (in conversations and excerpts from their diaries), archival footage, and newsreel, the filmmakers explore the women's homecoming and include flashbacks to combat the women faced in Ramadi in the spring of 2004.

In this documentary, Colonel William Brinkley is credited with establishing and naming the first Lioness Team (Figure 3.2). While the name "Shield Maidens," which evokes Scandinavian myth, was apparently considered, Brinkley settled on the animal moniker. Whether he was thinking of predatory or literary connotations is not known, but the comparison of women to lions—whether ancient or modern—is evocative of victory, vengeance, and mourning after battle.

While the film is a straightforward documentary, it threads images of prey and predator throughout its narrative. The first image is a shot of a fawn looking directly into the camera, before turning and running away in fear. On one level, the fawn sets the scene in the countryside of Mena, Arkansas, where the first section of the film, focusing on Shannon Morgan, takes place. But does the fawn stand in for the Lioness or for her

Figure 3.1 Sergeant Michelle Brookfield Wilmot on guard duty in Ramadi, Iraq in April 2005.
Photograph by Spc. Miranda Mattingly.

Figure 3.2 Lionesses Cynthia Espinoza, Ranie Ruthig, Shannon Morgan, and Michelle Perry in Ramadi, Iraq in July 2004.
Photograph by Lloyd Francis, Jr.

prey? Shannon at home is a hunter, but also someone who remembers being hunted.

In spite of the legal prohibition against women on the battlefield in effect at the time, the members of Team Lioness often found themselves in combat situations when they accompanied male soldiers during raids to find hidden weapons in the houses of suspected insurgents. Captain Manning, director of the Women in the Military Project based at the Women's Research and Education Institute, observes in the film that the Lionesses were forced to violate the policy in place at the time in order to do the jobs assigned to them. The Lionesses had no official status, and their actions were not documented, since the US Army could not acknowledge the presence of women in combat situations. The role played by the Lionesses in Iraq and Afghanistan and the difficulties they encountered on their return must have played an important role in Defense Secretary Leon Panetta's decision (at the unanimous recommendation of the Joint Chiefs of Staff) to overturn the ban on women in battle in the US military, a welcome corrective to the earlier practice, which resulted in a lack of recognition of the women's actions and unfair discrimination, especially for returning female veterans in need of treatment for physical or psychological injuries experienced during combat.[10]

Ordering untrained female soldiers into situations that could involve battle came with its own set of dreadful dilemmas: Army support soldiers are, by definition, not trained for combat, making hazardous situations even more dangerous; moreover, the Lioness team was composed of female Army soldiers who were sent to the battlefield with Marines, who function according to different rules and often speak what amounts to a different language.

Specialist Shannon Morgan, a mechanic, describes the shock of her first experience of accompanying a firing team of Marines during raids against insurgents. Because Shannon has the skills to fire a squad automatic weapon (SAW), the Marines wanted her to cover their rear. As they made their way through the city, the firing team came under attack, and Shannon, for the first time in her life, found herself in a combat situation. As bullets flew by, Shannon noticed one of the other Lionesses, Staff Sergeant Ranie Ruthig, also a mechanic, signaling to her from the top of a nearby building:

> And all of the sudden I looked, and everybody was gone. I was the only one in the street, there were insurgents all around me, firing at me. I'm like son-of-a-bitch! You know? I didn't know what to do . . . Ranie's like—going like this, like, trying to get my attention, "get over here," or something, "run." Because in Army, you tap back. You tap every man back and you let them know you're moving. These bastards didn't say nothing to me, just left me there. So I ran for my damn life and caught back up with my firing team—when I

got there I kicked the squad leader right in the nuts for leaving me. I
sure did. (*Lioness*, chapter 10, at 40:03)

The Lionesses lacked not only the training necessary for combat, but also
the very language to communicate effectively with the Marines to whom
they were assigned. While Shannon was doing the job assigned to her
according to the training she received, communication failure causes her
to be left behind in mortal danger.

Communication plays a central role in the Lionesses' experience of war
and subsequently in their homecoming, when finding ways to tell their
story brings the women some solace. While soldiers returning from war in
the twenty-first century have a variety of media at their disposal from diaries to film, in Homeric epic, women use weaving to tell their experience.
Women and men occupy different realms in Homer, and women's place is
by their looms, as Telemachus reminds Penelope when he asks her to go
back to her loom while the men focus on talk and the contest of the bow
that determines Penelope's fate (1.356–359 and 21.350–353). Weaving is
singled out as a female activity, but it is also the means through which
women are able to tell their story.[11] While Telemachus contrasts the loom
with the power (*kratos*, 21.353) invested in the male head of the household,
it is striking that the narrative of the *Odyssey* subtly undercuts his attempt
to keep male and female realms separate by using the same word, *polupeuo*
("to complete," "to bring to an end"), to describe Penelope's weaving and
Odysseus' completion of the war, thereby suggesting that Penelope is both
essential to, and participates in, her husband's successful homecoming.[12]
In both the *Iliad* and the *Odyssey*, both Helen and Penelope are portrayed
as master weavers whose weaving encapsulates the different ways in which
they react to the war and its aftermath.

In the *Iliad*, Helen weaves what she sees:

…ἣ δὲ μέγαν ἱστὸν ὕφαινε
δίπλακα πορφυρέην, πολέας δ' ἐνέπασσεν ἀέθλους
Τρώων θ' ἱπποδάμων καὶ Ἀχαιῶν χαλκοχιτώνων,
οὕς ἕθεν εἵνεκ' ἔπασχον ὑπ' Ἄρηος παλαμάων·

(*Iliad* 3.125–128)

…she was weaving a great web,
a red folding robe, and working into it the numerous struggles
of Trojans, breakers of horses, and bronze-armored Achaians,
struggles that they endured for her sake at the hands of the war god.

This arresting image of Helen at the loom presents her as both cause and
observer of the war. Helen's visual narrative encompasses not only the
sufferings and the great deeds of the Greek heroes, but the "struggles"
of both sides, mirroring the *Iliad* itself and its insistence on depicting

war as devastating to both victors and losers. Helen bears witness to the carnage she has caused and is observing from a distance but she remains seemingly unaffected by the events she watches. While Helen becomes a poet of sorts, her web is full of paradoxes: her storytelling is so private that it is addressed to no audience but herself; and while she depicts events that she notionally caused, she is noticeably absent from the scene she creates.

Penelope, by contrast, uses weaving to control events as she faces the consequences of the war and her husband's long absence. At home in Ithaca, Penelope sees nothing of the slaughter on the Trojan plains. Nevertheless, the war and its aftermath are for her a source of constant grief. She cannot bear, for example, to hear the singer Phemius sing "of the Achaians' bitter homecoming /from Troy, which Pallas Athene had inflicted upon them" (Hom. *Od.* 1.326–327). Lattimore's choice of the adjective "bitter" to describe the Achaians' homecoming captures the double-edged nature of the Greek *lugron*, "baneful, mournful." The *nostoi* of the Achaians are bitter for them to experience, but also bitter for others to remember, and to Penelope, they bring "unforgettable sorrow" (1.342). Telling the suitors that she will remarry only when she has completed the burial shroud for her (still living) father-in-law, Penelope uses weaving—and unweaving—to deal with the consequences of the Trojan War in Ithaca. Unlike Helen, Penelope shows no interest in recording the events that surround her, and has no wish to memorialize her suitors' sordid feasts, but her weaving, like Helen's, is also a way to tell her story and shape her future memories. By unweaving at night what she wove in the daytime, she is able to postpone giving an answer to the suitors who want to marry her and thereby gain a measure of control over her own fate. Penelope's weaving is a symbol of her cunning, but also her way of controlling the narrative of her life.[13] Helen's and Penelope's weaving thus stresses two important problems for women who face war and its consequences: how to tell a story for which there is no audience; and how to control and tell the story that has not yet been written.

For the members of Team Lioness, the ambiguity of their mission—to give support in combat situations that they, strictly speaking, are not expected to be in—marks both their experience in war and their homecoming. The ambiguity of their position is reminiscent of Penelope's ambiguous social position in Ithaca during Odysseus' absence, when she is both a wife and not a wife. For Penelope, it is essential to maintain her ambiguous status so she can control events, delay an eventual remarriage, and wait for Odysseus. For the Lionesses, the ambiguous nature of their position protects the men who order them in battle while it creates problems for the women when they come home. How does one come back from, and come to terms with, an experience that is not supposed to have happened at all? How can the former Lionesses find ways of telling their stories, which for many of them are too painful to be told? Because of what Captain Lory Manning describes as "the big disconnect right now between what the policy says women can do and what women are doing," the members of Team Lioness faced further hardships when they returned home to a society that did not recognize what they experienced. The film gives the Lionesses a voice, but there was no official mechanism to help these women gain access to professional recognition for their actions or to the treatment they might need. This of course has many harmful consequences for both their professional and personal lives.

In Homeric epic, warriors are compensated for their sufferings in war by becoming immortalized in poetry. Women suffer in, and as a consequence of, war, but they remain marginal characters in epic. While the *Iliad* stops short of describing the sack of Troy, the *Odyssey* explores the female experience of war in a famous simile in Book 8, describing Odysseus' reaction to the song just sung by the Phaiakian singer Demodocus. Demodocus' song glorifies the Greek victory at Troy, but Odysseus surprisingly breaks down when he hears the singer's praise of his own endurance in battle:

> ... αὐτὰρ Ὀδυσσεὺς
> τήκετο, δάκρυ δ' ἔδευεν ὑπὸ βλεφάροισι παρειάς.
> ὡς δὲ γυνὴ κλαίῃσι φίλον πόσιν ἀμφιπεσοῦσα,
> ὅς τε ἑῆς πρόσθεν πόλιος λαῶν τε πέσῃσιν,
> ἄστεϊ καὶ τεκέεσσιν ἀμύνων νηλεὲς ἦμαρ·
> ἡ μὲν τὸν θνήσκοντα καὶ ἀσπαίροντα ἰδοῦσα
> ἀμφ' αὐτῷ χυμένη λίγα κωκύει· οἱ δέ τ' ὄπισθε
> κόπτοντες δούρεσσι μετάφρενον ἠδὲ καὶ ὤμους
> εἴρερον εἰσανάγουσι, πόνον τ' ἐχέμεν καὶ ὀϊζύν·
> τῆς δ' ἐλεεινοτάτῳ ἄχεϊ φθινύθουσι παρειαί·

(*Odyssey* 8.521–530)

> ...but Odysseus
> melted, and from under his eyes the tears ran down, drenching
> his cheeks. As a woman weeps, lying over the body
> of her dear husband, who fell fighting for her city and people
> as he tried to beat off the pitiless day from city and children;
> she sees him dying and gasping for breath, and winding her body
> about him she cries high and shrill, while the men behind her,
> hitting her with their spear butts on the back and the shoulders,
> force her up and lead her away into slavery, to have
> hard work and sorrow, and her cheeks are wracked with pitiful
> weeping.

Listening to Demodocus' song, Odysseus cries for himself, his lost companions, and for the violence and suffering he has experienced in the past 20 years. While the passage describes a martial victory, the poet of the *Odyssey* offers a tragic scene that focuses on the human costs of war.

The song also evokes a specific event in the Trojan War, to which I will
return below. The woman in the simile is a victim of war—the Trojan
Princess Andromache, Hector's widow, immediately comes to mind—
and Odysseus is also in some sense crying for her and the violence and
suffering he has caused. This is a crucial moment in the *Odyssey*, in which
the victor is described as seeing the war from the point of view of the most
vulnerable of his victims.

Yet it is also striking that the woman to whom Odysseus is compared is
nameless: the anonymous woman who embraces her dying husband, and
who, like the women on the losing side of the Trojan War, loses everything, including her identity. The passage in fact functions as an identity
marker for Odysseus: his role during the sack of Troy signals him as a war
hero, but his tears also liken him to a combat victim, and shortly after his
breakdown Odysseus finally reveals his name and identity to his hosts.
But while the passage establishes Odysseus as a hero, the ancient poet also
stresses throughout the *Iliad* and the *Odyssey* that war—and the memory
of war—always conjures loss and hence tears for the men involved (see
chapter 2 in this volume).

The Homeric poems include many descriptions of weeping warriors,
in a stark contrast with the gendered meaning ascribed to tears in modern
US military culture.[14] Kate Guttormsen, the only female company commander at Ramadi who came to be in charge of choosing the women sent
on Lioness missions, confesses that she thinks women soldiers are better
equipped to deal with strong emotions than men because they are less
afraid to express them:

> I don't think my experiences were any different than my male coun-
> terparts. I think some of my coping mechanisms were different. For
> example, I'm sure I cried more than my male counterparts—behind
> closed doors.[15]

For Guttormsen, as for Odysseus and Achilles, tears are a natural reaction
to some of the events she witnessed. I will return below to what she calls
elsewhere "the emotional side" of war and the ways in which it affects
female soldiers.

In Homeric epic, women experience war from a distance. Helen is the
only woman to come back from Troy, but in contrast to the heroes whose
homecoming becomes the subject of song, she returns to a world in which
remembering her actions in Troy is a source not of storytelling and epic
kleos ("fame") but of grief. When Telemachus visits Sparta to gather information about his father in *Odyssey* 4, he finds Menelaus and Helen living
in extraordinary luxury, but the beauty of their palace and its furnishing
cannot hide the lack of harmony between the spouses. Their conflicting
memories of the war are so painful that they can only reminisce about the
past after taking a *pharmakos*, a drug in Helen's possession that counteracts
grief.

After Helen and her husband partake of the *pharmakos*, both remember episodes from the war that draw attention to less heroic moments away from the battlefield. Helen tells how she recognized Odysseus when he made a foray into the city disguised as a beggar. While Helen remembers trying to help the Greeks, Menelaus counters with his memories of her trying to trick the Greek warriors out of the Trojan horse by imitating their wives' voices, tempting them to forget war for wives, and inspiring them with a yearning for home so powerful that it almost causes them to abandon their mission at the most dangerous moment possible. But ultimately, Menelaus' story is about Odysseus' power of restraining the other men hidden in the horse and Helen's motivations remain mysterious.

The difficulties faced by Helen when remembering her role at Troy are mirrored in the modern Lionesses' troubles in remembering and telling their stories.[16] Because memories are intricately linked with identity, telling one's story is an important way of recovering from trauma. Yet traumatic memories are difficult to narrate precisely because they are dominated by nonverbal components such as sounds, sights, and emotions that are difficult to translate into a connected narrative. Traumatic memories can further cause individuals to lose a sense of the coherence of their entire life narratives, and lead to confused memories, as in the case of Helen and Menelaus, or to memories that are impossible to put into words.[17]

Trying to communicate what she has been through to her parents, Shannon finds it difficult to find words (Figure 3.3): "I didn't really know

Figure 3.3   Shannon Morgan on her parents' porch in Mena, Arkansas.
Photograph by Stephen T. Maing.

what to say." She finds some solace with her uncle, a veteran from the Vietnam War, as they sit together, "not saying a word," yet understanding one another because of their common experience in war. The Lionesses find it not only difficult to recount their experiences after they return, but also at the time because they did not wish to be a source of worry for their families. Shannon explains how even when she had the opportunity to tell her mother on the phone what she was doing in Ramadi, she could not tell her because she feared her mother would be so worried that it might affect her health. For Ranie Ruthig, her inability to manage her memories after her return results in bursts of uncontrollable anger typical of PTSD that leave her feeling both psychologically exhausted and full of guilt toward her family, especially her young daughter.[18] Ranie finds it particularly difficult to transition from her role as soldier to her role as mother.

When Helen and Menelaus talk of their memories at Troy, they both in different ways stress the notion of war as transgression. The role played by Odysseus and the other Greeks is ambivalent at best: they lurk, hide, and trick the Trojans into utter defeat, but the Greeks' victory is marred by its deceptive nature. Let me return to the song sung by Demodocus that provokes Odysseus' tears in *Odyssey* 8:

ἤειδεν δ' ὡς ἄστυ διέπραθον υἷες Ἀχαιῶν
ἱππόθεν ἐκχύμενοι, κοῖλον λόχον ἐκπρολιπόντες.
ἄλλον δ' ἄλλῃ ἄειδε πόλιν κεραϊζέμεν αἰπήν,
αὐτὰρ Ὀδυσσῆα προτὶ δώματα Δηϊφόβοιο
βήμεναι, ἠΰτ' Ἄρηα, σὺν ἀντιθέῳ Μενελάῳ.
κεῖθι δὴ αἰνότατον πόλεμον φάτο τολμήσαντα
νικῆσαι καὶ ἔπειτα διὰ μεγάθυμον Ἀθήνην.

(*Odyssey* 8.514–520)

He sang how the sons of the Achaians left their hollow
hiding place and streamed from the horse and sacked the city,
and he sang how one and another fought through the steep citadel,
and how in particular Odysseus, went, with godlike
Menelaus, like Ares, to find the house of Deiphobus,
and there, he said, he endured the grimmest fighting that ever
he had, but won it there too, with great-hearted Athene aiding.

At Odysseus' request, Demodocus sings of the wooden horse and the destruction of Troy. I have already discussed Odysseus' reaction to the song and the comparison of the hero to a captive woman, but his reaction is even more surprising given that the trick of the Trojan horse, and hence the sack of Troy, is celebrated as Odysseus' greatest victory. Yet taken together, Demodocus' song and Odysseus' tears offer a compressed version of the war and of the typical Homeric way of remembering war, which always acknowledges the indissoluble connection between battle and lament. Consider the *Iliad*, with its celebration of martial deeds that always lead to mourning, which becomes increasingly prevalent in the later parts of the poem. Achilles, accompanied by his mother and the Nereids, mourns the loss of Patroclus in Book 18, while the Trojans lament Hector in Book 22. Mourning takes center stage in Book 23 with the funeral of Patroclus and culminates with the tears of sorrow shared by Achilles and Priam in Book 24. Victors and losers mourn alike in the *Iliad*, and not even Zeus is immune to the grief brought upon by war, reacting to the death of his son Sarpedon with tears of blood (16.459).

Odysseus' tears in *Odyssey* 8 are also connected to the specific events, "the grimmest fighting" he ever endured, which took place at Deiphobus' house during the night of the sack of Troy. Demodocus does not give any details about what Odysseus did there, but the ancient audience would have known Deiphobus as the Trojan prince whom Helen marries after the death of Paris. When Menelaus and Odysseus go to Deiphobus' house, it is for one very specific reason: to get Helen back. And Helen plays a central role in what happens there.

To get a glimpse of that "grimmest" of battle, we have to turn to Vergil's *Aeneid* 6, where Aeneas encounters the dead Deiphobus in the underworld and hears the Trojan's version of the same events: Deiphobus recounts how Helen betrayed the city, leading the Trojan women into an ecstatic dance while simultaneously signaling to the Greeks to come out of their hiding place. While Deiphobus is asleep, Helen prepares for the Greeks' arrival by removing all weapons from his house. She then summons Menelaus and Ulysses inside, and they brutally mutilate and kill Deiphobus. The Roman Vergil to be sure presents a perspective that is as anti-Greek as possible—his Helen helps Menelaus and Ulysses to torture and slaughter her defenseless Trojan husband. When earlier in Book 2 Aeneas describes his own encounter with Helen during the sack of Troy, he portrays her as a dreadful presence, crouching in the shadows of Vesta's shrine, in fear of both the Trojans' and the Greeks' wrath. Aeneas is enraged at the sight of the hated woman whom he describes as the "Erinys," the vengeful curse bringing destruction both her own country and his own (2.573).

While the *Odyssey* does not describe the scene in the house of Deiphobus in any detail, the word Demodocus uses to describe the fighting is *ainotaton*, "the grimmest" or "the most dreadful," a word that connotes a transgression of some kind. Odysseus uses the same word to warn his companions of the "most dreadful evil" (*ainotaton kakon*) that awaits them on the island of Helios, where his companions will find death after they consume the forbidden cattle of the sun god (12.271–276). Yet the *Odyssey* remains silent on the events that take place at the house of Deiphobus, during the battle to recover Helen, which is in some sense at the center of the narrative of the Trojan War. And Helen at Sparta is depicted as a potential traitor whose past actions are so painful that they can only be remembered by her and her husband when they are drugged. Whatever the reasons for Demodocus' reluctance to mention Helen—whether he is unwilling to mention her second Trojan marriage or loath to ascribe any part of Odysseus' success in a war to a woman's help—we are left with a flickering and tantalizingly inconsistent image of Helen at Troy and at home: was she there at all or did she remain in Egypt, as Euripides has her do in his *Helen*, while the Greeks pursue her ghostly image to Troy? Is she always the enemy?

Helen's disappearing act finds its counterpart in some contemporary documentaries telling the story of the Iraq War. In *Lioness*, we witness a reunion of the team during which they watch together "Battlecry Iraq: Ramadi," an episode from the History Channel's series *Shootout*, which focuses on reconstructing famous historical battles. "Battlecry Iraq: Ramadi" depicts the struggles faced by US Marines in the spring of 2004 as they faced insurgents on the streets of Ramadi, including the same battle in which the Lioness teams were involved and which they recount in the central section of *Lioness*.[19] Although both films center on the same events, the contrast between the two versions could not be more striking. "Battlecry Iraq" of course belongs to a subgenre of war documentary that filters historical events through a traditional view of battle as the business of men: "witness real life-and-death combat, house-to-house, block by block, told for the first time, by the men who were there," announces the narrator at the beginning of the documentary. But while the documentary details the skirmishes between Americans and Iraqis in Ramadi and purports to tell of real events, using archival footage and interviews, it has no place for the untraditional Lionesses who were, in fact, there, and simply elides their presence. Women—whether American or Iraqi for that matter—are completely absent from the narrative. The omissions of "Battlecry Iraq" contribute to the documentary's generic and unproblematic vision of war, which has nothing to offer to the Lionesses who are still struggling to come to terms with their experiences in Iraq. Like Helen who comes home from a city at war only to find her experience muted through the *pharmakos*, or Penelope, whose role as narrator is severely curtailed in the *Odyssey* after Odysseus comes home and retakes control of the household (and the story), the women of Team Lioness come back from Iraq to find that their experience is neither acknowledged nor remembered. [20]

While some of the bluster is typical of the *Shootout!* series, the men also tell their stories in their own words, which reflect their different training and reactions in the face of combat. A soldier describes discovering an insurgent's silhouette against a lighted background as "a dream come true" because he could easily aim at and kill his target. *Lioness* by contrast brings to the forefront the moral dilemmas faced by soldiers and the *ainotaton*, the "grimmest," dimension of war. As they break into the houses of presumed insurgents to seek hidden weapons and information, the Lionesses have to trust that they are acting on trustworthy information. Ranie Ruthig imagines what it would be like to be at the other end of the search missions, which mostly took place between 11 p.m. and 5 a.m.: "I felt like the Gestapo. You know, all I could think of was what would I do if they did this to me?" Similarly, Anastasia Breslow writes in her diary that she finds the search missions unsettling: she imagines how she herself might react: "If someone rammed my gate down in the middle of the night I might be inclined to plot. We just have to have faith in the intel that these people are doing wrong."

Upon her return, Shannon Morgan continues to struggle with the implications of having killed another human being in the streets of Ramadi. She knows she had no choice and had to kill the man who was aiming at her before he shot her. She says that she is happy to be alive and to be back home, but also feels like she lost a part of herself when she took a human life in Iraq. Kate Guttormsen quotes what she wrote in her diary the day on which Shannon Morgan killed the insurgent and remembers another officer's reaction:

> I cannot imagine the feelings that she [Shannon] must be experiencing. Gave her a huge hug and didn't say anything. Chief Warrant Officer at the time came up to me because he saw me give her a hug and he said, "Remember, you're in charge." Which really bothered me because there's still an emotional side, you know, which I found, while I was over in that environment, that the women deal with much better than men, you know? I tried not to do it in front of people, but I would get teary-eyed when there were bad days, and I would break down when there was a bad day. I'd try to do it behind closed doors but you can't always do that. (*Lioness*, chapter 10, at 49:56)

What comes through again and again in *Lioness* is the difficulty for the team members to talk about what they have been through. Words are not enough: Kate Guttormsen "didn't say anything," while Shannon Morgan didn't know "what to say." Yet, while it may be impossible to find words adequate to recollect their painful experiences, the Lionesses are also keenly aware of the importance of telling their stories. The film is framed by Shannon Morgan's emphatic statement, "you don't ever forget," which functions as both introduction and conclusion, and both an explanation and an imperative: Shannon cannot forget what happened to her, but neither should we. Where both "Battlecry Iraq: Ramadi" and *Lioness* and both male and female soldiers agree—even if they do it in different ways—is on the absolute necessity to remember, and more particularly to remember fallen soldiers.

By way of conclusion, let me go back to the *Odyssey*, and its home-bound leonine heroine. Although she never leaves her house, Penelope is singled out by the ancient poet for both her struggle and her achievement. The epic *kleos* that is denied to unfaithful wives such as Helen (or Clytemnestra) instead goes to Odysseus' steadfast companion. Just after their final reunion, Odysseus breaks down:

> ὣς φάτο, τῷ δ' ἔτι μᾶλλον ὑφ' ἵμερον ὦρσε γόοιο·
> κλαῖε δ' ἔχων ἄλοχον θυμαρέα, κεδνὰ ἰδυῖαν.
> ὡς δ' ὅτ' ἂν ἀσπάσιος γῆ νηχομένοισι φανήῃ,
> ὧν τε Ποσειδάων εὐεργέα νῆ' ἐνὶ πόντῳ
> ῥαίσῃ, ἐπειγομένην ἀνέμῳ καὶ κύματι πηγῷ·
> παῦροι δ' ἐξέφυγον πολιῆς ἁλὸς ἤπειρόνδε
> νηχόμενοι, πολλὴ δὲ περὶ χροΐ τέτροφεν ἅλμη,
> ἀσπάσιοι δ' ἐπέβαν γαίης, κακότητα φυγόντες·
> ὣς ἄρα τῇ ἀσπαστὸς ἔην πόσις εἰσοροώσῃ,
> δειρῆς δ' οὔ πω πάμπαν ἀφίετο πήχεε λευκώ.
>
> (*Odyssey* 23.231–241)

She spoke, and still more roused in him the passion for weeping.
He wept as he held his lovely wife, whose thoughts were virtuous.
And as when the land appears welcome to men who are swimming,
after Poseidon has smashed their strong-built ship on the open
water, pounding it with the weight of wind and the heavy
seas, and only a few escape the gray water landward
by swimming, with a thick scurf of salt coated upon them,
and gladly they set foot on the shore, escaping the evil,
so welcome was her husband to her as she looked upon him,
and she could not let him go from the embrace of her white arms.

In the end, the *Odyssey* does grant Penelope her share of heroism. This powerful double simile, which suggests that men's and women's experiences can be reconciled, also stresses the ways in which *nostos* always remains an incomplete tapestry woven and unwoven by both those who leave and those who remain. Shuttling back and forth between modern and ancient experience, we weave new narratives of war and homecoming that include those who have been marginalized by ancient poets and those who are neglected by contemporary institutions. While Homeric epic gives the "female race" a circumscribed role, it also gives us a lioness heroine who is remembered as undergoing a heroic *nostos* of her own, and, in so doing, provides us with a model for contemporary and future homecomings.

Notes

1. For a study of Homeric epic and PTSD in the twentieth century, see Shay (1994, 2003). For the reception of Homer in the twentieth and twenty-first centuries, see Graziosi and Greenwood (2010) and Hall (2008).
2. All translations of Homer are by Lattimore (1951, 1967).
3. See Heubeck et al. (1990, 243) for Stephanie West's summary of the scholarly reception of the simile, which she concludes is "inept;" for the ways in which the lion similes connect Penelope and Odysseus, see, for example, Moulton (1977, 123); see also Magrath (1982, 207), who notes that the poet highlights "Penelope as the passive mate for Odysseus as the active lion." I examine this simile in greater detail in a forthcoming article.
4. There are seven lion similes in the *Odyssey* (or five, if we discount repetitions): Odysseus the lion coming back to his lair, 4.333–340 = 17.124–131; Penelope the lion, 4.787–794; Odysseus compared to a lion during his encounter with Nausicaa, 6.127–137; Polyphemos eating Odysseus' men compared to a lion, 9.287–295; Odysseus after the slaughter of the suitors, 22.402 = 23.48.
5. Tablet VIII.56–63. Translation by Foster (2001).
6. The connection between lionesses and maternal love and vengeance is perhaps linked to the strange belief about real lionesses only giving birth to one cub recorded by Herodotus, *Histories* 3.108.4: "On the one hand there is this sort of thing, but on the other hand the lioness, that is so powerful and so bold, once in her life bears one cub; for in the act of bearing she casts her uterus out with her cub. The explanation of this is that when the cub first begins to stir in the mother, its claws, much sharper than those of any other creature, tear the uterus, and the more it grows the more it scratches and tears, so that when the hour of birth is near seldom is any of the uterus left intact" (Godley 1982). How and Wells (1989) note in their commentary on these lines that "Aristotle without naming H. (Hist. An. vi. 31. 579 a 2) rightly styles this story as to the lioness ληρώδης; it was invented, he says, to account for the scarcity of lions. The lioness breeds once a year, and has usually three cubs. H. fails to explain how under his system the race of lions survives at all."
7. See West (1997, 342–3), where he notes that both "nēši 'lion' and nēšti 'lioness'" are found in different versions of the Akkadian epic, "but the sex of the creature in any case matters little."
8. For more on the ways in which Greek soldiers, and Achilles in particular, see their affection for each other in terms of similes involving maternal motifs in Homeric epic, see Dué and Ebbott (2012); see also Shay (1994, 42).
9. *Lioness* (Room 11 Productions, 2008). More information on the film can be found at http://lionessthefilm.com
10. Bumiller and Shanker (2013). For the ways in which the practice of using Lionesses went against policy (and may have played a role in making a change necessary), see, for example, Shingle (2009, 155–77).
11. Weaving in ancient Greek is also metaphorically associated with poetry and the art of narrative (as it also is in the English "text," derived from "textile") and with marriage. See, for example, McNeil (2005, 1–17).
12. On this key verb and its role in the narrative of the *Odyssey*, see Levaniouk (2011, 267).

13. In the words of the literary scholar Heilbrun (2002, 108), Penelope is faced "with an as-yet-unwritten story: how a woman may manage her own destiny when she has no plot, no narrative, no tale to guide her."

14. See, for example, Monsacré (1984). All the Greek heroes weep in Homeric epic, with the striking exception of Odysseus, who does not shed a single tear in the *Iliad*; see Pache (2000).

15. Interview with Kate Gutttormsen available on http://www.pbs.org/indepen-dentlens/lioness/guttormsen.html

16. For the connection between memory and trauma, see, for example, Kenny, Bryant, et al. (2009, 1049–1052).

17. For the connection between traumatic memories and storytelling, and further references to the literature on traumatic memories, see Hunt (2010, 118–20, 126). Cf. Shay (1994, 188–93).

18. For outbursts of anger as one of the criteria used to diagnose PTSD, see the American Psychiatric Association's Diagnostic and Statistical Manual of Mental Disorders (*DSM-V*); see also Shay (2003, 39–40).

19. *Shootout!* Season 1, Episode 11, "Battlecry Iraq: Ramadi," (A & E Television Networks, 2006).

20. On Penelope's diminished importance as a narrator after Odysseus' return, see Nieto (2008, 39–62).

Bibliography

Bumiller, Elisabeth, and Thom Shanker. 2013. " Equality at the Front Line: Pentagon Is Set to Lift Ban on Women in Combat Roles." *New York Times*, January 24.

Dué, Casey, and Mary Ebbott. 2012. "Mothers-in-Arms: Soldiers' Emotional Bonds and Homeric Similes." *War, Literature and the Arts* 24, http://wlajournal.com/24_1/pdf/DueEbbott.pdf

Foster, Benjamin, trans. 2001. *The Epic of Gilgamesh*. New York: Norton.

Godley, Alfred D., trans. 1982. *The Persian Wars. Volume 2*. Cambridge, MA: Harvard University Press.

Graziosi, Barbara, and Emily Greenwood, eds. 2010. *Homer in the Twentieth Century: Between World Literature and the Western Canon*. Oxford: Oxford University Press.

Hall, Edith. 2008. *The Return of Ulysses: A Cultural History of Homer's Odyssey*. London: I.B. Tauris.

Heilbrun, Carolyn. 2002. "What Was Penelope Unweaving?" In *Hamlet's Mother and Other Women*. New York: Columbia University Press.

Heubeck, Alfred, Stephanie West, and J. B. Hainsworth, eds. 1990. *A Commentary on Homer's Odyssey: Volume I: Introduction and Books I–VIII*. Oxford: Oxford University Press.

How, W. W., and J. Wells. 1989. *A Commentary on Herodotus: With Introduction and Appendices Volume I (Books I–IV)*. Oxford: Oxford University Press.

Hunt, Nigel C. 2010. *Memory, War and Trauma*. Cambridge: Cambridge University Press.

Kenny, L. M., Bryant, R. A., Silove, D., Creamer, M., O'Donnell, M., and Alexander C. McFarlane. 2009. "Distant Memories: A Prospective Study of Vantage Point of Trauma Memories." *Psychological Science* 20: 1049–1052,

Lattimore, Richmond, trans. 1951. *The Iliad of Homer*. Chicago, IL: University of Chicago Press.

———. 1967. *The Odyssey of Homer*. New York: Harper and Row.

Magrath, William T. 1982. "Progression of the Lion Simile in the 'Odyssey'." *The Classical Journal* 77: 205–12.

Monsacré, Hélène. 1984. *Les larmes d'Achilles*. Paris: Albin Michel.

Moulton, Carroll. 1977. *Similes in the Homeric Poems*. Goettingen: Vandenhoeck and Ruprecht.

Nieto, Pura. 2008. "Penelope's Absent Song." In *Penelope's Revenge. Essays on Gender and Epic*, *Phoenix*, 62.1: 39–62.

Pache, Corinne. 2000. "War Games: Odysseus at Troy." *Harvard Studies in Classical Philology* 100: 15–23.

Shay, Jonathan. 1994. *Achilles in Vietnam: Combat Trauma and the Undoing of Character.* New York: Simon and Schuster.

———. 2003. *Odysseus in America: Combat Trauma and the Trials of Homecoming.* New York: Scribner.

Shingle, Jennifer. 2009. "A Disparate Impact on Female Veterans: The Unintended Consequences of Veterans Affairs Regulations Governing the Burdens of Proof for Post-Traumatic Stress Disorder Due to Combat and Military Sexual Trauma." *William & Mary Journal of Women and the Law* 16: 155–77.

West, Martin Litchfield. 1997. *The East Face of Helicon.* Oxford: Clarendon Press.

CHAPTER FOUR

"Ravished Minds" in the Ancient World

LAWRENCE A. TRITLE

In 1917 and while recuperating from the intense traumas common to the battlefield experiences of a frontline infantry officer, Wilfred Owen wrote his powerful poem, "Mental Cases," with its memorable lines, "these are men whose minds the Dead have ravished."[1]

Some two thousand years earlier, another poet, and like Owen also a soldier who had experienced war's violence, Sophocles, wrote in his famous drama *Antigone* that "the strongest mind can not but break under misfortune's blows" (563–4: *nous tois kakōs prassousin, all' existatai*).[2] Separated in time and place, yet these authors reflect the trauma of war and how the mind can be no less affected than the body.

How can this be? While some acknowledge the traumatic effects of war on veterans and others who experience trauma of one kind or another, the very idea of posttraumatic stress disorder, commonly referred to as PTSD, continues to be challenged. Not long ago a writer in the UK newspaper *The Independent* suggested it was not until after the Vietnam War when soldiers "began to describe their symptoms primarily in terms of intrusive thoughts, memory avoidance and uncontrollable anxiety and arousal...the core of the PTSD diagnosis."[3] The implication of such an argument is that battle trauma and responses to it are somehow new—an assertion preposterous if it was not so tragic. One needs to look no further in writers as different as Ambrose Bierce (a Civil War Tim O'Brien) and Homer to see the folly in such a claim.[4]

More will be said of Homer below, but note that Bierce's writings of the Civil War came in the decades following the war. H. L. Mencken referred to these as the first realistic writings of war, while Daniel Aaron (1987) characterized them as "replete with disgusting ugliness," that Bierce "not only choked on the blood of the Civil War, he practically drowned in it."[5] All this can be seen in just one detail of "What I Saw at Shiloh" (1881): a sergeant dying from an oozing brain wound prompted one of Bierce's men to ask about bayoneting the man to end his suffering. Bierce replied that though he was "inexpressively shocked by the cold-blooded proposal, I told him I thought not; it was unusual, and too many were looking" (in Duncan 2002, 103–4).

While the comments of newspaper writers can be easily shoved aside perhaps, learned criticisms, like those of anthropologist Allan Young, for example, are more challenging. Young asserts that PTSD is not "timeless" or uniform.[6] The idea of traumatic memory, he argues, is "man-made," something originating in nineteenth-century thought: "Before that time, there is unhappiness, despair, and disturbing recollections, but no traumatic memory, in the sense that we know it today." In short, it is a culturally conditioned response to trauma

> glued together by the practices, technologies, and narratives with which it is diagnosed, studied, treated and represented, and by the various interests, institutions, and moral arguments that mobilized these efforts and resources.[7]

These conclusions, and the argument for a conceptual and ideological foundation for PTSD, will be examined further, but for the moment it seems worth noting that the findings of neuroscience today suggest a different picture. Neuroscientist David Eagleman (2011, 126), for example, notes that the amygdala, one of two important memory sites in the brain, records memories independently of the hippocampus (another memory site) and these "are difficult to erase and they can pop up in 'flashbulb' fashion—as commonly described by rape victims and war veterans." Moreover, this happens with incredible immediacy—less than one-twentieth of a second according to Stanford neuroscientist Robert Sapolsky—"a time so short that you aren't even aware of what you saw."[8]

That such recollections are expressed in culturally available terms and images is hardly surprising. Briefly noted below is the story of the Athenian soldier Epizelus, who went blind at Marathon and afterwards framed his story in mythic terms of a giant warrior who passed him by and killed the next man. Such an explanation was the only way that he and his contemporaries could comprehend a case of immediate blindness, what clinicians until the 1980s labeled "hysterical," now defined as functional somatic syndrome(s), or more simply, a conversion disorder.[9] An explanation that his blindness resulted from psychic intervention upon his physiology—his optic nerve intervening with his brain—would have left him and contemporaries speechless.[10]

Additionally, Young's claim that there is no such thing as "traumatic memory" might well astound readers of Homer's *Odyssey*. On hearing the "Song of Troy" sung by the bard Demodocus at the Phaeacian court, Odysseus dissolves into tears and covers his head so others do not notice (8. 322).[11] Such a response to a memory should seem to qualify as a "traumatic" one, but Young would evidently reject Odysseus' tears as "traumatic" and other critics are no less coldly analytic. The authors of the

Oxford commentary to the *Odyssey*, for example, limit their remarks on this passage to textual and academic exegesis. One would never get the idea that Odysseus's response could be a real human response to trauma, such as happened to American and German veterans seen leaving theaters after watching *Saving Private Ryan* in 1998. That inhabitants of the Greco-Roman world might respond to trauma like people in the modern seems to such critics a remote and improbable reality.

Views such as these follow from a combination of specialized academic focus on the one hand and a narrowness of perspective on the other. Some classicists, for example, continue to focus their studies on the same canon of texts (mostly) that have been under scrutiny since the eighteenth century, often with the same concerns as the founding fathers of the discipline. As historian T. C. McCaskie notes (2012, 163–4), "This makes for conservatism and a consensus in which history writing is more than usually encoded within its established and received narratives" or, to paraphrase Napoleon, history becomes a fable agreed upon. Moreover, departing from this comfort zone is made difficult by a scholarly penchant to see the conduct of affairs, the very essence of life, as rational. This "rationalist fallacy," as Anthony Stevens puts it (2004, 12–13), has led historians, for example, to define the causes of modern wars in terms of nationalism or imperial rivalries rather than to consider the nature and effects of war itself.

Scholarly detachment further complicates such views. Stéphane Audoin-Rouzeau and Annette Becker, two of the 1992 founders of the *Historial de la Grande Guerre*, a First World War study center, note the long-standing reticence of French historians to study the violence of warfare, to come to grips with what really happens in battle (Audoin-Rouzeau and Becker 2002, 15–16). They argue further that

> as a rule, French historiography of warfare has been unconcerned with the violence of the battlefield, the men in the arena, the suffering they endure, the perceptions of the men who try to survive and, in a nutshell, the immense stakes that are crystallized in the combat zone.

Their observation applies equally, in my view, to many historians and academics today. Too often these find war's realities and the rough and hard edges of soldiers a disturbing and nasty topic and so distance themselves from any close consideration of what really happens in war and the human consequences of wartime violence.

I have to admit a personal stake in this topic. Over the past 15 years I have explored in my teaching and writing the impact of war and violence on culture and society. As one who experienced war firsthand, I have a special interest in, and some understanding of, the nature of the battle experience and its impact on the veteran and those around him, and especially in the years since 2001, as we see increasingly today. In the American Civil War, soldiers called the battle experience "seeing the elephant." Perhaps it was this that later led to soldiers, since the Vietnam era to refer to War as the "Beast." Elephant or Beast, soldiers are burdened always with the memories of that experience. As Tim O'Brien says, "The bad stuff never stops happening: it lives in its own dimension, replaying itself over and over" (O'Brien 1990, 32)—as Demodocus reminded Odysseus in the land of the Phaeacians.

This is no less true today of those Americans living with the legacy of Iraq or Afghanistan whose memories are little different from those of novelist O'Brien. For that matter they differ little from the dramatist Aeschylus, who cared not that his dramatic accomplishments be noted on his grave stele, but rather that he had faced the Mede, who remembered the experience no less.[12]

> At Gela, rich in wheat, he died, and lies beneath this stone:
> Aeschylus the Athenian, son of Euphorion.
> His valour, tried and proved, the mead of Marathon can tell,
> The long-haired Persian also, who knows it all too well.

Such narratives and stories as these are universal or, as dramatist and classicist Peter Meineck rightly suggests it, ancient stories intersecting with modern lives.[13] In other words, the idea of post-battle trauma, PTSD, should be seen as a reality in the classical Greek world, one with which we too are familiar today.

Battlefield Traumas in the Ancient World

The traumas of war come in many forms, but as George Santayana said of ebullient but war-weary Oxford students in the 1920s, "only the dead have seen the end of war."[14] Oxford historian John Ma's photograph of the Theban soldier "Gamma 16" killed at Chaeronea (338/7 BC), his face nearly sliced away by a cavalryman's sword, makes this brutally clear. Other ancient battle casualties such as the Spartan heroes discovered in their tomb in the Athenian Kerameikos, one found buried with the spearhead that killed him, show war's horrors just as clearly.[15]

Additional battlefield sights and sounds can be seen in the second-century AD collection of military stratagems, the *Strategemata* of Polyaenus. While his purpose is to present a collection of military stratagems to the emperors Marcus Aurelius and Lucius Verus, Polyaenus incidentally makes mention of the stresses and horrors of battle. In his account of the Athenian General Iphicrates (a brilliant commander and tactician of the fourth century BC), Polyaenus mentions pale and trembling soldiers (9.1), others throwing away their weapons (9.4), and a chattering of teeth before battle so loud that it evoked a response from Iphicrates (9.8). Elsewhere the Epicurean philosopher Lucretius tells of

(Roman?) soldiers struggling to fight forward even after losing limbs to scythed chariots (3.634–656), a reference perhaps to Sulla's battle with Mithradates VI at Chaeronea (86 BC).[16] E. M. Remarque (1929/1984, 126) provides a modern counterpart of this, soldiers running for their lives on the stumps of their feet.

Death in battle is the end, but surviving battle and living with its sights and sounds is lifelong. Years ago when I began studying the trauma of war, Dr. Chaim Shatan, one of the guiding figures of the "Bible" of modern-day psychiatric study, the *Diagnostic and Statistical Manual of Mental Disorders*, commonly abbreviated *DSM*, told me that just one encounter with violence was enough to break a psyche.[17] At Marathon in 490 BC, the Athenian Epizelus watched as the man next to him—a neighbor or kinsman most likely—was struck down by a gigantic enemy soldier (as he later told). Instantly he became blind (Herodotus 6.117.2–3).[18] This instance of conversion is the same response to danger that afflicted many on the Western Front of World War I and left airborne trooper Albert Blithe temporarily blind the early morning hours of June 6, 1944.[19] What happened to Epizelus should not be imagined as exceptional. From the corpus of Epidaurian miracle inscriptions, a text records the life experience of one Anticrates of Cnidus:

> This man had been struck with a spear through both his eyes in some battle, and he became blind and carried around the spearhead with him, inside his face. Sleeping here, he saw a vision. It seemed to him the god pulled the dart and fitted the so-called girls (i.e., the pupils of the eyes) back into his eyelids. When day came he left well.[20]

Another example of conversion disorder amid the frightful sights and sounds of battle is mutism, what the Greeks referred to as *aphonia*. Treatises belonging to the Hippocratic corpus discuss medical conditions in which *aphonia* occurs, and the Epidaurian miracle inscriptions record such a case, though not of a soldier.[21] Herodotus provides an apposite but complementary example of a mute moved to stress-induced speech: the son of Croesus speaks for the first time warning off a Persian soldier from killing his father (Herodotus. 1.87.1).

These ancient accounts of psychic trauma inducing various kinds of conversion disorders have modern counterparts. These range from the fictional character of Billy Prior in Pat Barker's *Regeneration* to the Japanese flyer surviving a hail of American anti-aircraft fire off Guadalcanal, who returned to his carrier unable to speak coherently (Hornfischer 2011, 231). John Huston's powerful and long-suppressed post-World War II film, *Let There Be Light* (1946), depicts returning American GIs unable to speak, to walk, whose return to civilian society was delayed by months or years.[22]

In his Peloponnesian War era exhibition speech, *The Encomium of Helen*, the Sicilian Greek philosopher and rhetorician Gorgias absolved the infamous beauty of any responsibility for starting the Trojan War.[23] In passing,

Gorgias alludes to soldiers so shaken by their wartime experiences that some suffer from debilitating illnesses while others are unable to work:

> when warriors put on their armor and weapons, some for defense others for offense, the mere sight of these terrifies the souls of some, who flee panic-stricken even from anticipated dangers as if these were really present. . . . And [later] some of these [men] lose presence of mind, and others become unable to work, suffering terrible diseases or incurable madness.
>
> (Text and translation in MacDowell 1982/1993: 16–17. I have adapted the translation to make its sense clearer.) [24]

While today instances of conversion disorder and related psychic-induced trauma are easy enough for us to diagnose, contemporaries of these men would not have known or understood the underlying physiology that produced these reactions. Herein lies the value of Gorgias's testimony. He actually senses a connection, though he could not have explained it, between the effects of going into battle and seeing horrific things, and how these affect the mind and change the man. Essentially, Gorgias describes the change of character that results from battlefield trauma and. if put alongside psychiatrist and author Jonathan Shay's list of symptoms of PTSD, would match up favorably in many respects Two of these in particular —"loss of authority over mental function—particularly memory and trustworthy perception" and "chronic health problems stemming from chronic mobilization of the body for danger" jump out at the reader straight from Gorgias's text (Shay 1994, xx).

Other accounts in the ancient literature corroborate Gorgias's testimony. Xenophon's famous description of the march of the 10,000 into the heart of the Persian Empire offers the intriguing story of the Spartan commander Clearchus. Xenophon describes a veteran soldier whose character and actions are little different from the dysfunctional lives that Gorgias relates. Xenophon lived with Clearchus and had ample opportunity to observe this battle-hardened soldier he called *philopolemos*, or "war-lover," a man who could have lived in peace but chose instead to make war. In describing Clearchus' character, Xenophon notes traits that are strikingly reminiscent of PTSD. Clearchus began his career as a mercenary commander after refusing to follow orders from Spartan authorities, choosing to provoke a war with the Thracians, an act that led to his exile. This clash and other instances of social alienation and betrayal reflect what Jonathan Shay terms the "persistent expectation of betrayal and exploitation" and the "destruction of the capacity for social trust" (Shay 1994, xx). In fact, Clearchus dedicated his whole life to the pursuit of war, preparing for it in every way possible, even relishing the experience of battle. Xenophon says that on going into battle his "forbidding look seemed positively cheerful" (*Anabasis*. 2.6.115, discussed more fully in Tritle 2004, 32–9).

What Gorgias relates, and what the example of Clearchus reveals, is that the trauma of war manifests itself differently. Some, like those mentioned by Gorgias, are left debilitated physically and psychically. Today newspapers report stories of another generation whose responses to the experience of war in Afghanistan and Iraq are no different: suicide rates in excess of the national average, whose violent homecomings have inspired films. This, however, would not have surprised Gorgias, perhaps the first intellectual in the Western tradition to observe and make a connection between war and its traumas, what we would today define as PTSD.

PTSD, Past and Present

But as the critics cited above would argue, does such a thing as PTSD exist? Is it a phenomenon of the modern age imposed upon the past by those who wish to remake the past in the image of the present? There are some classicists and ancient historians who think just that. Classicist J.-C. Couvenhes rejects the possibility of PTSD in antiquity. He claims, without argument, that those ancient historians—including this author, as his footnote cites only my study *From Melos to My Lai*—who write about the trauma of war in the ancient world do so as some sort of idiosyncratic personal obsession without application to the classical world.[25] Such criticism hardly reflects the academic reticence of some, as noted above by Audoin-Rouzeau and Becker, to come to grips with the violence of the battlefield, to understand how that violence affects combatants, not only amid the chaos of battle but when the fighting ends.

In asserting the modernity of PTSD, critics such as J.-C. Couvenhes and Allan Young could easily point to the ambiguity of clinical terminology in the accounts of military physicians prior to the mid-nineteenth century.[26] In the years before World War I, soldiers suffered from conditions vaguely described as nostalgia, soldier's heart, sometimes also called Da Costa's syndrome. Often physicians attributed these conditions to the privations of military campaigning in places far from home (so nostalgia) or to the hard life that soldiers of the eighteenth and nineteenth centuries led (so "palpitation" or DAH, "disordered action of the heart"). First diagnosed in the Crimean War, DAH remained a ready description of soldierly ailments for some 80 years, largely because "the heart was a no-go area for surgery, while medication for cardiac disease was limited" (Jones 2006, 540). Such limitations suggested to some cardiologists that heart disease stemmed from morbid anatomy (e.g., deformed valves) and that such factors, worsened by the lifestyle of soldiers (smoking, alcohol) and the conditions of service (marching with heavy loads for long distances with poorly designed equipment), resulted in DAH.

The killing fields of World War I brought a new dimension to wartime trauma, shell shock, the best known of all war syndromes, at least prior to the later twentieth century's ostensible discovery of PTSD. While nostalgia and palpitation failed to grip the popular imagination, minds ravaged by shell shock and expressed in the poetry of Wilfred Owen and Siegfried Sassoon, since popularized in Pat Barker's moving novels, *Regeneration* (1991), *The Eye in the Door* (1993), and *The Ghost Road* (1995), have done just that. Symptoms of shell shock were seemingly physical, ranging from tics and tremors to nightmares, mutism, memory loss, and fatigue. Explanations were no less diverse: the result of sustained and intense combat, the failure of adaptive repression, or simple cowardice. In Britain the nature and condition of shell shock was studied extensively: opinions regarding its causation varied, with some concluding that it resulted from poor training, others ascribing it to the increased use of substandard troops (see further Jones 2006, 537).

In the 1920s American psychiatrist Abram Kardiner embarked on a period of work and study that would lead to the publication of *The Traumatic Neuroses of War* (1941). Several strands informed Kardiner's work: psychoanalysis carried over from the year spent in Vienna where Freud had analyzed him, along with extensive study of social theory and anthropology. While Kardiner concluded that war neuroses represented a form of hysteria, he realized that the pejorative connotations of the word discredited those so afflicted. *"Physioneurosis"* became his preferred definition of the response to trauma, and the terms commonly attached to PTSD today—startle reactions, hyperalertness, vigilance, and psychosomatic complaints—were established.[27]

Kardiner's notion of *physioneurosis* soon found new testing grounds in the battlefields of World War II. Within a short time of the war's outbreak, medical personnel in Britain noted the widespread occurrence of gastrointestinal and digestive problems that remained major problems throughout the war. Perhaps the best-known American study of combat stress was that of psychiatrists Roy Grinker and John Spiegel, *Men Under Stress* (1945), which observed that "gastrointestinal symptoms flourish in an abundance and variety" unlike the cardiac syndromes observed in World War I (254–5); within the ranks of German military forces similar problems were encountered, with the *Wehrmacht* even establishing "stomach" battalions (*Magenbattalionen*) of the chronically ill (see further Binneveld 1997, 93). Numerous hypotheses have been advanced to explain this surge in gastrointestinal and digestive problems. Edgar Jones (King's Centre for Military Health Research) discounts "pure chance" and suggests that contemporary and popular health fears and the limits of medical science influenced the scientific community to focus on conversion disorders, that is, on what was once known as hysteria (Jones 2006, 538; see also above, n. 9).

Kardiner's research and conclusions were elaborated by those of Grinker and Spiegel among others. This body of mid-twentieth-century scientific research aimed at explaining wartime psychic traumas in the context of what was happening to the body and at showing how disorders of the body reflected underlying combat stress. This linkage reflects similar developments in combat medicine and improvements in the treatment of wounds: in World War II, the Korean, and Vietnam Wars, for every combat death there were two or three wounded; in Iraq (2003–2010) and Afghanistan today that ratio is 1:7. Dr. Ron Glasser has studied extensively the treatment of combat wounds from Vietnam to Afghanistan, including the traumatic brain injuries (TBIs) inflicted by today's powerful improvised explosive devices (IEDs). He has suggested that while the twentieth century was medically speaking the century of the body, the twenty-first is the century of the brain.[28] Kardiner's physiological argument remains viable, but with one critical twenty-first- century qualification—the role of neurological damage in producing the disorders noted by the medical community.

This finding seems especially appropriate with respect to understanding how combat stress affects the brain and how the brain remembers trauma (i.e., basically how memory works), whether as the result of powerful explosives or the daily stress created by the dread of battle. Increasingly neuroscience and biochemistry are providing whole new perspectives on how to explain and understand psychic trauma. Clinical studies conducted over the last 15 years and more, including those of Robert Sapolsky and Emory University physician J. Douglas Bremner, demonstrate the reality of changes brought to brain cells by biochemical and physiological arousal.[29]

A vast body of ongoing medical and scientific research demonstrates that traumatic stressors —especially the biochemical reactions of adrenaline and other hormones (called catecholamines that include epinephrine, norephinephrine, and dopamine)—hyperstimulate the brain's hippocampus, amygdala, and frontal lobes and obstruct bodily homeostasis, producing symptoms consistent with combat-stress reactions. In association with these, the glucocorticoids further enhance the impact of adrenaline and the catecholamines. The effects of these biochemicals are not insignificant. The amygdala, for example, as a critical site of memory, functions differently from the hippocampus. As noted above, neuroscientist David Eagleman (2011, 126, 153) notes the difficulties involved in erasing memories recorded by the amygdala which often pop up in "flashback" fashion, as rape victims and war veterans commonly report —in other words, it records memories associated with strong emotions, both positive and negative. The amygdala, when damaged, also leads to a variety of symptoms including lack of fear, blunting of emotion, and overreaction.[30] Traumatic events beyond understanding resist incorporation into the memory: as a result, "the event demands perpetual replay," with the psyche attempting and often failing to control the trauma through flashbacks, hallucinations, and other displaced anxieties (cf. Dawes 2013, 29).

These studies show that the nature of brain change (and how this affects memory) need not be the result of the catastrophic impact of IEDs, as in Iraq and Afghanistan over the last ten years, or like those sailors who died from concussive effects of naval gunnery in World War II, that is dead but without so much as a mark on them (so described by Hornfischer 2011, 319). In fact, all the necessary agents for stress-induced changes in the brain are to be found in the biochemical makeup of our blood.

In short, the tremendous strides made in medicine both in treating the physical wounds of war and the psychic undercut the skepticism of critics like Allan Young who question the reality of PTSD by emphasizing its modernity and suggesting that traumatic memories were only discovered in 1980 with the publication of *DSM-III.*[31] This then-latest version of the manual made clear that calling attention to the trauma of war was essential given the situation current in the United States with ongoing problems of Vietnam veterans. Interestingly, however, this was not the first time that the *DSM* had listed such conditions. Study of combatants in World War II and Korea apparently influenced some psychiatrists to define war trauma in *DSM-I* (1952) as "gross stress reaction."

With war and war trauma seemingly a thing of the past, however, the 1968 edition of *DSM-II* omitted any reference to this category of psychic distress. But it was not long, however, before psychiatrists then working with growing numbers of troubled Vietnam veterans, Chaim Shatan and Robert Lifton among others, realized that this decision had been premature. Shatan, for example, in 1972 wrote a *New York Times* op-ed piece in which he coined the phrase "Post-Vietnam Syndrome," used to describe those veterans afflicted with rage, guilt, and alienation, among other things. In collaboration with others, Shatan and Lifton worked to restore and update the "gross stress reaction" and impact of war trauma of *DSM-I*, and it was this that resulted in the addition of PTSD to the *DSM-III.*[32]

How PTSD Is an Ancient Reality

Critics debate the extent to which PTSD can be a universal condition, one that could apply to everyone across time and place. Readers considering this question might examine closely one reality: how is it possible for humans as far apart in time, place, and culture as the Greek soldier Epizelus and those Cambodian women, survivors of the Pol Pot terror of the 1970s, to become "hysterically" blind as the result of wartime psychic trauma?[33] The answer seems to be in the underlying human physiology, a constant for the last 200,000 years, as science has demonstrated over the last several decades. This research has explored and identified the age and ancestral origins of "modern man," that is, our ancestors defined as "anatomically modern humans" by anthropologists (Dunbar 2004, 32–3). Researchers focused first on mitochondrial DNA, that which traced the maternal lineage, and so identified "Mitochondria Eve," the "Ur-mother" of modern man, in Africa some 150,000 years ago. Similar research into Y-chromosome DNA has only recently identified the "Ur-father" of modern man, again in Africa at a comparably remote time (Poznik 2013, 562–5). The ability of scientists to trace human DNA to its remote origins by sequencing the DNA of living humans argues for the continuity of human biology—and so the universality of trauma —over the last 150,000 years. As Anthony Stevens notes, we humans today are little different from our Paleolithic ancestors of 50,000 years ago, as the brain that once made stone axes today sends spacecraft out of the solar system (see Dunbar 2004, 33–4; Stevens 2004, 48; Garbutt 2006, 15–3).

That an exploding IED can ignite in crescendo fashion injuries now known to us as TBI is hardly surprising given today's knowledge of physiology and neuroscience. But what of the subtleties of simple combat stress—living every day on the edge of the abyss wondering when this moment is your last? Combat soldiers of every era know these things too well. In his gripping novel *Billy Lynn's Long Halftime Walk*, Ben Fountain notes the randomness of war, "living the Russian-roulette lifestyle every minute of the day," how "fractions, atoms, and...all this [was] random, whether you stopped at a piss tube this minute or the next, or skipped seconds at chow, or were curled to the left in your bunk instead of the right..." (2012, 53).

These realities were no less for soldiers in the classical Greek world as readers surely by now have detected: the Athenian Epizelus at Marathon, Anticrates of Cnidus in some unknown engagement, both blind as the result of the combat stress of battle, with others so gripped with fear that their teeth chattered audibly. Men like these were those Gorgias tells of who after the experience of battle became unable to work as they suffered terrible diseases or incurable madness. Gorgias and his contemporaries may not have used Kardiner's terminology, terms like startle reactions, hyperalertness, vigilance, and psychosomatic complaints (cf. Herman 1992/1997, 35), but not to connect these to Gorgias's report seems a denial of what is plainly evident.

As Dr. Glasser notes, the twenty-first century is the century of the brain. Neuroscience with its increasing understanding of the brain, as well as studies in evolutionary biology and biochemistry, should be seen as useful ancillary tools for the modern scholar. For those who seek a broad and deep understanding of what happens to those caught up in the violence of the battlefield, doing so without this body of knowledge must be seen as telling only part of the story (on these topics, see further Wilson 1978/2004, x–xvii; Dunbar 2004).

The Fight or Flight Experience, or Life after Battle[34]

The death of Patroclus was a sobering moment for Achilles: he had failed to protect his friend. He knew now that his own death awaited him, and soon. In reflecting on his friend's death, he recognized the insidious nature of battle, how its sweetness gripped the soul, and how he wished this could go away, but clearly it would not (*Iliad* 18.98–110).[35] The Spartan commander Clearchus too sensed this sweetness as he went into

battle smiling, even happy. Though able to function "normally," organizing armies and otherwise performing the usual duties of a wartime
commander, Clearchus's social skills were impaired. On several occasions
he "lost it," exploding uncontrollably, though often later regretting the
harsh actions that followed such outbursts: in short, his dedication to wartime pursuits suggests that "normal" life had eluded him. While clearly
Clearchus functioned at a higher level than the unhappy men depicted
by Gorgias, still years of war had changed his character (p. 92). There is
also the example of the soldier Socrates: though a survivor of hard-fought
battles, Plato (*Charmides* 153 B–C) suggests that Socrates was like many
a veteran survivor, one who preferred not to talk of what he had seen
despite friendly inquiries.

Socrates and Clearchus both survived the battles of the Peloponnesian
War, but their veteran lives diverged considerably. Socrates became the
great philosopher, able to live with the trauma of war, though if Plato's
accounts are accurate, not forgetting war's realities. Clearchus survived
too, but became hooked on war's violence and, as Xenophon tells, was
drawn to a life of war like a moth to the flame, driven, like Homer says,
to taste again the sweetness of battle. The postwar lives of both men attest
what recent studies of combat stress have suggested that there are degrees
of psychic postwar trauma. In his 2004 study *Odysseus in America*, Shay
suggested that PTSD be qualified as "simple" and "complex" (2004, 4),
and the Canadian military establishment has adopted a close parallel,
identifying a formula of battle trauma that includes combat stress reaction
(CSR), acute stress disorder (ASD), and PTSD.[36]

Conclusion

The Greek philosopher Heraclitus once remarked (c. 500 BC) that "war is
the father of all things," a sentiment later echoed by Winston Churchill:
"The story of the human race is War" (cited in Winter and Prost 2005,
175). These unhappy but true verdicts find confirmation in the scientific
study of the human condition, the biochemical and physiological secrets
of which—and their impact on us humans—continue to be revealed
almost daily. The problem is that too few in the humanities pay attention
to these. No less important, scientists and other researchers in the medical community focus on the recent past to explore the varied responses
to battle while also ignoring literature, whether Homeric, Greek drama,
or that of the World Wars and Vietnam, which record and preserve perhaps the truest voices of trauma and memory.[37] Of these voices, it is clear
that those from the ancient world—Homer and Herodotus, the philosophers Gorgias and Lucretius, and the unknown witnesses recorded on the
Epidaurian miracle inscriptions—while separated by millennia provide
examples not only of battlefield horrors, but how those horrors continued
into life after the battle (cf. Binneveld, 1997, 197).

Notes

1. Owen (1973, 98–9, 131). Hibberd, Owen's editor, suggests that the poem reflects Owen's stay at Craiglockhart as well as an earlier piece, *Purgatorial Passions*, from 1915/1916.
2. While the chronology is a bit unclear, Sophocles served as a general or *strategos* during the Athenian war with the island city-state of Samos, c. 442–438 BC. In the course of this campaign the Athenians executed a number of Samian officers, first crucifying them and then beating to death the survivors whose bodies were left exposed as a lesson to other would be rebels (see further Plut. *Per.* 25–28.3; Tritle 2010, 13–18). Watling's translation in the Penguin edition (1947/1974) perhaps expresses Sophocles's language most clearly.
3. E. Watters, "The Invisible Division: US Soldiers Are Seven Times More Likely as UK Troops to Develop Post-Traumatic Stress." *The Independent*, April 8, 2011. Scholarly critiques of the reality of PTSD include Young (1995) and Fassin and Rechtman (2009). Both studies might be characterized as presentist and neither looks closely at the intersection of trauma and literature. Cf. Binnevelde (1997, 197).
4. Jones (2006, 534–5) notes that the reporting of flashbacks (or "dissociative episodes," so Young 1995, 121) increases with the Vietnam War. Such views, however, pay too little attention to what we find in literature, including Homer and Bierce, which may be the truest effort to understand trauma (cf. Dawes 2013, 30).
5. See further Duncan and Klooster (2002, 20–1, 103).
6. Young (1995, 5) argues that PTSD has been shaped by the "social, cognitive, and technological conditions through which researchers come to know their facts and the meaning of facticity," yet acknowledges that "suffering is real; PTSD is real." While the caveat seems well intentioned, it lends support to those who would deny the reality of wartime trauma, whether in the ancient or modern world. Cf. Fassin and Rechtman (2009, 6).
7. Young (1995, 141, 5). The argument that PTSD is a social-cultural construct is weak. To assert that it is a social-cultural construct establishes nothing, and the argument is further undermined when scientific evidence demonstrates the biochemical changes triggered by stress that actually change the brain. A body of compelling scientific evidence will be noted below: neither Young (1995) nor Fassin and Rechtman (2009) cite, for example, studies by R. Sapolsky and J. Bremner.
8. R. Sapolsky, "Is Racial Prejudice Hard-Wired?" *Los Angeles Times*, July 28, 2013, p. A3.
9. See Tritle (2000, 8, n.16, 159–60) for fuller treatment of the story of Epizelus. "Hysteria" is a nineteenth-century term describing what in some cases was everything that men found "mysterious or unmanageable" in women (Herman 1992/1997, 10). Since the 1980s hysteria has been displaced by more modern terminology including "functional somatic syndromes" or conversion disorders. See further Jones and Wessely (2005, 206–8, *DSM-5*, 318–21) and Herman (1992/1997, 10–20, 23–5, 35–6). Disorders such as these afflict not only vision, but speech and bodily controls, these latter manifesting themselves, for example, as paralysis. See also Weinstein (1995) and Solomon (1993, 31).
10. While debate rages over the nature of the Greek intellectual revolution "from Myth to Logos" (cf. the essays in Buxton 1999), philosophers, physicians, and even historians then attempted to understand their world rationally. We today should attempt no less.
11. At Hom. *Od.* 11.87 Odysseus tears up again at the sight of his mother in Hades. See Heubeck-West-Hainsworth (1988, 381–2) for discussion.

12. Paus. 1.14.5; Aeschylus's *Vita* 11 preserves the epitaph, its authenticity accepted by Sommerstein (1996, 24), who provides the translation.
13. See further Meineck (2009) and his organization of the NEH program *Page & Stage* and *Ancient Greeks/Modern Lives*.
14. Often attributed to Plato, Palaima (2013, 734–5) traces it to Santayana.
15. See further Ma (2008, 72–91); Spartan tomb: Wycherley (1978, 257); Rossiter (1981, 115).
16. Plut. *Sul.* 18.6. Within a few decades of Sulla's battle with Mithradates Lucretius wrote *On Nature*, perhaps drawing from this famous encounter examples of soldiers suffering traumatic amputations, even decapitations.
17. This over lunch in a 1997 meeting. Chaim Shatan's role in the writing of the *DSM-III* (1980) will be discussed further below (see n. 32) and Young (1995, 109–10).
18. A kinsman or neighbor, most likely, as the Athenian military organization was tribal, relatives and neighbors serving side by side. See further Tritle (2000, 63–5) and similar conclusions reached independently by psychologist Louis Crocq (1999, 33).
19. See Ambrose (1992, 98) and depicted in the Tom Hanks–Stephen Spielberg HBO film version, *Band of Brothers*.
20. Edelstein and Edelstein (1945/1998, 235); the passage cannot be interpreted literally. Spearheads of this era were 12–18 inches in length, which makes it unlikely that Anticrates was physically wounded. His was most certainly psychic trauma. Other inscriptions also record conversion disorders involving sight (Timon, 237, and Valerius Aper, a Roman soldier of the second century AD, p. 251); wounded soldiers suffering from battle injuries (Gorgias of Heraclea, 235, and Euhippus, 232) and paralysis (Hermodicus of Lampsacus, 232–3).
21. Speechlessness the result of wounds: Hippoc. *Morb.* 1.4, 3; other references to speechlessness are the result of fever, for example, *Coan Prenotations* 77, 194, 240–4, for example, *Crises* (58), *Critical Days* (301), and nonmilitary mutism: Edelstein and Edelstein (1945/1998, 230–1). Ancient evidence clearly attests instances of conversion disorder; while certain cases of mutism for soldiers is lacking, its existence should not simply be rejected. Review of the evidence might reveal texts attesting mutism that have been overlooked or misunderstood. See Solomon (1993, 31) for reference to mutism among Israeli soldiers in the aftermath of the invasion of Lebanon (1982).
22. Further discussion in Shephard (2000, 271–8), though Shephard does not reveal that Huston's film was censored and not screened publicly until 1981 (at the Cannes Film Festival no less), and then only after the intervention of Vice President Walter Mondale (so Fassin and Rechtman 2009, 69).
23. From Leontini in Sicily, Gorgias arrived in Athens (c. 427 BC) on a diplomatic mission in the midst of the great Peloponnesian War, requesting aid against the aggressions of neighboring Syracuse. Evidently, he remained in Greece for some time, giving demonstration lectures of his rhetorical virtuosity (see Guthrie 1971, 270).
24. Discussion first appeared in Tritle (2009, 195–9), now in id. (2010, 158–60). Gorgias' primary goal is to expound on the nature of language and persuasion. To illustrate this he takes a lighthearted theme, defending Helen, employing an oblique argument based on what people see (to continue his own imagery) in the world around them, in this case the scourges of war. Skeptics might argue that Gorgias is just playing with words. Against this I would note that while an intellectual interested in philosophy and rhetorical theory, Gorgias was also a man of action: diplomat and otherwise experienced in real-world issues. Like his contemporaries, he knew what happened to those caught up in the bloody business of war and, as the stories told of the Athenian Epizelus and others, that while surviving were radically changed by the experience.

25. Couvenhes (2005, 431); cf. also Wheeler (2011, 73, n. 72), including the editors' dissenting note. Just to be clear, Couvenhes does not substantiate his argument with any reference to scientific or medical literature: his is a simple and unfounded assertion.
26. Yet the limits of medical science suggest caution in exaggerating what physicians in the nineteenth century knew about either physical or psychic trauma. In the aftermath of the battle of Antietam (1862), a number of wounded Union soldiers were laid out on the floor of a stable, no one knowing or imagining that this might endanger those so placed (cf. Morris 2000, 90–9); in 1881, when President Garfield lingered for three months before dying from a gunshot wound to the abdomen, none of the attending physicians thought it questionable procedure to probe his wound with unwashed hands (see Millard [2011, 140–2, 215–29] for some amazing details of Garfield's "treatment" and of the nature of medical science in the later nineteenth century). Practices like these suggest that understanding psychic trauma would have been difficult, if not impossible.
27. See discussion and sources cited in n. 9 above.
28. See Glasser (2011, 2013), preceded by his 1971 classic account of the Vietnam War, *365 Days* (New York: George Braziller).
29. Bremner (2002, 116); Sapolsky et al. (1990); and Sapolsky (1996). Bremner also presented his findings in a 2002 conference at UCLA, "Posttraumatic Stress Disorder: Biological, Clinical, and Cultural Approaches to Trauma's Effects."
30. See Shephard (2000, 387), who identifies doctors with interests in "biological" psychiatry seeking to establish the timelessness of PTSD. His quotation marks setting off biological seem just a bit prejudicial.
31. This on the publication of the third edition of the psychiatric community's handbook, the *Diagnostic and Statistical Manual of Mental Disorders*, commonly abbreviated as *DSM* (and now in its fifth edition, published 2013).
32. Noted by Young (1995, 98–9, 111) and discussed also by Shephard (2000, 364); Chaim Shatan, one of the psychiatrists involved in the writing of *DSM-III*, confirmed this to me.
33. Discussed first in Tritle (2000, 8, n. 16); the Cambodian women were the subject of the documentary *Ekleipsis* by filmmaker Tran T. Kim-Trang (1999).
34. The commonly understood response to a stressful situation is "fight or flight." But readers might be interested in a third—faint. See Natterson-Horowitz and Bowers (2013, 19–39) for discussion, and confirmed by a young Marine now at Dartmouth College, who told me of retrieving a faint comrade from the field and under fire (a conversation of May 2013).
35. See further Edwards (1991, 159), who notes that Achilles reflects not only on his own imminent death, but that of Patroclus as well.
36. See Garbutt (2006) for the comprehensive structure of operational stress injuries (OSIs) distinguishing levels of battle trauma now used by Canadian armed forces.
37. See, for example, the essays in Laurence and Matthews (2012), which offer a wide survey of manifold dimensions of military psychology, but with little attention to wartime traumas before the mid-nineteenth century.

Bibliography

Ambrose, S. 1992/2001. *Band of Brothers*. New York: Simon and Schuster.
American Psychiatric Association. 2013. *Diagnostic and Statistical Manual of Mental Disorders*. 5th ed. Washington, DC: American Psychiatric Publishing.

Audoin-Rouzeau, S., and A. Becker. 2002. *14–18. Understanding the Great War*. New York: Hill and Wang.

Barker, P. 1991. *Regeneration*. London: Penguin Books.

———. 1993. *The Eye in the Door*. London: Penguin Books.

———. 1995. *The Ghost Road*. London: Penguin Books.

Binneveld, H. 1997. *From Shell Shock to Combat Stress*. Amsterdam: Amsterdam University Press.

Bremner, J. D. 2002. *Does Stress Damage the Brain?* New York: W.W. Norton.

Buxton, R. 1999. *From Myth to Reason? Studies in the Development of Greek Thought*. Oxford: Oxford University Press.

Couvenhes, J.-C. 2005."De disciplina Graecorum: les relations de violence entre les chefs militaire grecs et leur soldats." In *La violence dans les mondes grec et romain*, edited by J.-M. Bertrand, 431–54. Paris: Publications de la Sorbonne.

Crocq, L. 1999. *Les traumatismes psychiques de guerre*. Paris: Editions Odile Jacob.

Dawes, J. 2013. *Evil Men*. Cambridge, MA: Harvard University Press.

Dunbar, R. 2004. *The Human Story. A New History of Mankind's Evolution*. London: Faber and Faber.

Duncan, R., and D. J. Klooster, eds. 2002. *Phantoms of a Blood-Stained Period. The Complete Civil War Writings of Ambrose Bierce*. Amherst: University of Massachusetts Press.

Eagleman, D. 2011. *Incognito. The Secret Lives of the Brain*. New York: Pantheon.

Edelstein, E. J. and L. Edelstein. 1945/1998. *Asclepius. Collection and Interpretation of the Testimonies*. Baltimore, MD: Johns Hopkins University Press.

Edwards, M. W. 1991. *The Iliad: A Commentary. Vol. V: Books 17–20*. Cambridge: Cambridge University Press.

Fassin, D., and R. Rechtman. 2009. *The Empire of Trauma. An Inquiry into the Condition of Victimhood*. Princeton, NJ: Princeton University Press.

Fountain, B. 2012. *Billy Lynn's Long Halftime Walk*. New York: ECCO Books.

Garbutt, P. F. C. 2006. "The Paradox of Fight or Flight—A Leadership Guide to Understanding and Mitigating Operational Stress Injuries." In *Human Dimensions in Military Operations—Military Leaders' Strategies for Addressing Stress and Psychological Support*. Proceedings RTO-MP-HFM, Paper 15. Neuilly-sur-Seine, FR.

Glasser, R. J. 2011. *Broken Bodies Shattered Minds. A Medical Odyssey from Vietnam to Afghanistan*. Palisades, NY: History Publishing.

Glasser, R. J. and C. Gordon, M.D. 2013. "Traumatic Brain Injury—The Invisible Injury." In *The Attorney's Guide to Defending Veterans in Criminal Court*, edited by B. Hunter and R. C. Elise, 199–221. Orlando, F L: DC Press.

Grinker, R. R., and J. P. Spiegel. 1945. *Men Under Stress*. Philadelphia, PA: Blakiston.

Guthrie, W. K. C. 1971. *The Sophists*. Cambridge: Cambridge University Press.

Herman, J. 1992/1997. *Trauma and Recovery. The Aftermath of Violence—From Domestic Abuse to Political Terror*. New York: Basic Books.

Heubeck, A., S. West, and J. B. Hainsworth. 1988. *A Commentary on Homer's Odyssey*. 3 vols. Oxford: Clarendon Press.

Hornfischer, J. D. 2011. *Neptune's Inferno. The U.S. Navy at Guadalcanal*. New York: Bantam Books.

How, W. W. and J. Wells. 1912. *A Commentary on Herodotus*. 2 vols. Oxford: Clarendon Press.

Jones, E. 2006. "Historical Approaches to Post-Combat Disorders." *Philosophical Transactions: Biological Sciences* 361(1468): 533–42.

Jones, E., and S. Wessely. 2005. *Shell Shock to PTSD. Military Psychiatry from 1900 to the Gulf War*. Maudsley Monographs 47. Hove: Psychology Press.

Laurence, J. H. and M. D. Matthews, eds. 2012. *The Oxford Handbook of Military Psychology*. Oxford: Oxford University Press.

Ma, J. 2008. "Chaironeia 338: Topographies of Commemoration." *Journal of Hellenic Studies* 128: 72–127.

MacDowell, D. M., ed. and trans. 1982/1993. *Gorgias. Encomium of Helen*. Bristol: Bristol Classical Press.

McCaskie, T. C. 2012 "'As on a Darkling Plain': Practitioners, Publics, Propagandists, and Ancient Historiography." *Comparative Studies in Society and History* 54: 145–73.

Meineck, P. 2009 "'These Are the Men Whose Minds the Dead have Ravished': Theater of War/ The Philoctetes Project." *Arion* 17: 173–91.

Millard, C. 2011. *Destiny of the Republic. A Tale of Madness, Medicine, and the Murder of a President.* New York: Doubleday.

Morris, R. 2000. *The Better Angel. Walt Whitman in the Civil War.* Oxford: Oxford University Press.

Natterson-Horowitz, Barbara, and K. Bowers. 2013. *Zoobiquity. The Astonishing Connection between Human and Animal Health.* New York: Vintage Books.

O'Brien, T. 1990. *The Things They Carried.* New York: Penguin Books.

Owen, W. 1973. *War Poems and Others.* Edited with Introduction and Notes by D. Hibberd. London: Chatto and Windus.

Palaima, T. 2013. "Epilogue. The Legacy of War in the Classical World." In *The Oxford Handbook of Warfare in the Classical World*, edited by B. Campbell and L. A. Tritle, 726–36. New York: Oxford University Press.

Poznik, G. D., et al. 2013. "Sequencing Y Chromosomes Resolves Discrepancy in Time to Common Ancestor of Males Versus Females." *Science* 341: 562–5.

Remarque, E. M. 1959/1971/1984. *Im Westen Nichts Neues.* Cologne: Kiepenheuer and Witsch.

Rossiter, S. 1981. *Blue Guide: Greece.* 4th ed. London: Ernest Benn.

Sapolsky, R. M. 1996. "Why Stress is Bad for Your Brain." *Science* 273: 749–50.

Sapolsky, R. M., H. Uno, C. S. Rebert, and C. E. Finch. 1990. "Hippocamphal Damage Associated with Prolonged Glucocorticoid Exposure in Primates." *Journal of Neuroscience* 10: 2897–902.

Shay, J. 1994. *Achilles in Vietnam. Combat Trauma and the Undoing of Character.* New York: Atheneum.

———. 2004. *Odysseus in America. Combat Trauma and the Trials of Homecoming.* New York: Scribner.

Shephard, B. 2000. *A War of Nerves. Soldiers and Psychiatrists 1914–1994.* London: Jonathan Cape.

Solomon, Z. 1993. *Combat Stress Reaction.* New York: Plenum Press.

Sophocles. 1947/1974. *The Theban Plays.* Translated with Introduction by E. F. Watling. New York: Penguin Books.

Sommerstein, A. H. 1996. *Aeschylean Tragedy.* Bari: Levante Editori.

Stevens, A. 2004. *The Roots of War and Terror.* London: Continuum.

Tritle, L. A. 2000. *From Melos to My Lai. War and Survival.* London: Routledge.

———. 2004. "Xenophon's Portrait of Clearchus: A Study in Post-Traumatic Stress Disorder." In *Xenophon and His World*, edited by C. J. Tuplin, 325–39. Stuttgart: *Historia Einzelschriften* 172, 2004.

———. 2009. "Gorgias, the *Encomium of Helen* and the Trauma of War." *Clio's Psyche* 16: 195–9.

———. 2010. *A New History of the Peloponnesian War.* Oxford: Wiley-Blackwell.

Weinstein, E. A. 1994–1995. "Conversion Disorders." In *Textbook of Military Medicine*, 4 Pts., edited by R. Zajtchuk, I, 4: 383–407. Falls Church, VA: TMM Publications Office of the Surgeon General.

Wheeler, E. 2011. "Greece: Mad Hatters and March Hares." In *Recent Directions in the Military History of the Ancient World*, edited by L. L. Brice and J. T. Roberts, 53–104. Publications of the Association of Ancient Historians, 10. Claremont: Regina Books.

Wilson, E. O. 1978/2004. *On Human Nature.* Cambridge, MA: Harvard University Press.

Winter, J., and A. Prost. 2005. *The Great War in History. Debates and Controversies, 1914 to the Present.* Cambridge: Cambridge University Press.

Wycherley, R. E. 1978. *The Stones of Athens.* Princeton, NJ: Princeton University Press.

Young, A. 1995. *The Harmony of Illusions.* Princeton, NJ: Princeton University Press.

CHAPTER FIVE

Beyond the Universal Soldier: Combat Trauma in Classical Antiquity

Jason Crowley

1.1 Introduction

Like an epistemological echo of Donovan's famous song *The Universal Soldier*, the belief that the combatant's susceptibility to posttraumatic stress disorder/combat stress injury[1] is diachronically universal is slowly gaining ground.[2] Gabriel, for instance, argues that the experience of close-quarters battle would leave ancient armies burdened with thousands of psychological causalities.[3] Shay offers an influential reading of the *Iliad* and the *Odyssey* as tales of both Achilles' and Odysseus' adverse psychological reactions to intense combat.[4] Tritle argues, similarly, that Epizelus, the uninjured Athenian hoplite who, according to Herodotus, went blind during the battle of Marathon, was suffering from conversion disorder;[5] that Aristodemus's voluntary death during the battle of Plataea was motivated by survivor guilt;[6] that Xenophon's portrait of the Spartan commander Clearchus is the description of a man suffering from Post Traumatic Stress Disorder (PTSD);[7] and that the unnamed individuals described by Gorgias who were terrified by the sight of warriors armed for combat, as well as those driven mad by the frightful things they had seen, were traumatized by their experiences of war.[8] Naturally, such retrospective diagnoses are not restricted to ancient Greece. The concept of PTSD/CSI (CSI, Combat Stress Injury) has been applied to individuals in seventeenth-century China,[9] Pepys's diary,[10] Shakespeare,[11] and even the Bible.[12]

Typically, such retrospective diagnoses rest on an implicit belief in historically transcendental human equivalence, that is to say, that since modern humans are the equivalent of ancient humans, they are not only both equally susceptible to PTSD, but the presence or absence thereof can be detected by the same diagnostic criteria, currently embodied in *DSM-V*.[13] This view has already been accepted by many leading theorists and clinicians,[14] and given the ongoing exponential increase in publications about PTSD/CSI, it seems likely that such studies will continue to proliferate until the universalist premise that underpins them becomes dogma.[15] Yet, while this premise, that susceptibility to PTSD/CSI is diachronically universal, to put the matter in Popperian terms, cannot be verified by the parade of white swans it has generated, it can be refuted by the production of one single black swan, and it is the aim of this chapter to provide just such a creature.[16]

1.2   Methodology

The methodology usually adopted by the universalists is characterized by the search for supporting sources that appear to describe conduct that could conceivably fit the current diagnostic criteria for PTSD/CSI, which, once identified, are deployed in support of a retrospective diagnosis thereof.[17] This methodology is admirably direct, yet it inevitably produces subjective and unfalsifiable readings of isolated pieces of ancient evidence,[18] and more importantly, it fails to recognize that PTSD/CSI results from the interaction of two variables, namely the human being and his or her environment.[19] This fact is critical, of course, because neither variable is historically transcendental: the attitudes and core beliefs adopted by combatants change, as does the sociomilitary environment in which they fight. This naturally allows for the possibility that although the modern combatant and his sociomilitary environment combine to produce a susceptibility to PTSD/CSI, a very different historically specific combination could just as easily reduce, suppress, or even eliminate that susceptibility.

To investigate this possibility, this chapter contrasts two combatants and their respective environments. Since the current diagnostic criteria for PTSD/CSI directly derive from the experiences of US Vietnam veterans, the first of these combatants has to be the modern, specifically the twentieth-century, American infantryman.[20] Similarly, since the American infantryman's adverse psychological reactions to combat have been retrospectively applied to ancient Greece, the second combatant will be the Athenian hoplite,[21] since he is one of the few warriors from classical antiquity for which a reasonable degree of narrative evidence survives. To maximize the force of the comparison and to avoid the charge that a modern apple is being compared to an ancient orange, these combatants have been chosen because they perform exactly the same tactical role, that is to say it is their grim task to close with and kill the enemy.

To ensure methodological clarity, the analytical distinction between the individual and his environment will be maintained throughout. Accordingly, examination of both the modern and ancient paradigms will focus on the combatant's core norms and values, since they determine what is or is not traumatic, as well as the three most pertinent aspects of the combatant's environment, namely the social environment, the tactical environment, and lastly the technological environment. Thereafter, the susceptibility of both paradigms to PTSD/CSI will be assessed and then compared. Finally, this chapter concludes by considering the implications of this comparison for the continued viability of the universalist position.

2.1   The American Infantryman and His Environment

Obviously it is important to acknowledge that significant points of continuity exist between the two historical case studies examined in this chapter. Like the American infantryman, the Athenian hoplite found the experience of combat intensely frightening,[22] and like his modern counterpart, he too suffered from exposure to the elements and all the other physical hardships associated with active service.[23] Nevertheless, the American infantryman carried into combat a highly specific set of norms and values shaped, regardless of personal belief, by the pervasive influence of the Judeo–Christian tradition.[24] Although once a fighting religion, by the outbreak of World War II, Christianity's former belligerence had been replaced by a nonviolent ideal stressing personal moral conduct,[25] mercy, love, and respect for human life,[26] with such principles most forcefully expressed in the duty to "turn the other cheek" and to "love thy neighbor" as well as, of course, by the commandment popularly translated as "Thou shalt not kill."[27]

Like the norms and values he adopted, the American infantryman's social environment was just as distinctive. In the US Army and Marine Corps, men served in military units comprised of complete strangers drawn from diverse geographical locations and socioeconomic circumstances.[28] Naturally, in such an environment, cohesion required time to develop. However, in American combat units, which, during the period under discussion, demonstrated a particular propensity for both poor performance in combat and PTSD/CSI, the process of interpersonal affiliation was retarded by the operation of three mutually reinforcing policies.[29]

The first of these policies was individual replacement, consequent to which, for instance, units that sustained casualties during World War II were not withdrawn from the line and reinforced, as was usually the case with the armies of Britain and Germany,[30] but kept up to strength by the allocation of individual replacements drawn from a replacement depot.[31] The second was individual rotation, which found its most famous manifestation during the Vietnam War. This policy operated on the principle that a soldier's ability to endure combat was finite,[32] and consequently, during the Vietnam War, soldiers were limited to a 12-month tour of duty,[33] with officers serving only six in order to facilitate the proliferation of command experience.[34] The third policy, aimed at increasing operational efficiency, assigned each ostensibly interchangeable and transposable combatant an MOS, a military occupational speciality, by which the military matched man to task,[35] consequent to which individuals were assigned and reassigned whenever and wherever units required their services.[36]

Whatever their current combat assignment, these individuals operated in a tactical environment determined by modern weapons systems, particularly the rifle, machine gun, and the artillery piece, which together produce what military theorists call the dispersed battlefield.[37] This deadly arena, traversed by red–hot, razor–sharp shrapnel and high–velocity gunfire, forced the soldier to seek safety in cover and concealment and, most importantly, to reduce the lethal effects of explosive and automatic weapons by remaining at all times physically distant from his comrades.[38]

Of course, modern weapons not only combine to produce a highly distinctive tactical environment, they, together with supporting military assets and equipment, also combine to produce a highly distinctive technological environment. Therein, the American infantryman faced a range of threats, not only from other similarly armed and equipped infantrymen, but also from armor, close–air support, and indirect fire weapons such as mortars and artillery pieces, not to mention tactical obstacles like landmines and improvised explosive devices.[39] In doing so, he was supported by sophisticated logistical systems and technological aids. His personal load-carrying equipment allowed for the efficient carriage of considerable amounts of his three basic staples—food, water, and ammunition—and when his supplies were expended, he could be resupplied in the field, usually, in the final quarter of the twentieth century, by helicopter. Consequently, the American infantryman could maintain contact with the enemy for extended periods, and since, from the Vietnam period onwards, he was typically equipped with tactical night–vision aids, he could also do so around the clock.[40]

2.2   The American Infantryman's Susceptibility to PTSD/CSI

It seems obvious therefore, that the twentieth–century American infantryman entered combat with a historically specific set of norms and values, and also operated in a historically specific social, tactical, and technological environment. What is not obvious, however, is that his prebattle socialization and every aspect of his environment combined to enhance his susceptibility to PTSD/CSI.

To start with, the American infantryman's received societal norms and values, stressing peace, mercy, and the sanctity of human life, were so stunningly incongruent with his tactical role, to close with and kill his enemy, that, as Marshall observed, during World War II such beliefs constituted a "handicap"[41] that inhibited the infantryman's ability to fight and to kill.[42] Naturally, this inhibition was militarily undesirable, and during the period under consideration the US military employed four main techniques aimed at overcoming it. First, it endeavored to resocialize its recruits, that is to say, to engineer the elimination of incongruous norms and values and their replacement with those designed to facilitate combat.[43] Secondly, it attempted to desensitize the soldier,[44] for instance, through the deification of killing, manifested by the worship of the "spirit of the bayonet"[45] and the chanting of mantras such as "kill, kill, kill."[46] Thirdly, it supported its soldiers' inclination to deny their lethal activities, by encouraging them to see combat as nothing more than a series of drills identical to those carried out during training.[47] Fourthly, as Grossman observes, after particularly poor performance during World War II, it sought to bypass any resistance to killing by embedding Pavlovian/Skinnerian conditioning techniques into skill-at-arms training, which henceforth presented the soldier with a stimulus in the form of a pop-up, man-shaped target, for which the conditioned response was swift and accurate engagement, positively reinforced through the fall of the target, as the enemy "died," and thereafter through progression in rank and associated privilege.[48]

Such techniques, during combat, when extreme stress often impairs high-level cognition, enhanced the American infantryman's ability to overcome his inhibition and kill, but they did so only at considerable psychological cost.[49] By killing, the American infantryman committed an irreversible act that transgressed his core values, and as psychologists recognize, such psychologically damaging transgressions are often closely associated with subsequent diagnoses of PTSD/CSI.[50]

The successful performance of his battlefield role was therefore psychologically toxic to the American infantryman, as, of course, was the social environment in which he was compelled to discharge it. As Schachter's experiments have demonstrated, when human beings perceive danger, they experience feelings of anxiety that stimulate the desire to affiliate with other human beings.[51] This interpersonal affiliation then reduces anxiety, and in sociomilitary contexts it enhances morale, endurance, psychological resilience, and small-unit cohesion, thereby enabling the soldier to withstand challenges which would break an unaffiliated combatant.[52]

For the combatant, then, affiliation offers profound protection against psychological breakdown. Given time and social stability, the vast majority of modern Western soldiers affiliate easily with their peers,[53] yet the operation of individual replacement, individual rotation, and the constant reassignments resulting from the MOS system effectively denied the American infantryman the same quality of opportunity.[54] Instead, he operated in a social environment characterized by chronic personnel turbulence, which revealed its deleterious effects most graphically during the war from which, tellingly, the very concept of PTSD is derived: Vietnam.[55] There, the operation of individual rotation and individual replacement resulted in a never-ending sequence of inexperienced officers to lead an ever-changing collection of troops whose incessant rotation and replacement inhibited affiliation precisely where it was needed most: in combat.[56] Naturally, such a social environment was perfect for the proliferation of PTSD/CSI, and unfortunately for the American soldier, this profound propensity was further exacerbated by his tactical environment.

In combat, the affiliative desire generated by intense fear produces an irresistible longing for the psychological support offered by the close physical proximity of other human beings,[57] the most visible expression of which is the irrational tendency of modern troops to "bunch" under fire.[58] Since this increases the lethal effects of both explosive and automatic weapons, modern infantry tactics require troops to maintain their personal intervals, and when under effective enemy fire to seek cover and concealment.[59] This offers effective protection against enemy weapons, yet, as each soldier goes to ground, his unit, no matter how cohesive, is transformed into a collection of mutually isolated individuals who engage their enemy alone, not only denied the comfort offered by the close physical proximity of their peers but actually segregated from them, and therefore bereft of the benefits offered by their protective presence. This tactical environment, then, virtually ensured that the American infantryman was psychologically most vulnerable precisely at the point of severest psychological stress.[60]

Worse still, this psychological vulnerability was further enhanced by the technological environment in which the American infantryman operated. This presented him with a range of threats, to which, as Lazarus demonstrated, he could respond in two very different ways, either by taking direct action to remove or escape the threat, or, if this was not possible, by taking palliative action to reduce its stressful effects through denial, drugs, alcohol, or humor.[61] Obviously, the type of response adopted by the infantryman is largely determined by two variables, namely the kind of threat facing him and his personal capacity to counter it. Thus, for instance, the infantryman can employ direct action against enemy troops, that is to say, by killing, suppressing, or breaking contact with them, but he is forced to rely on palliative action when under artillery bombardment, since his personal weapon cannot be employed against a target ten or more kilometers distant from his own position.[62]

This distinction is, of course, important because direct action removes the threat, and in consequence it is psychologically benign. In contrast, palliative action leaves the combatant in contact with the noxious agent, and as a result it is psychologically malignant.[63] This explains why, during World War II, as Stouffer and his colleagues discovered, American soldiers found the lethal threat presented by enemy crew-served weapons, such as MG34s and 42s, reasonably manageable, because they could respond with direct action, but they were intensely fearful of enemy artillery and air support, precisely because the only real response they had to this kind of threat was palliation.[64] Naturally, this enhanced the American soldier's psychological vulnerability, because, against the most lethal threats he faced, the only response available to him was psychologically toxic.

This vulnerability was further aggravated by extended exposure to combat. Typically well-trained and well-equipped, and supported by a sophisticated logistical apparatus, the American soldier was able and often expected to maintain contact with the enemy for many months at a time.[65] In addition, his ability to conduct operations during the hours of darkness ensured that the progressive exhaustion he experienced consequent to the physical and mental demands of extended campaigning was further compounded by sleep deprivation, which, as psychologists recognize, is a toxic combination that lowers the soldier's mental resilience and intensifies his vulnerability to psychological breakdown.[66]

The American soldier therefore demonstrated a profound propensity for PTSD/CSI as a result of a convergence of historically specific factors. Firstly, the societal norms and values he took to the battlefield ensured that the successful performance of his battlefield role was psychologically toxic. Secondly, his social environment reduced or even denied him the psychological benefits of protective affiliation. Thirdly, his tactical environment robbed him of the comfort he would otherwise have derived from the physical proximity of his peers and forced him to face his enemy alone, isolated and psychologically exposed. Fourthly, his technological environment presented him with threats that frequently required psychologically harmful responses, and the logistical and technological support he received during operations often compelled him to face those threats in an exhausted, sleep-deprived, and psychologically vulnerable condition. How then does this situation compare to that faced by the Athenian hoplite?

3.1   The Athenian Hoplite and His Environment

Like the American soldier, the Athenian hoplite carried into battle a highly distinctive set of norms and values. However, unlike those influenced by the Judeo-Christian tradition, these were profoundly pugnacious. The explanation for this, of course, lies in the peculiar geopolitical structure of classical Greece, where a thin veneer of cultural unity overlay an aggressive agglomeration of small, fiercely independent, and mutually antagonistic poleis.[67] In this singular environment, war, which the Greeks accepted as a legitimate tool of interstate relations,[68] proliferated unconstrained by enforceable international laws[69] or effective methods of conflict resolution.[70] Consequently, since the sovereignty and survival of his polis was secured by the warrior, the Greeks held nonmartial aspects of manhood secondary to battlefield bravery,[71] which they considered an unqualified social good that both defined a man and determined his social worth.[72]

Naturally, as Athenian society was profoundly performative,[73] a warrior had to demonstrate, rather than merely declare, his bravery,[74] either by dying on the battlefield[75] or by performing creditably in combat and earning the acclaim of those who witnessed his creditable conduct.[76] Accordingly, for the Athenians war was more than a means of defending or advancing the interests of Athens; it was a rite of passage marking the boundary between adolescence and manhood.[77]

Of course, although armed conflict was embedded in the Athenian *kosmos*, the Athenians were not blind to the allure of peace: they enjoyed both its benefits and its tranquillity, and they recognized that since war entailed destruction, loss, and sorrow, it should be avoided where possible. Nevertheless, despite this recognition, it is striking that expressions of humanistic sentiment are not only relatively infrequent in Athenian discourse, but most were generated by the Peloponnesian War, and those that were not are completely overshadowed by the dominant orthodoxy which fully acknowledged the human cost of war but wholeheartedly embraced it nonetheless.[78]

Again, this is easy to explain. Athens was an interventionist imperial powerhouse that ruthlessly deployed the institution of war to compete for dominance in one of the harshest geopolitical environments in history.[79] Unsurprisingly, since it formed the foundation upon which Athenian greatness was built, the Athenians venerated war,[80] and not just as an abstract concept, but also as a tangible human experience reduced to its three most basic components: fighting, killing, and dying, a triumvirate which together forms the most brutal distillation of war: combat.

For the Athenians, the ability to fight in close combat was the highest and most glorious expression of the masculine ideal.[81] Similarly, the desired end result of that engagement, the death of the opponent, was also something eagerly embraced. Such hardheartedness stems, in no small part, from a principle central to Athenian culture, namely that of helping friends and harming enemies, a doctrine not only deeply internalized by Athenian men, but also one they felt obliged to obey.[82] This exerted such normative force that Athenian men felt compelled to respond violently to their enemies, even if they were fellow citizens, with whom they were ideally expected to collaborate.[83] Naturally, external enemies invited not collaboration but elimination, and so on the battlefield lethal violence was not only morally unambiguous, but also utterly unconstrained.[84]

The Athenians, however, did not only kill their enemies, they were also killed by them, and so many men would have witnessed the deaths of their comrades at close hand on more than one occasion.[85] Yet while such losses were lamented,[86] the Athenians nevertheless chose to construe death in combat not as a premature end, but as a timely culmination.[87] Accordingly, at Athens, the war dead enjoyed a special social significance. Having demonstrated their unimpeachable courage, they reflected undying glory on both state and surviving family,[88] and in return for their sacrifice, they escaped mortality and, as something close to heroes, they were immortalized by inscriptions and annually honored by the spectacular state funeral Athens held for her fallen.[89] Thus, for the Athenians, death, far from dimming the bright glory of combat, was instead its most glorious aspect.

These bellicose views also received religious amplification. Admittedly Ares, who personified the more sinister aspects of war, appears to have revolted the Greeks.[90] Furthermore, religious sentiments, by underpinning the respect normally accorded to temples, truces, heralds, holy days, and enemy dead, undoubtedly offered a welcome degree of amelioration.[91] Nevertheless, there is no hint of pacifism in Greek religion, and the gods with whom men communed, usually through the medium of animal sacrifice, during which, tellingly, the victim had its throat cut with an edged weapon,[92] were often warriors themselves, and as such they both approved of the institution of war[93] and accepted its utility in interstate relations.[94] As a result, for the Greek warrior the gods were a potential source of support, and if their favor could be obtained by means of offerings and promises,[95] they could be induced to work for him and against his enemies.[96]

This ensured that the Greek warrior's relationship with his gods was both profound and pitiless, as two particularly grim examples offered by Xenophon demonstrate. In the first, he recounts how the Athenians promised to sacrifice a goat to Artemis for every Persian they killed at Marathon. The goddess, however, was so generous that the slaughter of Persians outstripped the supply of animals, and although the Athenians subsequently sacrificed by annual instalments of 500 goats, their blood debt was so great that, according to Xenophon, it was still being paid nearly a hundred years after it had been incurred.[97] In the second, even more dreadful example, Xenophon describes an awful Spartan massacre of corralled and utterly helpless enemies, which, in his view, was not only something that a Greek warrior might legitimately pray for, its successful execution, signified in this instance by "heaps of corpses," could actually be considered a "gift of heaven."[98]

Although shocking to a modern reader, Xenophon's ruthless religious Weltanschuung is entirely understandable. His formative years had been spent in the shadow of his city's patron, Athena, the warrior goddess par excellence. Her citizens paraded their military power in her honor during her festival, the Panathenaea.[99] They depicted her in Athenian art as the personification of Athenian martial virtue,[100] standing both with and for the Athenian hoplite, not only fighting at his side, but also celebrating his victories and grieving for his losses.[101] Most revealingly, they portrayed her, in the warrior-departure scenes often found on Attic pots, displacing the hoplite's wife or mother in order to assist him while he armed himself for battle against those hostile to her polis.[102]

Certainly then, the norms and values the Athenian hoplite carried with him into battle were strikingly different from those of the American infantryman, and so too was the social environment in which he fought. As a convergence of evidence demonstrates, the Athenian hoplite mobilized, deployed, and fought alongside his fellow demesmen.[103] This is significant because the deme, the smallest subdivision of the Athenian body politic, was also by far the most socially cohesive.[104] Most were small, rather internally focused face-to-face communities whose members were religiously, economically, politically, and socially integrated.[105] As a consequence, affiliation among demesmen was so profound and normative[106] that any damage to this affiliative relationship was, for the unfortunate demesmen concerned, not merely transgressive, it was actually shameful.[107]

The tactical environment in which these men fought was also very different. The Athenian hoplite was a heavy infantryman who sacrificed speed and agility in order to maximize his capacity for close-quarters combat. To protect himself from enemy troops, such as cavalry and light infantry, whose capacity for tactical mobility surpassed his own, he fought in a phalanx, a close-order formation predicated on mutual protection and tactical interdependency.[108] Insofar as its table of organization can be reconstructed, the Athenian phalanx seems to have been subdivided by ten medium-sized subunits, called *taxeis*, with each *taxis* in turn subdivided by an unknown number of smaller units called *lochoi*.[109] As the evidence suggests, demesmen were assigned to the same *lochos*, and deployed in tactically distinct files of men, usually eight deep, laterally arranged to produce eight serried ranks. Consequently, when the Athenian hoplite met his enemy, he did so surrounded by, and in close order with, his comrades.[110]

The technological environment in which the Athenian hoplite fought was largely determined by muscle-powered weapons and was also highly distinctive.[111] As he discharged his main tactical duty, to close with and kill enemy hoplites, the principal threat the Athenian hoplite faced was from the stabbing spears and slashing swords of similarly armed and equipped opponents.[112] Moreover, since he was normally protected by friendly cavalry and light infantry during deployment, the advance to contact, and while in contact with the enemy, if he was victorious, the weapons wielded by enemy hoplites were the only threat he would face on the battlefield.[113] However, if he was ineffectively screened by supporting arms, or if that protective screen was dispersed, or his own phalanx atomized by defeat, he might find himself exposed to the javelins thrown by enemy cavalry and light infantry, as well as the sling stones and arrows of enemy slingers and archers.[114]

In comparison to the modern infantryman, then, the range of threats faced by the Athenian hoplite was relatively restricted, and so too was the logistical and technological support he received. Typically, he mobilized with only a few days' worth of self-supplied rations,[115] and after they were consumed, he was forced to live by purchasing food from nearby markets when in neutral or friendly territory, and by plunder when in that of the enemy.[116] Accordingly, since he could live by plunder only when enemy crops were ripe, extended operations in enemy territory, such as those conducted by the Athenians on Sicily, were difficult to sustain. In addition, without the technological aids required for the amplification of ambient light, night operations, like the disastrous Athenian attack on Epipolae, were extremely risky, and therefore also comparatively rare.[117]

3.2 The Athenian Hoplite's Susceptibility to PTSD/CSI

It therefore seems obvious that the Athenian hoplite entered combat with a historically specific set of norms and values, and that he operated in a historically specific social, tactical, and technological environment. What is not obvious, however, is that his prebattle socialization and every aspect of his environment combined to produce a historically specific resistance to PTSD/CSI.

Clearly, the religiously amplified and militarized norms and values internalized by the Athenian hoplite were stunningly congruent with his tactical role, which was to close with and kill his enemy. Consequently, he did not require resocialization prior to active service since he was, from childhood, continually conditioned for combat.[118] Thus, instead of regretting the killing of his enemies, the Athenian hoplite gloried in their deaths. Xenophon, for instance, describes how, at the point when an enemy formation breaks and close-quarters combat gives way to the slaughter of fleeing and panic-stricken men, the emotion typically experienced by pursuing hoplites was unbridled joy. Furthermore, he adds, the pride men take in their own personal tally of kills tempts so many to exaggerate that their boastful claims exceed the actual body count.[119] The same feelings are also unambiguously expressed in a famous epitaph to Pythion of Megara. This claims Pythion was a good man because of his capacity to help his friends and harm his enemies, which he apparently demonstrated by helping to save three Athenian *taxeis*, which had been cut off near his homeland, probably in 446 BC, and by personally killing seven men in close-quarters combat. As Dover perceptively observes, the fact that, according to the inscription, Pythion then entered the underworld "having brought sorrow to no one among all the men who dwell on the earth"[120] demonstrates that the sorrow of enemies was not merely inconsequential, it was actually beyond reflective consideration.[121]

The successful performance of his battlefield role was therefore not psychologically toxic to the Athenian hoplite; nor was he forced to perform it without the full support from his social environment. On the contrary, he mobilized, deployed, and fought together with his fellow demesmen, and so, unlike the American infantryman, whose military service entailed the ongoing disruption of his social environment, the Athenian hoplite met his enemy surrounded by the men of own cohesive community whose protective affiliation both shielded him from the corrosive effects of apprehension and enhanced his psychological resilience.[122]

This psychological resilience was further reinforced by the Athenian hoplite's tactical environment, which virtually ensured the close physical proximity that combatants crave. Unlike the American infantryman, who sought safety in dispersion and often met his enemy isolated from his peers, the Athenian hoplite sought salvation in close order, and consequently, when he met his enemy, he was able to do so while deriving the maximum comfort from the close physical proximity of his surrounding comrades.[123]

Finally, the Athenian hoplite's psychological resilience was further enhanced by the technological environment in which he operated. Two aspects of this environment are especially notable. The first is that during conventional operations, the main threats he faced, that is, those presented by other warriors armed with muscled-powered weapons, could be countered by the most psychologically benign Lazarus response, namely direct action. Specifically, during main-force encounters, the Athenian hoplite could eliminate the threat he faced from enemy hoplites by closing with and killing them or, if overmatched, he could break contact under the cover of friendly cavalry and light infantry.[124] Indeed, even during a tactical worst-case scenario, in which his own phalanx was atomized and relentlessly pursued by more tactically mobile troops, the only option available to the hoplite, uncontrolled flight, usually facilitated by the abandonment of the shield, was itself a form of direct action.[125]

The second notable aspect of the technological environment is the limited duration in which the Athenian hoplite had to cope with the stresses and strains of the ancient battlefield. Main-force encounters were mercifully brief, and in the absence of sophisticated logistical support, the Athenian hoplite was not typically expected to conduct extended operations; nor was he, without the ability to amplify ambient light, usually required to fight during the hours of darkness.[126] Admittedly, because the Greeks generally lacked the technology for breach and the will to storm, siege operations, normally conducted by circumvallation, did entail continuous contact with the enemy, and in consequence such operations undoubtedly required a psychologically toxic Lazarus response, namely palliation.[127] Nevertheless, during conventional operations the Athenian hoplite was largely protected against progressive exhaustion and sleep deprivation, and all the subsequent psychological vulnerabilities entailed thereby.[128]

The Athenian hoplite was therefore profoundly protected against PTSD/CSI as a result of a convergence of historically specific factors. First, the martial norms and values he took to the battlefield ensured that the successful performance of his battlefield role was not psychologically harmful. Secondly, his social environment allowed him to receive all the benefits that protective affiliation could provide. Thirdly, his tactical environment almost guaranteed him all the comfort he could derive from the physical proximity of his peers. Fourthly, his technological environment enabled him to confront the threats he faced during conventional operations with the most psychologically benign response, and to face those threats with his psychological resilience largely unaffected by the insidious effects of exhaustion or sleep deprivation.

4.1   Conclusion

The American infantryman and the Athenian hoplite both performed the same tactical role, and this sometimes tempts even the most impressive modern scholars to read evidence in way that equates their experiences. Nevertheless, despite the apparent similarity of these combatants, it is clear that the norms and values they carried into combat, and the social, tactical, and technological environments in which they fought, were both historically specific and radically divergent. Furthermore, it would appear that these historically specific and radically divergent circumstances left the American infantryman critically vulnerable to PTSD/CSI while the Athenian hoplite was effectively immunized against the same risk. In Popperian terms, then, the Athenian hoplite is a black swan. Consequently, no matter how many white swans are marshalled in support of the universalist position, it seems that Donovan and his academic admirers are mistaken: the soldier is not, and indeed, can never be, universal.

Notes

1. This terminology, of course, reflects not only the value judgments attracted by this contentious subject, but also the breadth of human experience it covers (see, for instance, Shay's foreword to Figley and Nash (2007); also Nash (2007a, 33–63)). For the sake of analytical clarity, and to avoid the confusion entailed by the adoption of often indistinct and overlapping typologies (such as combat-related PTSD, combat shock, battle fatigue, perpetration induced PTSD, etc), this chapter uses both terms as shorthand for the full range of adverse psychological reactions to combat.
2. See Shephard (2001, 385–99) and especially Summerfield (1999, 1449–62), which both challenge the presumption that PTSD is universal and context independent, and the Western psychological neo-colonialism that underpins it. For further discussion specific to the ancient world, see Melchior (2011, 209–33).
3. Gabriel (2007, 12–15).
4. See Shay (1995, 2002), respectively.
5. Herodotus 6.117.2–3 with Tritle (2000, 64).
6. Herodotus 9.71.1–4; cf. 1.82.1–8; 7.231.1–232.1, 9.71.1–4; Pausanias 2.38.5; Thucydides 5.41.2, with Tritle (2000, 74–7).
7. Xenophon *Anabasis* 2.6.1–16, with Tritle (2000, 55–78). Consider also Tritle (1997, 123–36).
8. Gorgias *Helen* 15–17, with Tritle (2009, 195–9). Additional discussion of this intriguing text can also be found in Tritle (2010, 158–60), as well as Tritle's contribution to this volume and that offered by Raaflaub.
9. Struve (2004, 14–31).
10. Daly (1983, 64–8). Interestingly, although Daly acknowledges the possibility that PTSD is a historically contingent sociocultural artifact, his diagnosis of Pepys leads him to accept "the temporal constancy of post-traumatic stress disorder."
11. Trimble (1985, 5–14).
12. Haughn and Gonsiorek (2009, 833–45).

13. An acronym referring to the 5th edition of the American Psychiatric Association's *Diagnostic and Statistical Manual of Mental Disorders* (Washington, 2013). Scholarship which predates this publication naturally refers to earlier editions, namely *DSM-III* (1980) and *DSM-IV* (1994). For the evolution of the diagnostic criteria set out in both, as well as the controversial revisions now embodied in *DSM-V*, see Shephard (2001, 355–68); with Adler et al. (2008, 301–8); Gersons and Carlier (1992, 742–8); and Schnurr (2008, 1–2, 2009, 1–2, 2010, 1–2).

14. Consider, for instance, March and Greenberg (2007, 247–60); also Nash (2007a, 33–63) and Spira, Pyne, and Wiederhold (2007, 205–18).

15. Emergence of dogma: Melchior (2011, 209–23). Proliferation: Schnurr (2010, 1–2). As Schnurr observes, this increase in interest, reflected in the number of PTSD-focused publications, which grew from only 900 in 1984 to nearly 9000 in 2010, is simply phenomenal. Furthermore, as the source of these figures reveals (the United States' Department of Veterans' Affairs' Published International Literature On Traumatic Stress (PILOTS) Database, which can be found at www.ptsd.va.gov), this trend is continuing.

16. For this methodology, see Popper (1959).

17. For paradigmatic examples, see Daly (1983, 64–8) and Tritle (2000, 64, 74–7, 123–36).

18. Tritle's interpretation of Aristodemus' death (2000, 74–7) is an excellent example. His interpretation is perceptive, persuasive, and consistent with the ancient evidence, but so too is its most obvious competitor, that Aristodemus chose a glorious death in combat instead of a life degraded by the irrevocable destruction of his social status (cf. Xenophon *Constitution of the Lacedaimonians* 9.1.6, with additional discussion in Crowley (2012, 86–8, 106–7, 117–19)).

19. Aldwin (1994); Lazarus (2000, 39–64); and Szalma (2008, 323–57); also Nash (2007b, 11–31, 2007a, 33–63).

20. See above, Section 1.1, n. 13, with Moore and Reger (2007, 161–81); also Shephard (2001, 355–68). Of course, American soldiers were not fundamentally dissimilar to those troops fielded by other Western nations, nor were their responses to the experience of combat. Earlier drafts of this paper, in fact, proposed the "Western soldier" as the modern point of comparison, but the American soldier was eventually adopted for three reasons: firstly, it was his experiences that generated the current debate regarding adverse reactions to combat; secondly, the available evidence over-whelming relates to American troops; thirdly, it was hoped the focus on one specific combatant during one specific time period would help minimize, to some degree at least, the kind of analytically unhelpful generalizations unavoidably entailed by encompassing different cultures and time periods. Similar reasons explain why the Athenian hoplite was adopted as the ancient point of comparison, instead of a more general "Greek" warrior.

21. See above, Section 1.1, ns. 3–8. For the nature of hoplite combat, see especially Schwartz (2009); also Anderson (1970); Grundy (1911, 267–73); and Hanson (2000). Note, however, the competing model ably advanced by van Wees (2004, 184–97). For a summary of the debate between adherents of both positions, see Crowley (2012, 53–62).

22. A wide convergence of evidence attests not only to the experience of fear (Aristophanes *Birds* 289–90, 1470–81, *Clouds* 350–5, *Peace* 444–6, 673–8, 1172–85, 1295–1304, *Wasps* 10–30, 592, 820–5; Euripides *Bacchae* 303–4; Lysias 9.8–9, 12, 21–4, 16.17; Thucydides 4.34.7, 7.80.3; Tyrtaeus 11.22; Xenophon *Hellenica* 4.3.17), but also to the appearance of its physical manifestations (Aristophanes *Knights* 1055–6,

Peace 239–41, 1179–81; Herodotus 7.231; Homer *Iliad* 13.279–83; Plutarch *Agesilaus* 30.2–4, *Aratus* 29.5; Polyaenus *Stratagems* 3.4.8; Thucydides 6.10.8; Xenophon *Hiero* 6.3.7).

23. Aristophanes *Peace* 348; Thucydides 2.58.1–3, 7.47.1–3, 59.2–87.6; Xenophon *On Hunting* 11.2, *Constitution of the Lacedaimonians* 4.7.

24. Marshall (2000, 78); also Holmes (2003, 58, 71); McManus (1998, 154–5, 229–35, 279); and Stouffer et al. (1949b, 172–91).

25. Ehrenreich (1997, 163, 165–74); Hogg and Vaughan (2002, 460–2); and Holmes (2003, 289).

26. Bourke (1999, 224); Ehrenreich (1997, 165–6); and Keegan (1993, 48–9).

27. *Deuteronomy* 6.4–21; *Exodus* 20.1–17; *Luke* 6.31; *Mark* 12.31; and *Matthew* 7.12, with further discussion in Bourke (1999, 215–41).

28. See especially Holmes (2003, 82, 79–93). For extended discussion and an extremely valuable collection of evidence, see Stouffer et al. (1949a).

29. Gabriel and Savage (1978, x-9, 29–41, 50, 55–8) and Henderson (1985, 31–2). See also Wesbrook (1980, 274–6).

30. Shils and Janowitz (1948, 287–8) and Creveld (1982, 42–60, 74–9, 90–1); also Glenn (2000, 85–6).

31. Stouffer et al. (1949b, 242–89) and van Creveld (1982, 75–7, 90–1, 166–8).

32. See especially Wilson (1987, xvi); also Nash (2007a, 48–59) and Shephard (2001, 143–60).

33. Extended to 13 months for marines, for which see Lewy (1980, 102–3).

34. Gabriel and Savage (1978, 3–28, 70–2); Hoiberg (1980, 232–4); and Lewy (1980, 102–3). Note, however, the argument offered by Gabriel and Savage (1978, 3–28, 51–96), namely that this policy, despite its stated aim, was actually motivated by careerism.

35. Hauser (1980, 187–8, 204–5) and Hoiberg (1980, 213–14).

36. Gabriel and Savage (1978, 117–43); Henderson (1985, 18); Hauser (1980, 194–5, 204–5); Kellet (1982, 43); Sorley (1980, 73–89); and Wesbrook (1980, 266–7).

37. Bourke (1999, 92); Gray (1998, 136); and Marshall (2000, 60).

38. Consider, for instance, the British Army's Section Battle Drills, for which see Anon. (1991, 110–12), with further discussion in Bourke (1999, 77); Marshall (2000, 22, 46, 145); and van Zanten (1993, 9–10, 15). For the grim consequences of transgression, see, for example, Sajer (1991, 321–4).

39. See above, Section 2.1, n. 38.

40. Holmes (2003, 115–35); Nash (2007b, 18–22); and van Creveld (2005, 341–63); also MCRP *6–11C* (2000, 55–75). For an overview of modern infantry combat and the role of rotary-wing aircraft, see Cacutt (1992, 11–55, 122–57).

41. Marshall (2000, 67, 76–9).

42. Marshall (2000, 78) and Stouffer (1949b, 77), with further discussion in Baron and Byrne (2004, 453); Bourke (1999, 224, 247, 251, 260); Ehrenreich (1997, 10, 165–74); Hogg and Vaughan (2002, 460–1); and Nash (2007a, 48–59).

43. Bidwell (1973, 1); Glenn (2000, 1–126); Grossman (1996, xxiii–xxii, 1–4, 249–61); Bourke (1999, 69–102); Henderson (1985, 18, 49, 51, 75–6); Holmes (2003, 7–18, 36–73, 136–75, 204–69, 270–359); Kellet (1982, 67–78); Caputo (1977, 8–10); Shalit (1988, 110); and Stouffer et al. (1949a, 472–3, 1949b, 85–6). For notable examples, see Caputo (1977, 8–10, 36); O'Brien (1995, 51); and Sassoon (1966, 16–17).

44. Grossman (1996, 248–61); with Section 2.2, n. 43, also Bidwell (1973, 61–3) and Watson (1980, 181–3). For the concept of "battle inoculation" generally, see Bourke (1999, 87–8); Holmes (2003, 53–4); and Watson (1980, 141–4).

45. See, for example, O'Brien (1995, 51); cf. Sassoon (1966, 16–17), with additional discussion in Bourke (1999, 87–8, 92–3, 153–4).

46. Grossman (1996, 251–2). For instance, in an attempt to enhance their ability to kill in the jungles of South Vietnam, Caputo's hatchet-wielding and war-crying sergeant ordered his nervous recruits to chant "ambushes are murder and murder is fun." See Caputo (1977, 36).

47. Grossman (1996, 233, 256); cf. Bourke (1999, 225–35) and Holmes (2003, 366). This, of course, would also explain the widely attested calls of "endex" (military shorthand for end of exercise) by British troops when hostilities ceased on the Falklands, for which see Bramley (1991, 173); cf. Gray (1998, 136).

48. Grossman (1996, xxiii–xxii, 1–4, 177, 249–61, 313) and Watson (1980, 49–57, 89–104). For Marshall's influence on these reforms, see Bourke (1999, 69–102) and Holmes (2003, 7–18, 36–73, 136–75, 204–69, 270–359), also Glenn's introduction to Marshall (2000, 1–11), together with his own application of Marshall's theories in Glenn (2000, 1–126).

49. Grossman (1996, xviii, 233); also Grossman and Christensen (2008, 2–137); with O'Brien (1995, 50–1) and Holmes (2003, 41–2).

50. Bourke (1999, esp. 221–71); Grossman (1996, 356–64); MacNair (2002, esp. 1–29); Maguen et al. (2010, 86–90); Nash (2007a, 48–59, 2007b, 25–7); Shephard (2001, 369–76); Shay (2002, 19–34, 107–12, 231–41); and Stouffer et al. (1949b, 77, 172–91); with extended discussion in Shay (1995).

51. For these experiments, see Schatcher (1959); with Kellet (1982, 98–103, 287, 320–1); also Ehrenreich (1997, 22–95); Henderson (1985, 108, 163); Shalit (1988, 159); Stouffer et al. (1949b, 96, 99–100, 130–49); and Wilson (1987, 127).

52. du Picq (1987, 125, 136); Ehrenreich (1997, 22–95); Glenn (2000, 114); Kellet (1982, xix, 41, 45, 98–101, 277–9, 300, 320–1, 331); McManus (1998, 273–6, 278, 286–8); Shalit (1988, 115); Shils and Janowitz (1948, 284–5, 302); Stouffer et al. (1949b, 80, 100, 107, 130–49); van Creveld (1982, 91–100); Watson (1980, 91); Wesbrook (1980, 252); and Wilson (1987, xvi, 94, 174).

53. See above, Section 2.1, n. 28, with additional discussion in Kellet (1982, 42, 123, 320) and Stouffer et al. (1949b, 278–80), and for one particularly swift example, see McManus (1998, 280).

54. See above, Section 2.1, ns. 29–36.

55. See above, Section 1.1, n. 13.

56. Gabriel and Savage (1978, 3–41, 50–96); also Beaumont and Snyder (1980, 46); Glenn (2000, 84–108, 115–9); Hauser (1980, 192–4, 205); Henderson (1985, 18), Hoiberg (1980, 231–4); Lewy (1980, 102–3); and Shalit (1988, 170); cf. du Picq (1987, 122–3).

57. Cooley (2005, 23–42); du Picq (1987, 110–14, 125, 141); Kellet (1982, 320); Marshall (2000, 41, 141, 145); Trotter (1921, 140–3); and Wesbrook (1980, 251–2). See also Section 2.2, n. 51.

58. Holmes (2003, 24–5); Kellet (1982, 98, 100, 320–1); McManus (1998, 276); Stouffer et al. (1949b, 283–4); and van Zanten (1993, 9–10, 15); cf. Thucydides 5.71.1.

59. See, for instance, the British Army's No.2 Section Battle Drill, reproduced in Anon (1991, p.111); cf. Bransby (1992, 13), with Section 2.1, ns. 37–8, Section 2.2, n. 58.

60. Marshall (2000, 47, 124–7, 129), with Section 2.2, n. 52.

61. Lazarus (1966), with a good overview of this theory outlined in Buskist, Carlson, and Martin (2004, 723–4).

62. See, especially Holmes (2003, 28–30), with Section 2.1, ns. 37–8, and Section 2.2, n. 59.

63. Bourke (1999, 159, 248–9); Holmes (2003, 28–30, 139–40, 211–12, 230–2, 255, 261); Keegan (1976, 70–1); Kellet (1982, 256, 277, 300); Richardson (1978, 53); Shephard (2001, 33–51); Watson (1980, 154–6); Wilson (1987, 38). The obvious exception to this dichotomy is where direct action involves killing, in which case the psychological benefit derived from the removal of the threat is potentially tainted by the moral transgression entailed thereby (see Section 2.2, n. 50).

64. Stouffer et al. (1949b, 83, 232–41).

65. See above, Section 2.1, n. 40.

66. Grossman and Christensen (1996, 14–29, 1996, 69–73); Holmes (2003, 115–35); Nash (2007b, 18–22); MCRP *6–11C* (2000, 55–75); and Stouffer et al. (1949b, 73–7).

67. See Herodotus 8.144.2; Isocrates 4.43, 81; and Plato *Republic* 5.470c–d, with Low (2007, 33–73) and van Wees (2004, 6–18). For extended discussion, see especially Hall (1989) and Isaac (2004); cf. Gruen (2011).

68. Consider especially Plato *Laws* 1.625e–26a; with Finley (1985, 67–70); Low (2007, 108, n. 111); and van Wees (2004, 3–5, 19–33); also Dover (1974, 160–1, 310–6); Garlan (1975, 18); Momigliano (1966, 112–26); Tritle (2000, 28–9); and Zampaglione (1973, 1–18, 28–35, 60–4).

69. Bederman (2001, 154–5, 174, 177); Low (2007, 77–128); Mitchell (1997, 41, 44); Phillipson (1911b, 28, 30, 32, 43, 58); and Sheets (1994, 54–6, 62); cf. Herman (1990, 84) and Koh (1997, 2604).

70. Although arbitration clauses often appeared in Greek treaties (see, for instance, Thucydides 5.79.1; with Tod (1913, 174–5); Low (2007, 105–8); and Phillipson (1911a, 129–30, 138)), in the absence of effective means of enforcement, they rarely achieved their aim (consider, e.g., Thucydides 1.78.4, 85.2, 5.15.4; with Ager (1993, 8, 10–11); and Tod (1913, 189), also Adcock and Mosley (1975, 230–2, 239, 244); Bederman (2001, 164–5, 177); and Zampaglione (1973, 18, 28–35).

71. Adkins (1960, 73, 156–68, 231, 340); Cairns (1993, 147–77); Dover (1974, 67, 161); and Roisman (2002, 127–8).

72. For this argument in full, see Crowley (2012, 86–8); with Adkins (1960, 73, 249); Bassi (2002, 25–58); Christ (2006, 47–8, 88–142); Cohen (2002, 144–65); Dover (1974, 41, 161–7); Pritchard (1998, 44–9); Rademaker (2002, 115–25); Roisman (2002, 126–43, 2005, 1–2, 7–8, 67, 84–101, 105–6, 188–92, 205–14); Runciman (1998, 740–2); and Zampaglione (1973, 60–4).

73. Adkins (1960, 153–6); Christ (2006, 10–12, 38–9, 112–8); and Roisman (2002, 127, 2005, 95–6).

74. Xenophon *Symposium* 8.43; Lycurgus 1.104; Lysias 18.24, 30.26; and Xenophon *Hellenica* 7.1.21, 4.32.

75. Demosthenes 60.37; Lysias 2.1–2, 67–70, 79–81; Thucydides 2.42.2–3; Liddel (2007, 288); Roisman (2005, 67–71, 111, 205–14); and Yoshitake (2010, 359–77).

76. Crowley (2012, 66–9, 86–8); with Christ (2006, 12, 82–142); Adkins (1960, 198–214); Bassi (2002, 55–6); and Roisman (2002, 126–43, 2005, 109–11).

77. Crowley (2012, 86–8); also Christ (2006, 112–8); Finley (1985, 68); and Roisman (2002, 127–9, 2005, 163–85).

78. Crowley (2012, 88–92); with Karavites (1984, 162–5); Low (2007, 2, 161–73); Garlan (1975, 15–16); Momigliano (1966, 113–23); Roisman (2002, 132, 2005, 113–7); Runciman (1998, 742–3); and Zampaglione (1973, 71–106); also Section 3.1, n. 70.

79. Low (2007, 177–211); Ober (2008, 1–79); and Raaflaub (1998, 15–41); also Section 3.1, ns. 68–70.

80. As, indeed, did the Greeks generally. Consider, for instance, Aristophanes *Knights* 565–80; Herodotus 1.1.0; Isocrates 12.250–9, 15.60–1, 119–20, 306–7; Pausanias

1.15.3–4; Plato *Laches* 182c, *Laws* 8.831e, *Protagoras* 354a–b, 359e–360a, *Republic* 10.599c–d, 12.950e-51a; Thucydides 2.64–2–6, 6.41.3, 7.56.2, 59.2, 66.1, 70.6–8, 71.1, 86.2–3, 8.2.1–2; Xenophon *Anabasis* 7.6.31–33, *On the Cavalry Commander* 8.7, *Economics* 4.4, *Hellenica* 4.5.6, 5.1.17, 6.5.23, *Hiero* 2.15–16, and *Memorabilia* 4.6.13–14; with Crowley (2012, 88–92); Hölscher (1998, 153–83); Lissarrague (1989, 39–51); Pritchard (1998, 48–9); Raaflaub (2001, 307–56, 1998, 18, 39); Rademaker (2002, 115–25); Roisman (2002, 132–6, 2005, 113–7, 134–5); Runciman (1998, 731–51); and Zampaglione (1973, 71–82).

81. Aristophanes *Wasps* 1114–21; Plato *Laws* 1.641b, *Republic* 2.375a–d; and Sophocles *Antigone* 640–81; cf. Plato *Laws* 8.828d–829a and Plutarch *Pelopidas* 17.6, with further evidence and discussion in Crowley (2012, 86–8, 92–6).

82. Aeschylus *Eumenides* 465–7, 745–54, *Libation Bearers* 264–300, 1024–31; Aristophanes *Birds* 420–1; Demosthenes 18.280, 292; Euripides *Bacchae* 878–80, *Electra* 807, *Ion.* 1045–7, *Orestes* 665–70, *Medea* 807–10; Isocrates 15.99; Lysias 1.15–17, 44–5, 7.40–1, 9.20, 32.22, II.8; Plato *Meno* 71e, *Republic* 1.331e–34b, 2.375a–d; Plutarch *Aristeides* 10.8; Sophocles *Antigone* 643–4, *Oedipus Colonus* 27–272; and Xenophon *Anabasis* 1.3.6, 9.11, 7.7.46, *Cyropaedia* 1.4.25, 5.13, *Economics* 4.2–3, *Hiero* 2.2, *Memorabilia* 1.6.9, 2.1.3, 19, 6.35, 5.5.10; with Dover (1974, 180–4) and Roisman (2005, 59–63); also Low (2007, 38–43).

83. Demosthenes 54.13–14, 18–19, 34–6, 42, 21.2, 20, 28, 40, 74, 76, 120, 141; cf. Andocides 1.56 and Plato *Republic* 8.560d–e; with Fisher (1998, 68–97); Liddel (2007, 155); and Roisman (2002, 136–41, 2005, 71–9, 170–3); cf. Herman (1990, esp. 410–14).

84. See above, Section 3.1, n. 82.

85. For instance, in Aetolia in 426 BC (Thucydides 3.94.1–98.5), Delion in 424 BC (Thucydides 4.89.1–101.2), and of course, on Sicily, in 413 BC (Thucydides 7.83.1–85.4). Given that the Military Participation Ratio (for which see Andreski 1968) was so high at Athens, such experiences would have been particularly widespread.

86. Demosthenes 60.37; Lysias 2.71; and Thucydides 2.34.4, 44.1–46.2.

87. Aeschines 3.154; Demosthenes 18.205, 50.63; Isocrates 8.39; Lysias 2.79, 21.24, 27, 31.5–7; Plato *Laws* 9.874e–875c; and Thucydides. 2.41.5–42.4. For this idea generally, see Aristotle *Nicomachean Ethics* 1116b; Demosthenes 60.37; Euripides *Trojan Women* 400–2; Isaeus 6.9; Lycurgus 1.47–8; Lysias 2.79–81, 18.26); Tyrtaeus 12.21–26; Xenophon *Anabasis* 6.3.17–19, *Hellenica* 1.6.32, 2.4.17, 4.4.6–7, with additional discussion in Bassi (2002, 55–6); Cairns (1993, 147–77); Karavites (1984, 162–5); Liddel (2007, 288); Lissarrague (1989, 49–51); Roisman (2002, 128–9, 2005, 67–71, 111, 205–14); and Zampaglione (1973, 64–71).

88. Herodotus 1.30.3–5; Demosthenes 60.37; Euripides *Trojan Women* 400–2; Lycurgus 1.47–8; and Thucydides 2.41.4–43.4; with Section 3.1, n. 87.

89. See especially Thucydies 2.34.1–46.2 and *IG* I³ 1162, also Lysias 2.80, with Bradeen (1964, 16–62, 1969, 145–59); Jacoby (1944, 37–66); and Loraux (1986, esp. 15–131).

90. Fisher (1992, 504–5); also Deacy (2000, 285–98); and Zampaglione (1973, 18–23).

91. Garlan (1975, 23–77); Goodman and Holladay (1986, 151–71); Krentz (2002, 23–39); and Low (2007, 96–7, 126); and Ober (1996, 53–71); cf. Thucydides 4.97.2–3 and Xenophon *Hellenica* 3.5.23–4.

92. Homer *Odyssey* 3.430–63 and Euripides *Electra* 774–843, with Burkett (1983, 1–12, 293–7).

93. Antiphon 4.1.2; Lycurgus 1.99–101; Plutarch *Nicias* 18.1; and Thucydides 3.56.2; with Burkett (1983, 35–48); Connor (1988, 18–29); and Dover (1974, 255–7).

94. Demosthenes 4.45; Onasander *Strategicus* 10.25–7; Plato *Laws* 1.631c–d, 7.803e, 7.823c–824c; Thucydides 1.123.1–2; Xenophon *Anabasis* 1.4.18, 3.1.19–23, 2.9–13, 5.2.9–11, 6.3.17–18, *Cyropaedia* 7.1.10–15, 20, *Hellenica* 3.4.18, 7.1.4–5, 8–11, with Goodman and Holladay (1986, 151); Lissarrague (1989, 39–51); Roisman (2002, 132).

95. Aristophanes *Knights* 841–59; Diodorus 15.85.1, 16.22; Herodotus 6.76.1–2, 8.64.1, 9.61.2–62.1; Isocrates 7.10; Lysias 10.27–8; Pausanias 9.13.4; Plato *Laws* 7.803c–e, *Republic* 5.469e–470a; Plutarch *Aristeides.* 9.1–2, 10.3–5, 17.6–18.3–5, 19.6, 20.4, 21.1, *Pericles* 17.1–2, *Themistocles* 8.2–3, 13.2–3, 15.2; Thucydides 1.32.2, 118.3, 6.30.1–32.2, 69.2, 7.69.2; Xenophon *Anabasis* 3.2.9–13, 4.3.17–19, 5.2.9–11, 22, 6.4.12–25, *Cyropaedia* 7.1.35, *Economics* 5.19–20, *Hellenica* 1.6.11, 3.5.7, 4.2.20, 3.21, 7.2, 7, 7.2.20–1, with Goodman and Holladay (1986, 152); Jackson (1991, 228–49); Jameson (1991, 197–227); Parker (2000, 299–314); Pritchett (1979, 296–321); and Runciman (1998, 738–40).

96. Demosthenes 18.324 and Thucydides 1.118.3, also Herodotus 8.64.1–2; Thucydides 1.86.5, 123.1–2; Xenophon *Anabasis* 3.2.10, 4.3.8–15, 5.2.24, *Cyropaedia.* 7.1.11, *Economics* 5.19–20, *Hellenica* 4.4.2–3, 12, 6.4.7–8, 7.2.21, 5.9–10, 13, 26, *Memorabilia* 2.1.32–3; Lissarrague (1989, 42).

97. Xenophon *Anabasis* 3.2.10–14; cf. Herodotus 6.117.1. For similar examples, see Xenophon *Anabasis* 3.2.9, 4.8.25 and Diodorus 13.102.2.

98. Xenophon *Hellenica* 4.4.12 (trans. C. Brownson); cf. § 7.1.32–2, with *Cyropaedia* 7.1.11–13; also Thucydides 1.106.1–2.

99. Connor (1987, 48–9); also Connor (1996b, 79–90); Maurizio (1998, 297–317); and Neils (1994, 151–60). For similar manifestations of militarism in the Great Dionysia, see Connor (1996a, 217–26, 1996b, 79–90) and Goldhill (1990, 97–129).

100. Consider especially Plato *Laws* 7.796b–c; also Deacy (2000, 285–98); Finley (1985, 68–70); Hölscher (1998, 153–83); Raaflaub (2001, 326, 1998, 15–41); and Zampaglione (1973, 23–6).

101. Herodotus 5.77.4 and Pausanias 1.15.3–4; with Hölscher (1998, 173–6) and Villing (1992, 32–3, esp. n. 73).

102. See especially Lissarrague (1989, 42–8); also Boardman (1989, 220); Holmberg (1990, 85–103); Matheson (1995, 269–76, 2005, 23–35); and Pemberton (1977, 62–72).

103. For the evidence itself, see especially Lysias 16.14, 20.23 and Petrakos (1984, 197–8) (which discusses a collective military dedication made by the demesmen of Rhamnous), and for admittedly later corroboration, see Isaeus. 2.42 and Theophrastus *Characters* 25.3. For the argument in full, see Crowley (2012, 46–9), with similar views expressed in Jones (1999, 58); Osborne (1985, 82); Sekunda (1992, 311–55); Whitehead (1986, 225–7); and Wyse (1904, 268).

104. Lysias 16.14, 20.13, 23, 23.2–3, 31.15 and Thucydides 2.16.1–2; with Whitehead (1986); also Andrewes (1967, 84); Jones (1999, 122, 171, 297); and Osborne (1985, 88–104).

105. See especially Whitehead (1986), with additional discussion in Crowley (2012, 43–6).

106. Aristophanes *Clouds* 210–11, 1321–4, *Ecclesiazusa* 1023–4, 1114–9, *Knights* 319–20, *Peace* 79, *Wealth* 253, 322; Aristotle *Constitution of the Athenians* 21.4, 42.1–2; Lysias 6.53, 27.12.

107. Aristophanes *Clouds* 1215–20; Isaeus fr. 4; Lysias 20.13; and Whitehead (1986, 228–31, 234, 338); cf. Demosthenes 57.63–5 and Isaeus 1.39, 2.37.

108. Aristotle *Politics* 4.1297b; Demosthenes 3.17; Euripides *Heracles* 190–4; Plutarch *Aristeides* 18.3, *Moralia* 220a; Thucydides 1.63.1–3, 3.108.1–3, 4.126.1–6, 5.66.1–4, 69.1, 71.1; Tyrtaeus 10–11; Xenophon *Hellenica* 4.2.18–19, 5.1.12, 7.5.22, *Memorabilia* 3.1.7, with Section 1.2, n. 21.

109. *Taxeis*: Aristotle *Constitution of the Athenians* 41.3; Herodotus 6.111.1; Lysias 13.79, 16.15; Plutarch *Aristeides* 5.1–5, *Cimon* 17.3–5; Thucydides 2.79.4–5, 6.98.4, 101.5, 8.92.4. *Lochoi*: Aristophanes *Acharnians* 575, 1073–4; Lysias 452–4; Aristotle *Constitution of the Athenians* 41.3; Plutarch *Aristeides* 14.2–3; Xenophon *Hellenica* 1.2.3, *Memorabilia* 3.1.5, 4.1; cf. Isocrates 15.116; Plutarch *Moralia* 186f; Thucydides 5.66.2–4; and Xenophon *Constitution of the Lacedaimonians* 11.4.

110. See above, Section 3.1, n. 103.

111. For an experimental assessment of the power generated by the hoplite's weapons, see Gabriel and Metz (1991, 51–6), with additional discussion in Jarva (1995, 139–44); Schwartz (2009, 79–95); and Snodgrass (1967, 56).

112. For the mechanics of close-quarters battle, see Hanson 1991, 63–84; Lazenby 1991, 87–109.

113. For the tactical role of cavalry and light infantry, see Adcock (1964, 14–28, 47–53); van Wees (2004, 61–71); and Wheeler (2007, 186–223); with detailed additional discussion in Best (1969) and Worley (1994).

114. See above, Section 3.1, n.113. This explains why most hoplites were killed during the pursuit, for which see Thucydides 6.69.1–3; Plato *Laches* 181a–b, 189b, *Laws* 12.961e–62a, *Symposium* 221a–c; Plutarch *Alcibiades* 7.3.

115. Aristophanes *Acharnians* 197, 1073–142, *Peace* 311–2, 1181–2, and *Wasps* 243; cf. Thucydides 1.48.1.

116. Thucydides 2.101.5, 4.6.1, 6.44.1–4, 50.1–2, 8.95.4, with Anderson (1970, 43–66); Pritchett (1971, 30–52); and van Wees (2004, 102–8).

117. See above, Section 3.1, n. 116, also Foxhall (1995, 134–45). For the operations conducted during the Sicilian Campaign, see Thucydides 6.64.1–72.5, 96.1–97.5, 100.1–3, 7.5.1–4, 6.1–4, 43.1–45.2, 75.1–86.5, and for the difficulty and danger inherent to operations at night, see especially Thucydides 7.44.2–45.2.

118. See above, Section 3.1, ns. 81–102.

119. Xenophon *Hiero* 2.15–16.

120. *IG* I³ 1353/ML 51/Fornara 101/Tod 41 (trans. K. Dover); cf. Diodorus 12.5–7; Plutarch *Pericles* 22.1–3; and Thucydides 1.114.1–115.1.

121. Dover (1974, 280–2), with additional discussion in Crowley (2012, 92–6). For further corroboration, see especially Xenophon *Anabasis* 4.1.22–26 and *Hellenica* 4.4.12, with Anderson (2005, 273–89); Fisher (1992, 510–11); and Green (1999, 97–110).

122. See above, Section 3.1, ns. 103–10; cf. Section 2.1, ns. 28–36, Section 2.2, ns. 51–6.

123. See above, Section 3.1, ns. 108–10; cf. Section 2.1, ns. 37–8, Section 2.2, ns. 57–60.

124. See above, Section 1.2, n. 21, also Section 3.1, ns. 112–13.

125. For the pursuit, see Section 3.1, n. 114, and for abandonment of the shield in the course thereof, see Aristophanes *Acharnians* 1129, *Knights* 367, 389–94, *Thesmophoriazusae* 812–24, 830–45; Lysias 10.8–9, 12, 21, 22–4, 27–30, 4–8, 10, 16.15, 21.20; Xenophon *Symposium* II.8–19.

126. See above, Section 3.1, ns. 115–17, with the comparative brevity of combat discussed in Schwartz (2009, 201–22).

127. Consider, for example, the siege of Plataea (429–427 BC) (Thucydides 2.71–78, 3.20–24, 51–68) and that of Syracuse (415–413 BC) (Thucydides 6.52–104, 7.1–85). For siege warfare generally, see Strauss (2007, 237–47) and van Wees (2004, 138–50).

128. See above, Section 3.1, ns. 115–17, Section, 3.2, n. 126.

Bibliography

Adcock, F. 1957. *The Greek and Macedonian Art of War*. London: University of California Press.

Adcock, F., and Mosley, D. 1975. *Diplomacy in Ancient Greece*. London: Thames and Hudson.

Adkins, A. 1960. *Merit and Responsibility: A Study in Greek Values*. Oxford: Clarendon Press.

Adler, A. et al. 2008. "A2 Diagnostic Criterion for Combat-Related Posttraumatic Stress Disorder." *Journal of Traumatic Stress* 21: 301–8.

Ager, S. 1993. "Why War? Some Views on International Arbitration in Ancient Greece." *Echos du monde classique/Classical Views* 12: 1–13.

Aldwin, C. 1994. *Stress, Coping, and Development: An Integrative Perspective*. New York: Guildford Press.

Anderson, J. 1970. *Military Theory and Practice in the Age of Xenophon*. Berkeley: University of California Press.

Anderson, M. 2005. "Socrates as Hoplite." *Ancient Philosophy* 25: 273–89.

Andreski, S. 1968. *Military Organization and Society*. London: Routledge and Kegan Paul.

Andrewes, A. 1967. *The Greeks*. London: Hutchinson.

Anon. 1991. *The Volunteer's Pocket Book*. Beverley: Military Pocket Books.

APA. 1980. *Diagnostic and Statistical Manual of Mental Disorders*. 3rd ed. Washington, DC: American Psychiatric Association.

———. 1994. *Diagnostic and Statistical Manual of Mental Disorders*. 4th ed. Washington, DC: American Psychiatric Association.

———. 2013. *Diagnostic and Statistical Manual of Mental Disorders*. 5th ed. Washington, DC: American Psychiatric Association.

Baron, R., and Byrne D. 2004. *Social Psychology*. New Delhi: Prentice-Hall.

Bassi, K. 2002. "The Semantics of Manliness in Ancient Greece." In *Andreia: Studies in Manliness and Courage in Classical Antiquity*, edited by R. Rosen and I. Sluiter, 25–58. Boston: Brill.

Beaumont, R., and Snyder, W. 1980. "Combat Effectiveness: Paradigms and Paradoxes." In *Combat Effectiveness: Cohesion, Stress, and the Volunteer Military*, edited by S. Sarkesian, 20–56. London: Sage Publications.

Bederman, D. 2001. *International Law in Antiquity*. Cambridge: Cambridge University Press.

Best, J. 1969. *Thracian Peltasts and Their Influence on Greek Warfare*. Groningen: Wolters-Noordhof.

Bidwell, S. 1973. *Modern Warfare: A Study of Men, Weapons and Theories*. London: Allen Lane.

Boardman, J. 1989. *Athenian Red Figure Vases: The Classical Period*. London: Thames and Hundson.

Bourke, J. 1999. *An Intimate History of Killing: Face-to-Face Killing in Twentieth Century Warfare*. London: Granta.

Bradeen, D. 1964. "Athenian Casualty Lists." *Hesperia* 33: 16–62.

———. 1969. "The Athenian Casualty Lists." *Classical Quarterly* 19: 145–59.

Bramley, V. 1991. *Excursion to Hell: The Battle for Mount Longdon*. London: Bloomsbury.

Bransby, G. 1992. *Her Majesty's Vietnam Soldier*. London: Hanley Swan.

Burkett, W. 1983. *Homo Necans: The Anthropology of Ancient Greek Sacrificial Ritual and Myth*. Berkeley: University of California Press.

Buskist, W., Carlson, N, and Martin, G. 2004. *Psychology*. London: Pearson.

Cacutt, L. 1992. *Combat*. London: David and Charles.

Cairns, D. 1993. *Aidōs: The Psychology and Ethics of Honour and Shame in Ancient Greek Literature*. Oxford: Clarendon Press.

Caputo, P. 1977. *A Rumor of War.* New York: Holt, Rinehart and Winston.

Christ, M. 2006. *The Bad Citizen in Classical Athens.* Cambridge: Cambridge University Press.

Cohen, E. 2002. "The High Cost of *Andreia* at Athens." In *Andreia: Studies in Manliness and Courage in Classical Antiquity*, edited by R. Rosen and I. Sluiter, 114–65. Boston: Brill.

Connor, W. 1987. "Tribes, Festivals and Processions: Civic Ceremonial and Political Manipulation in Archaic Greece." *Journal of Hellenic Studies* 107: 40–50.

———. 1988. "Early Greek Land Warfare as Symbolic Expression." *Past and Present* 119: 3–29.

———. 1996a. "Civil Society, Dionysiac Festival and the Athenian Democracy." In *Demokratia: A Conversation on Democracies Ancient and Modern*, edited by J. Ober and C. Hedrick, 217–26. Princeton, NJ: Princeton University Press.

———. 1996b. "Festivals and Athenian Democracy." In *Colloque International: Démocratie Athénienne et Culture*, edited by M. Sakellariou, 79–90. Athens: Académie d'Athènes.

Cooley, C. 2005. *Social Organization: A Study of the Larger Mind.* New Brunswick: Transaction.

Crowley, J. 2012. *The Psychology of the Athenian Hoplite: The Culture of Combat in Classical Athens.* Cambridge: Cambridge University Press.

Daly, R. 1983. "Samuel Pepys and Post-Traumatic Stress Disorder." *The British Journal of Psychiatry* 143: 64–8.

Deacy, S. 2000. "Athena and Ares: War, Violence and Warlike Deities." In *War and Violence in Ancient Greece*, edited by H. van Wees, 285–95. London: Duckworth.

Dover, K. 1974. *Greek Popular Morality in the Time of Plato and Aristotle.* Oxford: Blackwell.

du Picq, C. A. 1987. *Battle Studies: Ancient and Modern Battle* (=*Roots of Strategy Book 2: 3 Military Classics*). Mechanicsburg: Stackpole Books.

Ehrenreich, B. 1997. *Blood Rites: Origins and History of the Passions of War.* London: Virago.

Finley, M. 1985. "War and Empire." In *Ancient History: Evidence and Models*, edited by M. Finley, 67–87. London: Chatto and Windus.

Fisher, N. 1992. *Hybris: A Study in the Values of Honour and Shame in Ancient Greece.* Warminster: Aris and Phillips.

———. 1998. "Violence, Masculinity and the Law in Classical Athens." In *When Men Were Men: Masculinity, Power and Identity in Classical Antiquity*, edited by L. Foxhall and J. Salmon, 68–97. London: Routledge.

Foxhall, L. 1995. "Farming and Fighting in Ancient Greece." In *War and Society in the Greek World*, edited by J. Rich and G. Shipley, 134–45. London: Routledge.

Gabriel, R. 2007. *Soldiers' Lives through History: The Ancient World.* London: Greenwood Press.

Gabriel, R., and Metz, K. 1991. *From Sumer to Rome: The Military Capabilities of Ancient Armies.* Westport, CT: Greenwood Press.

Gabriel, R., and Savage, P. 1978. *Crisis in Command: Mismanagement in the Army.* New York: Hill and Wang.

Garlan, Y. 1975. *War in the Ancient World: A Social History.* London: Chatto and Windus.

Gersons, B., and Carlier, I. 1992. "Post-Traumatic Stress Disorder: The History of a Recent Concept." *The British Journal of Psychiatry* 161: 742–8.

Glenn, R. 2000. *Reading Athena's Dance Card: Men against Fire in Vietnam.* Annapolis: Naval Institute Press.

Goldhill, S. 1990. "The Great Dionysia and Civic Ideology." In *Nothing to Do with Dionysos?: Athenian Drama in its Social Context*, edited by J. Winkler and F. Zeitlin, 97–129. Princeton, NJ: Princeton University Press.

Goodman, M., and Holladay, A. 1986. "Religious Scruples in Ancient Warfare." *CQ* 36: 151–71.

Gray, J. 1988. *The Warriors: Reflections on Men in Battle.* London: Harper and Row.

Green, P. 1999. "War and Morality in Fifth-Century Athens: The Case of Euripides *Trojan Women*." *AHB* 13: 97–110.

Grossman, D. 1996. *On Killing: The Psychological Cost of Learning to Kill in War and Society.* London: Back Bay Books.

Grossman, D., and Christensen, L., 2008. *On Combat: The Psychology of Deadly Conflict in War and Peace.* New York: Warrior Science Publications.

Gruen, E. 2011. *Rethinking the Other in Antiquity.* Princeton, NJ: Princeton University Press.

Grundy, G. 1911. *Thucydides and the History of his Age.* London: J. Murray.

Hall, E. 1989. *Inventing the Barbarian: Greek Self-Definition through Tragedy*. Oxford: Clarendon Press.

Hanson, V. 1991. "Hoplite Technology in Phalanx Battle." In *Hoplites: The Classical Greek Battle Experience*, edited by V. Hanson, 63–84. London: Routledge.

———. 2000. *The Western Way of War: Infantry Battle in Classical Greece*. Berkeley: University of California Press.

Haughn C., and Gonsiorek, J. 2009. "The *Book of Job*: Implications for Construct Validity of Posttraumatic Stress Disorder Diagnostic Criteria." *Mental Health, Religion and Culture* 12: 833–45.

Hauser, W. 1980. "The Will to Fight." In *Combat Effectiveness: Cohesion, Stress, and the Volunteer Military*, edited by S. Sarkesian, 186–211. London: Sage Publications.

Henderson, W. 1985. *Cohesion: The Human Element in Combat: Leadership and Societal Influence in the Armies of the Soviet Union, the United States, North Vietnam, and Israel*. Washington, DC: National Defense University Press.

Herman, G. 1990. "Treaties and Alliances in the World of Thucydides." *Proceedings of the Classical Philological Society* 36: 83–102.

Hogg, M., and Vaughn, G. 2002. *Social Psychology*. Harlow: Pearson.

Hoiberg, A. 1980. "Military Staying Power." In *Combat Effectiveness: Cohesion, Stress, and the Volunteer Military*, edited by S. Sarkesian, 212–43. London: Sage Publications.

Holmberg, E. 1990. *The Red-line Painter and the Workshop of the Acheloos Painter*. Jonsered: Åström.

Holmes, R. 2003. *Acts of War*. London: Weidenfeld and Nicolson.

Hölscher, T. 1998. "Images and Political Identity: The Case of Athens." In *Democracy, Empire, and the Arts in Fifth-Century Athens*, edited by D. Boedeker and K. Raaflaub, 153–83. London: Harvard University Press.

Isaac, B. 2004. *The Invention of Racism in Classical Antiquity*. Oxford: Princeton University Press.

Jackson, A. 1991. "Hoplites and the Gods: The Dedication of Captured Arms and Armour." In *Hoplites: The Classical Greek Battle Experience*, edited by V. Hanson, 228–49. London: Routledge.

Jacoby, J. 1944. "*Patrios Nomos*: State Burial in Athens and the Public Cemetery in the Kerameikos." *Journal of Hellenic Studies* 64: 37–66.

Jameson, M. 1991. "Sacrifice Before Battle." In *Hoplites: The Classical Greek Battle Experience*, edited by V. Hanson, 197–227. London: Routledge.

Jarva, E. 1995. *Archaiologia on Archaic Greek Body Armour*. Rovaniemi: Societas Historica Finlandiae Septentrionalis.

Jones, N. 1999. *The Associations of Classical Athens: The Response to Democracy*. Oxford: Oxford University Press.

Karavites, P. 1984. "Greek Interstate Relations in the Fifth Century BC." *Parola del Passato* 216: 161–92.

Keegan, J. 1976. *The Face of Battle: A Study of Agincourt, Waterloo and the Somme*. London: Pimlico.

———. 1993. *A History of Warfare*. London: Pimlico.

Kellet, A. 1982. *Combat Motivation: The Behavior of Soldiers in Battle*. Boston, MA: Kluwer-Nijhoff.

Koh, H. 1997. "Why Do Nations Obey International Law?" *Yale Law Journal* 106: 2599–659.

Krentz, P. 2002. "Fighting by the Rules: The Invention of the Hoplite Agōn." *Hesperia* 71: 23–39.

Lazarus, R. 1966. *Psychological Stress and the Coping Process*. New York: McGraw-Hill.

———. 2000. "Cognitive-Motivational-Relational Theory of Emotion." In *Emotions in Sport*, edited by Y. Hanin, 39–64. Champaign, IL: Human Kinetics.

Lazenby, J. 1991. "The Killing Zone." In *Hoplites: The Classical Greek Battle Experience*, edited by V. Hanson, 87–109. London: Routledge.

Lewy, G. 1980. "The American Experience in Vietnam." In *Combat Effectiveness: Cohesion, Stress, and the Volunteer Military*, edited by S. Sarkesian, 94–106. London: Sage Publications.

Liddel, P. 2007. *Civic Obligation and Individual Liberty in Ancient Athens*. Oxford: Oxford University Press.

Lissarrague, F. 1989. "The World of the Warrior." In *A City of Images: Iconography and Society in Ancient Greece*, edited by C. Bérard et al., 39–51. Guildford, NJ: Princeton University Press.

Loraux, N. 1986. *The Invention of Athens: The Funeral Oration in the Classical City.* London: Harvard University Press.

Low, P. 2007. *Interstate Relations in Classical Greece: Morality and Power.* Cambridge: Cambridge University Press.

Maguen, S. et al. 2010. "The Impact of Reported Direct and Indirect Killing on Mental Health Symptoms in Iraq War Veterans." *Journal of Traumatic Stress* 23: 86–90.

MacNair, R. 2002. *Perpetration-Induced Traumatic Stress: The Psychological Consequences of Killing.* Westport, CT: Praeger.

March, C., and Greenberg, N. 2007. "The Royal Marines' Approach to Psychological Trauma." In *Combat Stress Injury: Theory, Research, and Management*, edited by C. Figley and W. Nash, 247–60. London: Routledge.

Marshall, S. 2000. *Men against Fire: The Problem of Battle Command.* Oklahoma: University of Oklahoma.

Matheson, S. 1995. *Polygnotos and Vase Painting in Classical Athens.* London: University of Wisconsin Press.

———. 2005. "A Farewell with Arms: Departing Warriors on Athenian Vases." In *Periklean Athens and Its Legacy: Problems and Perspectives*, edited by J. Barringer and J. Hurwit, 23–35. Austin: University of Texas Press.

Maurizio, L. 1998. "The Panathenaic Procession: Athens' Participatory Democracy on Display?" In *Democracy, Empire, and the Arts in Fifth-Century Athens*, edited by D. Boedeker and K. Raaflaub, 297–317. London: Harvard University Press.

McManus, J. 1998. *The Deadly Brotherhood: The American Combat Soldier in World War II.* Novato, CA: Presidio.

Melchior, A. 2011. "Caesar in Vietnam: Did Roman Soldiers Suffer from Post-Traumatic Stress Disorder?" *Greece and Rome* 58: 209–33.

Mitchell, L. 1997. "*Philia*, *Eunoia* and Greek Interstate Relations." *Antichthon* 31: 28–44.

Momigliano, A. 1966. "Some Observations on Causes of War in Ancient Historiography." In *Studies in Historiography*, edited by A. Momigliano, 112–26. London: Weidenfeld and Nicolson.

Moore, B., and Reger, G. 2007. "Historical and Contemporary Perspectives of Combat Stress and the Army Combat Stress Control Team." In *Combat Stress Injury: Theory, Research, and Management*, edited by C. Figley and W. Nash, 161–81. London: Routledge.

MRCP. 2000. *6–11C.* Washington: Department of the Navy.

Nash, W. 2007a. "Combat/Operational Stress Adaptations and Injuries." In *Combat Stress Injury: Theory, Research, and Management*, edited by C. Figley and W. Nash, 33–63. London: Routledge.

———. 2007b. "The Stressors of War." In *Combat Stress Injury: Theory, Research, and Management*, edited by C. Figley and W. Nash, 11–31. London: Routledge.

Neils, J. 1994. "The Panathenaia and Kleisthenic Ideology." In *The Archaeology of Athens and Attica under the Democracy*, edited by W. Coulson, O. Palagia, T. Shear, H. Shapiro, and F. Frost, 151–60. Oxford: Oxbow Books.

Ober, J. 1996. "The Rules of War in Classical Greece." In *The Athenian Revolution: Essays on Ancient Greek Democracy and Political Theory*, edited by J. Ober, 53–71. Princeton, NJ: Princeton University Press.

———. 2008. *Democracy and Knowledge: Innovation and Learning in Classical Athens.* Princeton, NJ: Princeton University Press.

O'Brien, T. 1995. *If I Die in a Combat Zone.* London: Flamingo.

Osborne, R. 1985. *Demos: The Discovery of Classical Attika.* Cambridge: Cambridge University Press.

Parker, R. 2000. "Sacrifice and Battle." In *War and Violence in Ancient Greece*, edited by H. van Wees, 299–314. London: Duckworth.

Pemberton, E. 1977. "The Name Vase of the Peleus Painter." *The Journal of the Walters Art Gallery* 36: 62–72.

Petrakos, B. 1984. "Anaskaphē Rhamnoūntos." *Praktika tes en Athenais Archaiologikes Hetaireias* 59: 197–8.

Phillipson, C. 1911a. *The International Law and Custom of Ancient Greece and Rome, Vol. I*. London: McMillan.

———. 1911b. *The International Law and Custom of Ancient Greece and Rome, Vol. II*. London: McMillan.

Popper, K. 1959. *The Logic of Scientific Discovery*. London: Taylor and Francis.

Pritchard, D. 1998. "The Fractured Imaginary: Popular Thinking on Military Matters in Fifth Century Athens." *Ancient History:* 28: 38–61.

Pritchett, W. 1971. *The Greek State at War, Part I*. Berkeley: University of California Press.

———. 1979. *The Greek State at War: Part III*. Berkeley: University of California Press.

Raaflaub, K. 1998. "The Transformation of Athens in the Fifth Century." In *Democracy, Empire and the Arts in Fifth-Century Athens*, edited by D. Boedeker and K. Raaflaub, 15–41. London: Harvard University Press.

———. 2001. "Father of All, Destroyer of All: War in Late Fifth-Century Athenian Discourse and Ideology." In *War and Democracy: A Comparative Study of the Korean War and the Peloponnesian War*, edited by D. McCann and B. Strauss, 307–56. London: M. E. Sharpe.

Rademaker, A. 2002. "'Most Citizens are *Europrôktoi* Now': (Un)manliness in Aristophanes." In *Andreia: Studies in Manliness and Courage in Classical Antiquity*, edited by R. Rosen and I. Sluiter, 115–25. Boston: Brill.

Richardson, F. 1978. *Fighting Spirit: A Study of the Psychological Factors in War*. London: Cooper.

Roisman, J. 2002. "The Rhetoric of Courage in the Athenian Orators." In *Andreia: Studies in Manliness and Courage in Classical Antiquity*, edited by R. Rosen and I. Sluiter, 126–43. Boston: Brill.

———. 2005. *The Rhetoric of Manhood: Masculinity in the Attic Orators*. Berkeley: University of California Press.

Runciman, W. 1998. "Greek Hoplites, Warrior Culture, and Indirect Bias." *The Journal of the Royal Anthropological Institute* 4: 731–51.

Sajer, G. 1991. *The Forgotten Soldier*. London: Orion.

Sassoon, S. 1966. *Memoirs of an Infantry Officer*. London: Faber.

Schatcher, S. 1959. *The Psychology of Affiliation*. Stanford, CA: Stanford University Press.

Schnurr, P. 2008. "The First 20 Years." *Journal of Traumatic Stress* 21: 1–2.

———. 2009. "The Changing Face of PTSD Diagnosis." *Journal of Traumatic Stress* 22: 1–2.

———. 2010. "PTSD 30 Years on." *Journal of Traumatic Stress* 23: 1–2.

Schwartz, A. 2009. *Reinstating the Hoplite: Arms, Armour and Phalanx Fighting in Archaic and Classical Greece*. Stuttgart: Franz Steiner Verlag.

Sekunda, N. 1992. "Athenian Demography and Military Strength 338–322 BC." *ABSA* 87: 311–55.

Shalit, B. 1988. *The Psychology of Conflict and Combat*. London: Praeger.

Shay, J. 1995. *Achilles in Vietnam: Combat Trauma and the Undoing of Character*. New York: Touchstone.

———. 2002. *Odysseus in America: Combat Trauma and the Trials of Homecoming*. New York: Scribner.

Sheets, G. 1994. "Conceptualising International Law in Thucydides." *American Journal of Philology* 115: 51–73.

Shephard, B. 2001. *A War of Nerves: Soldiers and Psychiatrists in the Twentieth Century*. Cambridge, MA: Harvard University Press.

Shils, E., and Janowitz, M. 1948. "Cohesion and Disintegration in the Wehrmacht in World War II." *Public Opinion Quarterly* 12: 280–315.

Snodgrass, A. 1967. *Arms and Armour of the Greeks*. Ithaca, NY: Cornell University Press.

Sorley, L. 1980. "Prevailing Criteria: A Critique." In *Combat Effectiveness: Cohesion, Stress, and the Volunteer Military*, edited by S. Sarkesian, 57–93. London: Sage Publications.

Spira, J., Pyne, J., and Wiederhold, B. 2007. "Experiential Methods in the Treatment of Combat PTSD." In *Combat Stress Injury: Theory, Research, and Management*, edited by C. Figley and W. Nash, 205–18. London: Routledge.

Strauss, B. 2007. "Naval Battles and Sieges." In *The Cambridge History of Greek and Roman Warfare, Volume I*, edited by P. Sabin, H. van Wees, and M. Whitby, 223–47. Cambridge: Cambridge University Press.

Stouffer, S. et al. 1949a. *Studies in Social Psychology in World War Two, Volume I: The American Soldier: Adjustment during Army Life*. Princeton, NJ: Princeton University Press.

———. 1949b. *Studies in Social Psychology in World War Two, Volume II: The American Soldier: Combat and Its Aftermath*. Princeton, NJ: Princeton University Press.

Struve, L. 2004. "Confucian PTSD: Reading Trauma in a Chinese Youngster's Memoir of 1653." *History and Memory* 16: 14–31.

Summerfield, D. 1999. "A Critique of Seven Assumptions behind Psychological Trauma Programmes in War-Affected Areas." *Social Science and Medicine* 48: 1449–62.

Szalma, J. 2008. "Individual Differences in Stress Reaction." In *Performance under Stress*, edited by P. Hancock and J. Szalma, 323–57. Burlington, VT: Ashgate.

Tod, M. 1913. *International Arbitration amongst the Greeks*. Oxford: Clarendon Press.

Trimble, M. 1985. "Post-traumatic Stress Disorder: History of a Concept." In *Trauma and Its Wake I: The Study and Treatment of Post-Traumatic Stress Disorder*, edited by C. Figley, 5–14. New York: Brunner/Mazel.

Tritle, L. 1997. "Hector's Body: Mutilation of the Dead in Ancient Greece and Vietnam." *Ancient History Bulletin* 11: 123–36.

———. 2000. *From Melos to My Lai: War and Survival*. London: Routledge.

Trotter, W. 1921. *Instincts of the Herd in Peace and War*. London: T. F. Unwin.

van Creveld, M. 1982. *Fighting Power: German and U.S. Army Performance, 1939–1945*. Westport: Greenwood Press.

———. 2005. "Technology and War II: From Nuclear Stalemate to Terrorism." In *The Oxford History of Modern War*, edited by Charles Townshend, 341–63. Oxford.

van Wees, H. 2004. *Greek Warfare: Myths and Realities*. London: Duckworth.

van Zanten, W. 1993. *Don't Bunch Up (and Some Notable Exceptions): One Marine's Story*. Connecticut: Shoe String Press.

Villing, A. "The Iconography of Athena in Attic Vase-painting from 440 BC–370 BC." MPhil. Diss., University of Oxford.

Watson, P. 1980. *War on the Mind: The Military Uses and Abuses of Psychology*. Harmondsworth: Penguin.

Wesbrook, S. 1980. "The Potential for Military Disintegration." In *Combat Effectiveness: Cohesion, Stress, and the Volunteer Military*, edited by S. Sarkesian, 244–78. London: Sage Publications.

Wheeler, E. 2007. "Land Battles." In *The Cambridge History of Greek and Roman Warfare, Volume I*, edited by P. Sabin, H. van Wees, and M. Whitby, 186–223. Cambridge: Cambridge University Press.

Whitehead, D. 1986. *The Demes of Attica 508/7—ca. 250 BC: A Political and Social Study*. Princeton, NJ: Princeton University Press.

Wilson, C. 1987. *The Anatomy of Courage*. London: Avery Publishing Group.

Worley, L. 1994. *Hippeis: The Cavalry of Ancient Greece*. Oxford: Westview Press.

Wyse, W. 1904. *The Speeches of Isaeus*. Cambridge: Cambridge University Press.

Yoshitake, S. 2010. "Aretē and the Achievements of the War Dead: The Logic of Praise in the Athenian Funeral Oration." In *War, Democracy and Culture in Classical Athens*, edited by D. Pritchard, 359–77. Cambridge: Cambridge University Press.

Zampaglione, G. 1973. *The Idea of Peace in Antiquity*. London: University of Notre Dame Press.

CHAPTER SIX

Socrates in Combat: Trauma and Resilience in Plato's Political Theory

S. Sara Monoson*

Socrates was a combat soldier during the Peloponnesian War. This aspect of his biography is rarely placed at the center of an account of the enduring interest of the life of this celebrated philosopher. When it is the effect is striking. This is especially clear in the interpretation of Socrates by the Italian master of neoclassical sculpture Antonio Canova. In a series of four large bas-reliefs completed between 1789 and 1796 and now in the collection of the *Museo Canoviano* in Passagno, Canova addresses Socrates' trial and death.[1] In the first panel he depicts Socrates raising his arm and addressing the jurors while Meletus and Anytus, the historical accusers, hover in the background. Standing by Socrates is the boundary-crossing god Hermes ready to see him through dangerous circumstances and to the underworld (visually modeled on Alcibiades wearing a helmet[2]). The next three panels continue the story and bring out its psychological complexity. Canova shows us Socrates sending his family away and draws attention to his parting from his eldest child. The scene suggests Socrates' capacity for tenderness. It also presents Socrates' seated philosophical friends composed and unshaken. Following that Canova displays Socrates' calm and constancy under extreme stress. In this scene Socrates holds the cup of hemlock nearly to his lips with his left hand and, recalling the composition of the first relief, gestures upward with his right arm as he speaks to his friends. His philosophical partners now appear upset (they weep and hang their heads at the prospect of his imminent death). In the last relief of this series Socrates lies dead with friends in varying states of composure gathered around. At the center we see Crito leaning over to close Socrates' eyes.

The group is brilliantly conceived and executed yet Canova apparently believed it failed to capture fully the meaning of this figure. Within the year, and on the occasion of his election to the *Accademia di San Luca* in 1797, Canova added a fifth relief to the set. This extraordinary piece shows Socrates standing by a wounded Alcibiades during a hoplite engagement at

Potidaea 33 years before his trial (Figure 6.1). There is nothing hesitant about
Canova's composition. Socrates is an uncompromising warrior. His muscular
arms and legs are fully extended. He has a strong grip on his shield and projects
his chin forward. Canova places both the wounded Alcibiades and the viewer
of this work of art behind the protection of Socrates' shield. He is a powerful defender, ready to strike. The positioning of Socrates features "dynamic
diagonals" modeled on ancient battle reliefs and expresses martial prowess.[3]
The depiction of Alcibiades wounded is also defiant. Though an arrow is
fixed in his thigh and his helmet and sword lie on the ground, he sports a
fierce gaze and retains his shield. Furthermore, the arrangement of Socrates
and Alcibiades as a pair conveys the camaraderie and fortitude of these men.
Alcibiades' left leg nearly obscures our view of Socrates' left leg, suggesting
their cooperation. Three sides of a triangle are made by Socrates' arm, Socrates
sword, and then the combination of the head and shield of Alcibiades; another
triangle is formed by Socrates' extended right leg, Alcibiades' right arm, and
Alcibiades' sword on the ground. The fully extended legs of Socrates and
Alcibiades also combine with the ground to form a stable triangle (while their
opponent has a narrow stance and his right leg bows to form a compromised
triangle one side of which is formed by a dead soldier).[4]

Canova's portrait of Socrates, so unfamiliar to us today for its inclusion of
a vigorous combat soldier in action, is exquisitely faithful to Plato's account
of Socrates' distinctive excellence. In this chapter, I assemble the elements

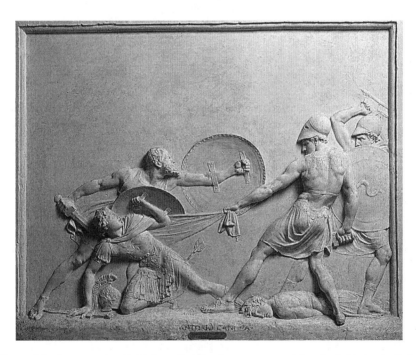

Figure 6.1 Socrates saving Alcibiades at Potidaea. Image courtesy of Accademia Nazionale di San
Luca, Rome.

of Plato's account of Socrates' military service at Potidaea and elsewhere, develop that portrait in light of evidence from Thucydides' account of these campaigns in his *History of the Peloponnesian War*, and consider the place of Socrates' conduct as a soldier in Plato's understanding of this philosopher's peculiar excellence. I propose, in particular, that Plato identifies Socrates' endurance of calamitous war experiences that could produce what today we call "war trauma" (with its attendant debilitating psychological symptoms) as constitutive of his excellence. Plato highlights Socrates' ability to remain himself under shifting and trying conditions, especially when moving between combat and home. Overall, Plato treats the conduct of Socrates in his capacity as a soldier as a visible sign of his achievement of an uncommon measure of "psychological health." This aspect of the portrait of Socrates engages myth (chiefly the figure of Ajax but also Achilles and Odysseus) and, in so doing, creates an archetype of resilience and "enlarges the significance of the philosopher's life."[5] I conclude by showing that the psychologically rich theory of justice elaborated in the *Republic* mobilizes the vantage point of a combat veteran.

Preliminary Methodological Considerations: The Historical vs. Literary Socrates and the Suitability of the Term "Veteran"

This essay examines Plato's portrait of Socrates the soldier on campaign, in combat and upon return home. I will not examine the evidence for Plato's own service.[6] Nor will I address the "historical Socrates" in relation to Plato's Socrates. All our evidence for Socrates' military service appears in Plato's dialogues. This is not a reason to question the veracity of its basic elements. I am satisfied that the fact of his service would have been impossible for Plato to fabricate and still maintain a credible portrait. In addition, the chronology assumed in Plato fits Thucydides' account of the relevant battles and scholarship does not cast doubt on the fact of his service. In order to address Plato's portrait of his military service in the least speculative way possible, I will restrict myself to the references in the dialogues to Socrates' own military experiences. I will not try to account for things such as how Socrates might have acquired his hoplite panoply.[7]

I am not examining a literary representation of an idealized soldier for its own sake. The figure of Socrates has exercised moral imaginations across the globe for centuries. In this essay I want to call attention to the very rarely noted fact that Plato places a capacity to endure with moderation harrowing military experiences and an array of linked psychological stresses at the very center of his account of what it means to struggle to sustain a "just soul." I also want to call attention to the fact that Plato's political theory draws on the inner life of a warrior to develop a portrait of Socratic practice. Moreover, Plato assumes that an adequate understanding of "justice in the city" must address the likelihood that, however usual and honorable, military service can expose a person to strains that can devolve into disabling distress and that a just society must recognize this, take steps to prevent and mitigate its occurrence, equip its members and communities to bear up under the stress, and craft civic practices that promote healing from any injurious consequences.

I will also use the term "veteran" with care in order to avoid suggesting a false parallel between ancient Athens and today. War was a permanent condition of life in the ancient city during Socrates' lifetime.[8] Moreover, "the Athenians perceived themselves as tough, courageous and bellicose, and were proud of it: military virtue was taken seriously by the population at large."[9] All able-bodied citizen men served episodically, regularly moving between campaigns, combat and home throughout their adult lives, or had to evade service one way or another.[10] It might seem to make sense to speak of Athenians who survived a particular campaign as "veterans" of that specific campaign (and notable for it), but it was not the way they referred to themselves. On the other hand, our sources attest to exceptional groups of fallen warriors sometimes gaining a laudable intermediary group identity (e.g., *Marathonomachoi* and *Plataiomachoi*[11]). It seems unlikely that the more general appellation, "veteran," that we use today to refer to someone formerly in the armed forces and now living as a civilian sensibly describes a condition of Athenian life. This is especially true as veterans today make up an ever-smaller slice of our population and the gap between soldiers and society has widened.[12] For the Athenians, in contrast, "there was no separation between civilian and soldier."[13]

"War Trauma" Can Provide a Frame of Reference for Examination of Plato's Portrait of Socrates

"War trauma" refers to catastrophic war experiences that can produce severe, persistent, and disabling anxiety commonly known as "posttraumatic stress disorder" (PTSD). The war experiences include exposure to extreme violence, gruesome physical injuries and bloodshed, intense suffering, brutality, extreme physical strain, and deprivations (hunger, filth), as well as prolonged separations from family and friends. In addition to these difficult experiences, clinicians today urge that grievous *moral* wounds must be added to this list of potentially upending experiences. Indeed, they emphasize that moral injuries often cause the most undermining and persistent symptoms. Moral injuries would include betrayal (e.g., incompetent or abusive commanding officers, disloyalty of a comrade, malfunctioning of a weapon, problems recovering bodies, and false representation of the cause for which warriors rally and kill), profound grief (especially the loss of someone close), terrible moral luck (a friendly fire episode, close call that kills a nearby comrade or being the proximate cause of collateral damage), and exposure to the suffering of civilians. The disabling symptoms range from consuming guilt, depression, social isolation and suicidal feelings, the persistence into civilian life of adaptations necessary to survive battle (e.g., hyper-vigilance), reduced mental function (lack of confidence in one's judgment and failing memory), addictive behaviors, and loss of one's capacity for social trust (and thus ability to sustain relationships), to outbursts of rage and episodes of going berserk. One prominent psychiatrist summarizes the symptoms of combat trauma worsened by moral injuries this way: "good character comes undone."[14]

War-related posttraumatic stress is today a formal diagnosis recognized by the medical establishment and veterans' affairs professionals. This is a recent development. It has long been known that war often subjects soldiers (and civilians) to traumatic experiences that can wreak havoc on their psyches as well as scar or destroy their bodies. We can find examples in antiquity and can point to accounts of "exhaustion" and "soldier's heart" among American Civil War soldiers as well as "shell shock" and "battle fatigue" in the World Wars.[15] But it was clinicians working with veterans of more recent conflicts, especially the Vietnam War, who identified a formal symptomatology.[16] We should observe, of course, that dreadful war experiences such as those detailed above do not necessarily produce trauma and debilitating posttraumatic stress. Some servicemen and women do come through it stable and capable. Precisely how and why they are so able when others suffer grievously is the subject of considerable study. What variables—personal and situational—can account for this? How is it possible to effectively and swiftly treat incipient and persistent posttraumatic stress? Can military practices and policies help protect soldiers from developing it?[17] How does the prevalence of trauma among veterans impact the public expression of morally justifiable outrage and political critique? These are, of course, urgent questions today as we recognize the high incidence of combat-related trauma among veterans of the wars in Iraq and Afghanistan and the heartrending consequences of such injuries for the individual soldiers, their loved ones, and their communities. Using the conceptual framework I refer to as war trauma to approach Plato, I do *not* mean to suggest that this ancient philosopher anticipated the modern psychiatric diagnosis. Instead, I mean to keep contemporary understandings of war trauma and posttraumatic stress front and center so as to alert us to features of Plato's depiction of Socrates' experiences on deployment, in battle, and upon return to Athens that have gone largely unnoticed for some time, thus enabling the recovery of a dimension of his work that resonates in important ways today. We do not need to assume that Greek culture constructed something akin to a modern medical diagnosis to find something familiar in its literature's attention to the physically and emotionally demanding aspects of military service and the sometimes debilitating psychological effects this can have on good people.

Plato Portrays Socrates Facing Severe Physical and Psychological Strains Common in War, Including Catastrophic Ordeals

Alcibiades' eyewitness account of Socrates on deployment to Potidaea and Delium in his encomium to him in the *Symposium* makes up the bulk of

Plato's explicit account of Socrates' behavior on campaign and in battle
(219e–221d). Plato offers only brief supplements in other dialogues. At
Charmides 153a–154b, the opening of that dialogue, we find Socrates in the
act of arriving home from the Potidaean expedition. At *Charmides* 156d
Socrates mentions having encountered foreign learning while on campaign
"there" (Potidaea). At *Laches* 181b Socrates' behavior during the retreat
at Delium is recounted by Laches, a general present on that campaign.
At *Apology* 28e Socrates proudly reminds the jury that he served in the
Athenian military on three campaigns, Potidaea, Amphipolis, and Delium.
And at *Crito* 52b Socrates (impersonating the *Laws*) recalls that he has never
left the city except with the army on campaign.

The basic outline of Socrates' military service drawn in these sources
can be stated simply. He was an Athenian hoplite during three significant
campaigns of the Peloponnesian War: the extended siege of Potidaea on the
distant isthmus of Chalcidice in northern Greece which started when he
was in his mid-30s (in 432), the strategic attack on Delium in very nearby
Boeotia about six years later (in 424), and the expedition north again to
defend Amphipolis just two years after that (in 423/2). All three were disasters for the Athenians. The campaign to Potidaea was an enormous drain
on resources and the Athenian forces suffered greatly—all for uncertain
military gains. Delium was an utter defeat on the battlefield for Athenian
hoplites with a large number of fatalities. Amphipolis was lost owing to
a tactical blunder. But Socrates' own personal behavior on campaign was
conspicuously exemplary. In particular, at both Potidaea and Delium he
remained steadfast at his post, holding his ground and bravely leading vulnerable—and also notable—fellow citizens (a young Alcibiades at Potidaea
and General Laches at Delium) through the bloody ordeal of close hoplite
combat and the chaos of retreat in the midst of collapsing Athenian lines
and fleeing, panicky troops.

Looking at these specific passages in Plato more closely, we find more
details of the combat experiences Socrates lived through. On the expedition
north to Potidaea the entire force confronted hardships that included serious deprivations (they were cut off from their supplies and suffered an acute
lack of food), prolonged periods of severe discomfort (including long periods of intense cold), and the stress of a protracted deployment (*Symposium*
220a–b). The expedition to and home from Potidaea included especially
fierce battles in which many personal friends of Socrates perished though
none are specifically named (*Charmides* 153b). Socrates witnessed his close
companion Alcibiades sustain a bad wound. He refused to leave Alcibiades'
side and rescued him from the battlefield, managing not only to extricate
Alcibiades but his armor as well (*Symposium* 220e). In addition, Plato reports
details that allow us to infer that twice Socrates suffered moral insults by
his own compatriots while on the Potidaean campaign. First, fellow soldiers
mocked Socrates' endurance of hardships (especially the cold) thinking it
an affront to them (*Symposium* 220d). Second, the commanders deliberately
ignored Socrates' act of valor in rescuing Alcibiades. Instead, they gave the

decoration to the one rescued, the ward of Pericles and well-connected young beauty, Alcibiades. In so doing they betrayed that their foremost concern was to curry favor with those who shared Alcibiades' social status, not fairly to recognize battlefield acts of valor (*Symposium* 220e). Furthermore, in the *Charmides* Socrates says that while on the Potidaean campaign a Thracian physician prompted him to question usual Athenian practices of healing (156d–157a). Turning to the account of Delium in the *Symposium* and *Laches*, we learn that Socrates' war experiences included additional challenges. On foot in hoplite armor he was caught in the middle of a lethal and disgracefully panicky Athenian retreat. Plato has the former general Laches report in his own voice that Socrates got him through the melee (*Laches* 181b). Plato also has Alcibiades report having witnessed Socrates' refusal to leave Laches' side during this horrible retreat (*Symposium* 220e–221a). Regarding Amphipolis, Plato places him there but provides no particulars (*Apology* 28e).

To fill out this picture we can consider what we might reasonably assume Plato's readers to have known about these campaigns. Looking at the evidence from Plato in the context of depictions of these specific campaigns in Thucydides' *History of the Peoloponnesian War* can give us some idea.[18] The Athenian action against the rebellious tribute-paying ally Potidaea is among the conflicts that initiate the Peloponnesian War. The Athenians first fight a fierce battle (during which Callias, one of the four Athenian generals on site, perishes) and the Potidaeans retreat behind their walls. The Athenians lay siege. And so Socrates likely had to participate not only in hoplite combat but also in the backbreaking work of building fortifications for a siege.[19] The Potidaeans held out for three years and so Socrates was likely away from home and living in severe conditions, possibly without leave, for a protracted length of time.[20] Among the things he had to endure was an outbreak of plague among the troops besieging Potidaea (2.58). And as if all this was not enough, we must also recall that Thucydides mentions that the Potidaeans became so desperate for food that they resorted to cannibalism (2.70.1). Seeing this, and surviving on barely adequate rations themselves, the Athenians finally agreed to terms of capitulation. On the way home, the forces fought a few smaller engagements.

Thucydides' accounts of the Athenians' debacles at Delium and Amphipolis provide more reason to believe that Plato's readers understood that Socrates' service would have surely exposed him to harrowing experiences. Delium was the first full-scale and certainly the bloodiest hoplite battle of the Peloponnesian War.[21] In this case the Athenians aggressively sought a stronghold in the heart of hostile Boeotia, just a day's march from central Athens, by fortifying the sanctuary of Apollo at Delium. Their tactical errors, humiliations, and gruesome suffering made this campaign infamous. Delium was the "only pitched battle of the Peloponnesian War fought in close proximity to Athens." Moreover, the "disaster of this Athenian 'home guard' must have quickly taken on mythic proportions and been recounted constantly throughout Athens."[22] Four details reported by Thucydides stand out. First, there was a "friendly fire" episode. In the midst of a hoplite battle in which the Athenians had gained a temporary upper hand, Thucydides reports, "some of the Athenians fell into confusion in surrounding the enemy and mistook and so killed each other"[23] (4.96.3). In the confusion they likely speared and hacked away and dozens of men "must have been impaled by their own brothers, fathers, friends."[24] Plato acknowledges that Socrates was caught right in the middle of this; Alcibiades says at Delium Socrates was remarkable for the way he was "looking out for friendly and enemy troops" (*Symposium* 221b)[25]. Second, Thucydides indicates that the disastrous retreat at Delium was initiated by Athenian errors, not Boeotian superior strength. Athenian forces were far larger but they were routed and fled in a chaotic fashion. Specifically, in the confusion of the friendly fire episode, Thucydides tells us that a smart tactical move on the part of the Theban General Pagondas "struck panic into the victorious wing of the Athenians…[and that] the whole Athenian army took to flight" (4.96.6), some to the ships and some over land. Third, Athenian losses remained on the battleground for 17 days. Because Athenians had violated a sanctuary by making it into a garrison and some Athenian troops had retreated into that space and therefore now still remained in Boeotian territory, the Boeotians refused to allow the Athenians to collect their dead until they abandoned the fortified temple (4.97.1–100.5). In effect, they held Athenian corpses hostage. The stalemate ended only after the Boeotians used a novel weapon on the holed-up Athenians in the offending garrison. This new weapon is the fourth special horror associated with Delium by Thucydides (4.100.1–5). The Thebans used a "flame-blowing contraption"[26] that allowed the enemy to set the wooden walls of the garrison ablaze from a relatively safe distance, incinerating some, driving out the rest, and striking terror in all.[27] After this, the Boeotians let the Athenians recover their dead, including the decomposing corpses from the earlier engagement. Thucydides reports that, at the end of the day, at Delium "not quite five hundred Boeotians fell in the battle, and nearly one thousand Athenians, including Hippocrates the general" (4.101.1–2). And so we can observe that Delium adds to Socrates' war experiences a grisly friendly fire episode, the sight of the rotting corpses of comrades, the deployment by the enemy of a fearsome new weapons technology, the combat death of another commanding general, and another episode of hand-to-hand combat in the middle of a disreputable retreat.

Soon after Delium, Socrates joined an Athenian expedition north to Amphipolis under the command of Cleon. Thucydides' account of that campaign mentions three things of importance in the current context. First, the Athenian forces were suspicious of Cleon's command skills and personal courage from the start and lost whatever small measure of confidence they might have had as the engagement progressed (5.7.2, 5.10.9). Second, this campaign ended not only in a decisive defeat of the Athenians but also in another full-blown rout and panic-stricken flight of Athenian forces (5.10.6) and slain commander. Thucydides' account of the troops' response to Cleon's position during the battle suggests a near case of what we might call "passive fragging" as they refrain from coming to his aid (5.10.9). Third, this is the expedition in which Thucydides (the historian) served as a general. He was in command of troops charged with reinforcing the Athenians on campaign to Amphipolis. He failed to get his forces there in time to make a difference. Judged incompetent by the Athenians, he was sentenced to a 20-year exile as punishment (5.26.5). And so, Amphipolis added to Socrates' war experiences moral injuries associated with service under the command of a known incompetent and failure to receive reinforcements due to poor leadership.

From the details Plato offers, read in historical context drawn from Thucydides, we can conclude that while Socrates did not himself sustain a bodily injury, his military service indeed exposed him to a whole array of war experiences that would place a person at significant risk of sustaining ruinous psychological wounds.[28]

Socrates Displays Uncommon "Resilience" on Deployment, in Combat and When Adjusting to Being Home Aagain

The physical affectations of the "historical Socrates" are well known from various sources—walking with a particular swagger, going barefoot, tolerating meager and poor food, wearing a single threadbare cloak in both winter and summer, abiding the privations of near poverty, having extraordinary powers of concentration as well as measure of commitment to philosophical examination that sometimes made him neglect ordinary things and thereby look silly. The sources attest to his display of these "mannerisms" both on the battlefield and in the streets of Athens.[29] Commentators ordinarily view the personal quirks as part of Socrates' odd (and irritating) asceticism. But their persistence in war and peacetime highlights an additional point: despite repeated exposure to the dreadful stresses of war, Socrates' character does not come undone. The continuance of his idiosyncrasies into combat zones and their prominent display at the very moment of his return home make this especially clear. This is apparent in Alcibiades' anecdotes about serving with Socrates at Potidaea and Delium recounted in his speech in the *Symposium*, the dramatic setting of the *Charmides* in which the reader encounters Socrates at the gymnasium only hours after having returned from Potidaea, and in Socrates' view of his own military service expressed in the *Apology*.

Alcibiades' account in the *Symposium* of what it was like to serve with Socrates on military expeditions immediately follows his account of Socrates' ability to resist all his amorous advances over the years. Frustrated, Alcibiades blurts out that his best efforts to "capture" Socrates have failed. Socrates is able to resist all inducements. Alcibiades laments that he cannot even count on offers of money to tempt Socrates because such things have always "meant much less to him than enemy weapons ever meant to Ajax" (219e). Although it is not entirely clear from this fluid translation of the sense of the passage, Alcibiades' comment refers to Ajax's extraordinary shield and its role in his ability to beat back enemy spears and swords.[30] When Alcibiades recalls Socrates' own military prowess, the reference to Ajax frames his story. In order to track the extent of the parallel, as Alcibiades invites listeners (and Plato's readers) to do, let me recall key details of the story of this Homeric hero.

Ajax is huge physically, very agile, swift, strong, and courageous. He fought in tandem with his bow-wielding brother Teucer, protecting him with the cover of an enormous shield. Moreover, though Ajax kills many, the *Iliad* celebrates Ajax's excellence at defensive maneuvers. He personally fights Hector but nightfall forces their duel to conclude before a victory is won. The exchange of gifts that follows (Ajax receives Hector's sword) is perhaps the strongest expression in Homer of the view that military ability does not require contempt for the enemy.[31] Overall, he obeys commanders and never sustains a physical wound at Troy. But Ajax does experience what we might call trauma exacerbated by moral injury. In the aftermath of Achilles' death, the commanders fail to honor Ajax's heroic actions appropriately by presenting him with Achilles' armor. Instead, Agamemnon requires Ajax to compete with Odysseus for the armor and sets up a contest the design of which—a contest of speeches—wholly favors honey-tongued Odysseus. In the Sophoclean tragedy *Ajax*, we get an account of the debilitating effects the trauma of Achilles' death, compounded by the moral injury of the unfair contest, has on this fine warrior. In this play, this exceptional soldier, the bulwark of the Achaeans, appears in agonizing psychological pain. Broken, Ajax becomes a berserker; in a fit of madness brought on by the moral injury of having been denied the armor outright and instead been made to suffer a humiliating slight at the hands of his own commander, he goes into a violent rage against his own compatriots. Only divine trickery saves him from massacring many of his own comrades (and fragging his commanders). Believing he is killing fellow Greeks, Ajax wildly slaughters livestock. When he regains his senses, his feelings of shame and fear only intensify and he descends into suicidal despair; he uses Hector's gift to end his own life. The story of his madness was well known in Plato's time. It not only was recounted in Sophocles' play but was part of the *Little Iliad*, a now lost part of the epic cycle that was as familiar at the time as the *Iliad* and *Odyssey* of Homer.[32]

As we imagine ourselves listening to Alcibiades tell stories about Socrates' behavior on lengthy deployments and in battle, the comparison with Ajax can order our thoughts. Like Ajax, in battle Socrates is a bulwark. He fiercely protects his comrades in arms (particularly Alcibiades whom Socrates treats, despite his advances, "like a brother"[33]—language that recalls Teucer), stays calm and determined in the heat of battle, does not himself sustain a physical wound, and obeys commanders. And, like Ajax (though on a vastly smaller scale than that of the Homeric hero), he is dishonored by an unjust decision by commanders (the Athenian commanders at Potidaea award the prize to Alcibiades/Agamemnon awards the armor of Achilles to Odysseus). But, while Ajax experiences severe psychological pain, rage, shame, and suicidal despair,[34] Socrates appears buoyant in the aftermath of battle (and remain so when he faces trial, imprisonment, and execution by his fellow citizens).

All of Alcibiades' anecdotes regarding Socrates at war stress continuities between home and war zones and his exceptional personal endurance (καρτερίαν *Symposium* 219d7). For example, he explicitly remarks on continuities between Socrates' behavior at war and back at home. He starts by saying that their odd erotic relationship predated their service together and continued on deployment: "All this had already occurred when Athens invaded Potidaea, where we served together and shared the same mess" (219e).[35] Alcibiades also elaborates on Socrates' attitude toward food. When they were cut off from their supplies at Potidaea, Alcibiades says of Socrates, "no one else stood up to hunger as well as he did" (καρτερεῖν 220a1). This reminds him of Socrates' attitude toward wine back at home; though he didn't much want to drink, when he had to, he could hold his liquor (220a). Turning to more general conditions, Alcibiades reports that Socrates not only endured the extreme cold at Potidaea (καρτερήσεις 220a6) but also did so in his usual bare feet and light cloak. He invokes the endurance of Odysseus to applaud Socrates' odd and marvelous ability to conduct philosophy while on campaign (calling him καρτερὸς ἀνήρ at 220c2 explicitly citing *Odyssey* IV.242). Alcibiades says that one warm day in Potidaea Socrates started thinking about a problem, and stood outside in the same spot, lost in thought, for a full 24 hours straight. After a few hours his comrades came out to watch him (and mock him), even taking their bedding outside to get a good view of the spectacle (220c).[36] This did not deter him any more than mockery interfered with his philosophical work at home. In addition, Alcibiades tells us that Socrates was wholly untroubled at having been passed over for a deserved prize for bravery in the battle of Potidaea when he rescued the young Alcibiades and his shield. At war, like at home, Socrates lacked interest in conventional honors (220e) and bore personal slights lightly.[37]

The last anecdote Alcibiades tells concerns Socrates' behavior during the retreat at Delium and again stresses healthy continuities between home and war. Alcibiades calls Socrates' constancy in this setting "a spectacle worth seeing" (220e9[38]), implying a comparison to dramatic performances and possibly recalling the praise of celebrated warriors by elegiac poets such as Simonides.[39] Alcibiades says that Socrates moved about in the midst of the battle "exactly as he does around town" and then, in an effort to drive home the substantive point, elaborates by openly quoting from Aristophanes' characterization of Socrates' in the *Clouds* saying that even during the retreat at Delium "you strut around like a grand gander [and] roll your eyes" (*Symposium* 221b citing *Clouds* 362[40]).

Plato depicts Alcibiades closing his discussion of Socrates in war by turning once again to myth. There is a parallel for everyone, Alcibiades comments. We might understand Achilles by referring to Brasidas or compare Pericles and Nestor or Antenor (221c). But it is possible, he submits, that

Socrates is so out of the ordinary that "search as you might, you'll never find anyone else, alive or dead, who's even remotely like him" (221d). And so Alcibiades himself suggests that his earlier reference to Ajax is most telling not for the ways in which Socrates is like Ajax, though these are revealing, but instead for the single most dramatic way in which the parallel breaks down and Socrates outshines this Homeric hero. Alcibiades' account of Socrates at war is playful. He delivers it in an inebriated state. And it is part of a larger story of Socrates' meaningful oddity. It is also a key element of how Plato mythologizes Socrates. Socrates offers a psychologically rich conception of warrior excellence that lauds resilience in the face of catastrophic combat experiences. [41]

The *Charmides* extends Plato's account of Socrates' resilience to his reintegration into life in Athens. The dramatic setting of the *Charmides* represents Socrates coming home after the lengthy deployment to Potidaea (153a–154b). The picture of Socrates home from war is one of easy re-entry and return to old pleasures. Socrates narrates this dialogue himself and so in his own voice we learn that he arrived home from the army at Potidaea only last night, has been away for a long period, and that only a short time ago had been in a significant battle (153b7). Without hesitation he adds, "After such a long absence I sought out my accustomed haunts [the palaestra where the youth congregate] with special pleasure." And he specifically denies feeling ill at ease in any way. As if to stress Socrates' oddity in this regard, he uses the language of mental instability to describe the unrestrained enthusiasm with which young men confined to the home-front, especially his young friend Chaerophon, greet him and pelt him with inquiries (μανικός 153b3). At first, Socrates answers Chaerophon's questions with very short, minimally informative lines. The tone and content of Socrates' responses are a bit strange given his self-described good mood. His initial comments very much resemble the cautious, terse way of speaking that clinical psychologists and contemporary veterans report is indeed characteristic of the way soldiers only recently back from a war-zone typically speak about their war experiences, especially their combat experiences. [42]

> *Chaerophon*: How did you survive the battle?
> *Socrates*: Exactly as you see me.
> *Chaerophon*: The way we heard it here the fighting was very heavy and many of our friends were killed.
> *Socrates*: The report is accurate.
> *Chaerophon*: Were you actually in the battle?
> *Socrates*: I was there.

Chaerophon urges Socrates to sit and give a full account of the battle. Socrates very quickly adjusts to more extensive talking. Socrates says he took a seat, "proceeded to relate the news in answer to whatever questions anyone asked, and they asked plenty of different ones." "When they had had enough of these things," he continues, "I, in my turn, began to question them with respect to affairs at home, about the present state of philosophy and about the young men, whether there were any who had become distinguished for wisdom or beauty or both" (153d). Answering all the questions about the recent battle, about injured and dead friends, and about conditions on the long deployment likely took up some time. Plato does not depict that conversation. Plato shows us a homecoming in which Socrates slips back into his usual life at Athens with little fuss or anxiety on his part. Plato's literary choices highlight Socrates' lack of hesitation about relating his war experiences.[43] His literary choices also show that Plato expected his readers to be familiar with returning soldiers indeed having difficulties traversing these spheres of life. He highlights the interlocutors' wonder at Socrates' composure and willingness to entertain so many questions. The opening of the *Charmides* is therefore striking in ways unappreciated in the scholarship. It stresses the ease with which Socrates resumes his usual practice of philosophical examination after two distinct kinds of stresses: experiencing combat and recollecting those experiences. The rest of the dialogue suggests how he does it. The substantive philosophical topic of the *Charmides* is the definition of "self-control" (σωφροσύνη), a virtue of considerable practical concern to a returning warrior because it is the virtue that equips an individual to resist temptations to act violently in pursuit of desires. Possessing it, Socrates models how a returning soldier can mentally work to "turn off" combat-honed habits of mind and behavior and, once again, think, argue, and act in ways appropriate to life in the city. What does Socrates do? He talks, forms his memories of the war into narratives, retells stories of combat to others who were not there, engages in dialogic examinations of moral questions—all therapeutically valuable and healing act according to today's clinical studies.[44]

Attending to the fact that Plato sets the discussion of self-control in the context of a warrior's homecoming also makes some sense of two other puzzling aspects of the *Charmides*: the account of Charmides' headache at the start of the text and the scheming conduct of Charmides and Critias that concludes the text. Charmides' headache comes up in this way. After Socrates completes his account of the Potidaean campaign, he inquires into what's been happening in his absence. He turns up that the most beautiful youth of the new generation, Charmides, is now of an age to undertake discussion and of course wishes to see him. Charmides' guardian, Critias, calls him to Socrates' side in a tricky way. Critias knows Charmides has been suffering from headaches and suggests Socrates is in possession of a cure (φάρμακον 155b2, c10, e8). When Charmides appears, Socrates is overcome by the sight of him (and by a glimpse inside his cloak, 155d) but recovers his wits quickly in response to Charmides' interest in his cure. Addressing Charmides, he stresses that the treatment he has to offer does not attend to the ailing body part in isolation but, instead, is in connection with the whole body, and also with the soul. Charmides agrees to try this strategy and, relieved, Socrates "regains his courage" (156d1) and begins to describe some healing practices he learned from a Thracian physician when he was away on campaign. In particular, he learned that treatment of the soul is by means of "charms," that is, by fine *words* that engender self-control (157a).[45] In this way Socrates directs Charmides' attention to the important issue of how *discussion* can support the development of self-control and can function as a remedy for ills (157d). Socrates takes self-control and its practical benefits seriously. But he also belittles precious Charmides' morning headaches. After all, Socrates is just back from war and has seen wounds and death, and he has just recounted at length stories of those horrors for Chaerophon and his friends. Socrates knows that there are kinds of "headaches" that actually need "curing" by means of hearing and telling stories and cultivating self-control. The aporetic ending of this dialogue (i.e., its failure to convince the interlocutors) is thus foreboding and realistic. At the close of the dialogue, Socrates worries that his healing charms have not worked on Charmides (and Critias) and that these two have not developed self-control or even a taste for it (175e). Charmides and Critias suggest they will keep at it (176b–c). But the dialogue does not end there. Instead, tacked on to the end is a seemingly peculiar depiction of Critias and Charmides scheming. Critias issues orders to Charmides, plots with him about secret matters, expresses a lack of interest in taking any counsel at all, and says he shall willingly embrace force to realize his plans (176c–d). It is not at all clear what they are doing. But, once we recall that the Plato and his readers knew that the historical analogs of the two characters depicted here were in reality leading figures in the conspiratorial and tyrannical rule of the Thirty at Athens at the close of the Peloponnesian War, an important layer of meaning in the final scene of the *Charmides* becomes clear. The historical Charmides (only a boy at the time of the dramatic setting of Plato's account of this conversation) was one of the Ten appointed by the Thirty to govern Piraeus. Critias was one of the Thirty. The closing scene of the *Charmides* asks readers to view the brutal regime of the Thirty in light of an utter failure of self-control. Perhaps we can even say that the *Charmides* proposes that the Thirty represents a moment in Athenian history when attitudes and behaviors appropriate to a warrior facing an enemy combatant marched unchecked into domestic politics.

Plato's account of Socrates' speech to the jurors at his trial in the *Apology* also mobilizes his war experiences to illustrate psychological health and its political consequences. In his speech, Socrates mentions his service at Potidaea, Amphilpolis, and Delium seemingly in passing (28e).[46] His reference to his service might even be mistaken for a simple rhetorical move on Socrates' part, that is, a contrivance designed to remind the jurors that he is a commendable veteran and deserves their compassion. After all, he seems to do something similar when he awkwardly engineers recollection of his position as head of a household with small children a little later in the speech (34d). Or the reference might appear a clear, if clumsy, effort to validate philosophy by associating it with a manly, high-status civic activity. But Socrates does not just briefly refer to his service in this *Apology* passage (28b–e).[47] The reference functions to weave together his life-long practice of philosophy and his repeat performances in battle into a single, integrated life-story. The references to his military service assert that he was not one man at war and another at home.[48]

Socrates in the *Apology* refers to his military service in the course of his response to what he takes to be a commonplace objection to his devotion to philosophy: it is a shameful activity that places one at risk of death (leaves one vulnerable to prosecution and either unable or unwilling to defend oneself in court). Socrates imagines being asked, "Aren't you ashamed to have engaged in the sort of occupation that has now put you at risk of death?" (28b). He responds by invoking the praiseworthy example of Achilles' decision to avenge the death of Patroclus in full awareness of the fact that his own death is fated to follow that of Hector. Socrates asks, "Do you really suppose Achilles gave a thought to danger or death?" when he set out to kill Hector (28d)? Socrates refers to a moral code appropriate to a war zone to explain his disposition as a citizen living in Athens. Socrates implicitly denies that different principles should apply to what is just in these two spheres of life (at war toward an enemy and in the city with fellows). His point is that one standard regarding what is shameful should guide men who traverse both of these fields of activity, war and philosophy, battle and disagreement. He stresses the same point in other dialogues as well. For example, in the *Laches* he insists that a single definition of courage must apply to "those who are courageous in warfare but also those who are brave in dangers at sea, and the ones who show courage in illness and poverty and affairs of state…and not only those who are brave in the face of pain and fear but also those who are clever at fighting desire and pleasure" (*Laches* 191d). To drive this point home in the *Apology*, he reminds his listeners that he is not speaking lightly; he has himself faced death on the battlefield during three campaigns—Potidaea, Amphipolis, and Delium. And, as he develops his argument, Socrates continues to refer to military affairs. He argues that being a warrior and doing philosophy *both* require obeying a commander and remaining at one's "station" (28d) over a period of time and in the face of grave dangers, even threats of death.[49]

Socrates challenges his listeners to see that his life would lack coherence if it were to be the case that, while repeatedly proving himself able to endure the risks associated with taking up weapons and positions in obedience to military commanders elected by the city, he should now prove himself unable to continue to endure the risks associated with taking up argument and examination in obedience to the gods (in obedience to the oracle and his daimon at *Apology* 33c).[50] Socrates does not liken philosophy to military service in the *Apology*. Socrates' reference to his own military service in the *Apology* does not propose an apt metaphor. Rather, Socrates indicates that his well-lived philosophical life has included exemplary military service. He assimilates the full arc of his life, not the single brave act of refusing to abandon philosophy at this moment, to the praiseworthy military conduct celebrated in elegiac poetry. Socrates also invites listeners to complete the comparison of himself to Achilles. Like Achilles, Socrates is impressively resolute in the face of his own impending death and, in this instance, displays a laudable understanding of what would be truly shameful behavior (abandon what's right to save one's skin). Like Achilles Socrates chooses to live fully rather than allow fear of death to paralyze him or diminish his ambitions. But, unlike Achilles, Socrates' good character does not come undone by anger and grief in the course of following through on that choice.[51] Socrates remains calm in battle and throughout the action of the *Crito* and *Phaedo*, that is, imprisonment and execution (beautifully rendered by Canova in artwork discussed earlier). Achilles' explosive wrath, in contrast, is of course the central theme of Homer's *Iliad* and culminates with his abuse of Hector's corpse.

Plato elaborates Socrates' singular resilience further. He additionally distinguishes Socrates from Achilles and invites new comparisons with other heroes. In his speech in the *Apology* Socrates introduces two senses in which he will endure death. First, he is confident that the example of his coherent life and unjust punishment will enter the Athenian collective memory. He expects the episode to linger in the Athenian conscience, allowing him to continue conducting interrogations of the Athenians from beyond the grave and thus enact deathless *kleos*. Second, he is personally confident of the immortality of the soul and conceives of Hades as a place where he can continue his philosophical labors. Impressively, the conversations in Hades he most looks forward to will be those in which he examines the quality of his own resilience. Hades is, he says,

> a place where I can converse with Palamedes, and Ajax the son of Telamon, and other heroes of old, who have suffered death through an unjust judgment; and there will be no small pleasure, as I think, in comparing my own sufferings with theirs. (41b)

Socrates does not minimize or mock the agonies endured by these heroes. Rather, he expects his own capacity for endurance to compare favorably. He specifically directs the listener to imagine a comparison of their respective "sufferings" and deaths, each brought on by an "unjust judgment" (in Shay's language, drawing on the directness of veterans' own words in clinical settings, brought on by "violations of what's right"[52]). Comparing his sufferings with those of Ajax would recall the similarity of their combat experiences and post-combat incidents of moral injury. In addition to the similarities detailed earlier, we observe now that both have close associates who try to dissuade them from accepting death (compare the pleadings of Ajax's wife Tecmessa and Socrates' friend Crito), both die by their own hands (Ajax buries Hector's sword in his chest, Socrates lifts the cup of hemlock to his lips) and both deaths are set in motion by unjust judgments by recognized authorities (Ajax's commanders, the Athenian jurors). But, in the end, it is their dissimilarities that stand out. Ajax is in despairing anguish. He remains in painful inner turmoil even after death; Ajax's shade in Hades is so broken that he remains furious and cannot even bear to speak with Odysseus when he visits the underworld (*Odyssey* 11.540). Ajax appears a cautionary tale of a great warrior who comes undone.[53] Socrates, on the other hand, is a model of a warrior who remains himself through it all.

Socrates's Capacity for Resilience Is Unaffected by a Lack of Conviction Regarding the Justice of the "Cause" for Which He Deploys, Suffers, and Kills

Plato never suggests that Socrates entertained the standpoint of what we would call a "conscientious objector" or showed any ambivalence about the moral legitimacy of killing enemy combatants in war. Loyalty to the city demanded service and that was sufficient reason to take up arms. His attitude is in this way thoroughly orthodox for his time and place.[54] Plato portrays Socrates confident that honorable conduct in war is possible regardless of any personal attachment, or not, to a "cause."[55] This is important because Plato's Socrates clearly lacks commitment to what we might call the "cause" behind Athens' embrace of the Peloponnesian War—preservation (and extension) of Athenian hegemony. Socratic moral philosophy questions deeply the material and ideological aims of war policies advanced by Pericles and other leaders. Plato explicitly depicts Socrates objecting to Athenian ambitions to secure glory, reputation, and wealth by developing an "empire" and undertaking the war with Sparta to secure it (e.g., *Gorgias* 515e–517a, 519a–b).[56] The very survival of the city as an independent entity was not the rallying cry for the campaigns in which he fought. Accordingly, we may say that Plato portrays Socrates fighting willingly but not entirely unburdened by doubts about the moral underpinnings of this particular war and the ugly appetites it unleashes.

The closest we come in the dialogues to any talk of Socrates trying to evade or resist military service is a joke at the opening of the *Gorgias*. In Greek, "War and battle" are the first words of the dialogue.

> *Callicles*: This is the way they say you ought to join a war and a battle, Socrates.
> *Socrates*: You mean we've missed the feast, as they say, and we're too late?
> *Callicles*: Yes, and a most elegant feast it was; for Gorgias put on many fine displays for us a little while ago.[57] (447a)

The humor pivots on Callicles' assertion that Socrates' late arrival at the gathering is in keeping with what "they say" about how one *ought* to join a war and a battle. Socrates plays along by making explicit what was implicit in Callicles' comment: Socrates says, "You mean we're too late?" This opening scene is funny and playful in a way that only makes sense if the reader knows Socrates to be no such "reluctant conscript"[58] but instead very much a reliably willing warrior in battle and in argument. As the dialogue progresses, the extent to which successive interlocutors (Gorgias, Polus, and Callicles) also prove willing to take risks and approach the battlefield of ideas fearlessly becomes an issue.[59]

The easy separation of conduct and cause in the portrait of how Socrates assessed the morality of combat has important consequences for how we understand Plato's portrait of his resilience. In particular, it brings out a difference between this account of Socrates and that of the conditions under which combat soldiers today struggle to cultivate resilience. Recent studies of American veterans indicate that particularly terrible anguish and post-traumatic stress afflict troops and veterans burdened by doubts about the justice of the war's larger cause. For example, one recent study shows that the psychic distress experienced by American servicemen and women over their individual accountability for the wars in Iraq and Afghanistan worsens significantly once they become ambivalent about, let alone furiously opposed to, American prosecution of these wars. The study details the "complexity of the inner moral landscape" they traverse, reporting that for these men and women "the moral oversight is internal" and might be best understood "as a soulful struggle with conscience." [60] The moral landscape troops traverse today includes feelings of having been "suckered"[61] by leadership (political and military) into having gone to war on "a pretext that camouflages other, actual causes"[62] as well as thus having become "tainted" as a result.[63] We have no reason to believe that something similar is at play in the story of Socrates' confrontation with questions regarding the morality of combat service. But we can imagine Socrates experiencing an "inner debate" or self-examination regarding his own culpability for his actions in combat (i.e., his own courage or cowardice toward comrades). This mental work is not complicated by worries about the justice of the cause. He disagrees with the war aims but there is no indication in Plato's portrait that he feels misled by leadership regarding what they are, nor that he feels abused. Plato's focus is on Socrates' control of his own conduct toward his compatriots, himself, and the enemy.

I have so far argued that Plato's depiction of Socrates' war experiences directs us to his observation of a layer of complexity in Socrates' extraordinary inner life. This dimension of Plato's portrait of an archetypal philosophical life provokes some questions. How is such resilience possible? What sustains it? What upends it? Does its practice have moral or political consequences? Can we get more precision and clarity regarding what it might mean to remain psychologically intact despite suffering trauma? Does resilience facilitate critique and philosophic labor? These seem very possibly to be among the questions that motivate Plato's moral psychology and theory of justice, especially in the *Republic*.

Signs That the *Republic* Is Alert to Psychological Challenges Peculiar to Experienced Combat Soldiers

The psychologically rich theory of justice elaborated in the *Republic* mobilizes the Socratic model of "resilience" in the face of war trauma in several ways. This is evident in the way, the long argument of the *Republic* gets started when Socrates and his dinner companions examine two commonplace definitions of justice. The apparently sensible definitions forwarded by Cephalus and Polemarchus in Book I quickly collapse into muddles as Socrates subjects them to scrutiny. Socrates' clever manipulation of these two interlocutors is the subject of much scholarly discussion. I only want to add that the definitions they offer crumble precisely when they fail to traverse war and peace. Specifically, at 331b–332a, the definition, "speaking the truth and paying debts," disappoints when Socrates asks Cephalus if it can apply to a hard case involving the use of weapons. Isn't it the case, Socrates inquires, that if a sane man gives his weapons to a friend for safe keeping and then asks for them back "when he is out of his mind," the friend "shouldn't return them, and wouldn't be acting justly if he did?" The situation suggests the case of a former soldier now suffering mental distress. Socrates insists that his friends owe him more than the repayment of a debt, that is, the mechanical application of a rule. He therefore objects to Cephalus' definition. Next, at 332e–334b, Socrates exposes as unsatisfactory Polemarchus' suggestion of a revised definition, "helping friends and harming enemies." In this case, the rule fails because its application denigrates "the clever guardian of an army" in the eyes of noncombatants. Socrates asks Polemarchus whether a good guardian of the army should be able to steal the enemy's plans and dispositions. When he sensibly answers, "Yes," Socrates observes that according to his revised definition of justice, "a just person has turned out to be a kind of thief"—an intolerable conclusion. My point is not that Socrates has at this point indeed refuted these traditional views of justice. Rather, I want to call attention to the fact that these passages depict Socrates and his interlocutors demanding that a definition of justice must address the anxieties that reasonably trouble good men moving between war zones and home. A definition that can guide behavior in only one sphere or that neglects the needs of experienced combat soldiers is taken to be patently unacceptable.

The *Republic* is also attentive to the vantage point of an active duty soldier when Socrates begins shaping the institutional structure of the ideal city and proposes a distinct class of "guardians." Socrates implicitly abandons the experienced amateur or citizen-soldier model familiar to Athenians and instead argues for creating a professional class of soldiers on the grounds that war, like other crafts, requires expertise and that "it is of the greatest importance that warfare be practiced well" (374c).[64] He proposes that the requisite expertise includes not only physical strength, courage, and command of the technical skills needed to design strategy and tactics, but also a sort of psychological agility that enables a soldier to enter a war zone with fierce confidence *and* to adjust with ease to being home and handling political and domestic responsibilities with gentleness. Consider this passage from Book II:

Socrates: The physical qualities of the guardians are clear.
Glaucon: Yes.

Socrates: And as far as their souls are concerned, they must be spirited.

Glaucon: That too.

Socrates: But if they have natures like that, Glaucon, won't they be savage to each other and to the rest of the citizens?

Glaucon: By god, it will be hard for them to be anything else.

Socrates: Yet surely they must be gentle to their own people and harsh to the enemy. If they aren't, they won't wait around for others to destroy the city but will do it themselves first....(375b–d)

The passage clearly acknowledges that intense psychological challenges characterize soldiering and that a just city must enable its troops to manage these stresses. Specifically, soldiers must be equipped to adjust to shifting contexts with the kind of nimbleness easily observable in a fine guard dog: "he is gentle as can be to those he's used to and knows, but the opposite to those he doesn't know" (375e).

It is important to note that the *Republic* does not rely on silver genetic material to produce such resilience among its guardians, as the myth of the metals might superficially suggest. Specific physical and musical training, education in censored myth and higher math, communal lifestyle, scheme of rewards and punishments for performance in combat (extra kisses and honors for valor as well as demotion to the farmer/artisan class for abandoning one's shield in battle, 468a–c), a confidence-inspiring command structure, and strictly enforced rules of engagement governing conduct on campaigns against other Greeks all work together to make sure that the just city's soldiers are minimally exposed to catastrophic war experiences (especially to moral injuries), thoroughly insulated from the family and economic stresses that accompany long deployments and maximally resilient psychologically in the face of war-related hardships—even calamities.[65] The *kallipolis* or "beautiful city" elaborated in the *Republic* will be able to "pursue war" in a way that reflects "her true character" (*Timaeus* 20b).

Resilience comes up again later in the argument of the *Republic* when Socrates turns to consider how the "philosopher-ruler" should be selected from among the population of the beautiful city. First, he makes it clear that the man or woman capable of being trained to rule and who will rule well must be selected from the guardian class (military), not separately raised. Socrates is also clear that great intellectual accomplishment alone cannot equip a fine member of the guardian class to become a philosopher-ruler. He does not hesitate to stress this in precise terms: "Our guardian must be both a warrior and a philosopher" (525b). To spot a potential philosopher this is what must be done. Once men have reached the highest level of rigorous training in abstract thinking, including mathematics,

Socrates: [Y]ou must make them go down again into the cave again, *and compel them to take up command in matters of war* and occupy the other offices suitable for young people, so that they will not be inferior to the others in experience. But in these too, they must be tested to see whether they'll remain steadfast when they're pulled this way and that or shift their ground.

Glaucon: How much is allowed for that?

Socrates: Fifteen years. Then, at the age of fifty, *those who have survived* (τοὺς διασωθέντας[66]) the tests and have been successful in both practical matters and in the sciences will…spend most of their time with philosophy, but, when his turn comes, he must labor in politics for the city's sake. (540a–b, my emphasis)

Those ready to serve as philosopher-rulers will be those who, over the course of repeated deployments marked by successively greater burdens of responsibility, excel not only in intellectual tests but in armed conflict as well. The philosopher-rulers will be "those among them [the guardians] who have proved to be best, both in philosophy and in warfare" (543a). In the *Republic*, good at warfare includes being fierce and gentle at appropriate times, enduring the hardships of deployments, remaining steadfast in combat, smartly utilizing math to plan strategy and tactics, observing rules of war between Greeks, and bearing psychological wounds lightly. For Plato, a history of conduct that exhibits what I have called "resilience" is an observable indicator of the condition of one's soul and evidence of a philosophic nature. [67]

War trauma and resilience also figure in Plato's startling suggestion in Book X that the beautiful city must prohibit the performance of dramatic poetry (especially tragedy) a grand and beloved Athenian cultural tradition. By this time in the text Socrates has completed his account of justice and the interlocutors have agreed that it's attractive. Socrates chooses to bring up some complicating issues that they had passed over earlier on. He says, "I think we omitted some things that then that we must now discuss" (603e). He points out that while their ideal city has cultivated an environment that will minimize exposure to trauma and nurture strong and resilient psyches, people will still experience grief and bereavement. This is unavoidable. And so he turns to detail how the institutional structure of the beautiful city can illuminate how to help good people experience measured responses to the pain of loss, especially of a child in war. Socrates explains:

Socrates: Grief prevents the very thing we need most in such circumstances from coming into play as quickly as possible.

Glaucon: What are you referring to?

Socrates: Deliberation. We must accept what has happened as we would the fall of the dice, and then arrange our affairs in whatever way reason determines to be best.[68] (603e–604c)

Socrates goes on to state that deliberation is not what happens in a "crowd gathered together in the theatre" (604e). Accordingly, Socrates affirms the exile of dramatic poetry from the ideal city (605b, 607b) unless or until it can defend itself by demonstrating how it can benefit a grieving person

struggling to sustain a just "constitution within him" (608a). While scholars today view Athenian dramatic festivals as providing rituals that support
the psychological well-being of soldiers and the "reintegration of veterans" into civilian life,[69] Plato only sees theater's capacity to stir emotions
and deliver superficial pleasures that, in his view, actually aggravate psychic
wounds and worsen potentially debilitating symptoms. Plato's remedy for
war trauma and other forms of psychological strain is the cultivation of
resilience through rational self-examination, deliberation, and storytelling,
not the "communalization of trauma" through the grand civic ritual of
dramatic festivals.[70]

Consideration of the relationship between living well, war trauma, deliberation, and resilience also features in the way Plato brings the long text of
the *Republic* to an end. In the closing passage known as "The Myth of Er"
(614b–621d[71]), Socrates tells the unnerving story of a foreign warrior's visit
to the underworld. He starts with a brief but vivid account of the treatment
of Er's corpse after he is slain in battle. Er's compatriots collected his corpse
from the battlefield on the tenth day, observing that unlike the others Er's
body had not begun to decay. Nevertheless, two days later they placed it
on the funeral pyre with all the others. While on the pyre Er revived. After
reviving he told what he had seen. Socrates then goes on to recount Er's
graphic descriptions of the peculiar topography of the other world and,
most remarkably, of the process that immortal souls undergo in preparation
for rebirth on earth. This process is extensive. It includes being judged based
on one's conduct on earth and awarded spectacular rewards or subjected
to severe punishments. Most important for tracking Plato's observation of
war trauma, this process also includes each soul being required to actively
choose for himself or herself a new life into which to be born. Among the
souls Er witnesses making a selection are five Greek soldiers of various ranks
and accomplishment who served in the Trojan War: Ajax, Agamemnon,
Thersites, Epeius, and Odysseus (620b–c).

The setting in which these figures must choose is simple. Er reports seeing the gods set a large assortment of possible lives before a sizeable gathering of souls. The gods explain that there are more good options than there
are souls gathered and so a good life-choice is within everyone's grasp. Each
option consists in a mixture of aspects of life (e.g., fame, nobility, sickness,
poverty, beauty, athletic prowess, etc.), so some deliberation is necessary to
choose well. Each soul can draw on his past experiences and skills developed
in his immediately prior life to assess the options. After choosing, each is
reborn with no memory of the process. Er reports seeing the great warrior
Ajax chooses to return a lion, remarking, "He avoided human life because
he remembered the judgment about the armor." Agamemnon chooses to
become an eagle. Er explains "His sufferings made him hate the human
race." Without comment Er mentions that Thersites (the frank speaking
common soldier assaulted by Odysseus in *Iliad* 2.211–277) opts for the
life of a monkey and that Epeius (a poor warrior but a good boxer and a
builder who worked on the Trojan Horse, *Odyssey* 8.493) picks the life of a
craft*swoman*.[72] Odysseus, last to choose, searches for a long time and selects

the life of a private man. Er reflects, the "memory of sufferings had relieved this soul of its love of honor." In sum, three are so psychologically wounded that they seek refuge in the animal kingdom, one is moved to be reborn a woman and one is determined to retreat from public affairs. All choose to avoid war at all costs. But we know that in the *Republic* Plato not only accepts that cities will experience war, but proposes that it is indeed possible for war to be practiced well and for combat to be a meaningful, even enriching, part of human experience. The Myth of Er's attention to these psychologically wounded soldiers of Homeric myth begs renewed attention to how that can be possible. It raises interest in the idea of Socratic resilience and its part in illuminating what it might mean to live well.

Conclusion

Writers have occasionally tried to conscript Socrates for pacifism. But to do so, these authors must take "extreme liberties" with Plato's texts.[73] Plato indicates that Socrates served willingly and honorably in the Peloponnesian War. Moreover, I have shown that Plato values combat service highly without romanticizing it and shapes his portrait of Socrates to feature the philosopher's multiple experiences of deployment, battle, and homecoming. Drawing on recent studies of "war trauma" to frame my inquiry and historical details culled from Thucydides to provide context for Plato's accounts, I have argued that Plato characterizes Socrates as exceptionally "resilient" in the face of calamitous war experiences and in this respect a wondrous or odd creature in the eyes of his fellow citizen-soldiers. I have stressed that this dimension of Plato's portrait of Socrates engages myth (Ajax, Achilles, and Odysseus) and in so doing creates an archetype of resilience. In the last section, I demonstrated that attention to the inner life of a combat veteran informs key elements of the psychologically rich theory of justice elaborated in the *Republic*. Together this material suggests that we should conclude, with Canova (Figure 6.1), that Socrates' conduct as a soldier is as fascinating and important philosophically as the manner in which he faced trial, imprisonment, and execution.

Notes

* I wish to thank Peter Meineck, David Konstan, Edith Hall, and Melissa Lane for encouraging me to take up this project. This work has also benefited from the comments of colleagues and students at New York University, University of Michigan, University of Wisconsin, University of Oxford, University of Sydney, University of South Carolina, and the Research Workshop in Classical Receptions at the Alice B. Kaplan Institute for the Humanities at Northwestern University.

1. Images of the series can be found in Albrizzi, Cicognara, and Missirini, 1824. Photographs of the pieces are online in various postings. One can be found at: http://www.corbisimages .com/stock-photo/rights-managed/MI001709/crito-closing-the-eyes-of-the-dead. Art

historians believe that Canova produced these four reliefs "for himself, rather than for any private patron or public display" (Lapatin 2009, 143). They were on occasion briefly available for inspection (Plant 2003, 18). Not all are finished. Perhaps he made them in personal consideration of the political upheavals of the day. Socrates was a symbolically potent figure during this tumultuous period. He was a hero of revolutionary France. Jacques-Louis David displayed his familiar *Death of Socrates* in the Paris salon of 1787. This painting is now on display at the Metropolitan Museum of Art in New York. For discussion, see Mainz (2007) and compare Pierre Peyron's (1787) "The Death of Socrates," now in *Statens Museum for Kunst*, Copenhagen. Perhaps Canova kept them private to protect his standing as an assiduously nonpartisan artist. Throughout his enormously successful career, Canova was unusual in that he "refused to work for one set of politically cohesive patrons" (Johns 1997, 4).

2. Athenian sculptors modeled their statues of Hermes setting out to escort someone safely through dangerous circumstances on Alcibiades (Clement of Alexandria *Protreptic* 4.53.6). Socrates' allusion to both *Iliad* 24.348 and *Odyssey* 10.279 at *Protagoras* 309b1–2 also suggests that Alcibiades' appearance calls Hermes to mind. See Denyer (2008, 66).

3. It also exhibits a strong reference to the Hellenistic sculpture by Agasias of Ephesus known as the "Borghese Warrior" that was recovered near Rome in 1611 and displayed at the Villa Borghese until 1807 when Napoleon Bonaparte had it, along with much else, removed to Paris where it remains today. See Lapatin (2009, 143). An image can be found at http://www.louvre.fr/en/mediaimages/fighting-warrior-known-borghese-gladiator

4. Canova's depiction of the relationship between Socrates and Alcibiades is unlike the treatments of this pair by his contemporaries. Prominent artists familiar to Canova passed over their military camaraderie and focused instead on the story of Socrates' erotic yet chaste interest in the company of a youthful Alcibiades and of Alcibiades' struggle with Socrates' admonishments to care less for physical pleasures (drawing on Plato's *Symposium* and Plutarch's *Life of Alcibiades*). They present Socrates attempting to save Alcibiades from the allure of sensual pleasures allegorically; a stern Socrates leads a hesitant Alcibiades away from the embrace of voluptuous, and nearly naked, women. See Pierre Peyron, *Socrate détachant Alcibiade des charmes de la volupté* (1782, now in a private collection) and Baron Jean-Baptiste Regnault's *Socrate arrachant Alcibiade du sein de la Volupté* (one in 1785 and now in a private collection and another in 1791 which was exhibited in the Paris salon of that year and is now in the Louvre).

5. Segal (1978, 321).

6. I have found no explicit reference to Plato's service in the sources. This is no reason to conclude that he did not serve. It would have been very odd had he not served at least on occasion. But he was too young to have gone on campaign during the Peloponnesian War.

7. Plato places Socrates on three campaigns of the Peloponnesian War. The evidence breaks down as follows: at Potidaea: *Apology* 28e, *Charmides* 153a–c, 156d; *Symposium* 219–221d; at Delium: *Apology* 28e, *Laches* 181b, *Symposium* 221a–c; and at Amphipolis: *Apology* 28e. Other Platonic dialogues present Socrates as familiar with battle and its consequences (e.g., *Menexenus*, *Republic*, *Laws*). Xenophon reports Socrates' own service only in general but does represent him conversing with a young Pericles about military issues (*Memorabilia* 4.4.1, 3.5.213) and commenting on Xenophon's decision to join the campaign with Cyrus (*Anabasis* 3.1). Diogenes Laertius in his *Life of Socrates* reports his part at Potidaea, Delium, and Amphipolis but his presentation of fuller historical details is muddled (see Woodbury 1971). On the historical Socrates' military service, see Calder (1961); Woodbury (1971); Planeaux (1999); Nails (2002, 264–265); Hanson (2003, 213–27); Anderson (2005); Graham (2008); Hughes (2010, 127–58); and Tritle (2010, 54–5, 233).

8. There is a large literature on Greek warfare. Key recent studies include Hanson (1989, 1991); Hamilton and Krentz (1997); McCann and Strauss (2001); Bekker-Nielson and Hannestad (2001); Chaniotis and Ducrey (2002); Van Wees (2004); Trundle (2004); Hodkinson and Powell (2006); Raaflaub (2007a, 2007b); Sabin, van Wees, and Whitby (2007); Pritchard (2010); and Crowley (2012).

9. Konstan (2010, 184). On the "belligerent *Weltanschauung*" of the Athenians, see Crowley (2012, 80–104).

10. On the evidence for evasion of conscription in ancient Athens, see Christ (2006). Many non-citizen residents, including slaves, were also pressed into service. See Brown and Morgan (2006).

11. Boedecker (2001b, 159).

12. For a recent discussion of the gap, see Wright (2012).

13. Crowley (2012).

14. Shay (1994), also (2002); on "moral injury," also see Maguen and Litz (2012). On the way "trauma is exacerbated by moral anguish and resentment that...trust was misplaced and abused" see Sherman (2013) (at p. 158).

15. Incidents of war-related post-traumatic stress in Greek sources include the story of Epizelus' loss of sight at Marathon in Herodotus (6.117) (King 2001), the report of Aristodemus' survivor guilt and suicidal behavior after Thermopylae in Herodotus (7.229, 9.71–3), the report of battle survivors' suffering psychological damage in Gorgias' *Helen* 16–17 (Tritle 2010, 127–8, 159–61) and the case of Clearchus in Xenophon's *Anabasis* (Tritle 2004). Less obvious are "hidden" examples reflected in tragedy, such as Heracles' violence against his own family as presented in Euripides' *Heracles* (Tritle 2010, 127–8), Ajax's suicidal despair in Sophocles' *Ajax*, and the depiction of the suffering of noncombatants in Euripides' *The Trojan Women*. Arguably, all extant tragedy addresses relevant themes. Recognizing that warfare was thoroughly integrated into every sphere of Athenian life and that the Athenian cultural practices were adept at producing combat ready psyches (see Crowley 2012) does not mean that every Athenian mobilization went well and that experienced killers could not suffer psychological injuries in combat situations. Note that Thucydides' account of the Peloponnesian War makes it abundantly clear that great upheavals and stresses horribly upset traditional practices and that war experiences could provoke even good character to unravel.

16. The diagnosis entered the *Diagnostic and Statistical Manual of Mental Disorders* (*DMS*) published by the American Psychiatric Association in 1980. The criteria have been revised in subsequent editions. Note that war experiences are not the only kind of traumas that can result in PTSD (others include criminal assault, sustaining or witnessing life-threatening injuries and natural disasters). The US Department of Veterans' Affairs established The National Center for PTSD in 1989. Some contemporary veterans' advocates raise concerns about the medical profession's reliance on the language of "disorder" because it obscures the point that the origin of the disability is an injury or wound (as opposed to it arising from an organic problem or personal deficiency). I will try to respect this concern though "PTSD" is entrenched in the literature and civic culture and thus hard to avoid.

17. Cf. discussion of the better design of military practices and institutions as the best prevention of trauma in Shay (1994, 195–209) as well as in the collection of studies presented in a special issue of *American Psychologist* on "Comprehensive Soldier Fitness: A Vision for Psychological Resilience in the U.S. Army," introduced by George W. Casey Jr., General, US Army Chief of Staff of (January 2011). On recovery, see Herman (1992). See Finkel (2013) for an unsettling account of efforts by US veterans of the wars in Iraq and Afghanistan to navigate available services.

18. Thucydides on Potidaea (1.56–67, 2.58.1–3, 2.701–4); Delium (4.89–101, 5.14.1); and Amphipolis (4.102–108, 5.6.1–16.1).
19. On the demands of ancient Greek siege warfare for all on campaign, see Kern (1999, 89–193).
20. Planeaux (1999) suggests the dramatic features of Plato's texts are consistent with the possibility that Socrates served without leave for three full years. See chapter 1 for discussion of the rotation of troops.
21. See Hanson (2003) for an account of the Battle of Delium.
22. Hanson (2003, 200, 213).
23. Translations from Thucydides are from Strassler (1996).
24. Hanson (2003, 181).
25. Unless otherwise noted, all translations of Plato are from Cooper (1997), modified to clarify who is speaking.
26. Mayor (2009, 219); also Crosby (2002, 89).
27. Thucydides explains the technology at 4.100.2–4. I suspect that the puzzling end of Aristophanes' *Clouds* might be an allusion to this episode of the battle of Delium (Strepsiades sets the Thinkery ablaze) and that Socrates' notable behavior in war might have contributed to playwrights' interest in him that year. The *Clouds* was produced in 423, the year following the disaster at Delium. Another comic play produced at the Dionysia that same year also featured Socrates as a central character (Ameipsias' *Connus*). Other reasons to suspect a link between the *Clouds* and Socrates at Delium include: (1) Alcibiades explicitly quotes *Clouds* line 362 in his account of Socrates' memorable behavior in the retreat at Delium at Symposium 221b and (2) similarities between Strepsiades' characterization of the Thinkery's cosmological teaching as "we are the hot coals in an oven" and Thucydides' account of the central role of hot coals in the operation of the Theban flamethrower (ἄνθρακες at both *Clouds* 97 and Thucydides 4.100.4). Another reason for suspecting that Aristophanes mobilizes his audience's knowledge of Socrates' military experience is the similarity of description of the Thinkery's students at *Clouds* 412–20 to Alcibiades' account of Socrates' notable behavior on campaign at Potidaea at *Symposium* 221a–b.
28. *Contra* Crowley (2012) and in this volume. I acknowledge that it is problematic to look for the elements of a culturally constructed modern medical diagnosis (war trauma, PTSD) in the ancient record and classify our sources accordingly. I do, however, remain confident that it makes sense to consider how war experiences, especially when they go catastrophically wrong, can stress the human psyche in ways that are recognizable.
29. Edmunds (2004, 195–6).
30. Translators Alexander Nehamas and Paul Woodruff (in Cooper 1997) add a note referring to Ajax's shield. Cf. Bury (1909) on *Symposium* 219e: "referring to the sevenfold shield of Ajax; cf. Pind.I.5.45; Soph. Af. 576." Bury 1909 is available on the *Perseus Digital Library*.
31. Shay (1994, 108–9). See also Kane (1996).
32. On Ajax in the *Little Iliad*, see Holt (1992) and Gregory Nagy's translation of Proclus' account of the *Little Iliad* at http://news.rapgenius.com/Gregory-nagy-proclus-summary-of-the-little-iliad-lyrics (produced by the Center for Hellenic Studies).
33. *Symposium* 219d1.
34. On the capacity of Sophocles' *Ajax* to speak to the experience of combat trauma, see the "Theater of War" programming developed by *Outside the Wire*, artistic director Bryan Doerries (http://www.outsidethewirellc.com/projects/theater-of-war/overview). They perform on military bases and hospitals as well as in civilian settings and receive funding from the Department of Defense and National Institute of Health as well as

private foundations. See also the programming developed by the Aquila Theatre of New York, artistic director Peter Meineck, for the National Endowment for the Humanities funded project, "Ancient Greeks/Modern Lives: A National Conversation" (http://ancientgreeksmodernlives.org/). For discussion, see Meineck (2009) and Lodewyck and Monoson (2015).

35. The friendship was erotically charged but, to Alcibiades' dismay, not physically realized.
36. On the capacity of Socrates' endurance to "convey to others an attitude of superiority" and thus elicit mockery, see Edmunds (2004, 196). He notes that a fragment of the *Connus*, a lost comedy of Amipsias that featured Socrates and was performed in the same competition as the *Clouds* soon after Delium, includes the phrase, καρτερικός γ'εἶ ("you are capable of endurance").
37. Cf. *Apology* 35e–36b where Socrates is not disturbed by his own conviction at trial.
38. Cf. *Republic* 328a7 (*re* the torch-race that prompts Socrates to stay) and 619e6 (*re* the sight of souls choosing lives in the myth of Er).
39. Boedecker (2001a, 2001b).
40. Trans. Meineck in Reeve (2002).
41. Plato's lively portraits of Socratic argument often employ allusions to Socrates' behavior in hand-to-hand combat situations at the moment an Athenian phalanx lines collapses, that is, to his "refusal to join the panicky frenzy that overtook most of the Athenian army" (Hanson 2003, 213). For example: *Crito* 51b–cb; *Phaedo* 88e–89a; *Laches* 188b and 191a; *Euthydemus* 307b; *Republic* 473e–474b, 471d. On argument as war see also *Gorgias* 513d and *Phaedo* 106c.
42. I owe this way of reading this passage to a conversation with L. A. Tritle.
43. Cf. Odysseus' reluctance to talk among the Phaeacians.
44. On the importance of converting fragmented memories into narratives, see Herman (1992). An anecdote is apt here. Tammy Duckworth was a helicopter pilot in the Iraq War. She was grievously injured in a crash and lost her legs. She recovered and went on to serve as assistant secretary of Public and Intergovernmental Affairs for the United States Department of Veterans Affairs from 2009 to 2011. In a public setting in 2012, she explained that she does not suffer from PTSD and she thinks that is due to the fact that part of her medical care post-crash involved repeated (nearly daily) efforts to tell her story and create a narrative that she could treat as a chapter in her life. She reported that some of the men on her helicopter who were far less seriously wounded physically on that terrible day still suffer from severe PTSD years later—something she attributes to their lack of similar opportunities to craft narratives about what they suffered. Author's notes from a "Talk-Back Session" following a "Theater of War" performance at the National Veterans' Art Museum, Chicago, January 25, 2012.
45. This visit with the Thracian physician might be the trip to the Isthmus *epi theorian* referred to at *Crito* 52b.
46. At *Apology* 28e Socrates lists the three campaigns out of historical order. On why see Calder (1961).
47. Contra Benardete (1963, 174): "he mentions his soldierly duty only to dismiss it."
48. Cf. Shay (1994, 169): "damaging personality changes" frequently follow severe trauma.
49. The language of obedience to commanders calls to mind Simonides' famous epitaph for the Spartans at Thermoplyae and the poet's case for their deathlessness. In the Scottish poet Robert Crawford's recent translation: "Stranger, take this message to our masters: we lie here dead. We did as we were told." McBeath and Crawford (2012, xiv).
50. Some peculiar features of the reference to Homer's *Iliad* 18.104 at *Apology* 28d might also confirm the importance Socrates attaches to a capacity to yield to "commanders" on deployment and in moral argument. See Benardete (1963, 174–5).

51. Cf. Metcalf (2009) and Hobbs (2000, 178) on Plato's comparison of Socrates to Achilles. Hobbs observes at *Crito* 44a–b a subtle allusion to Achilles' behavior in *Iliad* 9 that supports my reading: "Socrates emerges from the implied comparison not Achilles' equal but as his superior" (Hobbs 2000, 186).

52. Shay 1994. Also see Sherman (2013, 156–64).

53. How far the story of Palamedes (also noted at *Apology* 41b and quoted above) develops similar themes is hard to assess. Palamedes does not appear in the *Iliad*. Works of Aeschylus, Sophocles, and Euripides focused on his story survive only in fragments. Orators seem to have used his story to display their rhetorical chops (e.g., Gorgias, *In Defense of Palamedes*). The story of his death as related in later sources (describing accounts of lost early epics, see Apollodorus *Epitome* E.3.7) fits my account of Plato's interest in the figure. Palamedes was a hero at Troy who tangled with Odysseus. Palamedes exposes Odysseus' ruse to avoid conscription in the Trojan War (Odysseus feigned madness). Still furious nine years later, Odysseus maliciously accuses him of treason and manufactures false evidence. Palamedes is thus unjustly convicted and stoned to death.

54. See Crowley (2012) and in this volume. This does not preclude raising objections to specific policy decisions and actions performed during the prosecution of the war. See Socrates' objections to the treatment of the generals who served at Arginousae (*Apology* 32b).

55. Cf. *Protagoras* 359e–360a.

56. Socrates also mocks the postwar veneration of Pericles in the *Menexenus*. See chapters 3 and 7 of Monoson (2000). In *Apology* Plato has Socrates indicate that his moral objections to the appetite for empire were sometimes mistaken for disloyal, oligarchic (i.e., Spartan) sympathizing. Also see Connor 1991 on why some of Socrates' contemporaries might have mistaken his philosophical mannerisms for evidence of Spartan sympathies.

57. Trans. Irwin (1979).

58. I borrow this phrase from Christ (2006).

59. On *parrhesia* (frank speech) and philosophical examination in the *Gorgias*, see Monoson (2000, 161–5); Saxonhouse (2006); and Tarnopolsky (2010).

60. Sherman (2013, 143, 148).

61. Sherman (2013, 156–64).

62. Sherman (2013, 148).

63. Sherman (2013, 148 and *passim*).

64. Plato's discussion betrays a concern to understand how the psyche experiences combat and homecoming, not a partisan political admiration for oligarchic Sparta.

65. Nails (2012) sees a systematic response to the catastrophes of the Peloponnesian War evident in the structure of the *Republic*. Also see Schofield (2006, 203–12) and Saxonhouse (1983). The discussions of military practices across the dialogues betray sensitivity to precisely the kinds of problems, troubles, and mishaps Socrates encountered on campaign and their calamitous consequences for Athens. For example: Socrates' skill escaping the Boeotians at Delium is proof that young men should learn to use weapons (*Laches* 182a–b); Socrates reproaches Euthydemus for treating military service as a diversion from the search for wisdom instead of part of a philosophical life (*Euthydemus* 273c–274a); and Socrates chastises Ion for identifying competent generalship with familiarity with Homer (*Ion, passim*). Moreover, the military training outlined in the *Laws* includes learning to endure hardships such as poor food and extreme temperatures (*Laws* 942d–e), easily suggesting Socrates at Potidaea. The *Laws* also provides for extreme care to be taken when evaluating the quality of a soldier's service upon his return in ways that suggest appreciation of the ordeals endured and witnessed by Socrates. Prizes for valor should need the backing not only of commanders but also of

fellow soldiers, eyewitnesses, and other evidence (943b–c). Assessment of servicemen's behavior in battles that turned out to be calamitous for the army must pay very serious attention to the circumstances so as to distinguish between criminal neglect of duty and simple bad luck (943d–944e). On how far these texts influenced policy debates in Athens, see Allen 2010.

66. Cf. πῶς ἐσώθης ἐκ τῆς μάχης; at *Charmides* 153b (Chaerophon's question to Socrates upon his return from Potidaea).

67. Plato's expectation that excellence at war and philosophy will go hand in hand is evident in the opening scene of the *Theaetetus* (142a–c). There, a philosophical conversation conducted by a young Theaetetus is recalled on the occasion of the news that this great, now much older, philosopher has just returned from war grievously wounded. It is also evident in Plato's characterization of Socrates' main interlocutors in the *Republic*, Glaucon and Adeimantus. At *Republic* (368a), Socrates links his confidence in their intellectual sophistication to his knowledge of their honorable conduct in war. Also see Blondell (2002, 261). On the proximity of philosophy and war in Plato's *Republic* also see Nails (2012).

68. Τῷ βουλεύεσθαι, ἦν δ᾽ ἐγώ, περὶ τὸ γεγονὸς καὶ ὥσπερ ἐν πτώσει κύβων πρὸς τὰ πεπτωκότα τίθεσθαι τὰ αὑτοῦ πράγματα, ὅπῃ ὁ λόγος αἱρεῖ βέλτιστ᾽ ἂν ἔχειν. *Republic* 604c.

69. Shay (1995) and Meineck (2009).

70. See Shay 1994 on the "communalization of trauma." Plato rejects what Balot calls Athenian-style collective "grief-work" (2013, 187–8).

71. The Myth of Er has puzzled commentators for some time. An exception is Baracchi (2001) who links it to Plato's discussion of war.

72. At *Gorgias* 525d Socrates mentions that Thersites' actions in the *Iliad*, while wrong, do not amount to an incurable offence. And so the point here may be just to note that he is indeed among those who are reborn, not condemned to eternal punishment (as are tyrants, *Republic* 615d).

73. White (2007, 124). Bertolt Brecht, Georg Kaiser, and a little-known American playwright who dramatized Brecht's story (Levinson 1965) conscript Socrates for pacifism. Cf. Monoson (2011) on efforts to enlist Socrates as a symbol of democracy during World War II and the Cold War.

Bibliography

Ahbel-Rappe, Sara, and R. Kamtekar, eds. 2009. *A Companion to Socrates.* Oxford: Wiley-Blackwell.

Albrizzi, Isabella Teotchi, Leopoldo Cicognara, and Melchior Missirini. 1824. *The Works of Antonio Canova in Sculpture and Modeling, Engraved in Outline by Henry Moses.* London: H.G. Bohn.

Allen, Danielle S. 2010. *Why Plato Wrote.* Oxford: Wiley-Blackwell.

Anderson, Mark. 2005. "Socrates as Hoplite." *Ancient Philosophy* 25: 273–89.

Balot, Ryan. 2013. "The Psychology of Just and Unjust Wars: A Response to Sherman." In *Loyalty: NOMOS LIV*, edited by Sanford Levinson, Joel Parker, and Paul Woodruff, 175–91. New York: New York University Press.

Baracchi, Claudia. 2001. *Of Myth, Life and War in Plato's Republic.* Bloomington: Indiana University Press.

Bekker-Nielson, T., and L. Hannestad, eds. 2001. *War as a Cultural and Social Force: Essays on Warfare in Antiquity.* Copenhagen: Reitzel.

Benardete, Seth. 1963. "Some Misquotations of Homer in Plato." *Phronesis* 8(2):174–8.

Blondell, Ruby. 2002. *The Play of Character in Plato's Dialogues.* Cambridge: Cambridge University Press.

Boedecker, D. 2001a."Heroic Historiography: Simonides and Herodotus on Plataea." In D. Boedecker and David Sider 2001: 120–1.

———. 2001b "Paths to Heroization at Plataea." In D. Boedecker and David Sider 2001: 148–63.

Boedecker, D., and Sider, D., eds. 2001. *The New Simonides. Contexts of Praise and Desire*. Oxford: Oxford University Press.

Brown, C. L., and P. D. Morgan, eds. 2006. *Arming Slaves: From Classical Times to the Modern Age*. New Haven, CT: Yale University Press.

Bury, R. G. 1909. *The Symposium of Plato*. Cambridge: Cambridge University Press.

Calder, W. M., III. 1961. "Socrates at Amphipolis (*Ap.* 28e)." *Phronesis* 6(2): 83–5.

Chaniotis, A., and P. Ducrey, eds. 2002. *Army and Power in the Ancient World*. Stuttgart: Franz Steiner Verlag.

Christ, M. R. 2006. *The Bad Citizen in Classical Athens*. Cambridge: Cambridge University Press.

Connor, W.R. 1991. "The Other 399." *Georgica: Greek Studies in Honor of George Cawkwell, Bulletin, Institute for Classical Studies* (London), suppl. 58:49–56.

Cooper, John M., ed. 1997. *Plato. Complete Works*. Indianapolis, IN: Hackett.

Crosby, A. W. 2002. *Throwing Fire: Projectile Technology through History*. Cambridge: Cambridge University Press.

Crowley, Jason. 2012. *The Psychology of the Athenian Hoplite: The Culture of Combat in Classical Athens*. Cambridge: Cambridge University Press.

Denyer, Nicholas. 2007. *Protagoras, Plato*. Cambridge Greek and Latin Classics (Greek text and commentary). Cambridge: Cambridge University Press.

Edmunds, Lowell. 2004. "The Practical Irony of the Historical Socrates." *Phoenix* 58(3/4):193–207.

———. 2006. "What Was Socrates Called?" *Classical Quarterly* 56(2): 414–25.

Finkel, David. 2013. *Thank You for Your Service*. New York: Farrar, Straus and Giroux.

Graham, Daniel. 2008. "Socrates on Samos." *Classical Quarterly* 58: 308–13.

Hamilton, C. D. and P. Krentz, eds. 1997. *Polis and Polemos: Essays on Politics, War and History in Ancient Greece in Honor of Donald Kagan*. Claremont: Regina Books.

Hanson, V. D. 1989. *The Western Way of War: Infantry Battle in Classical Greece*. New York: Knopf.

———. ed. 1991. *Hoplites: The Classical Greek Battle Experience*. London: Routledge.

———. 2003. *Ripples of Battle*. New York: Doubleday.

Herman, J. L. 1992. *Trauma and Recovery: The Aftermath of Violence from Domestic Abuse to Political Terror*. New York: Basic Books.

Hobbs, Angela. 2000. *Plato and The Hero: Courage, Manliness and the Impersonal Good*. Cambridge: Cambridge University Press.

Hodkinson, S. and Anton Powell, eds. 2006. *Sparta and War*. Swansea: The Classical Press of Wales.

Holt, Philip. 1992. "Ajax's Burial in Early Greek Epic." *American Journal of Philology* 113(3): 319–31.

Hughes, Betthany. 2010. *The Hemlock Cup*. New York: Knoff.

Irwin, Terence. 1979. *Plato, Gorgias. Translated with Notes*. Oxford: Clarendon Press.

Johns, Christopher. 1997. *Antonio Canova and the Politics of Patronage in Revolutionary and Napoleonic Europe*. Berkeley: University of California Press.

Kane, Robert L. 1996. "Ajax and the Sword of Hector. Sophocles' *Ajax* 815–822." *Hermes* 124(1): 17–28.

Kern, Paul B. 1999. *Ancient Siege Warfare*. Bloomington: Indiana University Press.

King, Helen. 2001. "Recovering Hysteria from History: Herodotus and the First Case of Shell Shock." In *Contemporary Approaches to the Study of Hysteria*, 36–48. Oxford: Oxford University Press.

Konstan, David. 2010. "Ridiculing a Popular War: Old Comedy and Militarism in Classical Athens." In Pritchard 2010, 184–200.

Lapatin, Kenneth. 2009. "Picturing Socrates." In Ahbel-Rappe and Kamtekar 2009, 110–55.

Levinson, Alfred. 1965. "Socrates Wounded" [1959]. In *New American Plays*, edited by Robert W. Corrigan, 45–82. New York: Hill and Wang.

Lodewyck, Laura, and S. Sara Monoson. 2015. "Performing for Soldiers: 21st Century Experiments in Greek Theatre in the U.S." In *Oxford Handbook of Greek Drama in the Americas*, edited by Kathryn Bosher, Fiona McIntosh, Justine McConnell, and Patrice Rankine, chapter 37. Oxford: Oxford University Press.

Maguen, S., and B. Litz. 2012. "Moral Injury in Veterans of War." *PTSD Research Quarterly* 23(1).

Mainz, Valerie. 2007. "Bringing the Hemlock Up: Jacques-Louis David's Socrates and the Inventions of History." In Trapp 2007a, 249–67.

Mayor, Adrienne. 2009. *Greek Fire, Poison Arrows and Scorpion Bombs: Biological and Chemical Warfare in the Ancient World.* London: Duckworth.

McBeath, Norman, and Robert Crawford. 2011. *Simonides.* Edinburgh: Easel Press.

McCann, D. R., and B. S. Strauss, eds. 2001. *War and Democracy: A Comparative Study of the Korean War and the Peloponnesian War.* Armonk, NY: M.E. Sharpe.

Meineck, Peter. 2009. "These Are Men Whose Minds the Dead Have Ravished: Theater of War/The Philoctetes Project." *Arion* 17(1): 173–91.

Metcalf, Robert. 2009. "Socrates and Achilles." In *Reexamining Socrates in the Apology*, edited by Patricia Fagan and John Edward Russon. Evanston: Northwestern University Press.

Monoson, S. Sara. 2000. *Plato's Democratic Entanglements: Athenian Politics and the Practice of Philosophy.* Princeton, NJ: Princeton University Press.

———. 2011. "The Making of a Democratic Symbol: The Case of Socrates in North-American Popular Media 1941–55." *Classical Receptions Journal* 3(1): 46–76.

Nagy, Gregory. n.d. Translation of Proclus' account of the *Little Iliad*. http://news.rapgenius.com/Gregory-nagy-proclus-summary-of-the-little-iliad-lyrics. Center for Hellenic Studies: Washington DC.

Nails, Debra. 2002. *The People of Plato: A Prosopography of Plato and Other Socratics.* Indianapolis: Hackett.

———. 2012. "Plato's *Republic* in Its Athenian Context." *History of Political Thought* 33(1): 1–23.

Planeaux, C. 1999. "Socrates, Alcibiades, and Plato's *ta Poteideatika*. Does the *Charmides* Have a Historical Setting?" *Mnemosyne* 52: 72–7.

Plant, Margaret. 2003. *Venice: Fragile City, 1797–1997.* New Haven, CT: Yale University Press.

Pritchard, D. M., ed. 2010. *War, Democracy and Culture in Classical Athens.* Cambridge: Cambridge University Press.

Raaflaub, K., ed. 2007a. *War and Peace in the Ancient World.* Oxford: Oxford University Press.

———. 2007b. "Warfare in Athenian Society." In *The Cambridge Companion to the Age of Pericles*, edited by L. Samons, 96–124. Cambridge: Cambridge University Press.

Reeve, C. D. C. 2002. *The Trials of Socrates. Six Classics Texts: Plato, Aristophanes, Xenophon.* Indianapolis, IN: Hackett.

Sabin, P., H. van Wees, and M. Whitby, eds. 2007. *Cambridge History of Greek and Roman Warfare, Vol. I: Greece, the Hellenistic World and the Rise of Rome.* Cambridge: Cambridge University Press.

Saxonhouse, Arlene. 1983. "An Unspoken Theme in Plato's *Gorgias*, War." *Interpretation* 11: 139–69.

———. 2006. *Free Speech and Democracy in Ancient Athens.* Cambridge: Cambridge University Press.

Schofield, Malcolm. 2006. *Plato. Political Philosophy.* Oxford: Oxford University Press.

Segal, Charles. 1978. "'The Myth Was Saved:' Reflections on Homer and the Mythology of Plato's *Republic*." *Hermes* 106(2): 315–36.

Shay, Jonathan. 1994. *Achilles in Vietnam. Combat Trauma and the Undoing of Character.* New York: Scribner.

———. 1995. "The Birth of Tragedy—Out of the Needs of Democracy." *Didaskalia. The Journal for Ancient Performance* 2(2): 1–5.

———. 2002. *Odysseus in America. Combat Trauma and the Trials of Homecoming.* New York: Scriber.

Sherman, Nancy. 2013. "A Fractured Fidelity to a Cause." In *Loyalty: NOMOS LIV*, edited by Sanford Levinson, Joel Parker, and Paul Woodruff, 139–174. New York: New York University Press.

Strassler, R. B., ed. 1996. *The Landmark Thucydides.* New York: Free Press.

Tarnopolsky, Christina 2010. *Prudes, Perverts and Tyrants. Plato's Gorgias and the Politics of Shame.* Princeton, NJ: Princeton University Press.

Trapp, M., ed. 2007a. *Socrates from Antiquity to the Enlightenment.* London: Ashgate.

———. 2007b. *Socrates, in the Nineteenth and Twentieth Centuries.* London: Ashgate.

Tritle, L. A. 2004. "Xenophon's Portrait of Clearchus: a study in post-traumatic stress disorder," in C. Tuplin, ed., *Xenophon and His World. Historia Einzelschriften* 172: 325–39. Stuttgart: Franz Steiner Verlag.

———. 2010. *A New History of the Peloponnesian War.* Oxford: Wiley-Blackwell.

Trundle, Matthew. 2004. *Greek Mercenaries: From the Late Archaic Period to Alexander.* London: Routledge.

Van Wees, H. 2004. *Greek Warfare: Myths and Realities*. Bristol: Bristol Classical Press.

White, John J. 2007. "The Thorn of Socrates: Georg Kaiser's *Alcibiades Saved* and Bertolt Brecht's *Sokrates Wounded*." In Trapp 2007b: 119–40.

Woodbury, Leonard. 1971. "Socrates and Archelaus." *Phoenix* 25(4): 299–309.

Wright, James. 2012. *Those Who Have Borne the Battle: A History of America's Wars and Those Who Fought Them*. New York: Public Affairs.

CHAPTER SEVEN

The Memory of Greek Battle: Material Culture and/as Narrative of Combat

JUAN SEBASTIAN DE VIVO

Warfare in ancient Greece presents us with a fascinating insight not only into the workings of memory, but also into the intersections of memory, trauma, and material culture. From the *Iliad* to the Peloponnesian War and beyond, we constantly witness men at war, men who deliberated about war and commemorated it, who glorified it, denounced it, and incorporated it into their lives in countless ways. At each stage, not surprisingly, material culture served to underscore the process; whether as trophy, booty, armor, land, ships, money, monuments, and, even, temples, the aims, results, and consequences of warfare were deeply embedded within the material life of ancient Greece. Indeed, even the temples at the Athenian Akropolis, long a monument to Greek civilization, are redolent with material strategies to commemorate warfare.[1]

Though warfare was an ever-present feature of life in ancient Greece from the Bronze Age until the Roman conquest, I focus in this chapter upon late archaic and early classical Greece, the transition from the small "Dark Age" communities to the urban social structures of the polis. During this moment of transition, the rise of new technologies of battle had important repercussions for the subsequent understanding and narrative of the experience, particularly the Corinthian helmet and the *tropaion*, or battlefield trophy. I will argue that, given the form of the Corinthian helmet, the individual experience of battle was an inherently chaotic one, a consequence of the helmet's severe restriction of the individual's sight and hearing. Lacking the ability to apply to sensory experience, then, in order to build an account of the event, ready-made narrative structures *extrinsic* to the individual as a first-person participant became the means through which he represented, remembered, and communicated the event. Here, material culture became crucial. I therefore look at one particular means of materially concretizing and commemorating the event, the *tropaion*. I argue that the *tropaion* was the means through which the actual battle was first structured and understood by the individual. It was through the *tropaion,* in fact, that the first-person experience was systematically replaced by political and communal narratives of victory and defeat. What should have been a narrative of experience ("this happened to me") becomes a statement of political significance ("we were victorious in this battle"). As such, it becomes both a justification of the battle and an erasure of its potentially traumatic dimension.

The Corinthian Helmet and the Individual Experience of Battle

I should like to begin with the Corinthian helmet, and to focus upon one particular example (Figure 7.1). It is in the so-called Corinthian style, the iconic form that crowned the Greek hoplite panoply from the seventh to the fifth century BCE[2] Its form represents the gradual advance from early Near Eastern helmets in the form of a bowl or cone—protection for the wearer's head at its most basic level—that gradually descends to cover the wearer's ears, cheeks, and the back of the neck.[3] The earliest representation we possess, a bronze votive figurine from Delphi, is from the early seventh century BCE.

This particular example is a typical and even "middling" instance of its type.[4] It is of carefully worked bronze, with long curving lines that conform fairly closely to the shape of the head when worn, and allow it to rest

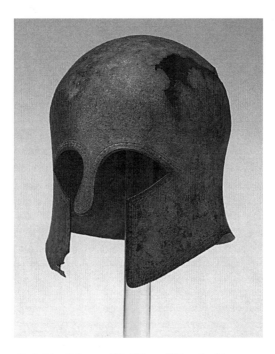

Figure 7.1   Bronze Corinthian Helmet, c. 700–500 BCE. Walters Art Museum, acc. no. 54.2304. Image courtesy of the museum.

somewhat comfortably on top of the head when not in actual use.[5] It has sharply outlined almond-shaped eyeholes and tapering cheek guards, covering virtually the entire head, face, and neck. It includes small perforations along its edges for the attachment of an inner lining, probably of leather or felt, that would have cushioned—if only slightly—against direct contact with the hard metal. The helmet has no decoration, no inscription, no relief work, or applied ornament that might signify ritual or elite connotations: this is a functional Corinthian helmet, pure and simple.

It was originally unearthed with the cheek guards and nosepiece twisted upward, a ritual practice meant to "kill" the helmet before it was dedicated and later buried at a Panhellenic temple, probably the Temple of Zeus at Olympia.[6] Many of the extant examples at Olympia exhibit similar wear. Though we know this much, we have no actual provenance for the helmet; it was most likely excavated in the nineteenth century expressly for the antiquities market, when the cheek guards and nosepiece were "repaired" for sale—basically bent back down.

This Corinthian helmet represents, in fact is the culmination of, a set of social processes that completely transformed Greece in the late eighth century BCE, processes deeply implicated with the rise of the hoplite and the massed battle formation of the phalanx.[7] These social, technological, and political revolutions in the realm of warfare resulted not just in a new *form* of warfare but in a material toolkit—the hoplite panoply—that was to alter profoundly the sociopolitical fate of the Mediterranean and Near Eastern Worlds. This hoplite panoply, underscored by an impetus toward increased defensive capabilities, consisted of a sword, javelin, a bronze bell-corselet or cuirass, bronze greaves, and guards for the upper and lower arms, thighs, loins, ankles, and feet, as well as the *hoplon* shield (from which the hoplite is supposed to have derived his name).[8] This shield, much larger than the preceding round shields of the earlier panoply, required an armband (the *porpax*) and a grip (the *antilabe*) upon the shield's edge, with which the hoplite could easily maneuver the shield into an oblique angle, thus avoiding cast weapons, and perhaps more importantly, distribute the weight of the shield throughout his left arm. This in turn allowed for easier movement of the right arm without sacrificing the extraordinary cover afforded by the shield, usually measuring about four feet across. All in all, the Greek hoplite entered battle with a level of defensive military capabilities that would, by the fifth century BCE, transform him into the most successful soldier in the Mediterranean and Near Eastern worlds, victorious even against the overwhelming manpower of the Persian Empire.[9]

Though it is impossible to estimate the prevalence of the Corinthian helmet in relation to other helmet types, we can advance tentative estimates based upon the data at hand. Finds from Olympia tend to take center stage, as they prove the most complete and well published (and indeed, among the most excavated: the site has been explored since the late eighteenth century and formally excavated since the middle of the nineteenth).[10] Today, on display and within its storerooms, the Olympia Archaeological Museum possesses approximately 250 helmets inclusive of all types and periods,[11] while Pflug estimates the total number of known Corinthian helmets at approximately 550, all in bronze (Pflug 1989). My own count at the Olympia Archaeological Museum arrived at 179 Corinthian helmets in storage against 22 Chalcidian and thirteen Illyrian, while on display there are 19 Corinthian, 2 Chalcidian, and 5 Illyrian examples, for a total of 198 Corinthian, 24 Chalcidian, and 18 Illyrian (not including fragments). An additional two Corinthian examples are on display at the Museum for the History of the Olympic Games at Olympia. Eero Jarva, in his own survey of the material, locates approximately 350 helmets excavated at Olympia (including examples no longer housed at the Olympia Archaeological Museum): of these, 250 are Corinthian helmets, 31 are *kegelhelme* (conical), 41 are Illyrian helmets, and 31 are Chalcidian (Jarva 1995). Based upon these figures, Jarva proposes a relatively straightfor-ward conclusion:[12] items for which low numbers have survived were not as prevalent as those for which we have higher numbers. So, given the scarcity of *kegelhelme*, for example, Jarva surmises their use was more limited, say, than Corinthian helmets.[13] Ultimately, Jarva argues (and I concur), the larger survival rate of Corinthian-type helmets testifies to its more widespread use against other types.

It is important to note that, although a more prevalent helmet type in comparison to others, we cannot speak in absolute numbers when it comes to the Corinthian helmet; we cannot know what proportion of the total fighting population owned and wore this type (the numbers required include total fighting population set against the number of helmet-wearers by period). Moreover, the Corinthian helmet was quite difficult to manu-facture and was probably made to order, thus making it quite expensive. Its method of production indeed was quite extraordinary: it was crafted from a single piece of bronze, a process that required a considerable amount of skill from the bronzesmith (Snodgrass 1967).

Though bronze-casting reached very sophisticated levels in Greece (Mattusch 1980, 1986), and had already done so in the Near East (Maryon 1949), the production of the Corinthian bronze helmet from around the late eighth century BCE proved an ingenious combination of metalworking techniques more akin to working in silver or gold (much softer metals and significantly easier to shape than bronze or iron) than to the manufacture of weapons, which, though noteworthy, is not entirely surprising, given the interconnected nature of metalworking crafts throughout the ancient world.[14] The actual production of the Corinthian helmet appears to be a variant of the standard beaten hollowware that had been practiced in the Near East at least since the third millennium BCE, consisting of an already cast, bowl-shaped cap that is laboriously hammered and thinned, constantly being reheated in order to remain malleable, without of course becoming too brittle and shattering.[15] Because the helmet was not of uniform thick-ness, simply hammering out the shape from an unworked bronze sheet is highly unlikely, as one could with gold or silver;[16] instead, the shaped cap or bowl was most likely cast in the lost-wax process with a basic variation in thickness already a part of the mold,[17] and with pin inserts within the pre-forms that would then become the perforations for the attachment of the helmet's inner lining.[18] Any attached parts, cast separately, would have then been affixed to the helmet (riveted or soldered), and decorative elements embossed, engraved, applied, or raised through repoussé, processes at which Greek bronzesmiths displayed considerable skill.[19] A Chalcidian helmet in the Olympia Archaeological Museum (inv. B6900), for example, displays particularly fine relief work, with figures of reclining bearded warriors on the sides, while a later Corinthian helmet (inv. B4691) includes similar relief work featuring ram's heads applied to the cheek guards.

In terms of cost, Aristophanes, in *Pax*, famously has the Armorer mention a price of ten minae for a bronze cuirass (Jackson 1987), a price certainly significant for an average hoplite, while Socrates, in conversation with the armorer Pistias in Xenophon's *Memorabilia*, mentions a fashion for orna-mented and gold-plated breastplates, certainly beyond the reach of all but a few (τοὺς ποικίλους καὶ τοὺς ἐπιχρύσους θώρακας: 3.10.14). The price for a full panoply is estimated by Meiggs and Lewis to be 30 Attic drachmae which, as Jackson points out, was still a substantial sum (Meiggs and Lewis 1969). We do not possess much data on the actual cost of the helmet itself.

Protection is the key to our understanding of this object. The Corinthian helmet afforded its wearer a remarkable and unprecedented level of pro-tection, covering virtually the entire head, including the cheeks, nose, and neck almost to the collarbone. A Greek hoplite could thus be reasonably safe from all but the most direct and forceful blows, and focus instead upon the immediate task of maintaining the integrity of the phalanx against the pushing and hacking of his opponents.[20] This protection, however, as I men-tioned earlier, came with a qualification: the more the head is covered, after all, the more the head is covered. So the Corinthian helmet, while affording important protection to the Greek hoplite, in battle severely restricted the wearer's vision and hearing.

Thus, the Corinthian helmet provides a suggestive account of the expe-rience of battle: it was, at the level of the first-person participant, inher-ently chaotic: fragmented, unruly, disjointed. The individual could see barely anything, after all, and hear only muffled thuds, clanks, and screams. There are no sensory data with which to build an account, except for a series of actions inflicted directly upon the body, and no narrative organizational principle to shape them, except for a strictly temporal one: "this, then this, then this happened to me." Though interpretive frameworks could be extracted and deployed to organize events with recourse to other agents beside the self—this person is attacking my unit by these means, for this reason, from this place—this immediately sets the experiencing body as audience, and removes him from the immediate flow of events as experi-enced in the first person. On the ground, at the individual level, one is cast in the midst of events registered only insofar as they have an immediate physical effect upon the body, and upon those in one's direct vicinity: only when the phalanx breaks, and the actual battle ends, do events again take significance beyond this chaos, and again become intelligible, narratable. The experience of battle, then, was inherently chaotic, and only afterward could it be organized. This is dramatized in Euripides' *Suppliant Women,* where the Messenger's account of the battle in 673–726—characterizing the Messenger as an *observer* who claims authority for his account by means of direct observation in (684)—is contrasted to that of Theseus, who, upon his return, declares that "when a man is face-to-face with the foe, he could hardly see even that which is his duty to observe" (856).

An experiment by Adam Schwartz of the University of Copenhagen bears this out. Schwartz used a reconstructed model of an average Corinthian helmet of the Myros-Gruppe in the Olympia Archaeological Museum (inv. no. M24), in order to determine the range of vision available to the wearer. He notes,

> Wearing the helmet, the test subject could relatively clearly discern objects at height of head one meter in front of her and within a radius of c. one meter to either side. Beyond this line objects quickly blurred and disappeared out of sight. At 0.5 m distance, only objects within 0.5 m to either side were visible. Without the helmet, the range of vision at a distance of one meter was more than 1.5 m to either side, and as much as one meter at 0.5 m distance. It is difficult to achieve complete accuracy; but it is certainly safe to say that a helmet of Corinthian type does restrict vision.

He continues:

> Moreover, as anyone who has tried on a domino mask will admit, eye-shaped and -sized apertures can easily block or obscure vision precisely *because* they are shaped after the eye: unless it is very securely fastened to the face, it takes only the tiniest of shifts for a domino mask to become dislodged and obscure vision or cut it off entirely. (Schwartz 2009)

Based upon principles methodologically justified by experimental archaeology and phenomenology, Schwartz makes two important contributions to the discussion at hand: first, the Corinthian helmet did significantly restrict the wearer's range of vision (as well as hearing); and second, this restriction was probably worsened by shifts in the helmet's position, mitigated in part by the chinstrap but nonetheless undoubtedly inevitable in actual battle.[21] Fit, then, was an important element, and one powerful reason to assume that helmets were made to order; it was a complex balance between a snug fit (attached padding included) to prevent slippage and a fit loose enough to allow the wearer to put it on quickly and take it off—in the case of pursuit—even quicker. My research at the Olympia Archaeological Museum points to a similar conclusion: while earlier helmet forms tend to have thinner edges and less substantial nose guards—in theory lessening their impact upon the wearer's vision—the actual total size of the eyeholes tends to be significantly smaller, mitigating any substantial potential gain in range of vision, which, as the form develops and matures, tends to hold steady. With the Myros-Gruppe in the seventh century BCE, we see significant thickening of the front edges of the helmet, particularly the eyeholes and nose guard, an evolution accompanied, however, by eyeholes made somewhat larger in response, thus maintaining a similar range of vision (albeit somewhat improved) to the earlier, cruder forms; in some instances of the Myros-Gruppe type, for example, we can see a thickness of 3–6 mm along the front edges.[22] It is not until the later Lamia and Hermione types of the sixth century that we are able to mark a significant change. Nonetheless, this tension remains an important problem throughout the form's history: the give and take between the helmet's defensive impetus (more coverage) and its restrictive nature (impeded vision).

The point remains: despite its defensive capabilities, the Corinthian helmet greatly restricted the individual's perception capabilities, making the experience of battle largely unnarratable. Barely able to see, his hearing muffled by clanks and screams, there was very little data in this "fog of war" from which the individual could construct a narrative of experience. It was only after the rout, once sight and hearing proved once again reliable means of perception, that the experience could be shaped into narrative. I discuss this further below.

Narratives of Battle

The aftermath of battle is never easy; no matter the outcome, the human consequences of warfare always rest upon the field, the dead and wounded of both sides. In classical Greece, for example, though casualties were comparatively light (5–14 percent according to Peter Krentz), once these are translated into human terms they cannot but become much more significant: depending upon the size of the armies fielded by the opponents, this could entail somewhere between 50 and 4,000 dead upon the field, not to mention the wounded.[23] Pamela Vaughn has identified the same gruesome aftermath of battle and locates it within the heavy task of identifying and retrieving the battle dead: both the victors and the vanquished must undertake "the grim misery of sorting and identifying the hoplite casualties" (Vaughn 1993). Faced with this field of death, how might the individual reframe this sight against the unnarratable experience immediately behind? What, in the direct aftermath, are the post-bellum practices, and how do these in turn serve to concretize the experience, to narrate it? How could Greek warriors transform the experience into something meaningful, particularly in light of the carnage that it must serve to justify? How, in other words, is the chaos from which the hoplite has just emerged shaped in relation to the horrors—and outcome—before him? Ultimately, I would suggest, the strategies of narration work as coping mechanisms against the potentially traumatic experience of battle in ancient Greece.

I argue above that a narrative of experience is problematic given the Corinthian helmet's effect upon the wearer. This, however, presupposes a direct correspondence between narrative and experience. Yet, why contend that sensory experience—sight and hearing—were in effect the means to build and validate an objective account of an event such as battle? Why, in other words, do I hold that the lack of sensory perception robbed the Greeks of the means to build an objective first-person account of their experience? Certainly a variety of discursive strategies were available to reframe experience, found in a variety of genres, from the rich symbolic discourse of myth and ritual (epic), to a performative tradition premised, in part, upon emotional engagement (theatre), to a poetic language able to reframe certain significant experiences (lyric). Tragedy, in particular, proves incredibly powerful in this respect; as Peter Meineck notes, it served in part as a "performance-based collective 'catharsis' or 'cultural therapy'." This was accomplished particularly through projection or reflection: the "traumatic experience faced by the spectators was reflected upon the gaze of the masked characters performing before them" (Meineck 2011). Tragedy, in other words, served as testimony by proxy, made especially significant given the mask's materiality: it served as container and mirror of the audience's emotional processes.

The tragic mask, moreover, presents a fascinating perspective on the interaction between materiality—particularly, the constricting nature of the mask—and experience. The mask, after all, functions in a manner quite similar to the Corinthian helmet; Meineck's interrogation of the tragic mask is ultimately a parallel to my own question on the Corinthian helmet: "Does the mask challenge normal human neural responses and produce a higher cognitive experience, more dependent on comprehending movement and processing language, and did the fixed and unmoving surface of the mask stimulate a profoundly personal, empathic visual experience that deepened the emotional response and accentuated the visceral experience of watching the drama?" The response, I would suggest, is affirmative: for the wearer, the Corinthian helmet cannot but create a state of physiological alertness, a different cognitive experience, made even more complex given the nature of the objects in his sightline. Armored and helmeted warriors become, in a sense, inhuman; their individuality as human beings (rooted, as Meineck argues, in the recognition of the face) is effaced by the Corinthian helmet.

Given this shift in the individual's ability to perceive his surroundings, I should now like to explore how this comes to affect his ability to narrate his experience. How, in other words, does experiencing combat in this manner affect the retelling of the experience? The notion of testimony, here, becomes important: can we locate the testimony of traumatic experiences in the Greek world? Does combat and its subsequent narrative constitute testimony? I use the term testimony loosely, informed largely by post-Holocaust memory studies; my interest, primarily, is in locating the narrative of difficult combat experiences in relation to the experience itself, that is, how testimony is constructed in relation to an unnarratable experience (again, the correspondence between narrative and experience).

This we find suggestively framed in Book 10 of the *Odyssey*, where Eurylochos returns to the ships after his companions are bewitched by Circe and transformed into swine: "Eurylochos came back again to the fast black ship, / to tell the story of our companions and of their dismal / fate, but *he could not get a word out, though he was trying / to speak, but his heart was stunned by the great sorrow, and both eyes / filled with tears, he could think of nothing but lamentation*" (10.244–248, my emphasis). Here we find testimony—the "story of our companions and of their dismal fate"—as a crucial strategy not only of survival, but of narration. Eurycholos, who returns to the ship to narrate a traumatic event, finds that he cannot speak, that, overwhelmed by what he witnessed (the disappearance of his companions), he can do nothing but lament. Only later is he able to speak, and here we find Odysseus' narrative in careful counterpoint to that of Eurylochos: the events that befell the party are narrated by Odysseus, while Eurylochos' own narrative includes a significant lacuna. As he tells it, the party entered the mansion and then vanished. What actually happened to them—their transformation—is unavailable to Eurylochos, much like the ability to speak, a result, one must suppose, of his "great sorrow". Only lament, then, can correspond to an experience of loss of this magnitude.

Now, the importance of testimony has long been recognized. Freud, in a short meditative paper entitled "Remembering, Repeating, and Working-Through," seeks to locate the value of testimony in the history of analytic techniques, from Josef Breuer's catharsis—what he terms "remembering and abreacting"—to free associations interpreted so as to reconstruct the narrative of the traumatic event, to a final tug of war between therapist and patient meant to identify resistances and thus formulate narrative testimony (Freud 1914). The same is the case today, where the treatment of posttraumatic stress disorder (PTSD) relies to a great extent upon the formulation and incorporation of narrative testimony: Mardi Horowitz makes this the first step in the treatment of stress response, after the patient has been evaluated and stabilized (Horowitz 2003).

All these strategies rely, to a great extent, upon the formulation of a narrative of experience grounded upon sensory data: What happened? What did I *see*? What did I *hear*? These are necessary before the event can be understood as such; this underscores the therapeutic technique that seeks to realign the event and its narrative, what Horowitz terms "telling and restructuring the story of the disastrous events as the therapist helps the patient to understand cause-and-effect sequences and to differentiate facts from fantasy." Were we to seek for this attempt at narrative within the Greeks' mediating genres (the only remnants, after all, of testimony as such), we would see a constant return to the senses, and sight in particular, as a means of narrating, of validating events. In our example above, in Book 10 of the *Odyssey*, once Eurylochos does tell his story, it is firmly grounded upon what he *saw,* vanishing companions likely the object of treachery. This establishes an authorial authority explicit earlier in the *Odyssey,* when Odysseus praises Demodocus, although in this example the qualification of learning from another privileges hearing as well as sight, given that others have seen the event and converted it into narrative:

> "Demodocus, I'd guess you're the best of any.
> You've learned from the Muse—Zeus' child—or Apollo—so well
> in order you sing the woes of the Achaeans.
> All that was done and endured and labored by them,
> *as if you had been there yourself or learned it from another.*"
> (*Odyssey* 8.487–491, my emphasis)

Similarly, in Herodotus one finds a constant interjection of authorial confirmation based upon sensory verification—"*I* myself saw this," "*I* myself heard this"—along with his own qualification regarding the truth value of accounts as he is told them, including his disavowal of those events and accounts he cannot himself evaluate—"it is said," "they say,"—and his use of indirect speech construction. Though we find this throughout the text, the trope is in full evidence in 2.3 and 2.12 (the Egyptian ethnography), where, for example, Herodotus mentions explicitly that he has confirmed *by sight* his contention that Egypt was a gulf based on comparative evidence. With Thucydides, we have this very same principle explicitly laid out in his programmatic statement in book I: "And with regard to my factual reporting of the events of the war…either I was present myself at the event which I have described or else I heard of them from eyewitnesses whose reports I have checked with as much thoroughness as possible" (I.22).

The abstraction of language, then, was constantly validated through description heavily grounded in material metaphors of sight, hearing, touch. This trope of creating a verifiable account of the world by means of sensory experience permeates Greek thought at the very least from the eighth century BCE, a trope which we must assume, with reasonable certainty, was available also to the individual as an organizational principle in his narrative of the experience of battle. The language, then, was there, the means for the individual to organize a narrative of battle in the first person, responsive to the events he experienced for himself.

Yet, here we find the principal rupture: though the individual would seek to privilege sensory data, when it came to the experience of battle there was, as we discussed, little such data available. What did he see, after all? What did he hear? There was thus no means for the individual to build a personal account of the experience, to construct a *testimony* faithful to the events he has undergone. Indeed, there was little but the contraction of time and space to an individual microcosm buried in the heaving mass of the phalanx. As the editors of the present volume mention, how could the individual Greek soldier not succumb to the temptation to organize experience along literary lines? Even the sixth-century soldier poet Archilochus, whose verse fragments are incredibly attentive to embodied experience and sensory data, ultimately communicates in lyric. His martial verses, which surely reflect his experience of battle, are ultimately elided, transformed into symbolism I discuss this further below.

How, then, to narrate the experience? How to understand it? It is here that we turn to material culture, specifically to the means by which material culture is engaged in order to create narratives of experience. How, I ask, is material culture embedded with a series of meanings that structure the individual's conception of himself, in relation both to himself and to others? How does it shape the memory of battle as narrative? I suggest that, much as Homeric discourse framed archaic and early classical conceptions of warfare, so too did Homeric understandings of material culture (particularly despoiled armor) wield tremendous influence upon the material concretization—indeed, commemoration—of battle well into the classical period. The erection of the battlefield trophy, or *tropaion,* is, I suggest, a continuation and adaptation of the semiotic charge of despoiled armor in the *Iliad* here translated to the communal context of the polis.[24] Where before a hero communicated individually by means of moral synecdoche, with the advent of the polis the same statement was undertaken in relation to the people at large.[25] In so doing, the *tropaion* serves to make an objective statement regarding the experience of battle, thus replacing a chaotic event with a tangible declaration of victory. The *tropaion* becomes the narrative.

Despoiled Armor and the Tropaion

In essence, the *tropaion* was merely the piling up on a wooden stand or tree trunk part of the vanquished army's weapons and armor, precisely at the spot where their phalanx broke and the rout began.[26] A stylized rendition appears on a red-figure *pelike* in Boston (acc. no. 20.187), dated to the mid-fifth century and marked by Beazley as the name vase of the "Trophy Painter"; it depicts a winged figure of Nike setting up a *tropaion,* with a detailed and quite complete hoplite panoply that includes a Corinthian helmet, corselet, javelin, *hoplon* shield, and a sword and scabbard. Examples from Athens (acc. no. 1683; 1447), Toronto (acc. no. 959.17.152), and Jena (acc. no. 386; 0467) display a similar (if less accomplished) motif.

There is still little agreement as to the origin and antiquity of the *tropaion.* As a form of votive practice—a ritual of thanksgiving to a deity—it is certainly linked to this ubiquitous act of worship, prevalent throughout the ancient world. By the Geometric period, the availability of tin had allowed for new modes of votive expression, quite early on linked to warfare; Langdon surveys early possible examples of warrior votives, later extensively discussed by Papalexandrou in the context of dedicatory and display practices (Langdon 1984; Papalexandrou 2005). We can surmise an early date for the actual practice of dedication on the battlefield (the *tropaion* as defined), although the term as such only makes its first appearance in Thucydides (discussed below). Thus, we can only say with certainty that it predates the Peloponnesian War.

The hoplite *tropaion* was constructed only after the defeated army had sued for the bodies of their dead, a public acknowledgment of defeat and therefore the granting to the victorious of the very right to construct the trophy. In this, it hearkens back to the uses of despoiled armor in the *Iliad*, where despoiled armor functions by moral synecdoche to signify not only victory, but the entirety of the values and virtues required of the victorious warrior within this epic framework. When a Homeric warrior displays despoiled armor, he is making a statement of victory as well as virtue, much like the term *agathos* would connote:

> the most admired type of man; and he is the man who possesses the skills and qualities of the warrior-chieftain in war and, as will be seen, in peace, together with the social advantages which such a chieftain possessed. To be *agathos,* one must be brave, skillful, and successful in war and in peace; and one must possess the wealth and (in peace) the leisure which are at once the necessary conditions for the development of these skills and the natural reward of successful employment. (Adkins 1960: 32–3)

In the epic, despoiled armor allows the heroes to embody, communicate, and commemorate themselves as successful in battle, and make use of this symbolic charge in order to locate themselves within the moral landscape of their community. When the Homeric heroes make use of despoiled armor, it is certainly as a trophy; however, unlike the *tropaion*, it does not function as a declarative to mark a *collective* victory in a particular battle and, with one possible exception, it is not location specific.

We can locate this possible exception in a critical passage that Kendrick Pritchett cites in order to date the *tropaion* earlier than the fifth century BCE (Pritchett 1974). In Book 10 of the *Iliad*, after Odysseus and Diomedes kill Dolon, they strip him of his cap, pelt, bow, and spear, which Odysseus then holds up for "Athena the Spoiler." He prays to her thus:

> Hail, goddess. These are yours. To you first of all the immortals
> on Olympus we will give your due share. Only guide us
> once again to where the Thracians sleep, and their horses.
>
> (463–464)

Having uttered his prayer, he continues:

> Lifting the spoils high from him he placed them
> upon a tamarisk bush, and piled a clear landmark beside them,
> pulling reeds together and the long branches of tamarisk
> that they might not miss them on their way back through the running
>   black night.
>
> (465–468)

The significance of this scene, beside the insight it grants us into practices of dedication, is quite far-reaching: it displays, even at this early period, the intersection of dedicatory practices and the memorialization of battle on the actual site of the encounter. Pritchett, whose monumental work on Greek warfare includes a study of the battlefield trophy, identifies this incident as the earliest example of a *tropaion* in the Greek world: "But the earliest example, although the word is not explicitly used, is surely in the Doloneia, where, after killing Dolon, Odysseus and Diomedes erect a kind of trophy in honor of Athena" (Pritchett 1974). Given the dedicatory language, the prayer to Athena the Spoiler, its form—armor hung upon a tree—and, of course, its location at the site of Odysseus' and Diomedes' victory over Dolon, this is fair conjecture to make.

However, Pritchett does not account for the fact that a few lines later, on their return to the Greek camp, Odysseus and Diomedes are explicitly said to stop and retrieve the spoils (10.528–529), and then, upon their arrival to the camp, to set them aside as a dedication to Athena at, one must assume, one of her temples back home: Odysseus "by the stern of the ship laid down the bloody / battle spoils of Dolon, to dedicate to Athene" (10.570–571).[27] Thus reframed, the despoiled objects become dedicatory and take much the same connotation as Hector's "fictional" vow in *Iliad* Book 4 to dedicate the despoiled arms of his defeated foe in the Temple of Athena at Troy.[28] If we assume the *tropaion* to be either a monument upon the battlefield or a permanent one in a civic or religious structure,[29] then it is clear that Odysseus' vow in the *Doloneia* is in fact an instance of the common dedicatory practice that survives into the fifth century BCE and beyond.[30]

As I mention above, the *tropaion* as a battlefield monument (and as a term) appears already fully articulated in Thucydides. There is thus a significant temporal gap between the despoilment of armor described in Homer and the full-fledged practice of the battlefield trophy. The dedications continue, certainly; Herodotus narrates, for example, the dedications of Gyges to Apollo at Delphi (1.50–52), and, as I noted earlier, we owe most of our extant armor examples to temple deposits at the great Panhellenic temples. I should like, however, to avoid this well-studied practice, and focus instead on the secular function of the *tropaion* and its consequences for the narrative possibilities offered the individual to frame his experience of battle.[31]

I suggest that the *tropaion* allows the individual to narrate his experience of battle as a declaration of victory. By doing so, he can locate himself by moral synecdoche within a social and ideological landscape, one that validates the horrors of battle and replaces them with a justificatory statement of identity ("we are victorious"). In other words, the *tropaion* allowed the individual a means to confront the trauma of battle by allowing him to say, in relation to this object, that he was victorious. Victory then justifies trauma. Whatever horrors characterized a particular battle, whatever losses, the victory of the polis stands as a monument justifying the horrors and losses faced by the individual warrior.

In order to fully realize the narrative significance of the *tropaion,* I should like to discuss Thucydides' conceptualization of the practice during the Peloponnesian War. Thucydides mentions the erection of a *tropaion* simply as that which the victorious army does after the battle; he offers no elaboration or discussion of the practice. This we find in 41 instances. Given the number of battles actually described in the *History of the Peloponnesian War,* it is not a large proportion, yet it does give the reader a fair characterization of the aftermath of hoplite battle in the classical period, perhaps one that, given the context, need not be repeated after every battle; Thucydides' audience, after all, would have been well acquainted with it (compare his remarks on the Corcyraean stasis: one description makes do for many). The gist is this: once one side prevails, a series of ritualized conventions come into force, whereby the defeated must formally request from the victors the bodies of their defeated compatriots, giving at this point the victor the right to erect a *tropaion.*[32] The victor also has right of despoilment over the defeated army's fallen (and, if a city, to the city itself). These formalities completed, the battle is then actually over, and the outcome set. In this way, the *tropaion* becomes a material concretization of the outcome of the battle, declaring one side the victor and grounding that victory upon the earth, literally where the victory was first performed (the turn, *trope,* of the defeated army).

Of the 41 instances of a *tropaion* in Thucydides, six mention specifically the despoilment of the enemy (3.112; 4.44; 4.97; 5.10; 5.74), drawing a clear link to the otherwise different practice in Homer. One states that the shield of Brasidas washed ashore and was later used for the *tropaion* (4.12), thus naming not only the defeated army but a specific (and famous) general. The other five specific references to a *tropaion* in the *History of the Peloponnesian War* include instances in which the erection of the trophy was contested by both sides. This is significant because it is when contested that everyday practices receive the attention and elaboration required in order to become comprehensible to subsequent historians. When we find the Greeks in dispute over the significance of the *tropaion,* we catch a glimpse of their understanding of this cultural phenomenon as it unfolds on the ground.

In 1.54 the Corinthians and Corcyraeans make competing claims to victory (the Corinthians having been victorious until nightfall and in possession of 1,000 prisoners and 70 sunk ships, while the Corcyraeans upon the arrival of Athenian reinforcements had retrieved their dead and sunk thirty ships, claiming as well that the Corinthians had retreated); in 1.105 an auxiliary force of Athenians meets a Corinthian force in Megara and both sides part with the impression they had been victorious, though it is the Athenians who set up a *tropaion,* with the Corinthians returning 12 days later at the urging of the elders to set up a *tropaion* themselves; in 4.134 the Mantineans and Tegeans meet, and one wing each routed the enemy opposite, so that, the outcome undecided, the Tegeans remain in the field and the next morning dedicate a *tropaion,* while the Mantineans return to set up their own afterward; in 7.34 a naval clash between the Athenians and Corinthians actually ends without a clear victor, with Thucydides here providing insight into the characterization of both peoples when he writes of "the Corinthians considering that they were conquerors, if not decidedly conquered, and the Athenians thinking themselves vanquished, because not decidedly victorious," with the result that the Corinthians set up a *tropaion* followed later by the Athenians; finally, in 8.24, the Athenians set up a *tropaion* in Milesian territory after defeating a small Spartan contingent, though, not being actually in possession of the field, it is taken down by the Milesians. Thucydides, then, only discusses the *tropaion* in disputed claims; elsewhere, it is simply described as a means to signify victory while here it becomes a means to challenge these claims. In no case do we find the *tropaion* not serving as a sign and symbol of victory.

Thus, the *tropaion* is both a sign and materialization of victory. As such, it activates a number of narrative possibilities both for the polis and the individual. Besides the obvious political repercussions explicit in the six contested instances above—that function at a communal level—they provide the individual with the possibility of constructing a narrative of his experience as a statement of victory. In the aftermath of battle, in the field littered with corpses and wounded, with a severely truncated perceptual experience of what actually transpired, the individual can look upon the *tropaion* and make a statement of fact: we were, I was, *victorious*. In this statement, the warrior's trauma is thus not only encapsulated but justified. This is nowhere made clearer than in Pericles' Funeral Oration, where, amidst the praises with which he seeks to inspire and indeed commemorate the Athenians, he remarks that:

> The admiration of the present and succeeding ages will be ours, since *we have not left our power without witness*, but have shown it by mighty proofs; and far from needing a Homer for our panegyrist, or other of his craft whose verses might charm for the moment only for the impression which they gave to melt at the touch of fact, we have forced every sea and land to be the highway of our daring, and everywhere, whether for evil or for good, *have left imperishable monuments behind us*. (2.41.4, emphasis mine)

Although these "imperishable monuments," I would suggest, both include and go beyond the *tropaion* (indeed, some might suggest the Athenian Acropolis in its entirety was a monument of war, as recent work by Joan Breton Connelly shows), it is clear that few carry the weight of materialized victory as effectively as the *tropaion*.

In every instance in the *History of the Peloponnesian War*, we find the *tropaion* functioning as a sign of victory and therefore in the same semantic range as despoiled armor in Homer. Much like despoiled armor, the *tropaion* allows the individual—here, of course, as part of a polis—to make a statement of victory that not only served to narrate his experience of combat, but also allowed him to justify it. Trauma is mitigated by means of material culture.

Thus, the rupture resulting from the introduction of the Corinthian helmet—from a Homeric conception of battle to the phalanx—makes it necessary to look to extrinsic narrative sources in order to conceptualize the experience of battle, and here we encounter the full communicative potential of material culture. The discursive range of despoiled armor in the *Iliad*, with all its attendant moral charge, is easily incorporated into the *tropaion*. In fact, though the transformation is invisible to us—as I mention above, from Homeric despoiled armor we jump to the fully realized, fully codified practice of erecting the *tropaion* in Thucydides—there is little difficulty in recognizing the same human impetus that lies behind both phenomena. The *tropaion* thus comes to function, alongside other means of commemoration, including epic, tragedy, votive dedications, and eventually the permanent battlefield memorials (particularly at Thermopylae and Marathon), as the means of transforming experience into narrative and therefore memory. It is also a means of transforming trauma into a narrative of justification.

In battle, unable to frame the experience on the ground, it is natural then that Greek hoplites would turn to material culture as a means to fix the event into an intelligible narrative. In becoming a narrative of victory, it carries the requisite moral charge to function as a total social fact— allowing its deployment in a variety of other contexts, social, political, etc.—as well as the emotional traction to justify what is, by all accounts, a difficult experience. This truism is only really explicitly challenged by Archilochus, whose iambic verses seek to turn the hoplite ideal on its head. In Fr. 5, the famous Shield Incident, he boasts of leaving his shield on the field in order to escape; though he loses the shield (he mentions it will delight some Saian who retrieves it, one must assume as a sign of victory), he escapes alive, to buy another just as good. Although at face value this appears a renunciation of the hoplite's heroic code (beautifully codified by Tyrtaeus' own elegiac lyrics), it is, really, a confirmation. Archilochus, as the fragment's poetic persona, claims that his life is worth more than victory (and, of course, his armor). For him to make this claim legitimately, there must be a convention against which the claim is being made. Therefore, Archilochus confirms a convention even as he seeks to undermine it.

How, then, does the *tropaion* function mediate the experience of battle? By serving as a symbol and narrative of victory, it allows the individual to narrate his experience not as a potentially traumatic experience, but as a statement of victory. So, a warrior whose experience at Marathon, for example, might have included wounding, the death of family and friends, or the intense barrage of negative emotions that mark battle (fear, hatred, disgust, etc.), could potentially turn to the *tropaion* and, instead of dwelling upon these calamities, or narrating his experience as one of wounding or loss, describe the victory that it symbolizes. By replacing the potentially traumatic narrative with one of victory, the *tropaion* serves to justify, mitigate, indeed mediate, the traumatic experience of combat.

Conclusion

In this chapter, I explore the intersections of material culture, battle, and narrative. I suggest, first, that the introduction of the Corinthian helmet—a new technology of warfare that coincided with the rise of the polis and the transformation of warfare to the communal phalanx—created an entirely new mode of experiencing battle. In particular, the restrictive nature of the Corinthian helmet made it nearly impossible for the individual warrior to access sensory data in order to construct a narrative of experience. Battle, therefore, became a chaotic "fog of war," a disorienting experience where the individual, in Theseus' words, can "hardly see even that which is his duty to observe."

Second, I survey the narrative possibilities for expressing the experience of battle in ancient Greece. I focus particularly upon the importance of sensory data in accounts of experience, where the trope of visual or oral confirmation appears again and again; from Odysseus, Eurylochos, and Demodocus in Homer's *Odyssey* to the programmatic statements of Herodotus and Thucydides, we find a continued emphasis upon visual and aural information as both building blocks as well as validation of narratives of experience. Given the difficulties that accompany the use of the Corinthian helmet, I therefore turn to material culture in order to explore the narrative possibilities therein.

With the advent of the *tropaion,* a positive means is found to lend the chaotic "fog of war" a distinct narrative shape. The *tropaion,* I suggest, presents a means to use material culture in order to shape and transform a narrative of experience: trauma becomes victory. It allows the individual to make a statement of victory that justifies the emotional and human consequences of combat. Combat as an intensely difficult and potentially traumatic experience, I suggest, is therefore justified in part through the battlefield trophy. Victory as a total social fact thus serves, in a sense, to replace a traumatic combat experience with a symbol and justification of that experience (*tropaion*). To a warrior who might dwell on the horrors of war, who might find the constricted experience of phalanx warfare overwhelming, the *tropaion* serves as testimony and reminder of his victory.

Notes

1. Breton Connelly (2014).
2. The Greek historian Herodotus mentions this helmet style once in the *Histories,* in IV.180, while describing a people in Libya, who, apparently, in the sort of bizarre ritual that Herodotus exults in describing, dress their prettiest young woman in a Corinthian helmet and Greek armor and parade her around a nearby lake. Interestingly enough, he speculates that Greek armor styles might have originally come from Egypt.

3. We possess a bronze panoply from a warrior's grave in Argos, dated to the seventh century BCE, comprising a helmet of the "Illyrian type" with a crest and a bell-corselet. This panoply represents a midway point in the helmet's evolution to the "Corinthian type," not surprising given Argos' geographical nearness to Corinth and Sparta. See Courbin (1957).

4. For a history of the form, see the definitive catalogue by Kukahn (1936), modified by Kunze (1961, 67) and Snodgrass (1964). Also discussion by Weiss (1977).

5. Cf. the Athena of the Velletri type.

6. Pritchett (1979). On the burial of the helmets, see the Olympia Excavation Reports, particularly Kunze (1961, 1967).

7. The coincidence of these two phenomena, giving rise to an infinitely entertaining question regarding precedence, and of course their relation to the polis and the rise in Greek democratic institutions, has been *extensively* discussed by historians and military historians. For a discussion of the hoplite evidence, and its possible repercussions upon Greek social structures, see Snodgrass (1965). Also van Wees (2000), who provides a useful summary of the main arguments.

8. But see Lazenby and Whitehead (1996). For an illustration of the full panoply, see Vikatou (2006). Snodgrass' work remains the standard on the subject of the panoply. See Snodgrass (1964). Homeric precedents described by Theveny (2009). The full hoplite panoply (including the additional arm, thigh, ankle, feet, and loin guards), weighing in at approximately 50–70 lbs., was not donned in its entirety; the hoplite soldier usually opted for the helmet, shield, and greaves, which themselves gradually became lighter and sleeker. At times, hoplites might have even gone into battle without a helmet or breastplate. Unlike the gradual movement toward the full-body protection of Medieval armor, Greek armor displayed a tendency over 250 years to become lighter, and later certain pieces were omitted altogether. Hanson (1989). van Wees (2004) describes the evolution of the hoplite panoply as an arc, culminating in the mid-seventh century BCE in the full hoplite panoply, and gradually devolving into the late fifth century, until finally in the fourth century the rise of mercenaries and light-armed soldiers made the cumbersome movements of the hoplite phalanx difficult to sustain.

9. Though this might seem a causal statement, it is obviously a gross oversimplification, which I will address throughout this work; suffice it to mention at the moment that, though there exist in fact countless factors affecting this state of affairs, there is little doubt that the hoplite panoply and the phalanx proved key factors.

10. Although helmets are catalogued in the Olympia Excavation Reports, the Corinthian type is specifically dealt with in volume VII. See Kunze (1961). See also Pflug (1988, 1989).

11. Including a handful of *kegelhelme* as well as one Assyrian example dedicated after the Persian Wars (supposed to be the only genuine votive dedication of armor from the Persian Wars, inscribed in stippled letters along the edge of the rim: DII ATHENAIOI MEDON LABONTES) and two Etruscan examples dedicated by Hieron of Syracuse with the same inscription: HIARON O DEINOMENEOS / KAI TOI SURAKOSIOI / TOI DI TURRANON APO KUMAS.

12. I should point out this is only an ancillary question within the much greater scope of the work, and should not detract from its achievement: it is an invaluable source for the study of ancient armor. Hans van Wees seems unnecessarily excessive in his critique, though he also acknowledges the work's strengths. van Wees (1997).

13. Here I must acknowledge that the relational nature of this statistical data, though obviously an important part of Jarva's argument, is here highlighted; Jarva also makes a

broader statistical claim, in this case that "something like 10 percent of Greek warriors of the Archaic Period must have worn the bronze cuirass." Given, as I mention, the difficulties in relating material survivals to ancient population statistics, I would be more hesitant in making a claim of this type, though the thrust of the argument—scarcer surviving objects were also in less widespread use at the time—remains largely sound. See Jarva (1995).

14. Silver has a Mohs hardness of 2.5 and a melting temperature of 961.78°C, while gold—among the most malleable of all metals—has a Mohs hardness of 2.5 and a melting temperature of 1064.18°C. The melting temperature of copper is 1084°C, while tin's is a remarkably low 232°C; depending upon the alloy, the melting temperature of bronze ranges between 1020°C for an alloy of 90 percent copper and 10 percent tin, and 750°C for an alloy of 70 percent copper and 30 percent tin. Given that most ancient bronze helmets range at 3–5 percent tin content, the melting temperature would be roughly 1050–1065°C. All this with the caveat, of course, that only the initial shape of the helmet was cast, while the bulk of the work consisted of hammering the metal into shape at a high—but not red-hot—temperature, as bronze at red-hot temperatures becomes brittle and would immediately break if hammered. See Rostoker and Gebhard (1980). For Near Eastern precedents, see Maryon (1949).

15. For a complete description of the helmet's manufacture, see Rostoker and Gebhard (1980). Most sources, including, surprisingly, Snodgrass, assume the helmet has been entirely hammered into shape, a method modified by Rostoker and Gebhard, who argue for a combination of methods. See also Fraser (1922); Coles (1962); Goldstein (1968); Williams (1977); Greenewalt and Heywood (1992); Richardson (1996); Dezsö (1998); and Rolley (2002).

16. This would have been the case with other parts of the panoply, particularly the corselet, armguards, and greaves. Given the remarkable realism which Greek bronze smiths attained in sculpting the human form, both in bronze and other materials, the creation of the "muscle cuirass" and other similar anatomically shaped defensive armor would have proved quite familiar; the techniques, after all, are the same. Cf. Richardson (1996).

17. One should note however that the central portion of the bowl, as the center from which the hammer's blows mold the helmet's shape, would therefore have been necessarily thinner; this is also the case when working with silver.

18. As Rostoker and Gebhard mention, actually hammering these after the helmet's completion would have proved virtually impossible. But see Rostoker (1986) for a technique whereby these could be punched into sheet metal, though of course for pieces without the thickness of a Corinthian helmet's nosepiece.

19. Rostoker and Gebhard (1980). The difficulty in drilling these perforations into the already completed helmet support their argument for a combination of metalworking methods, see above. For the decoration of the finished product, see the (albeit rather dated): Maryon (1949).

20. It is in fact in large part to these technological advances in Greek armor that Herodotus (IX.62) ascribes the latter's victory in the Persian Wars: "Eventually the two sides ended up grappling with each other, as the Persians caught hold of the Greeks' spears and broke them off short. In courage and strength the Persians wore no armour; besides, they did not have the skill and expertise of their opponents."

21. Schwartz's comparison of the Corinthian helmet to the domino mask is prescient: Peter Meineck's work on the mask in Greek theater points to the crucial phenomenological and, in this case, neurobiological aspects of vision, cognition, and movement while wearing a mask. Meineck's work in particular becomes important in seeking to develop

an understanding of how individuals make sense of their surroundings, of themselves in relation to others, of emotions in relation to an event. See Meineck (2011).

22. See, for example, inv. nos. B59, B4170, and 2770 at the Olympia Archaeological Museum. In the case of inv. no. B59, it was published by Kunze (no. 42 in his catalogue) citing the thickness of the edges as 3 mm (a number I would presume averaged, given the variation in the edge thickness), and of the noseguard as 8 mm. Kunze (1961).

23. Krentz (1985).

24. Though closely related to dedications at both Pan-Hellenic and local temples, the significance of this act of display lies outside the scope of this study. For the Archaic period, however, see the excellent study by Papalexandrou (2005). He notes, within the context of tripods and their anthropomorphic attachments, a drive to memorialize *kleos* through the act of dedication and display: "tripods and their dependent images played a catalytic role in the dissemination of the *kleos* of individuals" (111–3).

25. Obviously, with differing levels of inclusion: the Spartiates and Spartans cannot be tied to the *perioikoi* as the recipients of the moral weight of a victory—and a *tropaion*—while the Athenians, though more inclusive, did not by any means include *all* Athenians.

26. I should mention, of course, that our evidence is quite late, and there exists controversy also regarding the nature and composition of the *tropaion*.

27. They would have been lost in Odysseus' travels back to Ithaka.

28. Odysseus' vow, as well as Hektor's, is later found expressed in much the same terms in Aeschylus' *Septem*, where Eteocles promises, should he prevail, to give sacrifices to the gods and "θήσειν τροπαῖα πολεμίων δ' ἐσθήμασι / λάφυρα δαΐων δουρίπληχθ' ἁγνοῖς δόμοις / στέψω πρὸ ναῶν πολεμίων δ' ἐσθήματα: "to set up *tropaia* with the enemy's garments, spoils spear-pierced of war, and I will crown the holy temples with the garments of the enemy" (277).

29. Since Woelcke (1911) this remains an operative distinction, between the battlefield monument and the religious dedication at a city of sanctuary. Both are characterized as *tropaia*.

30. Though its context and shape (hung upon a tree) of course is quite suggestive in light of much scholarship focused upon the *tropaion* as a dedication. On the *tropaion* and its development as well as its nature as a religious dedication, see especially Pritchett (1974). He discusses the work of Woelcke, Janssen, Picard, and Nilsson. With the exception of Woelcke, who endeavors to collect the available testimonia and representations, most work on the *tropaion* addresses its origins and its religious significance. Rouse (1902) is representative of both views: on the dedication, he notes "so when the strife was won, the victorious host would testify their gratitude by some offering to their own deity, in the chief shrine of their own city, or in a national sanctuary like Delphi or Olympia" (96); while, on the *tropaion* specifically, he writes "I do not doubt that this is an offering to the protecting deity, set up in that spot where he had proved his present power" (99).

31. See Jackson (1991) on the dedication of armor, particularly at Olympia. The most recent survey is Stroszeck (2004).

32. Vaughn (1993).

Bibliography

Breton Connelly, J. 2014. *The Parthenon Enigma*. New York: Knopf.

Coles, J. 1962. "European Bronze Age Shields." *Proceedings of the Prehistoric Society* 28: 156–90.

Courbin, P. 1957. "Une Tombe Géométrique d' Argos." *Bulletin de Correspondance Hellénique* 81: 322–86.

Dezsö, T. 1998. *Oriental Influence in the Aegean and Eastern Mediterranean Helmet Traditions in the 9th–7th Centuries B.C.: The Patterns of Orientalization*. Oxford: British Archaeological Reports.

Fraser, A. D. 1922. "Xenophon and the Boeotian Helmet." *The Art Bulletin* 4(3): 99–108.

Freud, S. 1914:1924. "Remembering, Repeating and Working-Through: Further Recommendations on the Technique of Psycho-Analysis II." *The Standard Edition of the Complete Psychological Works of Sigmund Freud, Volume XII (1911–1913)*, edited by James Strachey, 145–56. London: Hogarth Press.

Goldstein, S. 1968. "An Etruscan Helmet in the McDaniel Collection." *Harvard Studies in Classical Philology* 72: 383–90.

Greenewalt, C. and A. Heywood. 1992. "A Helmet of the Sixth Century B.C. from Sardis." *Bulletin of the American Schools of Oriental Research* 285: 1–31.

Hallo, W., and W. Simpson. 1998. *The Ancient Near East: A History*. San Diego, CA: Harcourt Brace.

Hanson, V. D. 1989. *The Western Way of War: Infantry Battle in Classical Greece*. New York: Alfred A. Knopf.

Homer. 1951. *The Iliad*. Chicago, IL: University of Chicago Press.

Horowitz, M. 2003. *Treatment of Stress Response Syndromes*. Washington, DC: American Psychiatric Publishing.

Hoskins, J. 1998. *Biographical Objects: How Things Tell the Stories of People's Lives*. London: Routledge.

Jackson, A. 1987. "An Early Corinthian Helmet in the Museum of the British School at Athens." *The Annual of the British School at Athens* 82: 107–14.

———. 1991. "Hoplites and the Gods: the Dedication of Captured Arms and Armour." *Hoplites: The Classical Greek Battle Experience*, edited by V. D. Hanson. London: Routledge.

Jarva, E. 1995. *Archaiologia on Archaic Greek Body Armour*. Rovaniemi: Pohjois-Suomen Historiallinen Yhdistys.

Krentz, P. 1985. "Casualties in Hoplite Battles." *Greek, Roman and Byzantine Studies* 26(1): 13–20.

Kunze, E., ed. 1961. *Bericht über Die Ausgrabungen in Olympia*. Berlin: Walter de Gruyter.

———. 1967. *Bericht über Die Ausgrabungen in Olympia*. Berlin: Walter de Gruyter.

Langdon, S. 1984. *Art, Religion, and Society in the Greek Geometric Period: Bronze Anthropomorphic Votive Figurines*. PhD Thesis, University of Indiana.

Lazenby, J. F., and D. Whitehead 1996. "The Myth of the Hoplite's Hoplon." *The Classical Quarterly* 46(1): 27–33.

Maryon, H. 1949. "Metal Working in the Ancient World." *American Journal of Archaeology* 53(2): 93–125.

Mattusch, C. 1980. "The Berlin Foundry Cup: The Casting of Greek Bronze Statuary in the Early Fifth Century B.C." *American Journal of Archaeology* 84(4): 435–44.

———. 1982. *Bronzeworkers in the Athenian Agora*. Athens: American School of Classical Studies.

Meiggs, R., and D. Lewis, eds. 1969. *A Selection of Greek Historical Inscriptions to the End of the Fifth Century B.C.* Oxford: Oxford University Press.

Meineck, P. 2011. "The Neuroscience of the Tragic Mask." *Arion* 19(1): 113–58.

Murray, A. 1974. "In Perspective: A Study of David Jones' *In Parenthesis*." *Critical Quarterly* 16(3): 254–63.

Papalexandrou, N. 2005. *The Visual Poetics of Power: Warriors, Youths, and Tripods in Early Greece*. Lanham: Lexington Books.

Pflug, H. 1988. *Antike Helme: eine Ausstellung aus Anlass des XIII Internationalen Kongresses für Klassische Archäologie in Berlin*. Mainz: Römische-Germanisches Zentralmuseum.

———. 1989a. *Antike Helme*. Köln: Rheinland-Verlag.

———. 1989b. *Schutz und Zier. Helme aus dem Antikenmuseum Berlin und Waffen anderer Sammlungen*. Basle: Antikenmuseum Basel und Sammlung Ludwig.

Pritchett, W. K. 1974. *The Greek State at War*. Berkeley: University of California Press.

———. 1979. *The Greek State at War*. Berkeley: University of California Press.

Richardson, E. H. 1996. "The Muscle Cuirass in Etruria and Southern Italy: Votive Bronzes." *American Journal of Archaeology* 100(1): 91–120.

Rolley, C. 2002. "Le Travail du Bronze à Delphes." *Bulletin de Correspondance Hellénique* 126(1): 41–54.

Rostoker, W. 1986. "Ancient Techniques for Making Holes in Sheet Metal." *American Journal of Archaeology* 90(1): 93–4.

Rostoker, W., and E. Gebhard. 1980. "The Sanctuary of Poseidon at Isthmia: Techniques of Metal Manufacture." *Hesperia* 49(4): 347–63.

Rouse, W. 1902. *Greek Votive Offerings: An Essay in the History of Greek Religion*. Cambridge: Cambridge University Press.

Schwartz, A. 2009. *Reinstating the Hoplite: Arms, Armour and Phalanx Fighting in Archaic and Classical Greece*. Stuttgart: Franz Steiner Verlag.

Snodgrass, A. M. 1964. *Early Greek Armour and Weapons: From the End of the Bronze Age to 600 B.C.* Edinburgh: University of Edinburgh Press.

———. 1965. "The Hoplite Reform and History." *The Journal of Hellenic Studies* 85: 110–22.

———. 1967. *Arms and Armor of the Greeks*. Baltimore, MD: Johns Hopkins University Press.

Sparkes, B. 1987. "Greek Bronzes." *Greece & Rome* 34(2): 152–68.

Stroszeck, J. 2004. "Greek Trophy Monuments." Myth and Symbol II Conference: Symbolic Phenomena in Ancient Greek Culture, The Norwegian Institute at Athens.

Theveny, J. 2009. *Le Temps des Achéens: Histoire de la Civilisation Achéenne selon l'Iliade et l'Odyssée*. Paris: Elzévir.

van Wees, H. 1997. "Review: Greek Armour." *The Classical Review* 47(1): 154–5.

———. 2000. "The Development of the Hoplite Phalanx: Iconography and Reality in the Seventh Century." In *War and Violence in Ancient Greece*, edited by H. van Wees, 125–66. London: Duckworth.

———. 2004. *Greek Warfare: Myths and Realities*. London: Duckworth.

Vaughn, P. 1993. "The Identification and Retrieval of the Hoplite Battle-Dead." In *Hoplites: The Classical Greek Battle Experience*, edited by V. Hanson, 38–62. London: Routledge.

Vikatou, O. 2006. *Olympia: The Archaeological Site and the Museums*. Athens: Ekdotike Athenon.

von Soden, W. 1994. *The Ancient Orient: An Introduction to the Study of the Ancient Near East*. Grand Rapids: William Eerdmans Publishing.

Williams, E. R. 1977. "A Bronze Matrix for a Cuirass Pteryx." *American Journal of Archaeology* 81(2): 233–5.

Woelcke, K. 1911. *Beiträge zur Geschichte des Tropaions*. Bonn: C. Georgi.

CHAPTER EIGHT

Women and War in Tragedy

NANCY SORKIN RABINOWITZ*

The ancient Greeks were acutely aware that war took place not only on the battlefield with the armed combat of male heroes, but also in the aftermath when the women and children of the enemy were taken captive, as Thucydides describes in his *History of the Peloponnesian War*.[1] Kathy Gaca's work (2014) has shown that this "was ancient populace-ravaging warfare: that included the focused martial use of aggravated sexual assault and other bodily and psychological torments against war-captive girls and women," a practice called "andrapodization" in the prose sources.[2]

Literary sources corroborate this picture. The *Iliad* focuses mainly on the men in war, but it also gives us a spectrum of women's experiences—from the wives of the Trojans to the concubines and prizes of war, those women won by the spear so involved in the epic's opening crisis.[3] Drawing for the most part on the mythic past and on the Trojan War, tragedy presents that material at another historical moment, when Athens was again at war.[4] War might be said to dominate the extant tragedies, and with the notable exception of Philoctetes, who at the beginning of Sophocles' play has been abandoned on his island and will return to the company of men only, each of the combatants in tragedy is surrounded by women, whether their own relations or those of the conquered peoples.

Structuralism, with its analysis of the deep structures that organize a culture, notably Claude Lévi-Strauss' "the raw and the cooked,"[5] has given rise in classics to an emphasis on binary oppositions such as public and private (*polis* and *oikos*), marriage and war. Jean-Pierre Vernant gives this classic statement: "Marriage is for the girl what war is for the boy: for each of them these mark the fulfillment of their respective natures."[6] The plays, especially those taking up the theme of war, consistently interrelate the so-called opposites. Thus there can be no separation, even when the male and female characters occupy separate spaces (see below on *Women of Trachis*).[7] By looking at tragedy, then, we are reminded that war was about women.[8]

It was also a war on women. Thus, modern genocidal warfare, with its use of rape as a tactic, is not something new.

While we may not see what we call "combat trauma" (a relatively recent term for what used to be known as "shell shock" or "battle fatigue") in any straightforward way in the ancient texts, our own awareness of these syndromes can enable us to see familiar elements there. For instance, looking at the plays from this perspective brings out the scenes of madness that may cause or be caused by war. Having thus examined the plays, we can perhaps add something new to contemporary conversations about violence and war. That is, we better understand that men in war are called on to do the unthinkable, and the consequences are traumatic not only for them but for women and children as well. Given the canonical status of these plays, ignoring the connection they draw between war and violence against women allows us to ignore the normalization of such extreme behaviors in our own day; acknowledging the connection may help us recognize it in the present.

What does this persistent intertwining of male and female experiences mean? What might it have meant when it was performed in Athens and what, in contrast, does it mean now? The festival of Dionysus in Athens was state-organized.[9] In the events surrounding the presentation of the plays, Athens honored the orphans of the war dead and received tribute from its subject cities. The festival also offered an opportunity for the city to display itself to foreign dignitaries. Given my topic, it is especially significant that the official structure of the event was all male (actors, chorus, judges, playwrights), and there is considerable debate over whether women were even in the audience. The fragmentary evidence suggests that women were present in some capacity, but it is hardly conclusive.[10] As Peter Meineck points out, veterans of the wars probably made up a large portion of the audience[11]; let us not forget that the women who attended would similarly have been through the wars—although in different ways and to different degrees.

Despite its state backing, however, tragedy raises questions and demonstrates cracks and fissures in the dominant ideology; as a result, the plays could have pressed citizens in the audience to consider the costs of the wars that they were themselves undertaking.[12] At the same time, they might have given the subordinated women in the audience another vantage point from which to look at themselves and their experience. A third perspective might have been that of the participants, actors and chorus, who had the opportunity to experience the many different kinds of suffering at stake.[13]

In this chapter, I will turn my attention to the broad ways in which tragedy represents war's effects on women: both the women left behind (Clytemnestra and Deianeira) and the women taken captive by the enemy, whether in the past (Tecmessa) or more recently (Iole, the women of Troy). These categories are not airtight, however, and, as we will see, different versions of Clytemnestra, for instance, reveal that the same "person" may have experienced different traumas; furthermore, by the process of identification, Deianeira can occupy the positions of both wife and concubine.

The magisterial and expansive *Oresteia* (458 BCE) takes the house of Atreus from the end of the war in Troy and the return of Agamemnon to Clytemnestra's revenge, to Orestes' divinely ordained murder of his mother, and thence to the establishment of the Areopagus in Athens as a court to deal with the matricide. The trilogy exposes both the madness of warriors and the consequences for the women and children.

The *Agamemnon* chorus open the trilogy by giving the background to the war that has just ended. Starting with the words "This is the tenth year since against Priam, a great opponent at law (*antidikos*), Prince Menelaus and Agamemnon" launched their expedition (Aeschylus *Agamemnon* 40–2), they indicate that the war has been both long and just.[14] Nonetheless, there are other dimensions of the expedition that make its costs apparent. The omen of eagles eating a pregnant hare that accompanies the army's setting out is ambiguous; there is both good and bad to report (145).

Aeschylus shows us the army's distress as it is paralyzed by stormy winds:

> The Greek force was unable to sail,
> And they started to suffer and starve,
> Sitting in their ships, off the coast of Chalcis,
> Rocked back and forth by the swelling tides of Aulis.
> Bitter winds blew down from the Strymon,
> Bringing hunger and delay to that wretched harbor,
> Driving the men to wander on the edge of insanity
> Wearing thin the cables and rotting the ships.
> Then the prophet cried out,
> In the name of Artemis,
> Proclaiming a remedy to soothe the storm,
> And the sons of Atreus
> Beat the ground with their scepters,
> Unable to hold back a flood of tears.
>   (Aeschylus, *Agamemnon*.184–204, trans. P. Meineck)

As Meineck's translation makes explicit, the army is mad (literally, "wanders in its mind"); they are afflicted by devastating winds. Those external winds lead to a similarly troubled mortal breath when Agamemnon is said to breathe with the forces that strike him (187). He is placed in a double bind as the leader, between two heavy fates (*ker* 206): how can he kill his daughter? But how can he abandon his troops as a general? Once he has made the decision to perform the sacrifice, however, he is represented as mad, that is, willing to do anything.

> When he donned the yoke of necessity,
> breathing an impious, unholy turning of will, sacrilegious,
> from that time he turned to contemplate the all-daring;
> for mortals are emboldened by that wretched madness,

origin of suffering (*talaina parakopa prôtopêmôn*), devising shameful
   things (*aischromêtis*);
he dared then to become the sacrificer of his daughter, an aid of the
   woman-punishing war and the first sacrifice [(*proteleia*) also a bridal
   rite] for the ships.

(Aeschylus, *Agamemnon* 218–7)

Her cries mean nothing to him when he is so deranged though she was
previously very dear to him (227–30). Agamemnon is represented as being
in a state of mania, having gone from debating between his two terrible
alternatives to being all-daring. The war requires that he break the norms
of the family in order to save his army. But the sacrifice (or murder) of
their daughter then gives Clytemnestra a strong motive for her murder of
Agamemnon. Thus, trauma leads to further violence.

The army is also driven outside the boundaries of normal peacetime
ethics; they are driven to do things they would not normally do.[15] The
violence implicit in the omen of twin eagles eating a pregnant hare (119)
is echoed in the vicious and excessive behavior of the army. Clytemnestra
introduces an image of an army in the grips of passion in her prayer: "May
no lust (*erôs*) jump on the army to sack what is not fitting for the victors"
(341–2); we later hear that the army did act in this way (destroying the altars
and paying the sons of Priam back doubly [527, 537]). Thus, although the
war is at first made to appear justified, a war fought in the name of Zeus to
uphold the laws of hospitality and the lawful exchange of women, it is also
a war for booty and the conquest of other women; it makes of its soldiers
men who take satisfaction and pleasure in killing. The princess Cassandra,
who was given the gift of prophecy by Apollo, is the visible sign of this
aspect of the war. She was first raped by Ajax and then taken as the prize
of Agamemnon, appearing on the chariot beside him when he enters the
scene. And of course Cassandra, as the woman brought into her house as a
slave, is another assault on Clytemnestra; she, like Iphigenia, brings in her
wake Clytemnestra's revenge.[16] The sexual practices that were considered
acceptable for the military in wartime have an adverse effect on the women
at home.

There is also the wife's isolation to consider. Clytemnestra welcomes
Agamemnon to the palace and delivers a duplicitous speech about the life
of the woman left behind. Of course, the audience knows that she is not
honest here—if she ever missed Agamemnon, she has long since gotten
over it; moreover, she is hardly typical in that she has ruled in Agamemnon's
absence for ten years. Nonetheless, what she says has to be plausible if it is
going to convince Agamemnon:

Men of the city, elders of Argos,
I feel no shame in telling you of my love for the man, shyness dies
   when one
Gets older. I will speak from the heart,

I will tell you how unbearable my life has been
While this man stood under Troy's walls.
To begin with, when a woman sits at home, parted from her husband,
    her loneliness is terrible,
And the rumors she hears spread like a disease...
These rumors ate away at me, to the point
that I had to be released, against my will, from the noose of suicide,
    more than once.

(Aeschylus, Agamemnon 855–75 trans. P. Meineck;
cf. Libation Bearers. 918, 920)

Clytemnestra has suffered. She evokes her feeling of abandonment at living apart from her man (*arsenos dicha* 861), shamelessly (and ironically) setting it in the context of her sexual desire (*philanoras tropous*, man-loving ways 856); she also stresses the problem of rumor, of not knowing what is actually happening, which would have afflicted women on the home front then (as it does now). Her wakefulness has a double meaning, too: while she couldn't sleep (and set the beacon to be forewarned about the arrival of Agamemnon), the more ordinary wife might well have had difficulty sleeping out of anxiety, as she claims she did (891–4). Women and men in the audience are made conscious of the double pain behind the revenge that she later exacts. She is the victim of trauma and is, like Agamemnon, maddened in her own way—at least according to the chorus (1407–11, 1426); her pleasure (*chairousan* 1391, *chlidêi* 1447) in the violence she enacts is as erotic as that of the soldiers overtaking Troy. Her pain at the loss of her daughter and at the introduction of a new woman to the house have caused her behavior.

Clytemnestra does not make an extensive defense in the *Libation Bearers*. She has a brief scene with Orestes in which she strongly claims her right as his mother (Aeschylus *Libation Bearers* 896–8) and objects to the double standard (Agamemnon took a mistress; she took a lover 916–8), but she does not mention Iphigenia at all. The later plays on the theme show Clytemnestra interacting with Electra.[17] In these scenes she reiterates her statement of what she has suffered. In Euripides' *Electra,* Electra has been married off to a farmer; in order for the revenge action to be completed, she sets up the ruse that she has had a child. When Clytemnestra arrives to perform her duty as a mother and grandmother, she delivers an apologia for her behavior in which she draws attention to the rhetorical problem she faces: "Whenever evil reputation takes a woman, there is a bitterness to her speech" (Euripides *Electra* 1013–4, literally tongue, *glossêi* 1014). And in truth we never know exactly how we are supposed to take this woman, for we see her in relation to her children, who are committed to killing her and vilifying her, and of course through the eyes of the male playwright and the body of the male actor.

In this version, Clytemnestra is not only represented as living in wealth, but she has also clearly benefited from the capture of Troy: she has Trojan slaves at her disposal, which she calls a "small prize" in exchange for her daughter (1000–3). The term used (*geras* 1003) refers to the gifts of honor associated with the men at war. Thus, it is not only men who get booty from war. The lines suggest female complicity and the benefits accruing to the women of the victorious side, no matter that it is linked to her suffering.

At the same time her speech makes clear the costs. The woman's anguish is based in part on the loss of her daughter and in part on the betrayal by her husband. Of the two, however, she gives more weight to the latter (1030–1). Clytemnestra again objects to the double standard, the fact that the war presents her with a rival for her husband's bed, but that she is castigated for taking on a lover (Euripides *Electra* 1039–40); in Aeschylus she also notes that he was not blamed for the death of Iphigenia while she is blamed for the death of Agamemnon (Aeschylus *Agamemnon* 1412–8). In Sophocles, on the other hand, Clytemnestra emphasizes the death of Iphigenia and never mentions Cassandra at all (Sophocles *Electra* 525–51). Electra rebuts her argument with the story that Artemis demanded the sacrifice because Agamemnon had hunted in her woods, and adds the claim that she is having children with Aegisthus to replace her and Orestes (558–76).

In Aeschylus, as well as in Sophocles and Euripides' *Electras,* we see the traumatic effects on the children who live.[18] While Orestes is changed into a mother killer, Electra has been stunted in her development by the murder of her father and her mother's marriage to Aegisthus. She remains behind, and in Aeschylus' *Libation Bearers* she laments, complaining that she is thrust aside and dishonored, like a dog, worth nothing (Aeschylus *Libation Bearers.* 444–5); indeed her mourning makes her the object of laughter, and she has to hide her tears (449). She stresses that she is unmarried and living at home (486–8). In Sophocles, she is explicitly aggrieved that she has been prevented from marrying and is in a state of limbo, while in Euripides, she is married in name only. The war that was started by a rupture of the marriage laws (as well as those of hospitality, see above) continues to disrupt the normative transition of Electra from a young girl to a mature, married woman. Tellingly, the end of Sophocles' version leaves her standing outside the house, on the margins, as a result of her trauma.

Euripides' *Iphigenia at Aulis* (405 BCE), the latest play on this cycle of myths, expands on the sacrifice of the child necessary for the war to take place. The playwright has Agamemnon use the device of Iphigenia's fictitious marriage to Achilles to bring her and Clytemnestra to the Argive camp in Aulis, thus emphasizing the contrast and relationship between war and women, and between men's and women's spheres.

The opening of the play focuses on Agamemnon's indecision and draws out his awareness of what is at stake in sacrificing his daughter. The leader of the troops is shown regretting his decision at the play's opening and then changing his mind again in dialogue with his brother Menelaus. His actions make him appear visibly mad—he is writing and rewriting, throwing his torch down, and his eyes are bulging (Euripdes *Iphigenia at Aulis* 34–41); he is called mad (*mainesthai* 41; cf. 136–40, 389). What is it that makes him mad or not in his right mind? The fact that he was willing to kill his daughter. With Menelaus he proclaims himself in his right mind now, having been wrong before; he argues that Menelaus is the one who is mad—with his lust for his wife (388–90, 401). Agamemnon reaffirms that he will not kill his children (396)—thus, not killing one's children becomes a sign of sanity. But of course war requires the death of many parents' children, so war itself would seem to be insane. When Agamemnon changes his mind and agrees to perform the sacrifice, however, he appears to be quite logical and pragmatic: he presents himself as acting under pressure from the army. With this, Euripides reveals that the appearance of sanity or realpolitik in war is that which would in normal circumstances be labeled insane.

Clytemnestra's initial role in this play is that of the mother of the bride.[19] When she discovers the falsity of that position, she makes an unusual point: in her speech to Agamemnon, she mentions an earlier marriage, which makes her into a war victim. She reminds Agamemnon (and us) that her first marriage ended with him killing Tantalus and the young son that she was still nursing; he then kept her for his bed. Clytemnestra paints herself next as the virtuous wife (1146–65); like some of the other non-Greek women, then, she has become compliant to her master. She furthermore expands on the motif of the comparison between Helen and Iphigenia, to highlight the needless killing of war and the sacrifice of her daughter (1167–70, 1201 esp., cf. Sophocles *Electra*).

This play works to show the possibility of transformation and change of role. Clytemnestra's misery as a result of Agamemnon's wartime behavior will turn her into the evil or insane woman (1184) familiar to us now, and in antiquity. While we might more easily think of what happens to the man at war, and how he will interact in peaceful society, we see here that non-combatants are not exempt from the brutalizing effects of war.

In these ways, the Atreus myth as presented in tragedy reveals that war takes its toll on the family structure that it was supposedly waged to protect—in Euripides' *Iphigenia at Aulis* it is specifically said that the Greeks must go to war lest barbarians rape and seize Greek women (1266, 1274). Men and women in Athens who were involved in devastating wars themselves could not have avoided looking within as a result of their experience in the audience; we do not know, however, what they saw when they performed that examination. After all, Iphigenia is persuaded by her father and ends up volunteering for the sacrifice; her behavior acts as a model for courage and affects Achilles powerfully; he is struck with desire for her (1404–7, 1410–1). Would the various members of the audience have seen themselves in the zeal for war represented there? Or would Iphigenia's reaction have been undermined by the questioning of the war effort that preceded it? We can unfortunately only speculate, but by asking these questions we are at least able to see the multiple positions possible for the audience to inhabit.[20]

Clytemnestra, especially in *Agamemnon*, is often compared to Deianeira in Sophocles' *Women of Trachis* (420–410? BCE). In each play a woman is confronted with her husband's new lover, won at war. Deianeira's apparent innocence can well be put in the context of Clytemnestra's self-conscious revenge.[21] *Women of Trachis* takes place at what should be the completion of Heracles' labors; Deianeira is waiting for him. Thus, it underlines the painful anxiety caused by the absence of men at war.[22] Deianeira's position as the legitimately married woman of the house is the result of earlier aggression and hostility; her current suffering is the result of a later war. As is the case with Clytemnestra in Euripides' *Iphigenia at Aulis*, the lines between rape and marriage are blurred.

The fearfulness of women dominates the Deianeira story. Thus, when she introduces herself, she speaks at length of the maiden she once was in her father's house. She always knew that her fate was to be unhappy; the old saying that you don't know a mortal's fate until he dies is not true in her case: "I know well that mine is unfortunate and burdensome" (*dustuchê te kai barun*) (Sophocles *Trachinian Women* 1–5). In short, the playwright sets the tone by having Deianeira open with her painful past, and the threat of sexual violence. She was reluctant to marry because her suitor was the shape-changing river god Achelous.[23] His fearsome masculinity is under-lined in the shapes he takes on—bull, snake, man-ox—and the fact that his beard shoots forth fountains of water. Loathing him, she preferred death to the marriage bed (1–17).

And though she says she was "joyfully" (18) rescued from the river god by Heracles, her marriage turns out to be no different from the one she rejected. Heracles won Deianeira in a fight (*agôn* and *machês* 20), making her a form of a war prize.[24] The contest is between men, as is typical of war as well as courtship in the context of the exchange of women, both being structures that deny women agency.[25] The struggle between them seems to have been as terrifying as Achelous himself; thus, she was afraid to look and kept her distance, "terrified lest her beauty bring her additional suffering" (24–5, cf. 533–5). As a result, she says that someone else who saw it will have to speak about it (22–3). She cannot. Deianeira later tells another part of the story, when she was assaulted and almost raped by Nessus, the centaur who was carrying her across the river (555–77). Heracles was once again simultaneously the killer and the savior of her honor, and she is once again the passive object.

The chorus also give us a version of her "courtship" (504–30). They add details about the battle, saying, in the end, "She, delicate and with fair eyes (or fair to look upon, *euôpis* 523), watched from afar to see who would be her husband" (523–5). This language reaffirms her fearfulness, as well as her naivete, her distance from the battle, and makes her similarly the passive victim of male aggression.[26]

Moreover, her woes continue in her married life. However desirable Heracles may have been in contrast to her previous suitors, her life does not seem to have been changed by his marrying her.[27] It is as characterized by fear (28), as was her reaction to the fighting of the two males (24). Since being rescued by Heracles, her life has been a lonely one, because Heracles wanders and completes his labors.[28] Much like Clytemnestra, she does not know where her husband is or what is happening to him. As a result, she is full of anxiety and dread. This then is the lawfully wedded wife's narrative.

The terror is justified, but the harm comes not from an enemy of Heracles' but from another woman, a literal war prize, who will take her place beside Deianeira in the marriage bed, as they are "clasped" under one cover (536–40). While most of Heracles' labors are not actual wars, in this episode, a war was fought to win the woman, later named Iole. We have two versions of her acquisition, and war is involved in both; the question is simply what was cause and what effect. First, Lichas, one of Heracles' servants, enters with a group of captive women and announces to Deianeira that Heracles has returned from his last (or most recent, since ironically the last is still to come) labor, but that he is not home yet because he must make sacrifices to the gods. He tells her and us that Heracles promised the offerings "when he was conquering and laying waste the country of these women who are before your eyes" (240–1). The military tradition of taking young women captive is underlined here by the use of words for seizing and driving victims from their homes (*hêirei, anastaton dori* 240).

When Deianeira asks if Heracles has been away fighting all this time, Lichas mentions that for part of the time he was serving Omphale, the Lydian queen, to whom he had been sold. Lichas then creates a plausible connection between the two: he fought because he served the queen. In this narrative, Heracles went to war in revenge against Eurytus, who had caused his servitude to Omphale, for which Heracles vowed to enslave him with his wife and child (257). The full story touches on themes of hospitality and revenge and practices of warfare. Heracles was visiting Eurytus, who taunted him about his skills in archery; Heracles retorted that Eurytus was a slave. He was thrown out of the house for drunkenness, and he subsequently tricked and killed Eurytus' son, Iphitus; Zeus made him pay for that deceitful murder by selling him as a slave to Omphale; the price went to Eurytus. As a result of Heracles' vengeance for the sale, the whole city is now enslaved (283).[29] The themes in this false version of the story are war and the enslavement of the defeated.

As is typical with such false reports (e.g., Sophocles, *Electra*), we can learn a great deal from the way the internal audience reacts. Deianeira responds immediately with pity for the women (298); she defines it as a "terrible" or "strange" (*deinos*) pity, and indeed it is. She sympathizes with the women she sees, and clearly recognizes that their position might have been hers. She understands that this fate is the fate of any woman in war, not just the barbarian or foreigner (296–305). Their status as victims of the practice of taking women and children alive and selling them into slavery is pronounced, for they are referred to women of the land Heracles razed (*anastaton* 240). They are slaves, belonging to someone, and chosen out especially by Heracles for himself and the god (245). The women as prize reflect his power and his role as the destroyer of the land (cf. Cassandra's position, and the *Iliad* plot).

Deianeira reiterates that she feels pity, especially for one girl, who is as yet unnamed but who attracts her attention (307–13). Deianeira and the chorus earlier made Iole's sufferings palpable to the audience, preparing us well for this outpouring of sympathy (27–48, 103–11). Deianeira identifies with Iole—seeing in her the girl she used to be. Both indicate their fear in the face of male aggression. Iole's traumatic experience, having lost her whole family (like Megara in *Heracles*), may be inferred from her silence (often a sign of shock), which is emphasized. Deianeira's position as the prize of a single combat strongly resonates with Iole's fate; her averted eyes as a girl parallel Iole's current silence.

Deineira stresses the girl's youth and inexperience (*neanidôn* 307, *apeiros* 309), which makes her more pitiable. Furthermore, she infers "Iole's" nobility from her bearing, and, as a result, she has more feeling for her: she assumes that a noble feels her affliction more intensely than the other ordinary women feel theirs. In emphasizing Deianeira and Iole, as Sophocles does, we must not forget that Iole is in a crowd of other women, all of whom have been captured. They all testify to the experience of the enslavement of the women of the conquered army, which was still a practice when Sophocles was writing (and is indeed still at work in war-torn cultures today).

There is, however, another version of the sacking of Oechalia, and a soldier who heard Lichas speak outside the city challenges him to tell the truth now. Under pressure, Lichas is forced to recant. In the new reports, Heracles was from the first the victim of an overmastering desire, thus a slave to Eros.[30] Here we have Heracles the man mad with longing (*pothos* 368). Indeed, we are told that "Eros alone of the gods softened him to do these warlike deeds" (354–5). Desire for Iole now appears as the cause of the war not its effect; the whole city was sacked for her sake. Since Heracles could not convince her father to give her to him for a "secret bedding" (*kruphion lechos* 360), he went to war for her. He killed her father (later, all the men, 282) and destroyed the city. From the anonymous messenger's point of view, Iole is not a slave; Heracles loved her (366); indeed, he says that Lichas announced that he was bringing her as "*damarta*," a very strong word for wife (428). But let us not be confused by this talk of love: these are girls taken by the spear (532); the force they experience is not the force of desire. This is a rape narrative in the context of a war story.

Now Deianeira realizes that she is faced with a rival who will challenge her status as wife. Deianeira recognizes that Iole's beauty (which is like her own 547–9) has destroyed her life and the city (465). Although she proclaims her sympathy, there is reasonable doubt as to her sincerity. She enters the house saying that she is going to give Heracles gifts to match the gifts he has sent her (492–6). And when she returns, she speaks openly of her pain. While she again asserts that she is not angry (543), she acknowledges that she is afraid of the girl, who is, she fears, no longer a maiden but is "yoked" (*korên ezeugmenên* 536, with implications of both slavery and marriage), and whom she thinks of as a bit of "destructive" "baggage" or trafficked merchandise (537–8). Iole has been brought on board, so to speak, and Deianeira will be expected to share her bed with her. The chorus ended their earlier speech describing Deianeira as a prize, *amphineikêton* (527), but in this speech she has been replaced by a new prize (550–1: Iole will be the mate because she is younger, 547–8). The structure emphasizes that both women are similarly battle prizes, whether married or not. The potential rape of Deianeira and the actual rape of Iole are not so different; men in war take women, and sometimes they call this prize their wife. The family structure is contaminated by the sexual dynamics of war.[31]

The gift is a robe anointed with the unguent given to Deianeira by Nessus when he was dying; it was made from the poisoned arrow with which Heracles killed him. When Deianeira acts on her fear, and consciously tries to make her husband fall in love with her again, she subjects him to flesh-dissolving tortures. While before he was mad with love for Iole, now he is maddened with pain. This is combat trauma with a vengeance. When still ignorant of his fate, the chorus commented that Heracles has been sent back to them by the war god, Ares, having been stung to insanity (*oistrêtheis* 653).[32] When he appears, he indeed seems like the war god, maddened by his physical and mental affliction. His pain is in direct contrast with his warrior past, as he emphasizes (993–5, 1010–5, 1046–8, 1057–61, for madness 999). He is undone; having conquered all his other enemies, he is finally brought down by a woman (1063) and made a girl (1071, woman 1075) by the ravages of the poison. His body is attacked (cf. Medea's magic and its effects).[33]

Heracles ends by asserting his will over Hyllos and Iole. In the play's conclusion, Iole (like Deianeira, whose death is "shrouded in silence")[34] is a cipher exchanged between two men to cement their relationship. Heracles' dying wish is that Hyllos marry his bedmate (1221–9). At first Hyllos refuses, citing Iole's role in his mother's death (1233–7), but the force of the patriarchy bears down inexorably, and he accedes to his father's wishes (1249–51). He will replace him at Iole's side. As little agency as Deianeira had, she at least was given voice. Iole is to the end an object, handed around by men. Her new role as wife cannot obliterate her past as a slave taken in the conquest of her city and her people. Or can it? Will their marriage constitute a life of rape, or will she (as Andromache resists doing in *Trojan Women*) get used to it? In fact her position reinforces the vulnerability of a woman in war: what would her fate have been if Hyllos refused?[35]

Euripides' *Heracles* (which is not securely dated, so we don't know its relation to *Women of Trachis*) shows another attack on and by the hero. The tragedians seem well aware of the relationship between violence directed outward and violence directed inward toward the family. Amphitryon's opening speech articulates the history of war that set the condition for the present action—Lycus has taken over Thebes, having killed the former king, Creon (Euripides *Heracles* 33), and he intends to kill Heracles' sons and wife out of fear of reprisals from the sons (165–9, 547). In the past, and memorialized on stage, is another war, a victory over the Minyans (50, 220, 560) in consequence of which Megara was married to Heracles (68). The play's beginning emphasizes the suffering of Megara; it has left her hopeless about the future (69–72, 94; cf. 539–61). When Heracles returns from his "last" labor in the land of the dead, he finds his wife, father, and children dressed for their death, the fate that awaits many of the survivors of armed conflicts (525–8, 534–7, 539, 548, 562). In the stichomythia between Megara and Heracles, we learn the relevant facts: they had no friends to support them in Heracles' absence; they were forced from their house (again as is the case in modern wars). As a mature woman, she is unlikely to have been one of those who would have been kept alive and enslaved by Lycus (see Gaca 2014).

Heracles immediately turns his thoughts to violence and revenge (565–73). The connection to his labors (*ponoi*) is made explicit: they were for naught if he does not save his family (575–82). He will regain his noble name only if he does this deed. The hero enters the house with a generalization about men loving their children, at the same time that he vows to protect his "little boats" (631–4). Of course, the word "*kallinikos*" (582) and the care he shows his family heightens the contrast with what will happen next when in a fit of madness he kills them all, except for his father.

The play shows very clearly and explicitly the interrelated nature of warfare, trauma leading to madness, and war on the family; while the onset of the avowed insanity is not explained as the result of a battle but as a continuation of Hera's anger at him, the language of the messenger's speech emphasizes its connection to the struggles Heracles has already gone through. Even before the killing, Amphitryon suggests the possibility that his son's recent acts of violence are making him mad: "Is it not the slaughter (*phonos*) of the corpses you have killed that makes you frenzied" (like a bacchant, *ebakcheusin* 966–7). And when Heracles awakens from his rampage, he indicates that he has fought a war against his family, but a war that is no war (*apolemon polemon* 1133).

At this point, Theseus, Athenian hero and Heracles' friend, arrives. Theseus first confuses the current mayhem with a war, offering his army (1164) to support his ally, but then he notices that the dead are Heracles' children. While he interprets that fact to mean that this was not a war (1176), the play enables us to see the ways in which children are indeed the casualties of war. Heracles' labors are capped by this final labor, the killing of his own family (1279–80); this is the finishing touch, the top layer of misery on his house (*paidoktonésas doma thrigkosai kakois* 1280). His labors and his children, which should have given him a fine reputation, are perverted. Heracles veils himself to prevent himself from being seen by his friend, a feminine gesture reflecting his shame;[36] Theseus then unveils Heracles in return for Heracles' having brought him back from the grave. Thus, a culture of male reciprocity is reestablished, and the relationship between the men promises to build a new and positive future in which Heracles will be purified and given a house and a share of Theseus' possessions (1322–5). The audience can see that this will not have a positive result for women and children, however, since the dead cannot be brought back.

Sophocles' *Ajax* (n.d.) also merges the hero's fate with that of his survivors.[37] The epic tradition makes it clear that Ajax was a fierce warrior and was rightfully furious when the arms of Achilles went to Odysseus and not him. Sophocles opens the play with Athena displaying Ajax to Odysseus in the midst of his attack on the cattle that he still thinks are the leaders of the Greek army, Odysseus, Menelaus, and Agamemnon. His mental illness is made a shameful spectacle (Sophocles *Ajax* 51–60, 66 *noson*). Different forms of madness are at stake here: that of the human being who would have turned against his own army, that of the confusion between the intended target and the actual one (81–3), and that of Ajax's mistaken and overweening confidence in his own power (96, 128). In the scene where Athena draws him out, revealing his mistake to the audience and chorus, Ajax's blood lust is elided with his current madness (e.g., 95, 97, 104–11).

Ajax's madness and consequent suicide powerfully express the consequences of war, but the picture would be incomplete without a study of what his trauma inflicts on Tecmessa. While Clytemnestra, Deianeira, and Megara are representations of the women left behind in war, Tecmessa is like Iole, a slave-bedmate, who follows her lord to war.[38] She enters with fresh evidence of Ajax's mental disorder. She defines him as follows: "Ajax, great, terrible and harsh in his strength (*ômokratês*), lies sick as if in a storm" (*tholerôi ...cheimôni* 205–7), words that imply both his special power and the turbulence that attacks him; she later adds that he was afflicted by some madness in the night (*maniai* 217).

War and family mix: Tecmessa is there in the camp with the child that she has borne to Ajax. She is not quite a concubine like Cassandra, or Briseis in the *Iliad*, but she is also not quite a wife; she was a war prize (*lechos dourialôton* 211), taken when Ajax killed her family, and her status is therefore insecure. She reveals these things, and in the process she poignantly reveals the effects of war on women. She was the daughter of a mighty Phrygian, and now she is a slave not only because of the will of the gods but also because of Ajax's strong hand (489–90). The fate of a youthful defeated woman is sexual in nature. She does not think of herself simply as a victim of rape, however; since she has shared Ajax's bed for some time, she is bound to him in loyalty (see above on Iole, and Andromache below).[39] Moreover, she prays to him on the basis of that bed, imploring him not to give her over to his enemies, to strangers. We learn of her lack of a future: since Ajax has destroyed her family (515–7), she has no recourse should he die. In short, she is totally dependent on him (cf. Iole above). Without his protection, she will once more be enslaved (499) along with their son, suffering anew the fate to which he had subjected her in the past. She quotes the insults that will be hurled at her; since she is his loyal companion, they will, of course, reflect on him as well (500–5).

Tecmessa understands her limited power. Therefore, she mentions what the impact would be on Ajax's parents, about whom he has expressed concern, and his son. Tecmessa assumes that their son will share a fate similar to hers, an orphan in the care of guardians who won't love him. She begs Ajax

to consider that "such is the evil you hand down to him and for me, whenever you should die" (512–3). In the end, however, Ajax is interested only
in other males. He will care for his son, but only his son (Heracles similarly
forgets about Megara). He dismisses her concerns. Having said that she will
gain his approval by obeying him, he further enjoins her silence—he does
not want to hear her laments (579–80, 586, 592). He orders her to bring
his son to him (530), whom she had sent away in fear that Ajax would kill
him in his troubles (*kakoisin* 532, *thanoi* 533). The importance of the male
is pronounced in other ways, as well. First, Ajax insists that the child must
become like the father, inured to blood; indeed his reaction will verify his
paternity: Blood won't frighten him (*tarbeséi gar ou, neosphagê touton ge pros-
leusssôn phonon* 545–6) if he is his offspring (*emos ta patrothen* 547). The scene
is reminiscent of Hector, Andromache, and Astyanax at Troy in the *Iliad*, but
the comparison makes clear the difference between the two women; while
it elevates Tecmessa by making her worthy of the comparison, it also points
out her double vulnerability.[40] In his deceptive speech where he tricks his
soldiers and Tecmessa into leaving him alone so he can commit suicide, Ajax
mentions her and the boy specifically as causes for his softening. At the end
of the play, however, Tecmessa is forgotten while Teucer and the boy remain
relevant.

War has controlled Tecmessa's life as a woman from the time that Ajax
killed her family and took her as a bedmate until his madness leads him to
attack his "fellow officers," and then turn on himself. For the woman taken
in war, the madness of war and the sanity of war are not so very different.

Iole and Tecmessa are victims of the overall strategy of taking women and
children captive. I turn now to the effects of the ancient policies of warfare on the women of defeated Trojan army—drawing on Euripides' *Trojan
Women* (415) and *Hecuba* (n.d.). These plays take the women victims of war
and put them at the center. In so doing, they ask the Athenian audience to
sympathize with their mythical eastern enemies, while they were treating
their current enemies in much the same way.

It is particularly important to note the ways in which taking women as
slaves and killing the male youth is represented in *Trojan Women*.[41] It is sensible to put the *Trojan Women* into the context of the Peloponnesian War,
although perhaps not specifically to the attacks on Melos and the Syracuse
expedition (416/415).[42] Euripides wrote this play when Athens was at war,
and the situation must have had echoes for the original audience.

Poseidon opens the play introducing the themes of suffering and rape
caused by war: the city's river echoes with the shrieks of the women
who have been "taken by the spear" and "allotted" to the Greek soldiers
(Euripides *Trojan Women* 28–9). The costs of defeat are clear: the god draws
our attention to the suffering Hecuba, who might have escaped the audience's notice because she lies huddled on the ground. He also informs
us of the death of Polyxena, Hecuba's youngest daughter, at the tomb of
Achilles. His speech suggests the prevalence of violence against women,
since Agamemnon, "abandoning piety will marry Cassandra by force in an

unlawful union" ([literally, shadowy, *skotion* 44] 43–4). Sexual aggression against women would seem to be thematic.

Rape and the sacrificial murder of Polyxena are not the only problematic Greek behaviors, however. As a result of the Greeks' hubris toward Athena and her temples (69)—when Aias raped Cassandra (literally, took her with force [*bia*]), the Achaeans did nothing [70, 71]—the goddess has abandoned them and made an alliance with Poseidon to cause storms that will mar their voyage home. Poseidon closes the prologue with this lesson: "He is stupid, whoever of mortals sacks cities, and temples and tombs, the holy places of the fallen, giving them to desolation, he will be destroyed later" (95–7). War, then, leads not only to excess violence and rape, but also to the pillaging of sacred sites; therefore, the doer will suffer in turn.

Euripides identifies the fall of the city with the rape of the women.[43] Clearly the play vividly recreates the evil of war in the suffering of Troy and specifically arouses pity for the women and children. The wailing and mourning of the chorus form the emotional backdrop to the action (especially 97–234, sung with Hecuba); Cassandra and Andromache represent specific kinds of losses, and the death of Astyanax embodies the horror of war and the cruelty of the Greeks.

Hecuba lies on the ground; she lifts her head and sings a lament with the chorus that focuses on the consequences of war for women. They are all victims, and as such they have a choice between life in slavery or death (the possibility of suicide by burning with the city is raised twice [301–2, 1281–2]). Hecuba stresses the gender of the victims (wives and maidens 143, 144); they will all be slaves (158, 165 [*mochthôn*], 192, 277, 422, 492, 507, 600, 678, 1271, 1280). But important differences of class and status emerge. Hecuba is enslaved, mourning with her head shaven, as the city she once ruled burns (140–3, cf. 9). Her lament is for the city and its wealth: Troy is no more, and she is no longer the Queen of Troy (99–100, cf. 194–6). She stresses her former wealth and grandeur (108, 196), and the songs she used to sing that were appropriate to her royal station. The ordinary women, on the other hand, remember not their possessions but their work at their looms (199–200).[44] There are also differences of age. As an old woman, Hecuba will be a nurse or doorkeeper (194–5); the younger women will be raped or become servants (or both): "I shall have greater labors than these, either approaching the beds of the Hellenes (May that night and its spirit disappear) or as a pitiful servant" (202–3).

If the women suffered slavery and rape in war, the male children of the defeated were killed. The Greek herald Talthybius enters and announces that the Greeks, persuaded by Odysseus, have voted to execute Astyanax, the last remaining child of the family. The immorality of the Greeks and the antiwar reading often rests on this murder, which is in effect part of a campaign to raze Troy to the ground forever: Troy must not rise again, so this child of a noble father must die (723). The violent death of Astyanax makes it clear that innocent noncombatants pay with their lives for decisions they never made. Attention to his sweet flesh highlights both the cost to the defeated and the cruelty of the winning army. Andromache says: "You Hellenes have discovered barbarian evils, why do you kill this child in no way to blame?" (764–5). Greeks distinguished between themselves and the barbarian other. Here Euripides has Andromache point up the fact that they have become the enemy in their behavior.

As Andromache called the Greeks barbarian for killing the child (764–5), now Hecuba scorns them as cowards, afraid of a little boy (1158–66). "What would a poet write on your grave? Here is the child that the Argives killed because they feared him? An inscription shameful to the Greeks!" (1188–91). The Greeks, however, were not irrational in their decision; they simply followed the dreadful logic of vengeance. Indeed, Hecuba hoped that Astyanax would reestablish Troy (703–5). If he had lived, Astyanax would likely have been driven by the heroic code of ethics to try to punish the aggressors. Euripides makes clear the costs of war, and shows how the victors become vicious.

The staged Trojans are not very different from historical Greeks. Not only do they accept "barbarian" as a slur, but Andromache praises herself for the very virtues that characterized Athenian womanhood—she was quiet and obedient, kept her eyes downcast, and did not leave the house (645–56). She hates women who get along with their new "husband," (667–8) but being raped may bleed over into compliance in sleeping with the enemy; Hecuba counsels such behavior (even though her new owner is the son of Achilles, who killed Hector [661–8]), and even sees it as part of Troy's rebirth (697–705). As seduction was a worse crime than rape in Athens, so here, Andromache does not want to be seduced into good behavior. The fate of Andromache echoes that of modern survivors of war as well.

The play required Greek men and women in the audience to sympathize with the enemy, at least for the duration of the action. The men might not have identified with the losers, especially since Athens is singled out for praise, but they might nonetheless have heard themselves in Talthybius when he says he unwillingly delivers his message consigning Astyanax to death (710). Could the experience of watching the play have convinced the soldiers to treat their enemies with more respect out of fear that this might happen to them? Of course we cannot say anything about ancient audience reactions with security, but we can use the play to take a more critical look at what we are doing in our own wars. Are we becoming like our enemy? Moreover, depending on the staging, the treatment of women in the play as sexual prey could lead the audience to reflect on rape as a weapon in modern warfare.

Hecuba (424? BCE) is a play divided between the deaths of the children and revenge by the mother. Euripides makes a compelling case for the dehumanizing effects of war—in the end, it is predicted that Hecuba will turn into a hound. That conclusion is an indictment of war in that she is shaped into a monster by what she has experienced at the hand of men, both Greek and Thracian.

The story of the sacrifice of Polyxena is told in *Trojan Women*; it is enacted in *Hecuba*. That the youngest daughter of Priam and Hecuba should be sacrificed on the tomb of the dead Achilles is paradigmatic of the waste of war. The heroic code and Achilles' glory demand the physical death of an exemplary virgin, not an old woman like her mother. Unlike Iphigenia, who chooses death and exalts the army in the process, Polyxena chooses death rather than be forced to die; she prefers it to the life of slavery that would otherwise have been her lot (Euripides *Hecuba* 357–68). She seems to be powerful, directing Odysseus to stop when she sees him (342) and directing her own death, as recounted by Talthybius. She might not have gotten her wish to die nobly, however, if her mother had not been vigilant. Though the army praises Polyxena, Hecuba is worried about what would happen if they should touch her and forbids their doing so (605). In short, the old queen does not trust the mob and emphasizes the fact that she is burying a bride for Hades, "a maiden who is no maiden" (612).[45] Even in death Polyxena could have been mishandled.

In the second half of the play, Hecuba devises her revenge, which is predictably double. Though Polymestor killed one of her children, Polydorus, for the gold that was meant to ensure his safety, she kills both of his. She does so in a particularly treacherous way because she uses the cultural assumptions about female weakness (Agamemnon doubts that as a woman she can actually take her own revenge, 883–5) as a trap. Hecuba and her women get Polymestor's children into their power by praising the handiwork of the Thracian women (1152–4), and then use the pins holding their clothes to blind Polymestor (1169–71). The inner space, the attention to cloth, and the weapon deployed all emphasize the femininity of the plot, driving home the point that the violence and greed unleashed in war produces violence beyond the combat zone.[46]

From this consideration of the plays, we can see both the madness of battle and the consequences for women (and children), who suffer their own form of combat trauma as a result of men's licensed warrior behavior. Women are used to represent all phases of military action: they may be sacrificed to make it possible (Iphigenia); they may be left at home (Clytemnestra, Deianeira); they may be taken as captive and enslaved, for sex or for labor (Cassandra, Andromache, Hecuba, Iole, the women of Troy); and they may be killed as a sign of male honor (Polyxena). They are not simply collateral damage; though noncombatants they are part of the war effort.

I have argued that women and men in ancient Athens could have seen these plays as revealing about their own lives. They were often engaged in armed struggles, and, it would seem, were well aware of the price to be paid. The sensitivity of the tragedians to the costs of war also makes these stories useful to us in a rich and powerful way. While we may consider the horror of Abu Ghraib and other stories of atrocity in Darfur or Rwanda exceptional, from the perspective of Greek tragedy they seem to be part of the cost of waging war. The plays show the loss of humanity involved by painting the relationship between combatant and noncombatant trauma clearly.

In downplaying the ways in which war affects both women and men in so many of the plays, we may participate in a cover-up of the reality of war. By the same token, perhaps watching and studying them attentively can help us to be more aware of what we are doing when we go to war.

Notes

*I want to thank the editors, David Konstan and Peter Meineck, for their suggestions, as well as Kathy Gaca for her generous reading of this chapter. I am grateful to Pangea Farm for two writing retreats where I was able to flesh out my arguments in peace and serenity.

1. On the killing of men and enslaving of women, see Thuc. 5.32.1; 5.84–116 (Melian dialogue); 3.68; 4.48; 5.3.4.
2. Gaca (2010, 129) points out that the two-part practice is first named as such in Herodotus, κτείνειν and ἀνδραποδίζεσθαι or φόνος καὶ ἐξανδραπόδισις 3.140.5, 3.147.1.
3. On the difference between fame of men at war and the female survivors, see Munteanu (2010), especially on the *Trojan Women*. On *Iliad* imagery, see Gaca (2008).
4. Vernant (1988).
5. Lévi-Strauss (1970 [1964]); see also his seminal work, *Elementary Structures of Kinship* (1969 [1949], 496) for a statement of the connection to women.
6. Vernant (1990, 34). See also Loraux (1981).
7. One role for women in society and the plays was lament; see, among others, Seaford (1994); Foley (2001); Holst-Warhaft (1992, 2000); Loraux (1998); and Dué (2006). Suter (2008) contests the exclusive focus on women's mourning, in, for instance, McClure (1999), noting that while women mourned in reality, we should not overlook the importance of male lament in tragedy.
8. Kathy Gaca's recent work on andrapodization, the historical practice of taking women and children prisoner in war, makes this very clear (Gaca [2010, 2014]; see also Solvang [2014], on the comparison to modern warfare in Rwanda). Their work has been a particular inspiration, urging me to look more carefully at tragedy for its evidence about the effects of war on the noncombatants.
9. For a summary of the discussion of the importance of the city in the festival, see Rabinowitz (2008, 34–5, 43–7); for early statements, see Goldhill (1990); Longo (1990).
10. This is a huge area of controversy; see Meineck (2012); Roselli (2011, 158–94) gives a thorough reconsideration of the evidence tending toward the view that women attended in some limited way; Goldhill (1994) argues that no women were present; Henderson (1991) takes a more open view; for the ancient testimony, see Csapo and Slater (1995).
11. Meineck (2012).
12. Segal (1986, 41): "The social context of the performance presupposes a safe, limited world hedged about by the order of rituals and stable community and communication, but the action of the performance explores what transgresses that order." As festival, it then "affirms the solidity of social forms," but the content reveals conflict. Zeitlin (1996, 364) argues that the "masculine values are tested" and found "inadequate" alone.
13. On the use of the feminine for the making of the masculine self in theater, see Zeitlin (1990, 1996). For a consideration of the apportionment of the actor among the roles, see Damen (1989).
14. Translations are mine unless otherwise noted; line numbers refer to the Oxford Classical Texts. For the classic statement on the justice of Zeus, see Lloyd-Jones (1983 [1971]); for a feminist rethinking see Zeitlin (1978).

15. Denniston and Page (1957), ad loc. Such excessive behavior is asked of soldiers in modern wars (or tolerated) as well.
16. Debnar (2010, 129–30) discusses Deianeira's status and her relationship to Iole as a parallel.
17. The relative dating of Euripides' and Sophocles' plays is not established, but they are definitely from later in the fifth century, probably around 410. In Sophocles' version, Clytemnestra mentions only Iphigenia as motive (Sophocles *Electra* 530–51).
18. For an extensive working out of the Electra theme, see Rabinowitz (2014). On the performance of trauma, see Griffiths (2011).
19. On ritual irony, see Foley (1985, 65–105).
20. Meineck (2012) proposes to use the modern audience's reactions to give us insight as to how the ancients might have responded. For my earlier reading of this play as leading the audience to praise Iphigenia, see Rabinowitz (1993, 38–54) with notes.
21. Goward (2004, 34); for a challenge and with further references, see Carawan (2000).
22. Critical discussion of whose play it is, summarized by Goward (2004, 33–5), is ultimately fruitless; of course it both of theirs. See Kitzinger (2012) on the division of the play into their two parts, citing critics who argue that "the one dies before the other appears; they occupy different worlds. These critics suggest that Sophocles has organized his play to contrast the mutually destructive worlds of men and women" (2012, 112). I would add that these are also the worlds of combat trauma and domestic injury.
23. On the marriage theme in the play, see Ormand (1999); on the theme of traffic and exchange, see Wohl (1998).
24. On Deianeira's lack of traditional marriage, see Ormand (1999, 41–2).
25. See Wohl (1998) and Ormand (1999) on male homosocial relations in the play.
26. As noted also by Goward (2004, 37).
27. On the similarity, see Easterling (1982, 133–4 on lines 497–530).
28. Ormand (1999, 38–45) on *eremia*.
29. Ormand sees the primary relationship as with Iole's father. That is not inconsistent with what I am arguing.
30. See Jebb (2004, 70–1, 77), on power of eros, on lines 441–50, 497–530. This is of course a standard trope, but it usually affects women, for example, Medea and Phaedra. Men who are mad for love are diminished in their masculinity; see above, however, on Menelaus, mad with love for his wife.
31. Thanks to David Konstan for his help on crystallizing this point.
32. Either Heracles is maddened, or Ares has been "stung to fury." The word can also refer to passion or to the attack on Oechalia. To add to the confusion, the chorus believes that Heracles/Ares is putting Deianeira out of her suffering (with a word that is related to that used for Heracle's labors, *epiponon* 654).
33. Zeitlin (1990, 72–5) on Heracles and Ajax. On Heracles' problematic virility and femininity, see Loraux (1990); Loraux (1995, 37–43) takes on the issue of femininity and Greek masculinity that are at stake particularly in Heracles; see (1995, 44–58) on the conflation of women's suffering and men's labors (*ponos*).
34. Kitzinger (2012, 112).
35. Thanks to Peter Meineck for this observation.
36. On the feminization of Heracles, see above, n. 33.
37. For a study of the surrounding characters, see Burian (2012).
38. For rape in war, see Rabinowitz (2011).
39. On this complicity, see Scodel (1998) on Andromache.
40. Burian (2012, 76).
41. I am developing here my work on rape and the reception of *Trojan Women* (Rabinowitz [2011, 2013a, and forthcoming]).

42. Kip (1987); for an early statement of the importance of Melos, see Murray (1905, 6–7); Murray (1913, esp. 130–1).
43. Rehm (2002, 182). On the politics, see Kovacs (1997). Loraux (2002, 8–13) argues that it is not only a political play but also lyric.
44. On class, see Rabinowitz (1998); DuBois (2004).
45. Bride to Hades, see Gregory (1999, 612). On the viewing of Polyxena and its implication in an erotic structure, see Rabinowitz (2013b).
46. Gregory (1999, ad loc).

Works Cited

Burian, Peter. 2012. "Polyphonic *Ajax*." In *A Companion to Sophocles*, edited by Kirk Ormand, 69–83. Malden, MA: Wiley-Blackwell.
Carawan, Edwin. 2000. "Deianira's Guilt." *TAPA* 130: 189–237.
Csapo, Eric, and William J. Slater. 1995. *The Context of Ancient Drama.* Ann Arbor: University of Michigan Press.
Damen, Mark. 1989. "Actor and Character in Greek Tragedy." *Theatre Journal* 41: 316–40.
Davies, Malcolm. 1991. *Sophocles* Trachiniae. Cambridge: Cambridge University Press.
Debnar, Paula. 2010. "The Sexual Status of Aeschylus' Cassandra." *Classical Philology* 105: 129–45.
Denniston, John, and Denys Page. 1957. *Aeschylus* Agamemnon. Oxford: The Clarendon Press.
DuBois, Page. 2004. "Toppling the Hero: Polyphony in the Tragic City." *New Literary History* 35: 63–81.
Dué, Casey. 2006. *The Captive Woman's Lament in Greek Tragedy.* Austin: University of Texas Press.
Easterling, P. E. 1982. *Sophocles* Trachiniae. Cambridge: Cambridge University Press.
Foley, Helene. 1985. *Ritual Irony: Poetry and Sacrifice in Euripides.* Ithaca, NY: Cornell University Press.
———. 2001. *Female Acts in Greek Tragedy.* Princeton, NJ: Princeton University Press.
Gaca, Kathy. 2008. "Reinterpreting the Homeric Simile of "Iliad" 16.7–11: The Girl and Her Mother in Ancient Greek Warfare." *American Journal of Philology* 129: 145–71.
———. 2010. "The Andrapodizing of War Captives in Greek Historical Memory." *TAPA* 140 [2010]: 117–61.
———. 2014. "Ancient Warfare and the Ravaging Martial Rape of Girls and Women." In *Sex in Antiquity: New Essays on Gender and Sexuality in the Ancient World,* edited by Mark Masterson, Nancy Sorkin Rabinowitz, and J. E. Robson. London: Routledge.
Goldhill, Simon. 1990. "The Great Dionysia and Civic Ideology." In *Nothing to Do with Dionysos: Athenian Drama in Its Social Context,* edited by John Winkler and Froma I. Zeitlin, 97–129. Princeton, NJ: Princeton University Press.
———. 1994. "Representing Democracy: Women at the Great Dionysia." In *Ritual, Finance, Politics: Athenian Democratic Accounts Presented to David Lewis,* edited by Robin Osborne and Simon Hornblower, 347–70. Oxford: Clarendon Press.
Goward, Barbara. 2004. "Introduction." *R.C. Jebb. Sophocles: Plays.* Trachiniae. London: Bristol Classical Press.
Gregory, Justina. 1999. *Euripides:* Hecuba. Introduction, Text, and Commentary. Atlanta: Scholars Press.
Griffiths, Jane. 2011. "The Abject Eidos: Trauma and the Body in Sophocles' *Electra*," In *Tradition, Translation, Trauma: The Classic and the Modern,* edited by Jan Parker and Timothy Parker, 229–43. Oxford: Oxford University Press.
Henderson, Jeffrey. 1991. "Women and the Athenian Dramatic Festivals." *Transactions and Proceedings of the American Philological Association* 121: 133–48.
Holst-Warhaft, G. 1992. *Dangerous Voices: Women's Lament and Greek Literature.* New York: Routledge.
———. 2000. *The Cue for Passion: Grief and its Political Uses.* Cambridge, MA: Harvard University Press.
Jebb, R. C. 2004. *Sophocles: Plays.* Trachiniae. London: Bristol Classical Press.
Kip, A. 1987. "Euripides and Melos," *Mnemosyne* 4.40.3–4: 414–9.

Kitzinger, Margaret Rachel. 2012. "The Divided Worlds of Sophocles' *Women of Trachis.*" In *A Companion to Sophocles*, edited by Kirk Ormand, 111–25. Malden, MA: Wiley-Blackwell.

Kovacs, David. 1997. "Gods and Men in Euripides' Trojan Trilogy." *Colby Quarterly* 33.2: 162–76.

Lévi-Strauss, Claude. 1969 [1949]. *Elementary Structures of Kinship.* Edited by Rodney Needham. Translated by J. H. Bell, J. R. von Sturmer, and Rodney Needham. Boston, MA: Beacon.

———. 1970 [1964]. *The Raw and the Cooked. Introduction to a Science of Mythology.* Vol. I. Translated by John and Doreen Weightman. London: Cape.

Lloyd-Jones, Hugh. 1983 [1971]. *The Justice of Zeus.* Sather Classical Lectures 41. 2nd ed. Berkeley: University of California Press.

Longo, Oddone. 1990. "The Theater of the *Polis.*" Translated by John J. Winkler. In *Nothing to Do with Dionysos: Athenian Drama in Its Social Context,* edited by John Winkler and Froma I. Zeitlin, 12–19. Princeton, NJ: Princeton University Press.

Loraux, Nicole. 1981. "Le lit, la guerre." *L'Homme* 21: 37–67.

———. 1990. "Heracles: The Super-male and the Feminine," In *Before Sexuality: The Construction of Erotic Experience in the Ancient World*, edited by David Halperin, John J. Winkler, and Froma I. Zeitlin. Princeton, NJ: Princeton University Press.

———. 1995. *The Experiences of Tiresias: The Feminine and the Greek Man.* Translated by Paula Wissing. Princeton, NJ: Princeton University Press.

———. 1998. *Mothers in Mourning.* Translated by Corinne Pache. Ithaca, NY: Cornell University Press.

———. 2002. *The Mourning Voice: An Essay on Greek Tragedy.* Translated by Elizabeth Rawlings. Ithaca, NY: Cornell University Press.

McClure, Laura. 1999. *Spoken Like a Woman.* Princeton, NJ: Princeton University Press.

Meineck, Peter. 2012. "Combat Trauma and the Tragic Stage: 'Restoration' by Cultural Catharsis." *Intertexts* 16: 8–24.

———, trans. 1998. *Aeschylus* Oresteia. Introduction by Helene Foley. Indianapolis, IN: Hackett.

Munteanu, Dana. 2010. "The Tragic Muse and the Anti-Epic Glory of Women in Euripides' *Troades.*" *Classical Journal* 106: 129–46.

Murray, Gilbert. 1905. *Trojan Women of Euripides.* London: Allen and Unwin.

———. 1913. *Euripides and His Age.* London: Williams and Norgate.

Ormand, Kirk. 1999. *Exchange and the Maiden: Marriage in Sophoclean Tragedy.* Austin: University of Texas Press.

Rabinowitz, Nancy Sorkin. 1993. *Anxiety Veiled: Euripides and the Traffic in Women.* Ithaca, NY: Cornell University Press.

———. 1998. "Slaves with Slaves: Women and Class in Euripidean Tragedy." In *Differential Equations: Women and Slaves in Greco-Roman Culture*, edited by Bridget Murnaghan and Sandra Joshel, 56–68. New York: Routledge.

———. 2008. *Greek Tragedy.* Oxford: Wiley Blackwell.

———. 2011. "Greek Tragedy: A Rape Culture?" *Eugesta* 1:1–21.

———. 2013a. "The Expansion of Tragedy as Critique." In *Classics in the Modern World: A Democratic Turn?*, edited by Lorna Hardwick and Stephen Harrison, 119–30. Oxford: Oxford University Press [Classical Presences].

———. 2013b. "Women as Subject and Object of the Gaze." *Helios* 40.1–2: 195–221.

———. 2014. "Melancholy Becomes Electra." In *Sex in Antiquity: Sexuality and Gender in the Ancient World*, edited by Mark Masterson, Nancy Sorkin Rabinowitz, and James Robson. London: Oxford.

———. Forthcoming. "Trojan Women," In *Blackwell Companion to Euripides*, edited by Robin Mitchell-Boyarsk. Oxford: Wiley-Blackwell.

Rehm, Rush. 2002. *The Play of Space: Spatial Transformation in Greek Tragedy.* Princeton, NJ: Princeton University Press.

Roselli, David. 2011. *Theater of the People: Spectators and Society in Ancient Athens.* Austin: University of Texas Press.

Scodel, Ruth. 1998. "The Captive's Dilemma: Sexual Acquiescence in Euripides' *Hecuba* and *Troades.*" *Harvard Studies in Classical Philology* Harvard Studies in Classical Philology 98: 137–54.

Seaford, Richard. 1994. *Reciprocity and Ritual: Homer and Tragedy in the Developing City-State.* Oxford: Oxford University Press.

Segal, Charles. 1986. *Interpreting Greek Tragedy: Myth, Poetry, Text*. Ithaca, NY: Cornell University Press.

Solvang, Elna. 2014. "Guarding the House: Conflict, Rape, and David's Concubines." In *Sex in Antiquity: Gender and Sexuality in the Ancient World*, edited by Mark Masterson, Nancy Sorkin Rabinowitz, and J. E. Robson. London: Routledge.

Suter, Ann. 2008. "Male Lament in Greek Tragedy." In *Lament: Studies in the Ancient Mediterranean and Beyond*, edited by Ann Suter, 156–80. Oxford: Oxford University Press.

Vernant, Jean-Pierre. 1988. "The Historical Moment of Tragedy in Greece: Some of the Social and Psychological Conditions." In *Myth and Tragedy in Ancient Greece*, translated by Janet Lloyd, 23–9. New York: Zone Books.

———. 1990. "City-State Warfare." In *Myth and Society in Ancient Greece*, translated by Janet Lloyd, revised paperback edition, 29–53. Antlantic Highlands, NJ: Zone Books.

Wohl, Victoria. 1998. *Intimate Commerce: Exchange, Gender, and Subjectivity in Greek Tragedy*. Austin: University of Texas Press.

Zeitlin, Froma. 1978. "The Dynamics of Misogyny: Myth and Mythmaking in the *Oresteia*." *Arethusa* 11. 1, 2: 149–84.

———. 1990. "Playing the Other: Theater, Theatricality, and the Feminine in Greek Drama." In *Nothing to Do with Dionysos? Athenian Drama in its Social Context*, edited by John J. Winkler and Froma Zeitlin, 63–96. Princeton, NJ: Princeton University Press.

———. 1996. *Playing the Other: Gender and Society in Classical Greek Literature*. Chicago: University of Chicago Press.

CHAPTER NINE

"He Gave Me His Hand but Took My Bow":* Trust and Trustworthiness in the Philoctetes and Our Wars

NANCY SHERMAN

The Moral Injury of Betraying

On April 21, 2007, army captain Josh Mantz died in Baghdad and came back to life after flatlining for 15 minutes—long past the time doctors routinely mark as the cut-off point for lifesaving measures, given the likely damage to the brain without vital signs. Not only did Josh survive, but he returned to his unit five months later to resume his platoon command. Yet despite the remarkable revival and media tour as the resilience poster boy for the Department of Defense, Josh emotionally crashed four years later. "It's the moral injury over time that really kills people," he told me. "Soldiers lose their identity. They don't understand who they are anymore." And he added, "Society is oblivious to what soldiers go through."[1]

What specifically weighs on Mantz is that he survived, but his staff sergeant Marlon Harper did not. The details are wrenching: Mantz was guiding his troops near the Shiite rebel stronghold of Sadr City when a sniper fired a round of bullets that penetrated Harper's left arm, severing his aorta. The hot molten round fused with Harper's armor-plate, forming a projectile the size of a human fist that ricocheted into Josh's upper right thigh and severed his femoral artery. Injured and dazed, Mantz administered first aid on Harper, as he waited for medical assistance. A young medic arrived and immediately went to work on Mantz, not Harper, probably because an aortal wound is less viable than a femoral wound. Having died and returned "didn't bring me closer to God," Mantz says. "'Ah, He must have great plans for you,' people say. 'But what about Staff Sergeant Harper?' I ask."

In *The Untold War*[2] I write about the moral injuries soldiers endure. Some are like those with which Josh Mantz still struggles, feeling the guilt of survival, of having had luck, miraculous luck, and state-of-the-art medical interventions on one's side, and yet experiencing that good luck as an awful betrayal of buddies. As Mantz's story makes clear, moral wounds demand moral healing. Experts in military and veteran mental health are now trying to articulate just what that healing would look like and how treatments overlap or are critically different from those routinely used in treating post-traumatic stress, where the psychological injury in the paradigmatic case has to do with exposure or witnessing life threats rather than moral damage.[3]

Philosophers have by and large been on the sidelines in exploring the nature of moral injury and moral repair, in general, and in soldiering, in particular.[4] Yet their contribution is important to understanding the nature of suffering moral damage, the emotions and attitudes expressive of it, and moral repair. In this chapter, I examine trust and trustworthiness as part of a notion of moral repair. As a case study to consider side by side with contemporary cases, I turn to Sophocles' *Philoctetes*.

One way to understand Mantz's narrative is as a tale of restoring his own sense of trustworthiness in the face of what he took to be his betrayal of his buddy. I am not here interested in whether his construal and emotions have warrant—that is, whether his guilt or shame is justified by what in fact happened and whether or not he in fact betrayed Harper. (I don't believe he did.) My focus is not on warrant, but rather on a more general understanding of reactions of holding self and others responsible, whether the transgressions are apparent or actual. To focus primarily on the fittingness of the emotion is to focus on a different and more limited question that can eclipse a fuller conceptual understanding of the nature of specific reactive attitudes.[5]

Trust as a Reactive Attitude

In contemporary philosophical literature, the notion of certain emotional attitudes as constitutive of holding self and others responsible is discussed in the context of reactive attitudes.[6] Broadly put, reactive emotional attitudes, like resentment, indignation, or guilt (on the negative side) and gratitude (on the positive side) are constitutive of holding persons responsible, in cases where we presuppose the plausibility of attributions of responsibility. As Hurley and Macnamara have put it recently, reactive attitudes are modes of praise or blame targeted at some recipient (others or self), in response to morally significant conduct that negatively or positively impinges on one's moral good functioning.[7] I insult you and you feel resentment. You give me a gift, and I feel gratitude for your caring about me. I intentionally harm you, and I myself feel guilt and reproach for the transgression. Sometimes, these attitudes are openly expressed, though not always. I may feel resentment at your slur, though I say nothing and show no irritation. In the self-reactive case, my guilt for real or apparent wrongdoing may be unconscious or masked by complicated defenses, but when it is felt it is manifest to me just by virtue of being felt. In such cases, I experience a sense of being punished or holding myself to account. In the interpersonal case, when I express my resentment to you, I may hold you responsible in my heart, but I also, in this expression, hold you to account publically through my blame. Expressed emotional attitudes are overt practices of crediting and punishing.[8]

Thinking of trust as a reactive attitude is not straightforward. It is not primarily backward-looking, as in the case of the paradigm (negative) reactive attitudes of resentment, indignation, or guilt. In each of these we react (or have the tendency to react)[9] to something that has been done to us (or that we have done to another) that violates due regard or a norm. Gratitude, a positive reactive attitude, is also backward-looking, and recognizes that another has exceeded a norm or minimum regard due to us.[10] Trust, in contrast, is primarily forward-looking; it is anticipatory, and broadly speaking takes the form of a confidence or expectation about a person that falls short of sure belief and involves some exposure to vulnerability and risk-taking. It is not just reliance or reliability that could be filled by nature or a machine, or even by a person's dependable habits (such as relying on Kant's daily Königsberg walk for setting one's watch). Rather, it is a signal to another that one is counting on her to recognize and respond to one's dependency (or entrustment) in a certain domain.[11] Given its future orientation, trust is perhaps better thought of as primarily "projective" than "reactive," and specifically, normatively projective of an attitude of responsiveness: it calls out to another that one is counting on her to recognize and respond to one's need.[12] In this, trust enlists and elicits responsiveness in another with respect to a certain domain.[13]

Depending on the theoretical account, a trustor trusts a trustee on the basis of belief in the goodwill (or benevolence) of the trustee;[14] or, in the case of friendship or the solidarity of battle buddies, on the basis of a belief in the goodwill constitutive of those relationships;[15] or, in the case of other roles and duties, on the basis of presumed trustworthiness that flows from the conscientiousness of the trustee in fulfilling a given role. The ground of trustworthiness may also be much weaker and based on self-interest, because it is in a trustee's self-interest to maintain a trust relationship and so in her interest to "encapsulate" the trustor's interests within her own,[16] or because it is in a trustee's self-interest to nurture the self-esteem that comes from being regarded as trustworthy by others.[17] Some of these, though not all, may be backward-looking (reactive) reasons that support one's projection of trust in another with regard to the future, that is, a trustee exhibited goodwill in the past, or showed solidarity before, is a reason to trust her now and deem her more or less trustworthy.

Most recently, though, Karen Jones has critiqued these various motives, as either too restrictive to cover a broad range of cases, or as too unstable and transient to motivate trust.[18] Her suggestion is that what does the unifying and characteristic work of motivating trustworthiness (and which in turn motivates trust) is simply the consideration "that someone is counting on you."[19] Trustworthiness, in her view, is "active engagement with the fact of our dependency."[20] From the standpoint of a conceptual function or role argument, we have a "pressing interest," James rightly claims, "in there being people who will take the fact that others are counting on them to be reason-giving in their practical deliberations."[21] When we trust others, we are counting on them to recognize that we are counting on them. We are counting on them to be responsive to our trust and to mirror that trust through trustworthiness.

This is important background to my interests in the moral psychology of soldiering. Trust and trustworthiness are irreducible elements in the fabric of military solidarity and unit cohesion. A soldier goes to war trusting that his buddies will cover his back. The anguish of not fulfilling that expectation can bring on crippling self-reproach and self-doubt about one's trustworthiness as a battle buddy, as Mantz's case painfully illustrates. Soldiers, of course, also extend their trust upward toward command, and betrayal by command (or by incompetent, behemoth bureaucracies of which command is a part) is all too common a theme and a significant cause of moral injury in war and after.[22]

In what follows I want to consider the aftermath of one such betrayal and abandonment by command, the festering resentment that follows, and the critical recuperative role a trust relationship plays in restoring the hope that others can be responsive to one's dependency. The strange trust relationship I take up is that between Philoctetes and Neoptolemus in Sophocles' tragedy, *Philoctetes*.

Trust and Trust Responsiveness in **Philoctetes**

The story is familiar to many readers.[23] Philoctetes is a Greek warrior marooned for ten years on the island of Lemnos, abandoned by his Greek commanders as they headed on to Troy. He was left behind because of a fetid foot wound he suffered as the result of a bite from a poisonous snake guarding the tomb of the goddess Chryse. He was left to die with his "weeping disease," (6) shunned by his command and by a fleet that couldn't tolerate the putrid smell of his mutilated foot or his anguished wailing.[24] But ten years into his solitary confinement, Philoctetes, or more properly his bow, becomes critically necessary for the victory of the Greeks against the Trojans. And so Odysseus, trickster and cunning speechifier, enlists a boy warrior, Neoptolemus, with the right credentials and ancestral lineage (he is son of the deceased and glorious Achilles), to do Odysseus' and the Greek army's bidding. The two arrive at the island, Odysseus keeping out of sight as he coaches Neoptolemus to capture the bow through a snare of trust, "You know I could never speak to him as you can / He will trust you, and you will stay safe" (70–1).

Like a good interrogator, Neoptolemus is to build trust in order to exploit it. Of course, it is not intelligence that he will gather, but the "unassailable weapon" itself (77). He is to say that he too has a grudge against the Greek commanders for not holding him worthy of inheriting Achilles' arms. And from that sense of shared resentment, Philoctetes will begin to make himself vulnerable to Neoptolemus' overtures. He will begin to trust.

The trusting at first seems odd. Why should Philoctetes trust this young stranger who has pulled in from Troy and arrived so mysteriously on his island? Moreover, is it trust or just desperation that disarms him of caution? For he is miserable and lonely, and above all else craves safe passage home. He longs for human contact, and after a decade of solitary confinement thirsts for any news a messenger can bring of the battlefront and the fate of his fellow soldiers. In light of all this, is he just too ready to gain a friend, as a possible meaning of his name suggests (as "he who gains a friend" [673]).[25] Trust is an attitude born of dependency. But when the need is abject and the power others have over one is near total, trust is manipulated, not given. Indeed, Neoptolemus' narrative of betrayal by the Greek commanders might be seen as an ancient version of a rapport-building technique that a good interrogator uses. The good interrogator develops an intimate and empathic relationship with his subject, and may even sow the seeds for an erotic or idealizing "transference" onto himself that can then be exploited for further domination and advantage:[26] At very least, Neoptolemus makes clear the grounds for rapport:

Abused and insulted, I am sailing for home
Deprived of what is rightfully mine
By that bastard son of bastards, Odysseus.
I hold the commanders accountable.

(381–5)

Philoctetes is moved, as planned. We share a "cargo of common griev-ances," he says. "You and I sing the same song" (404–5).[27]

The trust is coerced by faked trustworthiness, or at least trustworthiness fashioned with bits and pieces of truth, designed to ensnare. That is the hoax, a kind of Trojan horse rolled onto this island, once again engineered by Odysseus, with the young warrior Neoptolemus (which is just what his name means) being initiated by his side in the sorts of treachery often mor-ally permissible in warfare, even if typically not directed against one's own. But is there any genuine trust and trustworthiness displayed in this play? Is there trust and trustworthiness that is not part of an intelligence scheme? I claim that there is. But it has to be developed. Moreover, its manifestation is critical for Philoctetes' moral repair from the double moral betrayal he suffers by his command (the first in the original abandonment by his com-manders, the second in this hoax).

The pivotal moment comes when Philoctetes, persuaded to leave the island with Neoptolemus and set sail for what he believes is home, gath-ers his few belongings, including his famous bow. Eager to get it his hands on the bow, Neoptolemus asks to see it. Without the slightest reluctance, Philoctetes begins to entrust Neoptolemus with the very bow that has kept him alive on this island, protected from predators and supplied with food. "I will grant your wish. There's nothing I wouldn't do for you," says Philoctetes (658–9). Neoptolemus gently demurs: "Is it allowed *(themis)?* If not, I will relent" (660). Philoctetes assures him that it is permissible, and more importantly, that he trusts him because he has shown him goodwill and kindness. In that, he says, he mirrors Philoctetes himself, who received the bow from Heracles as a gift for his demonstration of kindness.[28]

There are two wrinkles in this passage, however, and they mislead about what is most fundamental in the trust exchange. The first is the apparent worry about background norms, suggested by the question of whether it is right or permitted to hold the bow. Can he, Neoptolemus, really hold this sacred bow? Will it offend the gods? Is Neoptolemus really concerned about being in conformity with that external norm, or is he just exhibiting fake decency and politeness in order to mask his intention to steal? I suspect it is the latter. But whatever the answer, the basic trust isn't grounded in Philoctetes' expectation of Neoptolemus' compliance with some antecedent norm. Rather, I want to suggest that it is essentially grounded in Philoctetes himself, calling out to Neoptolemus saying, "I'm counting on you as competent here," and normatively expecting that here and now Neoptolemus will engage with that dependency and be responsive to it in respect to his own reasons for action. Moreover, that trust is projective. It elicits trustworthiness. It scaffolds trust, nurses it along, and helps it to grow through the expectation that one ought to be trustworthy. That is trust's cunning, and perhaps, why, at times, it can create not just trustees, but dependents, manipulated into collaboration.[29] The second wrinkle is that Philoctetes' own remarks bury this point. He suggests that his trust is based on his anticipation of Neoptolemus continuing to show goodwill and compassion toward him in his suffering. Neoptolemus has become a "priceless friend," (673) and friends act out of goodwill and benevolence. I can trust my bow with a friend, he thinks. He won't steal it. He won't "stab me in the back," as we would say. But even in this kind of case where trust imputes goodwill to the trustworthy, there is something more basic going on. Philoctetes is telling Neoptolemus that he is counting on him. And that expectation can itself, at times, motivate. So Philoctetes assures Neoptolemus, "Don't worry, *(tharsei,* have confidence), the bow will be yours to hold / And then hand it back to the hand that gave it" (667). He plies on additional reasons for his trust, namely friendship, goodwill, and compassion. And they too, no doubt, can incentivize and bring Neoptolemus around. But in a barer, more minimal way, Philoctetes is fostering trust simply by projection of his trust, implicitly saying I'm counting on you to keep safe the bow and then give it back. Being responsive to another's dependency is the bare bones of trustworthiness.

Moreover, in this staged case of trustworthiness, though Philoctetes presumes Neoptolemus' goodness, we as audience have an ironic distance that Philoctetes does not yet possess (and will have only in retrospect).[30] We know that despite the fact that he seems genuinely moved by the islander's suffering, Neoptolemus is still in the employ of Odysseus, and his goodness, even if native and genuine, may just be instrumentally deployed here. So we are suspicious, rightly, from our position of knowledge, that his antecedent goodness or good name is doing any work here other than that of ensnaring his prey.[31]

But, despite this, it would be hard to come away from this scene without seeing a genuine spark of trust and trust responsiveness being kindled. What we see, and probably what Philoctetes also picks up in Neoptolemus' response, is that he is answering an address to be trusted and trustworthy. He is responsive to the address, "I am counting on you." And recognizing that he is being so addressed, and acknowledging it, however thinly, back to Philoctetes, adds a new level of being counted on by him.[32] Put differently, Neoptolemus' "catching the ball" is the first step in the reciprocation.[33] And that acknowledgment, that you are being counted on, is thrown back and caught by the trustor and reinforces the trust.

There is much more to say about trust and trustworthiness in this play. Neoptolemus insists repeatedly on his trustworthiness with respect to the safekeeping of the bow, and his sincerity seems to grow the more he is exposed to Philoctetes' excruciating suffering.[34] Philoctetes' utter dependency on him makes it hard for Neoptolemus to carry through with the plot. And he opts to return the bow to Philoctetes, rather than continue as Odysseus' lackey, despite the consequences for the mission. It takes a deus ex machina, in the form of Heracles, to resolve the plot and assure Philoctetes that his (and the bow's) return to Troy will both bring victory to the Greeks and the cure of his noxious wound.

So goes the plot. The take-home lesson I wish to draw is that in this story Philoctetes, though traumatized by betrayal, still reaches out through trust, and thereby elicits trustworthiness in a potential enemy bent on subjecting him to yet more betrayal. Part of the work is done by the cunning of trust and not just by Philoctetes' generous and resilient spirit or by Neoptolemus' potential compassion, pity, and remorse.[35] These other factors no doubt play an important role in a richer trust relation that can be read into this play, but I don't want to overmoralize the story, or lose sight of a ubiquitous, more easily available form of trust that is also part of this story. I am intent rather on showing what a basic display of trust itself can do, by calling out that you are counting on another to do something (or be competent in a certain domain), and how the fact of dependency may become a compelling reason in that other's deliberations.[36] Whether it is an overriding reason is another matter. And what Neoptolemus must do is to figure out precisely what Philoctetes is counting on him for and whether he can comply in a way that minimizes conflict with his other important standing obligations, including trust relations. But the general point is that expressing trust can bootstrap trustworthiness. It projects onto another a normative expectation that can have a causal efficacy.[37]

Resentment, Reentry, and Trust after War

But trustors, of course, need to be wise, and make their addresses to those who are plausibly competent to aid and assist in the domains required. And those who are competent also need to signal their competencies, and in many cases contribute not just interpersonally, but institutionally, in networks of support. In the case of returning veterans, there can be a familiar shutting out of civilians, even family members, as potential recipients of trust: the thought is that those who don't put on the uniform can't fully understand the moral and psychic challenges of going to war. And that retreat of veterans to their own circle reinforces many a civilian's response to withdraw or believe that it is meddlesome or presumptive to think one might contribute in a dialogue with soldiers about what they have been through in a war zone.

I myself may have once, in a significant way, been complicit in this. And the insight speaks to a more general point about elicitations of trust responsiveness. My dad was a World War II veteran (an army medic) who died several years ago. I was left to clean up his effects in the hospital room. And in putting away his belongings, I found his key chain, with his dog tags (army identifications) attached. They were well worn, and his name, "Seymour Sherman," was just visible. They had been touched and rubbed and fingered for some 65 years. My mother said he had carried them their whole marriage. But I never noticed them before, and he never showed them to me. Perhaps it was a case of willful ignorance on my part, and willful concealment on his. But his war experiences were by and large not something to be shared with his children. They were his private burdens, not ours.

I mention this because many returning veterans do feel, as my dad did, that the inner landscape of war is for soldiers and not for the civilians to whom one returns. War presents myriads of complex, concrete questions about the moral permissibility of killing and being killed, of liability to lethal and nonlethal harming and being harmed, questions of whether one did enough to prevent harm to innocent civilians or was a good enough soldier and avoided undue risk to one's troops. Guilt, shame, and a sense of betraying others can easily commingle with adrenalized pride, bravado, and the overwhelming sense of purpose and meaning that participation in war, even an unjust or misguided war, can offer. The psychological and philosophical mess is hard to untangle, and easy to wall up. Opening yourself up to civilians who may not be able to bring all that back into their "own bosoms," as Adam Smith would say, is not something all service members have a taste for doing. In this regard, Philoctetes becomes a metaphor of sorts for the alienation and anomie of a veteran, war-wounded, resentful, and isolated.[38]

And yet trust embeds hope, hope in others, that they can be responsive to your need. And even if their empathy cannot access your inner emotional affect in the way that self-empathy at times can, it nonetheless can be connective, interpersonally and intrapersonally, connecting persons (and parts of self) walled off from each other.[39] And this responsiveness can come from civilians, too, who have not gone to war or put on a uniform. Part of the work of trust is to be open to making the overture, wisely, to those who have taken some of the burden off the trustor and signaled some competence and interest.

This doesn't always happen and soldiers can retreat. Or they can retreat and then reenter. Consider the experience of Phil Carter, an army reserve officer who served in Iraq and returned home to civilian life in spring 2006.[40] In his ears, the "thank-you's" and "hero" labels heaped on him rang hollow, given that what he had left behind were "thousands of Iraqis…dying each month in a hellish civil war. If we were really heroes, why was the war in Iraq going so badly?" He was alienated and withdrew from civilians, "even pushing away family," and tightening his web of trust to mostly other veterans, where there was a ready-to-hand sense of mutual trustworthiness, based on implicit loyalty, a common appreciation of sacrifice and military virtue, and a mutual appreciation that each could help the other:[41] "I even resented the strangers who thanked me. I suspected that they were just trying to ease their guilt for not serving. Instead of thanking me, I wanted them…to make some sacrifice greater than the amount of lung effort necessary to utter a few words." Words were cheap and action dear, especially the sort of action he valued as a military man.

In his case, trust in the civilian world required a mutual reaching out. Family and civilian friends continued to signal their availability, interest, and competence to support him, and he, through self-reflection and therapy, began to monitor and revise the evaluations implicit in his resentment. He came to see some civilian displays of gratitude as sincere and reflective attempts to be more connected with those on whom the burdens of military service fell. "I…began to empathize with those who had no personal connection to the military, but who still wanted to say something or do something to support those who served on their behalf…After a while, I came to accept their thank-you's." The acceptance expressed in "you are welcome" became his recognition and acknowledgment of (or responsiveness to) the "thank-you's," which in turn he came to see as a recognition and acknowledgment of (or responsiveness to) his service.

Laid out this way, the interpersonal structure of service, gratitude, and acceptance of gratitude has the reciprocal, reactive structure of trust. To trust is implicitly to address another and say, "I am counting on you here." That recognition of another as the object of your trust in a specific area seeks acknowledgment. The trustee can acknowledge privately, to himself, that he has been so recognized, but given the aspirations of trust, one would expect the exchange to be geared to a public expression to the trustor that he has received and acknowledges how he is being recognized and has accepted its normative burden, or as we put it earlier, accepted that that he is being counted on is a compelling reason for action.[42]

Similarly, serving one's country, and its citizens, in uniform, as Phil Carter has done, is, formally speaking (putting aside the substantive issues of just cause and conduct, or pacifism), to do one's fellow citizens a service. Gratitude, publically expressed to a service member in a "thank-you," is an approving acknowledgment of the receipt of that service, and a "you are welcome" is an approving acknowledgment of that expressed gratitude. The exchange, of course, can be faked (Carter's worry) simply to fulfill the expectations of etiquette or, instrumentally, to relieve guilt. But if the exchange is successful, the acknowledgment of gratitude is not just in conformity with what is expected, but is motivated by a genuine feeling of appreciation and thanks.[43]

In *De Beneficiis,* Seneca rehearses this very trope of recognition and acknowledgment (and its potential for iterative looping) through an analogy of a game of ball, an intuitive metaphor I have already used here. Seneca's context concerns the norms set up by doing favors (benefactions), but as I have suggested, the point holds more generally for trust interactions as well. The idea lays bare the calling out to another and the acknowledgment back of your reaching out. Knowing something about the recipient of your address and her competencies is critical in making a wise pass. But equally important is being ready to catch the acknowledgment thrown back, in the case of gratitude with a willingness "to listen to professions of gratitude" as if they were "actual repayments,"[44] and in the case of trust, I suggest, with a willingness to reinforce the original trust overture. All this is part of the normative (and growth) potential of the initial throw. The passage bears quoting at length:

> I would like to take up an analogy which our own Chrysippus drew with a game of ball. It falls to the ground through the fault either of the person throwing it or of the person receiving it, while it only remains in play by passing, properly thrown and caught, from one pair of hands to the other. A good player needs to send it off differently to a tall partner than to a short one. The same principle applies to a favour. Only if properly accommodated to both the persons involved, bestower and recipient, will it leave the one and reach the other as it should. Again, if the game is with a trained and practised player, we shall be bolder in throwing the ball. No matter how it comes, his hand will be ready and quick to drive it back. Against an untrained novice, we shall not throw it so hard or so vigorously but be more relaxed, aiming the ball right into his hands and simply meeting it when it comes back. We should use the same procedure when doing favours.[45]

Obviously, doing someone a good turn is best geared to what that recipient needs and is capable of using. As Seneca suggests, giving books to a country bumpkin or a heavy coat to someone in summer will not count as a wise pass likely to be caught with particular gratitude by the recipient![46] And similarly, trust given to someone who has signaled no competence or interest in that domain is not a wise exposure of vulnerability, or a likely way to scaffold deeper trust. And this again relates back to veterans. Many are right to be suspicious of public professions of gratitude that seem to be cover-ups for deeper, private disdain or at least selective insulation from soldiers' burdens. They are not sure that the pass thrown to them by the "thank-you" is really directed at them as gratitude for service rather than as pity for being suckered.[47] And if it is the latter, then a longer story needs to be told about the "thank-you" giver's role in that suckering. And that's not likely to happen except at a town meeting or the like designed specifically to air grievances and bridge military/civilian gaps. What can be mobilized at those meetings is not only greater interpersonal trust but also insight into how governmental and nongovernmental institutional structures can support or undermine that trust. Interpersonal trust, in all arenas of our lives, depends deeply on background institutional structures that can support that trust. In the case of veterans, pulled out of civilian society for a decade, this is especially so, given that they often come home with injury, and often without jobs, homes, and educational opportunities.[48]

Trust as Emotion

My remarks have been in broad brushstroke about trust as a kind of reactive attitude. But I have qualified that trust is forward-looking and so in a way is projective in normatively anticipating recognition and acknowledgment or responsiveness. If it is reactive, it is so only in the more restricted sense of responding to someone as presumed to be trustworthy, and so approving of them, if you will, as someone before whom to make yourself vulnerable. But trustworthiness, as I have said, is often elicited, or at least strengthened, by responsiveness to the initial trust. Gratitude is more properly reactive in responding to someone in virtue of what they have already done. It looks backward, even if it sets in motion a forward-looking anticipation of acceptance of your gratitude in a "you are welcome."

Reactive attitudes are typically thought of as emotions. At least that is the common understanding of the paradigmatic (negative) reactive attitudes of resentment, indignation, and guilt (cf. the very term pathos). But what about trust? Do we do well to think of it as an emotion? Even if it isn't a belief, in the sense that the reason we turn to trust is precisely because we lack the evidence that would ground firmer belief, still trust doesn't have that excitable feeling, the charge and strong valence (negative or positive affect) that characterizes many emotions. In the Aristotelian language of the *Rhetoric*, it isn't in an obvious way "accompanied with" pleasure and pain.[49] But of course many emotions are quieter in that regard, and an emotion's feel, as the critiques of William James[50] have suggested, is not a reliable indicator of emotion in general (as opposed to mere edginess, say) or a distinct type of emotion (resentment, e.g., rather than shame).

Rather than look at an analysis of emotion, however, I think we do better in thinking about trust as an emotion if we take seriously some of the roles emotions serve in practical agency. I have argued at length elsewhere

that emotions play various roles, (1) as modes of discerning or recognizing salience that direct, and indeed, rivet our attention to certain objects
of value we care about and take to be important for good living (modes
of attending to value); (2) as modes that signal those valuings to ourselves
and others (modes of conveying and expressing value); (3), related to (2), as
modes that can reveal values we were unaware we had, where the emotional
experience itself discloses to us and others that we have a deep interest here
and concern (modes of disclosing value); (4) as modes of establishing or
creating new values rather than tracking antecedent ones (modes of instat-
ing value); and (5), most familiarly, as motivators and mobilizers to which
we react, as when we act out of compassion or out of friendship. Emotions
stir us into action insofar as we take up the evaluations implicit in those
emotions—that I see his need or that he is my friend—as reasons for action
(modes of motivation).[51]

Now trust seems to fulfill many of these roles. First, to trust someone is
to organize one's attention in a certain way, to notice what another is signaling, to perhaps block out some doubts or suspend suspicion because of
the riveting power of that attending. As Peter Goldie puts it, emotions have
an epistemic tendency to build "an epistemic landscape" that coheres with
an evaluation that that emotion has. In Michael Brady's terms, emotions
have a "capture and consume" mode of directing attention and cognitive
resources.[52] Trust doesn't just see someone in a certain light. It makes an
investment in the other to do something with something that is entrusted.
And construing that person in that light unwittingly positions us to sum-
mon other features of the landscape as confirmation of the view. In a way,
trust digs us into vulnerability.[53]

Second, as we have said before, when we trust, we typically communicate
or express that to another, with an "I am counting on you," or in emotionally laden body language or facial expressions that show one's dependency
and expectation. Trust may not broadcast facially in the way that anger does
(in a furrowed brow or gruff voice), or compassion (in upturned lips or
kindly gaze), but it surely enlists a variety of narratives to communicate
expectancy, demand, dependence, and in its absence, betrayal. Third, and
relatedly, in trusting another, and in communicating that, we may be disclosing to ourselves and to others what we took for granted or were not
quite aware of as salient, but that now has moved to the foreground of our
concerns and interests. Fourth, trust in another may be de novo, a new way
of regarding another, and a way of initiating, or eliciting, as I've said before,
trustworthiness that is as of yet unproven and may be uncertain, but which
we are hoping to cultivate and establish through our display of dependence
and expectancy. Finally, trust can motivate. It can act as a motive for sharing
burdens, entrusting intimacies, overcoming resentments, and even terror. It
motivates connection to others and, in virtue of that, connection to ourselves. It takes seriously that others are capable of, and have an interest in,
mirroring our specific recognitions of them and of responding to those recognitions with an acknowledgment that they will take them up in action.

There is much more to say here, but this outlines a way to think about trust as a reactive attitude that is an emotion. Emotional trust tracks and conveys salient information about whom we take to be competent and worthy of reaching out to about our needs. Out of trust, we are motivated to expose ourselves to risk in significant ways, with the hope that others will respond to our calls.

Conclusion

Soldiering cannot exist without trust. No one would put his or her life at risk in war without considerable trust that others will be there with physical, emotional, and medical support. Of course, that trust can be betrayed in war. *Philoctetes* reminds us of how deep the betrayals and abandonments can go.

Philoctetes' wounds are, of course, physical as well as psychological. And presumably that festering, fetid leg is the cause and putative justification of the moral betrayal: he must be cut off from the whole, if the whole is to be saved—with a little utilitarian logic chop, the sacrifice of one soldier preserves the army of many. War always puts its human assets, and not just its materiel, at some risk; *Philoctetes is* just another case of balancing force protection against the exigencies of the mission.

But there is something insidious, haunting, cruel, and inhumane about Philoctetes' sacrifice. And it has to do with the trauma of isolation. Philoctetes has been a prisoner in solitary confinement for a full ten years. In his case, he has nature and the beasts as his companions. Not all are so lucky, especially those who have spent the past decade in the US detention center at Guantanamo, set up as a part of the "global war on terror."[54] Still, Philoctetes was put in solitary by his own side, by his own command, and that is perhaps the unkindest betrayal. And the reason why his trust in Neoptolemus is so fascinating. Why should Philoctetes trust this emissary sent by his betrayers? And why should Neoptolemus be moved to renege on his plot? I've argued that the moral address in this interaction, the signaling of dependency, and the projection that it will be recognized and acknowledged as legitimate, are the components of this new trust bond. Trust and trustworthiness are built here from the ground up, on the ashes of soul-shattered living. This is an ancient and abiding lesson for veterans coming home and for civilians to whom they return.[55]

Notes

⋆ *Philoctetes*, 942 (Sophocles [2007]).

1. From an interview with Josh Mantz, March, 2012.
2. See Sherman (2010).
3. See Litz et al. (2009). See also Nash et al. (2011); Nash and Westphal (2011).

4. For some noteworthy exceptions, see especially Walker (2006) and Brison (2002).
5. See D'Arms and Jacobson (2000) for an important disambiguation of moral and epistemic appropriateness. Aristotle, in discussing appropriate emotions, emotions that are *hôs dei*, leaves matters ambiguous. For further discussion, see Sherman (2010, ch. 4 especially).
6. See the classic article of Strawson (1962), and its discussions: Wallace (1996); Darwall (2006); Hurley and Macnamara (2011); Macnamara (2011, 2012); and Smith (2005).
7. Hurley and Macnamara (2011).
8. Note, Aristotle's notion of pathos (emotion) is, in many cases, reactive. But while reactive anger and its blaming *presupposes,* on an Aristotelian view, an attitude of holding persons responsible, that attitude of holding responsible is independent and prior, not itself constituted by the emotional attitude. The whole point of Strawsonian reactive attitudes is that they are constitutive of moral responsibility, and not a side effect of some independent, underlying belief in responsibility. That is the radical aspect of Strawson's position. For Aristotle on the link of anger or shame with blame see Aristotle (1984) *Nicomachean Ethics* (hereafter *NE*) 2.7 (see 1108b1–10 for the link between), *NE* 3.1 Rhetoric (hereafter Rh). (2. 2, 2.6, 2.9).
9. See Wallace (1996) on this dispositional account.
10. See Macnamara (2012).
11. I am here indebted to Karen Jones' recent account, which I fill out below (Jones, [2012]). Implicit in her account is acceptance of a three-place relation analysis of trust and trustworthiness: "A trusts B in a certain domain of interaction where B has competence." (2012, 70). Or, Jones, (2004), note 1. A trusts B to do Z: "A trusts B in domain of interaction D." She draws on Annette Baier's influential work on trust, specifically, "Trust and Anti-Trust," and the three-place analysis of, "A trusts B with valued item Z." (Baier [1986]).
12. See Karen Jones (2012) on the idea of trustworthiness as capturing the idea that others are counting on us.
13. On the idea of trust-responsiveness, see Pettit (1995). On a reactive attitude of resentment as a call for an RSVP, see Darwall (2006) and Walker (2006).
14. Baier (1986).
15. See Aristotle on goodwill as constitutive of friendship, *NE* 8.2, (Aristotle [1984]).
16. See Hardin (2002).
17. Pettit (1995 and 2004).
18. Aristotle says similar things, not surprisingly, of friendships based on utility and pleasure. They are unstable contexts for mutual recognition of goodwill and friendly feeling.
19. Jones (2012, 70).
20. Jones (2012, 65).
21. Jones (2012, 66).
22. See especially Sherman (2010, ch. 2). See also Sherman (2012).
23. I use throughout Peter Meineck and Paul Woodruff's translation and notes in their edition (Sophocles, [2007]).
24. For a plea not to minimize as a mere inconvenience the physical wound and the effect of Philoctetes' animal screams of pain on the Achaen troops, see Stephens (1995).
25. See Meineck and Woodruff's note, (Sophocles, [2007, 217]), on this possible translation. See also Daly (1982) for the name's related connotation: "a friend better than any possession." The traditional meaning is "fond of gain."
26. For a discussion of interrogation techniques based on building rapport, see Sherman (2010, chs. 5 and 6), with notes. For the army field manual on interrogation techniques in human intelligence collection, see https://www.fas.org/irp/doddir/army/fm2-22-3.pdf

27. For the theme of false and persuasive *logoi* used to lure Philoctetes, see Hoppin (1990).
28. When Philoctetes, as a young boy, lit Heracles' funeral pyre. See note to 671 in the Meineck and Woodruff edition, which fills out the background here. Also, see *Women of Trachis,* in the Meineck and Woodruff edition of *Sophocles: Four Tragedies,* note to 1214 (Sophocles [2007])
29. See Pettit (1995) for a brief discussion of just when in the play Philoctetes addresses Neoptolemus as "friend" (*philos*), see Konstan (2001).
30. See Peter Goldie on ironic narrative distance in Goldie (2003).
31. For a discussion of Neoptolemus' ultimate change of heart and his rejection of Odyssesus' "stratagems in favour of his natural honesty," see Gill (1980).
32. For this back and forth iteration of second personal address, see suggestive remarks by Jones (2012); Macnamara (2012); and Kukla and Lance (2009). For suggestive and complementary remarks here about the "restoration of communication between man and man," see Segal (1995).
33. See Seneca for an important "game of catch" metaphor constitutive of the giving gifts, accepting them with gratitude, and acknowledging that gratitude. *On Favours* 2, 19.3–7. Also, see the related metaphor of the three Graces' dance that "goes back on itself" (1.2.2–4). For a related perspective on this reciprocation of gift giving with "thank-you" and in return, "you're welcome," see Macnamara (2012).
34. For a complaint that Neoptolemus is motivated by an unexplained pity, see Sandridge (2008). For a more sympathetic view of the growth and motivational power of Neoptolemus' (and the Chorus') pity, see Konstan (2006).
35. See above note.
36. Again, I am indebted to Jones (2012, 71).
37. There is an overlap here with the psychoanalytic notion of projective identification. The rough idea, first developed by Melanie Klein, is that an individual splits off negative represented parts of self (or ego) onto another in order to distance and defend oneself against the anxiety those represented parts arouse. Projective identification is a defense mechanism. The projection I have in mind is not defensive, but more proactive and normative. It is a transference and then mirroring of one's own trust of another onto that other, with the aim of that target receiving, recognizing, and reciprocating (through trustworthiness) that trust investment. For a discussion of the history and meaning of projective identification, see Grotstein (1995).
38. For a wonderful psychoanalytic piece on Philoctetes and the sense of abandonment of Vietnam veterans see Lansky (2003).
39. On self-empathy, see my forthcoming, "Self-Empathy and Moral Repair" Sherman (2014). On hope as a reactive attitude, like trust, important in moral repair, see "Moral Recovery after War: Hope" (Sherman [2014], Forthcoming).
40. From an opinion piece Carter wrote in the *Washington Post* for Veterans' Day, 2011. See http://www.washingtonpost.com/opinions/for-veterans-is-thank-you-for-your-service-enough/2011/11/03/gIQA67hZmM_print.html. Phil Carter commented on a paper I gave on fidelity to cause at a meeting of the American Society for Political and Legal Philosophy, December 2007. He served in the first Obama administration as national veterans director.
41. See Pettit (1995, 208–12) on a mechanisms of loyalty, virtue, and prudence as bases of trustworthiness that can arouse and sustain trust. Friendship, is, of course, a privileged sphere of trust and, as Aristole notes, is motivated by similar reasons: virtue, pleasure, and utility. See *NE* 8. 2–3.
42. For this way of putting the matter, see the related discussion of Macnamara (2012). She draws on Kukla and Lance (2009).

43. On this, see again Macnamara (2012).
44. Seneca, *On Favours* [*De Beneficiis*], in Cooper and Procopé (1995, II.15.6).
45. Seneca, *On Favours* 2.17.3–4. For related analogy based on the looping back of the mutual reciprocations of the Three Graces, see *On Favours* 1.3.8 in (Cooper and Procopé [1995]).
46. See my discussion of Seneca on doing favours in Sherman (2006) and (2004).
47. For a discussion of being suckered, see Sherman (2010, ch. 2) and the narratives of Derek Vines, Iraq veteran, and Bob Steck, Vietnam veteran.
48. For the issue of homelessness among veterans, see http://www.huffingtonpost.com/2012/03/07/12-startling-statistics-veteran-homelessness_n_1327816.html. According to this report, one in seven of those homeless previously served in the military. For governmental initiatives aimed at post 9/11 GI veterans, see http://www.gibill.va.gov/benefits/post_911_gibill/.
49. *Rhetoric* (1378a31–33, 1383b13–19); relatedly (1385b12, 1386b17–30). See Aristotle (1984); Sherman (2004).
50. James (2003).
51. For a discussion of this, see Sherman (1995, 39–50).
52. See Brady (2007) and Goldie (2004, 99).
53. In this way, trust may be reactive to, or elicited by our construals; but that elicited trust in turn elicits trustworthiness, in the form of an acknowledgment or "uptake" by the trusted one that she is being counted on.
54. For a recent discussion marking the tenth anniversary of GITMO, see http://www.pbs.org/wnet/religionandethics/2013/09/06/september-6-2013-guantanamo-ethics/20043/.
55. I am grateful to Trip Glazer for his invaluable research assistance in the final stages of preparing this paper.

Bibliography

Aristotle. 1984. *The Complete Works of Aristotle: The Revised Oxford Translation*. Edited by Jonathan Barnes. Princeton, NJ: Princeton University Press.
Baier, Anette. 1986. "Trust and Antitrust." *Ethics* 96.2: 231–60.
Brady, Michael S. 2007. "Recalcitrant Emotions and Visual Illusions." *American Philosophical Quarterly* 44.3: 273–84.
Brison, Susan. 2002. *Aftermath: Violence and the Remaking of a Self*. Princeton, NJ: Princeton University Press.
Cooper, John M., and J. F. Procopé, 1995. "Selections from Seneca: Moral and Political Essays." In *Seneca: Moral and Political Essays*, edited by John M. Cooper and J. F. Procopé, 181–308. Cambridge: Cambridge University Press.
D'Arms, Justin, and Daniel Jacobson. 2000. "The Moralistic Fallacy: On the 'Appropriateness' of Emotions." *Philosophy and Phenomenological Research* 61.1: 65–90.
Daly, James. 1982. "The Name of Philoctetes: Philoctetes 670–73." *The American Journal of Philology* 103.4: 440–2.
Darwall, Stephen. 2006. *The Second-person Standpoint*. Cambridge, MA: Harvard University Press.
Gill, Christopher. 1980. "Bow, Oracle, and Epiphany in Sophocles' 'Philoctetes'." *Greece and Rome*, Second Series 27.2: 137–46.
Goldie, Peter. 2003. "One's Remembered Past: Narrative Thinking, Emotion, and the External Perspective." *Philosophical Papers* 32.3: 301–19.
———. 2004. "Emotion, Feeling, and Knowledge of the World." In *Thinking about Feeling: Contemporary Philosophers on Emotions*, edited by Robert Solomon, 91–106. New York: Oxford University Press.
Grotstein, James. 1995. *Splitting and Projective Identification*. Northvale, NJ: Jason Aronson.

Hardin, Russell. 2002. *Trust and Trustworthiness*. New York: Russel Sage Foundation.

Hoppin, Meredith Clark. 2003. "What Happens in *Philoctetes*?" In *Sophocles*, edited by Harold Bloom. New York and Philadelphia: Chelsea House.

Hurley, Elisa, and Coleen Macnamara. 2011. "Beyond Belief: Toward a Theory of Reactive Attitudes." *Philosophical Papers* 39.3: 373–99.

James, William. 2003. "What is an Emotion?" In *What is an Emotion? Classic and Contemporary Readings*, edited by Robert Solomon, 66–76. Oxford: Oxford University Press.

Jones, Karen. 2004. "Trust and Terror." In *Moral Psychology: Feminist Ethics and Social Theory*, edited by Peggy DesAutels and Margaret Urban Walker, 3–18. Lanham, MD: Rowman and Littlefield.

———. 2012. "Trustworwthiness." *Ethics* 123.1: 61–85.

Konstan, David. 2001 "Murder among Friends: Violation of 'Philia' in Greek Tragedy (review of Elizabeth Belfiore's book)." *American Journal of Philology* 122.2: 240–74.

———. 2006. *The Emotions of the Ancient Greeks: Studies in Aristotle and Classical Literature*. Toronto: University of Toronto Press.

Kukla, Rebecca, and Mark N. Lance. 2009. *"Yo!" and "Lo!": The Pragmatic Topography of the Space of Reasons*. Cambridge, MA: Harvard University Press.

Lansky, Melvin R. 2003. "Modification of the Ego Ideal and the Problem of Forgiveness in Sophocles' Philoctetes." *Psychoanalysis & Contemporary Thought* 26.4: 463–91.

Litz, Brett, Nathan Stein, Eileen Delaney, Leslie Lebowitz, and William P. Nash. 2009. "Moral Injury and Moral Repair in War Veterans: A Preliminary Model and Intervention Strategy." *Clinical Psychology Review* 29.8: 695–706.

Macnamara, Coleen. 2011. "Holding Others Responsible." *Philosophical Studies* 152: 81–102.

———. 2012. "Screw You" & "Thank You." *Philosophical Studies* 130.2: 893–914.

Nash, William P., Lillian Krantz, Nathan Stein, Richard Westphal, and Brett Litz. 2011. "Comprehensive Soldier Fitness, Battlemind, and the Stress Continuum Model: Military Organizational Approaches to Prevention." In *Caring for Veterans with Deployment-related Stress Disorders*, edited by Josef Ruzek, Paula Schnurr, Jennifer Vasterling, and Matthew J. Friedman, 193–214. Washington, DC: American Psychological Association.

Nash, William P., and Richard Westphal. 2011. *Trauma, Loss, and Moral Injury: Different Approaches for Prevention and Treatment*. Armed Forces Public Health Conference, Hampton, Virginia, March 23, 2011.

Pettit, Philip. 1995. "The Cunning of Trust." *Philosophy and Public Affairs* 224.3: 202–25.

———. 2004. "Hope and Its Place in Mind." *Annals of the American Academy of Political and Social Science* 592: 152–65.

Sandridge, Norman. 2008. "Feeling Vulnerable, but Not Too Vulnerable: Pity in Sophocles' Oedipus Colonus, Ajax and Philoctetes." *Classical Journal* 103.4: 443–48.

Segal, Charles. 1995. *Sophocles' Tragic World*. Cambridge, MA: Harvard University Press.

Sherman, Nancy. 1995. *Making a Necessity of Virtue: Aristotle and Kant on Virtue*. New York: Cambridge University Press.

———. 2004. "Virtue and Emotional Demeanor." In *Feelings and Emotions: Interdisciplinary Explorations*, edited by Anthony Manstead, Nico Frijda, and Agneta Fischer, 441–454. Cambridge: Cambridge University Press.

———. 2006. "The Look and Feel of Virtue." In *Norms, Virtue, and Objectivity: Issues in Ancient and Modern Ethics*, edited by Christopher Gill, 59–82. Oxford: Oxford University Press.

———. 2010. *The Untold War: Inside the Hearts, Minds, and Souls of our Soldiers*. New York: W. W. Norton.

———. 2013. "A Fractured Fidelity to Cause." In *Loyalty, Nomos. Volume LIV*, edited by Sanford Levinson, Joel Parker, and Paul Woodruff, 139–174. New York: New York University Press.

———. 2014. "Self-Empathy and Moral Repair." In *Emotions and Values*, edited by Sabine Roeser and Cain Todd. Oxford: Oxford University Press.

———. Forthcoming. "Moral Recovery After War: Hope." In *New Essays on the Ethics of War*, edited by Samuel Rickless and Saba Bazargain. New York: Oxford University Press.

Smith, Angela M. 2005. "Responsibility for Attitudes: Activity and Passivity in Mental Life." *Ethics* 115.2: 236–71.

Sophocles. 2007. *Sophocles: Four Tragedies*. Translated by Peter Meineck and Paul Woodruff. Indianapolis, IN: Hackett.

Stephens, J. C. 1995. "The Wound of Philoctetes." *Mnemosune* 48.2: 153–68.

Strawson, P. F. 1962. "Freedom and Resentment." *Proceedings of the British Academy* 48: 1–25.

Walker, Margaret Urban. 2006. *Moral Repair: Reconstructing Moral Relations after Wrongdoing.* New York: Cambridge University Press.

Wallace, R. Jay. 1996. *Responsibility and the Moral Sentiments.* Cambridge, MA: Harvard University Press.

CHAPTER TEN

Combat Trauma in Athenian Comedy: The Dog That Didn't Bark

ALAN H. SOMMERSTEIN

This chapter differs from most of the other contributions to this volume[1] in that it deals not with the ways in which the effects of combat trauma are described in ancient Greek literature, but with a branch of ancient Greek literature that seems to go out of its way to *avoid* describing them. Not only that, but it also, in very large measure, avoids reference to the types of situation likely to cause combat trauma, and to the types of person likely to experience it—and this although in one way or another it very frequently concerns itself with the subject of war and soldiering. The relevance of such avoidance to the theme of the book does not, I hope, require to be argued for: silence, or suppression, can be very eloquent.

The genre is Greek comedy—more specifically, Athenian comedy. The vigorous history of this form of drama lasted for more than two centuries, during which the number of plays produced ran into thousands, but there are only two periods, and two authors, that have left us complete or nearly complete plays. From Aristophanes (ca. 450–385 BC) we have 11 plays (out of about 40 that he wrote), the earliest dating from 425, the latest from 388. From Menander (342/1–291/0), thanks to papyrus discoveries over the last 170 years (which continue), we have one complete play, two or three others that are more than half complete, and substantial portions of several more (out of a total of just over a hundred); the complete play, *Dyskolos (The Curmudgeon)*, was produced in 316, and the rest, so far as we can tell, appear to span most of the dramatist's career. The structure, style, and subject matter of the genre had changed greatly in the century between Aristophanes and Menander, and scholars since antiquity have treated them as representing distinct phases in its history, often known as Old and New Comedy respectively. We need not here enter into the details of their differences, except insofar as they are relevant to our theme.

Both Aristophanes and Menander were writing in a world in which, as is described elsewhere in this volume, war was ubiquitous. Aristophanes'

career began in the early years of the great Peloponnesian War, the bloodiest conflict that the Greek world had yet known, and continued through
Athens'defeat and recovery into another war, the so-called Corinthian War
(395–387) in which the hegemony of Sparta was unsuccessfully challenged
by a coalition of most of the other leading Greek city-states. In Menander's
time these states had become little more than pawns in the disputes and
conflicts among the former generals, and would-be successors, of Alexander
the Great, and the dynasties they were beginning to found: whereas, therefore, in Aristophanes the typical soldier is a citizen conscript fighting for
Athens, in Menander he is normally a mercenary, a soldier by choice, often
of foreign citizenship or believed to be so, who campaigns in distant lands,
under nameless commanders, fighting for pay and booty. In both of them
military activities are much talked about. Every one of Aristophanes' surviving plays makes some reference to warfare currently in progress; in three of
them—*The Acharnians, Peace,* and *Lysistrata*—the main action of the play
consists in an attempt (always successful) by the hero or heroine either to
end the war or to opt out of it, and in two more—*The Knights* and *The
Frogs*—the public is told that the success of the fantasy plan around which
the play is built will result, among other things, in the making of peace. And
of the seven best-preserved plays of Menander, three—*Misoumenos (The
Man She Hated), Perikeiromene (The Girl with Cropped Hair),* and *Sikyonioi
(The Men from Sicyon)*—have a professional soldier as a major character, a
fourth—*Aspis (The Shield)*—is built around the fortunes of a young citizen
who takes mercenary service in order to raise a dowry for his sister, and in
a fifth—*Samia (The Woman from Samos)*—a young man who feels his father
has treated him badly *pretends* to be going abroad as a mercenary in order
to scare the old man.

In Aristophanes, almost all sympathetic characters detest the war—that is,
the ongoing conflict with Sparta; no one ever speaks against any *other* conflict, present or past, unless (like the Sicilian expedition of 415–413) it had
ended in obvious disaster. And a great deal is said about various evils associated with war, including (but not too prominently) the impact of casualties
on those left behind at home. But nothing whatsoever is said about the
impact of combat, its dangers and horrors, on the minds of those directly
exposed to them. The following is a complete listing of the specific sufferings of war affecting Athenians, as described in the three Aristophanic plays
most concerned with it, *The Acharnians, Peace,* and *Lysistrata*.

The Acharnians

(1) The discomforts of guard duty on the city walls…
(2) …and/or of having to live in makeshift accommodation in the town
     because the countryside was subject to repeated enemy invasions
     (alternative interpretations of 71–2; cf. 266–7)
(3) The presence in Athens of unruly foreign mercenaries (153–68)

(4) The destruction of crops, especially vines, by enemy action (183, 226–33, 512, 979–87)

(5) Being called up for campaigns (197, 251, 269)...

(6) ...even when gray-haired (600)

(7) Inability to trade with enemy states (623–5), especially resource-rich (and allegedly stupid) Boeotia (860–958)

(8) Plundering by enemy raiders (1022–36, 1076–7)

(9) Sexual deprivation (affecting both men and women) when men are on campaign (1049–68)

(10) Cold weather, when campaigning in winter (1075, 1140–1, 1146)

(11) Bad food (1097–117)

(12) Injuries (1174–80, 1190–227)—but the injured man, Lamachus, is an ultra-hawkish, fire-eating officer, who is *mocked* by the hero, Dicaeopolis.[2]

Peace

(1) The mutual destruction of Greek communities (58–63, 93, 105–6, 231, 236–54, 266, 1080–2)...

(2) ...to the benefit of their traditional common enemy, Persia (108, 406–13)

(3) Being called up for campaigns (303, 312, 1179–87)

(4) Having to obey arrogant officers (303, 1172–90; cf. 561)

(5) The destruction of crops, especially vines, by enemy action (308, 520, 612, 628–34, 916; cf. 702–3, 1322–4)

(6) Inability to travel abroad (341, 342)

(7) Sexual deprivation (341)

(8) Having to sleep rough when on campaign (348)

(9) Regular military training sessions (353–6)

(10) Injuries (443)—but the one specifically mentioned (an arrow wound in the elbow) is painful (and a little ridiculous) rather than traumatic

(11) Bad food (527–8, 1129)

(12) For the country people, having to leave their homes and fields (550–600, 866–7, 1130–71, 1329)

(13) Inability to trade with enemy states (999–1005).

Lysistrata[3]

(1) The mutual destruction of Greek communities (29–38, 1129–34)...

(2) ...to the benefit of Persia (1133)

(3) The absence of men from Athens (99–107)...

(4) ...resulting in sexual deprivation for the women (108–10, 591–2)

(5) The death of young men (cf. 391–7, 589–90)—but this is always referred to in an allusive manner

(6) A surplus of marriageable young women over available men (592–7)
(7) The presence in Athens of unruly foreign mercenaries (563–4)
(8) Inability to trade with enemy states, especially Boeotia (700–3)

From the men's point of view, then, warfare, for the individual soldier, is mostly a matter of discomfort rather than of death, mutilation, or even danger. Combat deaths are never even mentioned, and when we hear of wounds they are either minor (*Peace* #10) or the victim is one who is clearly felt to deserve it (*Acharnians* #12)—and even in his case the injuries seem to be treatable (cf *Acharnians* 1175–80, 1222–3) and we are probably meant to feel that he is exaggerating their gravity. In *Lysistrata,* characters are allowed to allude, but only allude, to the impact of casualties and the grief of their female kin. Despite the precedents of the *Iliad* and of tragedy, there is very little direct reference to the experience of battle; perhaps the nearest we get to it, in these three plays, is a vignette (*Peace* 1172–8) of an officer with a fancy cloak and crest who is the first to flee while the common soldiers stand firm.

Another notable feature of these three plays, considering their subject matter, is that actual fighting men are remarkably thin on the ground. In *Acharnians,* there are only Lamachus (and we know what we are meant to think of him) and—if we can count a character who is talked about but does not actually appear—the bridegroom spoken of in lines 1049–66. Dicaeopolis occasionally speaks as though he had served in the war currently being waged (e.g., *Acharnians* 197, 596), but he is several times described as an old man (397, 1129, 1130, 1228)—even by the chorus, who are themselves old men—and will of course have worn an old man's mask; and despite the apparent implication of 600 ("seeing gray-headed men in the ranks"), old men were not normally used in combatant roles (Socrates, e.g., is never made by Plato or Xenophon to refer to serving in any campaign later than that of Delium, when he was about 45). In *Peace* the chorus, though they can imply that they are (relatively) old (336, 558), also imply, considerably more often, that they have served on campaigns regularly throughout the war (303, 312, 336 again [ἐκφυγὼν τὴν ἀσπίδα], 347–8, 1128–9, 1172–90); but nobody else, hawk or dove, claims to have done so. *Lysistrata* contains a considerable number of males of active years, their vigor demonstrated (to their own embarrassment) by their massive penile erections; but whereas the old men of the chorus do recall taking part in conflicts long ago (*Lysistra* 271–85, 664–5), these younger men give no indication that they have ever done so. We see, then, relatively few actual soldiers of any age, and no actual *young* soldiers at all (let alone sailors and oarsmen, whose lives, during a naval expedition, were at least as much in jeopardy). One might say that while war figures prominently in Aristophanic drama, *warfare* does not. The idea of battle-fighting, it seems, carries other ideas with it, ideas with which a comic dramatist does not often wish to burden his audience.

In Aristophanes' other eight surviving plays, in which war is a less central theme, there is likewise virtually no reference to its major horrors. *Frogs*, produced early in 405, is much concerned with the naval battle of Arginusae, fought the previous summer. The battle was an Athenian victory, but 25 Athenian and allied ships were lost, and owing to a storm (and, as many believed, to negligence or worse on the part of senior officers) hardly any of their 5,000 crew members were rescued. Probably Arginusae saw the third greatest loss of Athenian lives of any campaign in the entire Peloponnesian War thus far. Arginusae is alluded to half a dozen times in *Frogs*—but nothing is ever said of the losses: only of the mobilization, and subsequent liberation, of slave rowers (*Frogs* 33, 191, 693–6), of the sinking of *enemy* ships (49–50), and of the subsequent political recriminations and maneuverings, which culminated in the execution of six of the fleet commanders (1196, also 538–41 on Theramenes' dexterity in avoiding blame).

Perhaps the only reference to war in Aristophanes that strikes a truly grim note is also to be found in *Frogs*, at the end of the *parabasis* (the passage in which the chorus address the audience directly). The chorus—or, to be precise, its leader—has been urging the Athenians to discard their current political leaders and "honour the honest again," and the final argument in support of this recommendation is as follows:

> That will be creditable for you if you are successful, and if you trip up at all, well, even if something does happen to you, at least discerning people will think it's happening "on a respectable tree!" (*Frogs* 735–7)

—alluding to a proverb that said something like "if you're going to hang yourself, at least try and hang yourself on a beautiful tree." Most unusually, this makes it virtually explicit, and treats it as a strong possibility, that even if the Athenians follow what the chorus regard as the best course of action, they may still go down to final defeat—which could mean, and in the event very nearly did mean[4], the total destruction of Athens and the death or enslavement of its population. At the end of the play this is forgotten, and the message is more hopeful. Dionysus says he wants a poet who can save Athens (1418–9, 1435–6), and chooses Aeschylus; the chorus sing that Aeschylus will be "bringing blessings to his fellow-citizens" (1487, 1530), and the underworld gods commission him to "save our city" (1501)—in part by the same method recommended in the *parabasis*, the removal of Cleophon and other currently dominant politicians (1504–14, 1532–3), which is expected to result in the making of peace or, as the chorus put it, in Athens being "rid of great sufferings and of terrible encounters in arms" (1531–2). It is striking that that last phrase, general and vague as it is, is the nearest Aristophanes ever comes to admitting that battle-fighting is a very nasty thing.

In Menander, as we have seen, soldiers are often major characters, but these are normally successful mercenaries who have enriched themselves sufficiently to retire from active service. They are, of course, the lucky ones, since they are always whole in body; but they never mention their less lucky comrades, and have virtually nothing to say about their military experiences. They are stereotypically thought to have a propensity to impulsive violence. Polemon (his name means "Warman") in *Perikeiromene* shears off the hair of his mistress, Glykera, when he believes (wrongly) that she has been unfaithful, and when she thereupon leaves him, he raises an armed posse (apparently of slaves) and tries to get her back by force. (Another character in the same play, a slave, humored by his young master with the idea of becoming a general or dynast, says he wouldn't like to be one because he'd probably be murdered by his troops: *Perikeiromene* 279–81.) Eventually it is discovered that Glykera is of citizen birth, the daughter of Polemon's friend Pataikos, and she and Pataikos agree that Polemon may take her in marriage; but Pataikos tells him that "in future you must forget that you're a soldier—no more headstrong behaviour!" (*Perikeiromene* 1016–17). The other two military professionals don't behave that way in the first place (Menander delights in thus creating characters of all kinds who refuse to be typecast).

In *Misoumenos*, when Thrasonides ("MacReckless") finds that his mistress (originally his captive), Krateia, is denying him her favors (because, as we later discover, she wrongly believes him to have killed her brother), he accepts that her "no" means "no," and merely laments his lot to the night air and to his male slave. We may have been given an account of the brother's experiences after this by an all-knowing deity, in a so-called delayed prologue, but nothing of this survives. Later in the play Krateia's father arrives from Cyprus, looking for members of his family which has been "dispersed in all directions by war, the common enemy of all" (*Misoumenos* 233–4 Sandbach = 634–5 Arnott). Thrasonides asks for Krateia's hand in marriage, is refused both by her and by her father, and his reaction is to threaten violence—but against himself; he is apparently saved when Krateia's brother turns up alive and well, and the marriage is duly agreed on. And in *Sikyonioi*, Stratophanes ("Army-bright") finds himself the owner of a young girl, Philoumene, whom he knows to be an Athenian citizen, and with whom he falls in love—but he respects her virginity, and is rewarded by discovering that he too is an Athenian citizen and then also discovering the identity of Philoumene's father, who is thus able to give her to him in marriage, according to the conventions that govern Athenian comedy. If it weren't for Stratophanes' mistress Malthake and his sidekick Theron (who end up getting hitched themselves), we would hardly know he was a soldier at all, and nothing in what survives of the play refers to any military activity, unless one counts the keeping of donkeys.

In *Aspis*, on the other hand, we hear a great deal about campaigning, including a detailed narrative of a military disaster (if a relatively small one). The play begins with the arrival in Athens from abroad of a slave, Daos, with a large quantity of booty and a battered shield (from which the play takes its name). He is the personal servant (*paidagōgos*) of a young man named Kleostratos, who had taken service as a mercenary (in Lykia, we later hear, in southwestern Asia Minor) in order to collect money for his sister's dowry. I translate his speech (minus some of the interruptions of the young man's uncle, Smikrines, who expresses perfunctory grief but is already thinking mainly of the possibilities of enriching himself by marrying his nephew's sister and heiress—which, as her next of kin, he has a legal right to do if he chooses to make a claim). Words in square brackets are conjectural (but probable) restorations of material missing through damage to the papyrus.

Daos: This is [a very sad] day for me, young master, and my thoughts are very different from the hopes with which I set out. I expected that you would return from campaigning safe and respected and able to live well in future, with the title of General or Chief of Staff. On your longed-for return home, you would give your sister—for whose sake you set out in the first place—to a bridegroom worthy of her, and I, as a reward for my loyalty, would have in my old age a rest from my long years of toil.[5] But now you're gone, Kleostratos, snatched away unexpectedly, and I, your attendant, have come back bringing this shield, which you kept safe so often but which didn't keep *you* safe. Because you were a brave man, if ever there was one....

Smikrines: How did he die? In what way?

Daos: For a soldier, Smikrines, the problem is to find an explanation for his *survival*; explaining his death is easy...There's a river in Lykia, called the Xanthus, near which we'd done well throughout quite a series of battles, so that the barbarians had made themselves scarce and left the flat country. Apparently it would have been better not to have had such unbroken good fortune: if you've stumbled, you take precautions. We'd come to despise the enemy, and that made us careless afterwards. Many of our men had left the fortified camp and were plundering the villages, laying waste the fields, selling their booty, so they all had plenty of money when they left...My young master, when he'd got together some six hundred gold pieces, a good lot of cups, and this crowd of captives that you see here with me, sent me off to Rhodes and told me to leave them with his friend there and then come back to him...I set off early in the morning. On the day of my departure, the barbarians had taken up a position behind a ridge where our sentries couldn't see them, having heard from some deserters that our troops were scattered. When the evening came and the whole force were back in their tents, after a day in a countryside which had an abundance of everything, what happened was what you might expect: most of them were having a high old time...And I suppose the enemy fell upon them and took them by surprise...I [had not got very far on my journey, and had camped for the night]. Round about mid[night], when I was walking about in front of my tent keeping [guar]d on the booty and slaves, I heard a noise—crying, running, wailing, people calling out each other's names—and I heard from them what had happened. Fortunately there was a strong point close by, a little hill. Up there we all gathered together, and others kept streaming in—cavalry, guardsmen, infantry, wounded…In the morning we threw up a palisade and stayed where we were, and we were continually reinforced by the men who had got scattered in the raids that I mentioned. Three days later we advanced again, back to our original camp, having learned that the Lykians were taking their captives up to the mountain villages.

Smikrines: And you saw him lying among the dead?

Daos: He couldn't be positively identified. They'd been lying out there for three days, and their faces were all bloated up.

Smikrines: So how do you know it was him?

Daos: He had his shield with him. It was so battered, I suppose, that none of the barbarians cared to take it. Our splendid commander wouldn't allow any individual cremations, because he thought it would take too long for everyone to gather up their ashes, so he piled them all up and burned them all together, buried the remains in great haste, and broke camp at once. We crossed first to Rhodes, stayed there for a few days, and then took ship back here.

(*Aspis* 1–81)

Daos answers some questions from Smikrines about the booty, and then goes into the house of Kleostratos' other uncle, Chairestratos, "to report this sorrowful news to those who least deserved to hear it" (91–2)—Chairestratos himself, his wife and daughter (cf. 126), his niece (Kleostratos' sister), and his stepson Chaireas (who was to have married her this very day, the dowry being provided by Chairestratos). There then appears a goddess, who at the end of her speech identifies herself as Tyche (Chance), and who tells us some things that Daos didn't know. The beginning of her narrative is badly damaged in the papyrus, but there is a reference to "another mercenary" (102) who, we may guess, was Kleostratos' tent-mate. Then the goddess proceeds:

When…the attack by the barbarians [occurred], the alarm kept sounding, and everyone rushed out to fight [straight away] armed with whatever happened to be lying near him. So it was that the man who at that moment was next to this slave's young master ran out carrying his shield, and fell at once. What with the shield lying among the corpses, and the young man's body having swelled up, the slave made a mistake. Kleostratos sallied out from there with a different set of arms and was taken prisoner, but he's alive and will come safe home very soon. (103–13)

This information of course remains unknown to the characters within the play, and they concoct an intrigue[6] with a view to making sure that

Smikrines does not marry Kleostratos' sister; this plot has advanced some way when it is overtaken by events, namely the return of Kleostratos safe and well. He can now end the play, in typical New Comedy fashion, with a double wedding, giving his sister in marriage to Chaireas while he himself marries Chairestratos' daughter.

Daos' narrative is exciting and graphic, particularly, as one might expect, the account of the episode in which he himself was involved (53–66). It will be observed, however, that it includes no description of any actual fighting: the story is so arranged that during the crucial period, Daos does not witness any. The attack on the camp took place in his absence, and there never was an attack on the improvised fort on the hill. There had been several battles earlier, but they are passed over in a single sentence (24–6). The fugitives who made a stand at the hill included wounded men (61–2), but their wounds cannot have been very serious, since they had managed to cover on foot a distance of, presumably, several miles (a day's journey, if perhaps a short one, for Daos and his prisoners and pack animals).

The dead, to be sure, lie unburied for three days, and by that time the bodies have deteriorated so badly as to be unrecognizable. We can imagine what Homer or Sophocles might have made of this. When Polyneices is left unburied for less than 24 hours, our attention is drawn to the decay of the corpse and to the evil smell as the guards take care to keep upwind of it (*Antigone* 410–2), and later we hear that it has been mauled by dogs (1198) and that Creon and his men cremated "whatever was left" (1202); Antigone had cried out like a bereaved mother-bird when she saw that the dust with which she had covered the body had been cleared away (423–8). In *Aspis* the sight of the obscenely bloated corpse, which he believes to be that of his much-loved master, does not seem to increase Daos' grief at all; it is simply a plot device to explain his mistaken identification of the body. Within a few lines (*Aspis* 84–5) Daos shows himself as sharp as a needle when, in response to Smikrines' questions about the booty, he addresses him as "Mr Inheritor" (*klēronome*), signalling his awareness that Smikrines is thinking less of the loss that the family has suffered than of the profit that he can now secure. In the goddess' speech, too, the death of Kleostratos' tent-mate, and the state his body was in three days later, are described because these facts need to be given to explain Daos' error, certainly not in order to arouse our sympathy for the dead man, or Kleostratos, or Daos himself. And so far as we can tell, the events of the campaign are never referred to again, except when a waiter (*trapezopoios*, a hired assistant at the planned wedding feast) makes fun of Daos for having brought the booty home instead of absconding with it (237–45). Kleostratos himself, when he returns, pretty certainly says nothing about it in his brief entrance-monologue (491–9), and after he has established his identity (508), his exit and the end of act 4 are less than a dozen lines away. In the opening scene Menander has given us a vivid narrative of an episode that ended many lives, and was felt as tragic by the narrator Daos, and yet he has kept it as free as he can of disturbing elements. The soldiers other than Kleostratos mean nothing to us as persons; we can already guess (this being a comedy) that Kleostratos himself will come back alive, even before the goddess confirms it; and as to the bloated corpses, which might indeed be disturbing, if the loyal and sympathetic Daos can take them in his stride, then so will the audience[7].

Thus neither for Old nor for New Comedy is war a taboo subject. But both to a considerable extent sanitize it and elide most of the features that actually make it horrific. In Aristophanes' *Acharnians* and *Peace*, about the worst things that happen in war are the evacuation of the countryside and the destruction of crops; actual military service seems little more disagreeable than military (or even athletic) training, and the soldier is hardly ever envisaged as actually facing the enemy. In *Lysistrata* it is acknowledged, if indirectly, that in war men die; but this recognition remains on an abstract level—none of the women claims to have actually lost a brother or husband or son, let alone to have one who is a disabled survivor.

In Menander, war is no longer part of the experience of the community but only of those individuals who choose to engage in it, balancing the risks against the potential profits—a hazardous career choice, like (e.g.) maritime trading, but with the advantage that if one survives, one can make a fortune fairly quickly[8] and can then retire from the profession. And it can be quite a fortune. Kleostratos' booty must have been taken in a single campaigning season (otherwise some of it would have reached home before now), and his "six hundred gold pieces" are equivalent to 12,000 drachmas, or 2 talents, in coin alone, without counting the plate, slaves, and clothing that Daos has also brought home (*Aspis* 35–7, 83–9). For comparison, a skilled workman in the 320s would earn two or two-and-a-half drachmas per day, so that assuming he was employed for 300 days a year, he would gross 2 talents in 16–20 years. The risks are rarely stressed—only, in fact, when a death is actually being reported; and then it is in the nature of the genre that the death usually proves not to have occurred after all (or, at any rate, that the victim is a person of no significance to the drama). Nor do we ever hear of close emotional ties between comrades-in-arms, such as induce warrior after warrior in the *Iliad* (above all Achilles) to take savage revenge for the death of a friend: Daos, to be sure, has a deep affection for Kleostratos, but Daos is not a soldier.

In New Comedy, as in Old, the true horrors of war are always either avoided or defused. They *are* a taboo subject, and they are not the only one. Notoriously, in comedy, no one dies, at least not after the action of the play has begun[9] (*earlier* deaths are often crucial to the mechanics of New Comedy plots). Characters may *pretend* to have died (like Chairestratos), or may be *believed* to have died (like Kleostratos), or may *threaten* to kill themselves (like Thrasonides), or may be threatened with death by others (like Euripides' in-law in Aristophanes' *Women at the Thesmophoria*)—but it never *actually* happens. Again, the great plague which, well into its fifth year, was still ravaging Athens while Aristophanes' *Acharnians* was being written,[10] is never mentioned in that play or in any other comedy. There are many aspects of Athenian human experience about which we hear only, or almost only, on the comic stage; but there are others to which comedy must resolutely shut its eyes, and the subject of this volume is one of them.

Notes

1. Compare however Konstan, this volume.
2. And though he apparently thinks he has been wounded by the enemy (1194, 1226–7), his injuries actually result from a fall into a ditch (1178–86).
3. In this play, since it is women who are attempting to end the war, the sufferings to which attention is drawn are mainly those affecting women left at home.
4. See Xen. *Hell.* 2.2.19–20 on the proposal of the Corinthians and Thebans, supported by "many of the other Greeks," that no peace should be made with the Athenians but that they should be destroyed (ἐξαιρεῖν—which the Spartans, in rejecting the proposal, take to be synonymous with ἀνδραποδίζειν "enslave"). Ironically, within a decade Thebes and Corinth were to be allies of Athens in a new war with Sparta.
5. That is, probably, he would be given his freedom.
6. The plot, devised by Daos, calls for Chairestratos to pretend to fall ill and die. This will make *his* daughter the heiress to a much larger estate, and Smikrines will be so eager to assert his right to marry *her* that he will give away Kleostratos' sister to the first person who asks—who will of course be Chaireas; once that has been done, Chairestratos can come back to life—leaving Smikrines with no bride and no inheritance.
7. Konstan (2013, 145–7) points to another traumatic happening that *Aspis* takes in its stride. Daos seems completely unmoved by the plight of the captives he has brought home—so recently free men and women, now doomed to lifelong slavery—regarding them merely as part of the property that will now fall to the lot of Kleostratos' heir; and the audience are apparently expected to take the same attitude. For a different view of the treatment of war in *Aspis* see James, this volume.
8. Particularly if one chooses the right kind of enemy—poorly organized and equipped "barbarians" in up-country districts (like Lykia in Daos' narrative) rather than the armies of Macedonian dynasts. Campaigning opportunities of this kind will have abounded in the vast territories of the former Persian empire.
9. An exception is sometimes made for persons whose loss (in the words of W. S. Gilbert's Lord High Executioner) would be a distinct gain for society at large. In Eupolis' *Demes* (fr. 99.112) Aristeides "the Just" may well have sentenced a *sykophantēs* to death (see Storey [2003, 167]); and in Aristophanes' *Frogs* (1504–14) Pluto commissions Aeschylus (who is returning to earth from the underworld) to supply Cleophon and others with the means of suicide and instruct them to "come quickly here to me and not waste time about it."
10. Having begun in the spring of 430 BC (Thucydides. 2.47.3) it continued virulently for two years, then abated (but without ever completely dying out) only to flare up again for "not less than a year" starting in the winter of 427/426 (Thucydides. 3.87.1–2). *The Acharnians* was produced during the winter of 426/425, in the month of Gamelion (January/February).

Bibliography

Konstan, David. 2013. "Menander's Slaves: The Banality of Violence." In *Slaves and Slavery in Ancient Greek Comic Drama*, edited by Ben Akrigg and Robert Tordoff, 144–58. Cambridge: Cambridge University Press.

Storey, Ian C. 2003. *Eupolis, Poet of Old Comedy*. Oxford: Oxford University Press.

CHAPTER ELEVEN

The Battered Shield: Survivor Guilt and Family Trauma in Menander's Aspis

SHARON L. JAMES*

Although Menander's generally sentimental theater, written in a period of prolonged political turmoil and regular outbreaks of war, is relatively apolitical and nontopical, it remains conscious of its larger social and cultural setting (see Konstan 1995 and Lape 2004, among many others).[1] In *Aspis*, I will argue, Menander depicts the very specific social realities of combat-related posttraumatic stress disorder (PTSD), survivor guilt, and family trauma—psychological issues that would have been familiar to many in his audience.[2] With this play Menander creates a space for such viewers to experience a very personal catharsis. Its extravagant metatheatrics notwithstanding, *Aspis* constantly recurs to loss, grief, and an ever-widening circle of survivors whose lives will be irremediably damaged by the soldier's death.[3] The happy turn, in which the warrior returns unharmed, offered a comforting wish-fulfillment for many viewers, a fantasy of family rescue and reintegration.

Before I lay out the elements of my analysis and approach, a summary: Kleostratos, whose father has long been dead, had taken his slave Daos, his former *paidagogos* (the domestic slave whose chief job is to take the family's son to school and training, and to oversee his education), to Lykia on a "freebooting" mission (Ireland 2010, 76; Groton 1982, 56; Gomme and Sandbach 1973, 65), seeking a dowry for his sister, who is betrothed to Chaireas, the stepson of Chairestratos, their younger uncle. As the play begins, Daos is leading a group of captives to Chairestratos' house, along with a large amount of loot and the titular shield, badly damaged. He tells Kleostratos' older uncle Smikrines, that Kleostratos had sent him to secure his booty away from the field of battle. Trapped nearby after a surprise attack on the Athenian encampment, Daos returned to be told that his master had been killed. The corpses were so engorged, after three days in the sun, that none could be individually recognized, but Kleostratos' battered shield served to identify him.

Because the unit commander ordered an immediate mass cremation and
burial, Daos could not look more closely at the body. He brought the shield
and the spoils back to the family, in grief for both his young master and for
himself—he had hoped to earn a rest from a long life of labor.[4] Smikrines
begins plotting to gain possession of his dead nephew's belongings (including Daos himself) by marrying Kleostratos' sister, who is now an *epiklēros*.[5]
As the eldest member of the family he has the right of first refusal.[6] The two
men exit, and the goddess Tyche (Chance) comes out to assure the audience
that Kleostratos is in fact alive (in the chaos of the enemy attack, the Greek
soldiers had grabbed any weapons at hand, so a fellow warrior had used
his shield) and that the repulsive Smikrines will get his comeuppance. The
viewers can then relax, knowing that the play will end happily.

Daos, Chairestratos, and Chaireas are stricken with grief at the young
man's death and horror at the prospect of the girl's having to marry her
unpleasant senior uncle. Chairestratos suffers a sort of fit, being prone (as
Daos says, 338–9) to melancholy, but is rescued when Daos proposes a charade: he will tell Smikrines that Chairestratos has died of grief; his daughter
too will be rendered an *epiklēros*, with an estate 15 times that of her cousin.
The greedy Smikrines will then demand her as wife instead. Kleostratos'
sister can be quickly married to Chaireas, after which point Chairestratos
can be revealed as alive. Both girls will be safe. Chairestratos assents.

Daos appoints himself playwright, director, and star.[7] Chaireas brings a
friend to play a doctor to diagnose the false illness. The womenfolk are
informed, so that they can act out laments for Chairestratos. A cook and
his crew provide comic interludes, during which Daos and a waiter discuss
ethnicity, masculinity, and loyalty in slaves. Much of the remainder of the
text is missing, but all is set right when Kleostratos eventually turns up alive
and well. The end of the play is lost, but the fragmentary lines 521–4 mention a double wedding—Chairestratos' daughter to Kleostratos, his sister
to Chaireas. This plot may be "fairly simple" (Gomme and Sandbach 1973,
63) but its emotional dynamics are not, and the engagement of viewers
must have been complex and delicate.

PTSD, Survivor Guilt, and Postwar Family Trauma

Although survivor guilt is generally considered a component of PTSD, I
treat it separately here. The terms "PTSD" and "survivor guilt" have been in
common use for some decades, applied to a broad range of circumstances,
including health crises, employment in emergency response, journalism,
nursing, and more; I limit my use of the terms to phenomena relating specifically to war.[8] Survivor guilt often has multiple causes, but I focus on
one stressor, the "death of a buddy" (Breslau and Davis 1987; Kubany 1997,
218–9, 228–30).[9] Herman sums up:

> Feelings of guilt are especially severe when the survivor has been a
> witness to the suffering or death of other people. To be spared oneself,

in the knowledge that others have met a worse fate, creates a severe burden of conscience. Survivors of disaster and war are haunted by the images of the dying whom they could not rescue. They feel guilty for not risking their lives to save others, or for failing to fulfill the request of a dying person. In combat, witnessing the death of a buddy places the soldier at particularly high risk for developing post-traumatic stress disorder. (Herman 1992, 54, with citations, 245: nn.10, 11; see also Shay 1994 and 2002, 78–82)

Lee, Scragg, and Turner (2001) distinguish between shame-based and guilt-based PTSD. They note that persons feeling guilt may attempt to make restitution to others, although "in certain circumstances (e.g., combat-related guilt), restitution cannot be made because the trauma led to death" (456). In veterans, this guilt can be overwhelming, and it may lead them to reach out to the families of their lost buddies, to offer help, support, or comfort.[10]

The effects of combat on family members are multiple. I focus on specific traumas in those whose menfolk die in combat, particularly grief compounded by guilt, and the prospect of a second life destroyed by the warrior's death—namely that of his wife or his fiancée. The grief of family members whose men do not return may be compounded by guilt if they feel responsible for the soldier's original departure to war. Further guilt may be added upon realizing that a young man's wife or fiancée has lost her anticipated future life.

These elements too can be glimpsed in *Aspis*, where Kleostratos' family suffers not merely grief but full-scale trauma, as the losses and disasters continue to mount: the news of his death, on what was to be the wedding day of his sister (for whose sake he had gone to war in the first place); the demands of Smikrines to marry the sister—demands that disrupt the family's grieving process by breaking up her intended marriage and adding a prospect for her that all parties view with horror; the loss of the intended marriage for Chairestratos' own daughter, who was to marry Kleostratos; Chairestratos' slide into a state of nonfunctional depression; the despair of Chaireas, at losing his bride and friend on the same day; and the agitation and survivor guilt of Daos.[11] As I will argue below, Chairestratos and his niece, the sister of Kleostratos, also suffer intense guilt by feeling responsible for his having gone to war. All these blows pile on, until the entire family is on the point of collapse. It is not necessarily the case that every family bereaved by a death in war would experience such trauma, but Kleostratos' family does.

Many, if not most, of the citizens in Menander's audience would have been personally touched by war, and all of them had been affected by it politically for many years.[12] I suggest that this play, whose plot absurdly, almost frantically, moves away from war and back into the bureaucracy of civic law, was designed to be experienced as both distressing, as it recalls the horrors of war, and comforting as it resolves problems and depicts a family working to keep itself together in the face of terrible loss. The comic masks, the distractions of the metatheatrical plot, and the reassurances of Tyche that

Kleostratos is not dead, allow viewers to reexperience their own war-based suffering and simultaneously enjoy a happy fantasy of the evaporation of that suffering in what is staged as virtually a deus ex machina miracle.[13] The onstage antics represent a common reaction to death, namely a desire to stay active and productive.[14]

My approach presumes that many viewers would have had a divided response to *Aspis*, seeing it both as reflecting their own experiences and fears, and as fulfilling their wishes both past and present (e.g., "my son was not killed in war," "my husband will come home safely"). Tyche's guarantees would allow them to relax and enjoy the fun, while also empathizing with the bereaved characters on the stage.[15] *Aspis* stages the kind of complex situations that could arise, on any given day, at the news of a young man's death at war: family mourning, disputes over property and estates, the prospect of an unappealing husband for a young *epiklēros*, whose life would be changed in an instant. The audience saw not an ancient myth but a common Athenian reality—one that would have been feared whenever a man went off to war, along with the general anxiety that families, especially women, experienced while he was away.[16] If the ultimate outcome of *Aspis* is wish fulfillment, along the way to its happy ending the play stages—and invokes—a set of grievous realities that were shared by a great number of its viewers. I turn now to considering those realities, and I do so, perhaps paradoxically, by beginning with modern Great Britain.

Daos: Social Class, Combat Trauma, and Survivor Guilt

Dorothy Sayers' fictional detective, Lord Peter Wimsey, suffered PTSD with a specific form of guilt beyond his shell shock: when he was a commander in World War I, his every order, for nearly four years, meant that a man was likely to die. More than a few of his soldiers did so, and after the war Lord Peter's guilt immobilized him, especially on the matter of issuing orders, or even expressing preferences on trivial matters. Nightmares and symptoms of trauma recurred periodically, and only his valet Bunter—formerly his sergeant—could understand and help. His mother, the Dowager Duchess, explains to his bride, Harriet Vane:

> "There were eighteen months...not that I suppose he'll ever tell you about that, at least, if he does, then you'll know he's cured...I don't mean he went out of his mind or anything, and he was always perfectly sweet about it, only he was so dreadfully afraid to go to sleep [...] if anybody can be said to have pulled Peter round again it was Bunter [...]"
>
> Harriet asked to be told about Bunter.
>
> "Well," said the Duchess, "he was a footman at Sir John Sanderton's before the War and he was in Peter's unit [...] they were in some [...] jam or other, and took a fancy to one another...so Peter promised

Bunter that, if they both came out of the War alive, Bunter should come to him. Well [...] Bunter turned up [...] He said he had succeeded in obtaining his demobilisation, and had come immediately to take up the situation Peter had promised him. Well, my dear, it happened to be one of Peter's very worst days, when he couldn't do anything but just sit and shiver...I liked the look of the man, so I said, 'Well, you can try—but I don't suppose he'll be able to make up his mind one way or the other.' So I took Bunter in, and it was quite dark, because I suppose Peter hadn't had the strength of mind to switch the lights on [...] Bunter said, 'Sergeant Bunter, my lord, come to enter your lordship's service as arranged'—and he turned on the lights and drew the curtains and took charge from that moment [...] he managed so that for months Peter never had to give an order about so much as a soda-siphon [...] it was really rather touching [...]"

"I'd come up to Town one morning early and looked in at the flat. Bunter was just taking in Peter's breakfast...and came out with a plate in his hand and said, 'Oh, your Grace! His lordship has told me to take away these damned eggs and bring him a sausage.'...He was so much overcome that he put down the hot plate on the sitting-room table and took all the polish off...From those sausages," concluded the Duchess, triumphantly, "I don't think Peter ever looked back!"

Harriet thanked her mother-in-law for these particulars. "If there is a crisis," she said, "when these Assizes come on, I'll take Bunter's advice. Anyway, I'm very grateful to you for warning me. I'll promise not to be wifely and solicitous."

(Sayers 1937, 364–5).[17]

In this scene, mother and new wife discuss several phenomena devolving from World War I combat trauma in the classed society of early twentieth-century Great Britain: Lord Peter's postwar trauma; its tendency to reappear unexpectedly; the understanding and tight bond between fellow warriors; the need of the PTSD sufferer for that very particular comprehension; the women's awareness that they do not understand the condition; and their recognition that they cannot heal it. They acknowledge that the lower-class Bunter, a servant, can do for the elite Wimsey something that his most intimate and devoted family members cannot, that employer and employee share a bond beyond explanation. Harriet already knows that at one point Wimsey was trapped at the bottom of a dugout, and saved when his men unearthed him. This information had come to her by way of a conversation between Wimsey and Padgett, the porter of the fictional Shrewsbury College at Oxford, when they met up and reminisced about their unit and their experiences as major and private in the same troop (Sayers 1935, 358–61). There too Harriet observed the tight bond of former soldiers, a bond that lasts well after the war has sent them off to very different lives, and—more importantly for my argument—a bond that crosses class divisions in a way not possible for civilians who have not experienced war together.

I have begun my consideration of Daos by quoting from Sayers's detective fiction because her British setting shares with Menander's Greece a crucial element, namely, a strongly classed society. Bunter is hardly Lord Peter's slave, but their social classes are sharply asymmetrical, and he therefore offers a rough analogue to Daos. Bunter appears not to suffer PTSD, but he understands it. The special relationship of the two veterans retains its classed structure in all Sayers's novels and short stories, but they share a close partnership and a wordless understanding. Bunter takes pride in seeing that all aspects of his employer's personal life are properly managed, and he greatly values his role as an assistant in Wimsey's investigations.[18] His intense attachment to Wimsey is made clear in his brief experience of being overcome at Lord Peter's request for sausages, and in his epistolary description of the wedding of Wimsey and Harriet: "Well, Mother, we were happily married this morning and a very pretty wedding it was" (Sayers 1937, 8). The first-person pronoun speaks volumes, as it is addressed not to Bunter's employer but to his mother, in private communication. Bunter's concern for, pride in, and loyalty to, his former commanding officer are not merely standard equipment for an English nobleman's valet, but hallmarks as well of the relationship of combat partners.[19]

We may glimpse much the same in one of the first remarks made by Daos, upon his return to the house that he knows will be devastated by the news he brings. His opening speech is an address to his missing master:

$$
\begin{aligned}
&] \text{ἡμέραν ἄγω,} \\
&\text{ὦ τρόφιμε, τὴν [νῦν,] οὐδὲ διαλογίζομ[αι} \\
&\text{παραπλήσι' ὡς τό[τ' ἤλ]πισ' ἐξορμώμε[ος.} \\
&\text{ᾤμην γὰρ εὐδο[ξο]ῦντα καὶ σωθέντα σ[ε} \\
&\text{ἀπὸ στρατείας ἐν βίῳ τ' εὐσχήμονι} \\
&\text{ἤδη τὸ λοιπὸν καταβιώσεσθαί τινι,} \\
&\text{στρατηγὸν ἢ σ[ύμ]β[ο]υλον ὠνομασμένον,} \\
&\text{καὶ τὴν ἀδελφήν, ἧσπερ ἐξώρμας τότε} \\
&\text{ἕνεκα, σεαυτοῦ νυμφίῳ καταξίῳ} \\
&\text{συνοικιεῖν ποθεινὸν ἥκοντ' οἴκαδε,} \\
&\text{ἐμοί τ' ἔσεσθαι τῶν μακρῶν πόνων τινὰ} \\
&\text{ἀνάπαυσιν εἰς τὸ γῆρας εὐνοίας χάριν.} \\
&\text{νῦν δὲ σὺ μὲν οἴχει παραλόγως τ' ἀνήρπασαι,} \\
&\text{ἐγὼ δ' ὁ παιδαγωγός, ὦ Κλεόστρατε,} \\
&\text{τὴν οὐχὶ σώσασάν σε τήνδ' ἐλήλυθα} \\
&\text{ἀσπίδα κομίζων ὑπὸ δὲ σοῦ σεσωμένην} \\
&\text{πολλάκις· ἀνὴρ γὰρ ἦσθα τὴν ψυχὴν μέγας,} \\
&\text{εἰ καί τις ἄλλος.}^{20}
\end{aligned}
$$

(1–18)

Today's [as sad a] day [as] I have spent,
Master, and all the thoughts that cloud my brain
Aren't what I hoped they'd be when we set off.

I thought you'd come back safe and rich in honour
From your campaign, and afterwards you'd live
Your future years in style. You'd have the title
Of General or Counsellor of State,
And see your sister, for whose sake you went
Campaigning, married to a man you felt
Was right, upon your glad arrival home.
And for me too, as I grew old, I hoped
There'd be a rest from these long labours, after all
I'd done for you. But now you're dead, snatched off
Against all reason, and, Kleostratos,
It's I who've come—your tutor, bringing back
This shield which didn't protect you, though you often
Protected it. You always showed fine spirit,
Second to none.

This language bespeaks a personal connection that transcends social status, and in this case, that close relationship goes back to the young master's childhood, presumably some 15 or 20 years earlier. Daos was Kleostratos' *paidagogos*, a position identified by Cox (2013, 160) as belonging to the top rank of the hierarchy of slavery in Athens.[21] Beroutsos notes that τρόφιμε underscores Daos'"affection for, and long association, with" his master, whose caretaker he had been.[22] Kleostratos, having neither father nor mother, may have felt especially close to Daos, who obviously reciprocates that emotion. His integral role in Kleostratos' undertaking is evident as soon as he speaks, especially as he is leading the young man's loot, including slaves, back from Lykia. After all, Daos could simply have made off with at least some of the spoils, a point driven home by Menander when the waiter abuses Daos precisely for not having done so (238–41)—and it is worth noting that this loot could have provided just the release from labor that Daos had hoped for, as he could have taken, say, the six hundred gold coins and gone home to Phrygia, to live in comfort and freedom. Instead, he faithfully returns all of it to Kleostratos' family, even knowing that he is almost certainly returning to continued labor.

Daos' fidelity also represents a standard owner-class fantasy of loyalty in slaves, but the special nature of his bond to Kleostratos is evident throughout, and I suggest that, as staged, it manifests the unity of men who went to war together. Daos' own life was at risk during the expedition, but he also stood to gain personally from the undertaking. Kleostratos had gone on campaign to benefit his sister rather than himself, and he was a raider, rather than a soldier representing or defending his country. But combat is combat, regardless of its purpose: master and slave were part of a military unit and they suffered its anxieties, difficulties, and risks together.[23] Some studies have found that, paradoxically, "a high level of unit cohesion in combination with high war-zone stress was associated with the highest levels of PTSD and psychopathology" (Fontana, Rosenheck, and Horvath 1997, 675).[24] From the moment he comes on stage, Daos shows particular closeness to his master and fellow soldier, and that degree of closeness helps to explain his high degree of survivor guilt.

Daos is Phrygian, as the play remarks more than once. As Konstan (2013, 146) notes, he must have been "captured and sold into servitude rather than raised as a slave from infancy." Moreover, he was old enough when enslaved that he still sees "Athenian customs and practices as foreign" (as in 206–8). Sherk notes a general reputation of Phrygians as "cheap and irresponsible slaves" (342), and the waiter says that a Phrygian is effeminate and no good (242: οὐδὲν ἱερόν· ἀνδρόγυνος), a view that Daos does not hold.[25] He asserts his ethnicity without reservation, but he is aware of its poor reputation, which he may be eager to disprove. Ethnicity, particularly membership in a minority group, is a further component relevant to combat trauma: numerous studies suggest that soldiers who belong to a minority group suffer greater degrees of war trauma, with culturally specific responses.[26] The existence and reported success of culturally sensitive treatment for trauma further supports the finding that there are culturally specific experiences of trauma.[27] Daos' ethnicity may play a role in his experience of war trauma.

Throughout his opening speech, Daos shows his close bond to his young master. Touches of pathos recur, in his reversed hopes for Kleostratos and himself, and his prior expectation that the sister would enter not merely into an advantageous match but into a marriage worthy of her brother, who had undertaken the expedition (visually marked as military by the captives and the titular shield itself) on her behalf.[28] Further elements of pathos include.Daos' characterization of Kleostratos' death as unfathomable and irrational (παραλόγως, 13), criticism of the shield as having failed its owner (16–17), and his praise of his master's lofty spirit (17–18). His remarks amount to a funeral eulogy, but they are also a returning warrior's confession of failure, as Daos and the shield both failed to protect their master.[29] He shows his unity with Kleostratos and the unit, using first-person plurals to describe their shared battle experience: τότ᾽ ἦμεν ἐπιεικῶς μάχαις | πολλαῖς διευτυχοῦντες…ἡμᾶς δ᾽ ἀτάκτους πρὸς τὸ μέλλον ἤγαγε | τὸ καταφρονεῖν ("There we saw some action, quite a lot, and we'd been lucky all the time…Over-confidence led us | Undisciplined towards the morrow," 24–5, 29–30). Daos' intermittent philosophizing (26–8) and explanations about how the enemy's surprise attack could have succeeded (45–8) represent a soldier's attempt to puzzle through, and make sense of, unanticipated and stunning disaster.

In the three days of waiting, on the defensive behind the hastily built palisade, Daos would have experienced great anxiety, fearing that Kleostratos had been captured, as the reports suggested (67–8). Upon arriving at the camp, he was confronted with one of the great horrors of war: an indiscriminate pile of bodies, so bloated (presumably scorched as well) after three days that they could not be recognized by feature or mark (70–2). Only Kleostratos' shield remained, so bent and useless that the enemy did not bother to take it, to serve as an identity token—the Greek narrative equivalent of dog tags.[30]

The unit commander, adding outrage to loss, ordered that all the bodies be swiftly cremated and that the ashes be buried immediately in a mass grave. This mandated speed prevented further chances for Daos to inspect the body—hence his sarcastic comment, ὁ δ’ ἡγεμὼν ἡμῶν ὁ χρηστός (75) ["our fine commander"].[31] Realistically, given the number of dead bodies, the operation could not have been completed speedily, as each of the necessary steps is time-consuming: digging a pit large enough to contain all the bodies and the burnt remains, acquiring adequate firewood, building a stable, high-heat fire, and finally covering the massed ashes with soil.[32] The whole process, given the number of dead bodies, must have taken more than a day. But Daos describes the cremation and burial as almost instantaneous, a perspective that I suggest arises from his survivor guilt.

The commander's decision, though logical and necessary, causes further trauma to Daos, as he cannot perform an appropriate ritual for his master and fellow combatant; Shay (1994) has described the increase in PTSD caused to survivors when commanders fail to acknowledge individual deaths or permit meaningful commemoration (see esp. 55–68). Daos' resentment of the unit's commander, for just this reason, is evident, especially in his emphasis on the speed of the operation (σπουδῇ πάνυ, 78; εὐθύς, 79) and the begrudging of the time for individual burials:

ὁ δ’ ἡγεμὼν ἡμῶν ὁ χρηστὸς καθ’ ἕνα μὲν
κάειν ἐκώλυσεν, διατριβὴν ἐσομένην
ὁρῶν ἑκάστοις ὀστολογῆσαι, συναγαγὼν
πάντας δ’ ἀθρόους ἔκαυσε· καὶ σπουδῇ πάνυ
θάψας ἀνέζευξ’ εὐθύς·

(75–9)

Our fine commander banned all separate
Cremations, for he realised how much time
Would be required for gathering, man by man,
The ashes; all the dead were heaped together
And burnt, then buried with all speed. Immediately
He broke camp.

As Beroutsos (ad 75) notes, Daos "would have preferred to return his master's ashes to his family."[33] Instead, he can only take Kleostratos' loot—human beings as well as luxury goods and coins—back to the family, along with the shield that now substitutes for the battered body of its owner.[34] His grief and guilt toward Kleostratos' family are evident in his final remark in the opening scene:

παράγωμεν εἴσω τὸν ταλαίπωρον λόγον
ἀπαγγελοῦντες τοῦτον οἷς ἥκιστ’ ἐχρῆν

(91–2)

...let's go inside to tell
This sorry tale to those who'd least deserved such news.

The postponed prologue of Tyche tells the audience that all will be well, because Kleostratos is alive, and soon to return. Strikingly, her account reinforces Daos' depiction of the dreadful scene, repeating its grim detail about the bloating (109) that caused the misidentification. Tyche is more interested in punishing Smikrines than in the chaos of battle (or the minor detail of how Kleostratos could free himself after having been captured).[35] She shifts the play's focus from the traumatized warrior-slave and his survivor guilt to the family of the dead warrior (now known, to the audience, as alive), by describing the care Chairestratos took as *kurios* for the sister of Kleostratos.

This shift in focus prepares the audience for the comic theatrics, which allow Daos to do important service for Kleostratos' family and to work off some of his survivor guilt. When he sees Chairestratos failing, he springs into action, beginning with a rebuke to the unhappy uncle, whose wealth and superior social status do not matter to the agitated slave veteran:

Χαιρέστρατ', οὐκ ὀρθῶς ποεῖς· ἀνίστασο·
οὐκ ἔστ' ἀθυμεῖν οὐδὲ κεῖσθαι. Χαιρέα,
ἐλθὼν παραμυθοῦ· μὴ 'πίτρεπε· τὰ πράγματα
ἡμῖν ἅπασίν ἐστιν ἐν τούτῳ σχεδόν.

(299–302)

Chairestratos, you're doing wrong! Get up!
You can't lie down and languish. Chaireas,
Come here and reassure him, don't let him
Succumb. The interests of us all may well
Be anchored in him.

His explanation of the ingenious charade leaves Chairestratos and Chaireas mystified until Daos explains that Smikrines will abandon his designs on Kleostratos' sister (349–59). When Chairestratos understands, he credits Daos not only with an excellent plot but also with having the right to take personal revenge on their common enemy: εὖ γ' ἐστ]ὶν ὃ λέγεις, Δᾶε, τοῦ τ' ἐμοῦ τρόπου | τιμωρί]αν δὲ τοῦ πονηροῦ τίν' ἂν ἔχοις | λαβεῖ] σφοδροτέραν; ("Daos, your idea's [fine (?)], just after my | Own heart. What sharper vengeance could you take | On that rogue?" (368–70). With such remarks, the right of Daos to a personal stake in representing Kleostratos' interests is taken for granted by all parties, and that stake provides the slave with energy and purpose that appear to begin healing his survivor guilt.[36] In acting to fulfill Kleostratos' original purpose for going to war, Daos fulfills his dead comrade's wishes.

When that dead comrade turns up alive, his opening speech, even tattered in our text, shows that his great hope is that Daos has returned safely:

ὁρῶ δεομεν[
εἰ δ' αὖ διαπ[εσὼν
ὁ Δᾶος, εὐτυ[χέστατον
νομίσαιμ' ἐμαυτό[ν.

(495–8)

I see [that I (?)] require [...]
But if Daos [escaped and got home safely, then (?)]
I'd think myself [of all the men in the world (?)]
The one most fortunate.

Here too the bond of fellow combatants is evident.[37] The scene is in shreds, but their reunion seems joyous indeed. The embrace of master and slave, fellow warriors, must have been very moving to viewers who had experienced such a homecoming: ἔχω σε cries Daos—"I hold you!" (508).[38] Their elation stages, for all to see, the close bond of soldiers whose trauma can be healed by each other alone, and it would have allowed some in the audience a vicarious similar experience. As Lord Peter Wimsey needs Bunter, so Kleostratos needs Daos, and not merely as a caretaker of spoils; and as Bunter finds purpose in serving his commanding officer's needs, so Daos finds purpose in making right all his master's plans and arrangements. I think it unlikely that Menander staged the two discussing their war experience—part of the special bond of soldiers here may be, as in Sayers' fiction, precisely that they do not articulate aloud the horror, fear, and danger they underwent. Because they experienced it together, they do not need to speak of it.[39]

Family Trauma

In addition to showing survivor guilt in Daos, *Aspis* stages the suffering of a family traumatized by the loss of a young man at war. This trauma is compounded by the instant legal crisis that Smikrines creates: a love match of two young people is broken up minutes after the sad news. The development is a lightning-fast version of what would have been a common, and commonly feared, scenario in which a girl's life is doubly ruined, first by the death of her primary male relative and then by the forcible breakup of her planned marriage.[40] The speed with which Smikrines asserts his legal rights over her represents yet another common family trauma after a war death. It is unknowable which of these two scenarios—loss of a *kurios* or a fiancé— would have been more common, but the death in war of one man could easily scar two families and put at risk the futures of two young women. The grief of Chaireas further represents the damage to family life: he has lost, he believes, both a dear friend and his own bride.

The first staged symptom of family trauma is Chairestratos' fit, but even earlier there would have been offstage sounds of grief, especially by women. Daos speaks backward into the house, as he comes to answer Smikrines' knock at the door:

πολλὴ μὲν ὑμῖν ταῦτα συγγνώμη ποεῖν,
ἐκ τῶν δ' ἐνόντων ὡς μάλιστα δεῖ φέρειν
ἀνθρωπίνως τὸ συμβεβηκός.

(164–6)

It's very understandable you should behave
Like this, but in the circumstances try your best
To bear what's happened reasonably.

We do not need to know a precise addressee to infer that the inhabitants are
reacting in shock and horror to the news of Kleostratos' death. The cook's
comically selfish complaint, shortly after, confirms the family's vocal woe,
complaining about the loss of the three drachmas he had been expecting for
preparing the wedding feast:

νεκρὸς
ἐλθών τις ἐκ Λυκίας ἀφῄρηται βίᾳ
ταύτας. τοιούτου συμβεβηκότος κακοῦ
τοῖς ἔνδον, ἱερόσυλε, κλαούσας ὁρῶν
καὶ κοπτομένας γυναῖκας...

(224–8)

And now a corpse has come
From Lycia and snatched them clean away.—You crook,
A blow like this falls on the house, when you
See women crying, battering their breasts.

Chairestratos' urgent negotiations with Smikrines show his escalating despair,
until he utters a suicidal thought: ἀπαλλαγῆναι τὴν ταχίστην τοῦ βίου |
γένοιτό μοι πρὶν ἰδεῖν ἃ μήποτ' ἤλπισα. ("Let me depart this life with-
out delay, | Before I see my dreams to nightmares turn," 282–3). He may be
manifesting his own survivor guilt, as he had approved his nephew's mission,
and had thought only belatedly of granting his niece a dowry.[41]
 When Chairestratos goes indoors, his distraught stepson Chaireas appears,
offering a degree of comic relief in the form of the young lover's certainty
that nobody is worse off than himself:

εἶέν· τὸ μὲν σὸν πρῶτον, ὦ Κλεόστρατε,
ἴσως ἐλεῆσαι καὶ δακρῦσαι κατὰ λόγον
πάθος ἐστί, δεύτερον δὲ τοὐμόν· οὐδὲ εἷς
τούτων γὰρ οὕτως ἠτύχηκεν ὡς ἐγώ.
ἔρωτι περιπεσὼν γὰρ οὐκ αὐθαιρέτῳ
τῆ[ς] σῆς ἀδελφῆς, φίλτατ' ἀνθρώπων ἐμοί,
οὐθὲν ποήσας προπετὲς οὐδ' ἀνάξιον
οὐδ' ἄδικον ἐδεήθην ἐμαυτῷ κατὰ νόμους
συνοικίσαι τὸν θεῖον ᾧ σὺ κατέλιπες
καὶ τὴν ἐμὴν μητέρα παρ' ᾗ παιδεύεται.
ᾤμην δὲ μακάριός τις εἶναι τῷ βίῳ,
ἐλθεῖν δ' ἐπ' αὐτὸ τὸ πέρας οἰηθεὶς σφόδρα
καὶ προσδοκήσας οὐδ' ἰδεῖν δυνήσομαι

τὸ λοιπόν· ἕτερον κύριον δ᾽ αὐτῆς ποεῖ
ὁ νόμος ὁ τοὐμὸν οὐδαμοῦ κρίνων ἔτι.

(284–96)

Ah well! Kleostratos, it's only fair
To mourn and sympathise with your fate first
Of all, perhaps; but secondly, with mine,
For none of them has suffered quite like me.
I didn't choose to fall in love with *your*
Sister, O dearest of mankind to me!
I've done nothing that's hasty or vile or
Unauthorised. I asked permission for
Her hand in marriage legally from your
Uncle with whom you left her, from my mother
In whose care she's being groomed. I thought I was
Lucky in my life, I fully thought and felt
I'd reached the very goal. In future I
Can't even see her. She belongs to another
By laws which now reject my claim outright.

In his self-pity, Chaireas articulates precisely the fate of his beloved: if he can never see her again, neither can she see him.[42] She, of course, cannot be staged, so his lament includes hers, which can be vocalized only in unscripted offstage wailing.[43]

The sinking fit of Chairestratos is nearly complete at this point. The displacement of his grief is notable: what turns his face to the wall is not Kleostratos' death, too tragic to be faced, but his elder brother's greed and intransigence. Thus, Smikrines' villainy distracts Chairestratos from his bereavement. Daos' plan both rescues Kleostratos' sister and engenders a stunningly complex enactment of grief both real and feigned. Daos begins by listing the family's unfolding trauma, and moves on to their play-acted trauma:

ὃ γὰρ ὑπεῖπας ἀρ[τίως
δόξαι σε δεῖ νῦν, εἰς ἀθυμίαν τινὰ
ἐλθόντα τῷ τε τοῦ νεανίσκου πάθει
τῆς τ᾽ ἐκδιδομένης παιδός, ὅτι τε τουτονὶ
ὁρᾷς ἀθυμοῦντ᾽ οὐ μετρίως ὃν νενόμικας
υἱὸν σεαυτοῦ, τῶν ἄφνω τούτων τινὶ
κακῶν γενέσθαι περιπετῆ· τὰ πλεῖστα δὲ
ἅπασιν ἀρρωστήματ᾽ ἐκ λύπης σχεδόν
ἐστιν· φύσει δέ σ᾽ ὄντα πικρὸν εὖ οἶδα καὶ
μελαγχολικόν. ἔπειτα παραληφθήσεται
ἐνταῦθ᾽ ἰατρός τις φιλοσοφῶν καὶ λέγων

πλευρῖτιν εἶναι τὸ κακὸν ἢ φρενῖτιν ἢ
τούτων τι τῶν ταχέως ἀναιρούντων.

(330–42)

> What you just said
> Must now come true for you—apparently.
> You slump into depression through the ordeal
> Of that young man and his intended bride,
> And through observing Chaireas sunk in
> Deep gloom, the boy you've looked on as your son.
> So you fall prey to one of those acute
> Afflictions. Grief's the likely cause of most
> Of this world's ailments. And I know you have
> This bitter side to you, this proneness to
> Depression. Next, a doctor will be called,
> An intellectual; "Pleurisy's the trouble,"
> He'll say, or "phrenic inflammation," or one of
> Those things that's quickly fatal.

Once the plan is established, the two chief conspirators make their final arrangements.

Δαος.   ταῦτα τὰ βεβουλευμένα·
             ἀπόθνησκ᾽ ἀγαθῇ τύχῃ.
Χαιρεστρατος. ποήσω· μηδένα
             ἔξω γ᾽ ἀφίετ᾽, ἀλλὰ τηρεῖτ᾽ ἀνδρικῶς
             τὸ πρᾶγμα.
Δαος.   τίς δ᾽ ἡμῖν συνείσεται;
Χαιρεστρατος. μόνῃ
             δεῖ τῇ γυναικὶ ταῖς τε παιδίσκαις φράσαι
             αὐταῖς ἵνα μὴ κλάωσι, τοὺς δ᾽ ἄλλους ἐᾶν
             ἔνδον παροινεῖν εἴς με νομίσαντας νεκρόν.

(380–6)

Daos: Follow our
              Plans. Die, and good luck to you!
Chairestratos: I'll do that.
              Let no one go out. Guard the secret with
              Determination.
Daos: Who'll be in the know with us?
Chairestratos: Only my wife and the two girls themselves
              Must be informed, to stop them flooding tears;
              The rest must think me dead, and be allowed
              To snipe at me indoors.

Chairestratos' presumption that the women would refrain from weeping, in the secure knowledge that he is not actually dead, is almost formally surrealist in its absurdity: they are already in tears, over Kleostratos, and now they must perform lamentation not for him but for the not-dead Chairestratos. Daos' assessment that their game will provide amusement and activity (308–9) marks its displacement function: the charade gives the men an active role in fending off worse fallout from the family's bereavement (although it can do nothing for Kleostratos' bereaved fiancée, the daughter of Chairestratos). Through their play-acting, the family members can both postpone their grief, while simultaneously expressing it and preventing the death from leading to a permanent trauma for Kleostratos' sister. Giving priority to the false death of Chairestratos allows them to avoid thinking about the real death (as far as they know) of Kleostratos. The speed and eagerness with which the entire family leaps into this program of evasion marks a symptom of trauma: they are unable to face the fact of his death, and the charade allows them to minimize, in advance, the effects of that death, even before they settle back into official mourning for him.

Observing these antics might well have been dizzying for viewers, anchored only by Tyche's assurance that all is to end happily. Daos' madcap quotations from tragedy, Smikrines' impatience, the exaggerated pseudo-Doric accent of the pretend doctor, the caterwauling indoors—all these antics could have been received by the audience as hilarious, while still representing the family trauma caused by a death in war. The collapse of a nervous older man at the catastrophic news, the precarious state of a house lacking its male heir, the emotional and psychic damage caused by the loss in war of a beloved relative—these staged behaviors are the family's response to the death.[44] The feigned grief enacts, displaces, and postpones real grief. Even in the middle of this elaborately staged lamentation, then, Smikrines' selfish interventions allow comic relief for the audience. For the family members, who do not know that Kleostratos is alive, the charade allows both displacement of their real grief for him, and a sense of working together to protect the family in the face of his loss.

Kleostratos' arrival, of course, turns grief to joy. Although we have only shreds of this part of the play, we can imagine that happy-sounding shrieks from offstage would have underscored the description of the women as joyous (γυ]ναῖκες ἄσμεναι, 518). The beginning of act 5 gives us the crucial details of a double wedding, of all four young people:

γί   ] νεται διπλοῦς γάμος
τὴν] ἑαυτοῦ θυγατέρα
      ] τὴν ἀδελφιδῆν πάλιν[45]

(521–3)

...a double wedding's being held
[He is giving] his own daughter [to Kleostratos to wed],
While [to Chaireas] on the other hand [he gives] his niece [away].

Thus ends the intelligible section of our text of *Aspis*.[46] In addition to its complex metatheater and fast-moving plot, this play stages all manner of

war trauma, from the horrors of combat to the grief of family, to lives damaged in the long aftermath of war. It is worth recalling that Athens' many
wars would have produced incalculably high numbers of traumatized veterans, bereaved families, confused and terrified *epiklēroi*, and ruined lives. That
Kleostratos' successful mission destroyed other lives is unspoken in the text
but witnessed in the form of his captives on stage. And the repetition of the
one detail of gruesome reality in all of extant Menander brings home to
Athens, briefly, the grim horrors of war, in the spectral vision of the unrecognizable bloated bodies of Athenian warriors.[47] Gaiser (1973, 132) asks if
Menander is playing with a "Horroreffekt," or merely varying the form of
the tragic messenger speech. But the combat that produces those corpses is
represented as a present-time event in the lives of the Athenians. It is not a
distant mythic battle, but one that could be part of daily reality in Athens. Its
repeated presence is striking, not least because as Beroutsos (2005, 11) points
out, the image is "without parallel in extant comedy."

Arnott concludes a study of Menander by focusing on just that traumatic
reality:

> It would have been possible …for a playwright of Menander's imagina-
> tive powers to devise a dozen different bromidic explanations for Daos'
> false assumption. But Menander lived in an Athens tortured by war,
> famine, and disease; and the explanation he chose was appropriate to
> his civilization and to his own harsh humanity. Even though he wrote
> comedies about the unimportant activities of unimportant people,
> he was not averse to reminding his audience of the more unpleasant
> aspects of contemporary life …The *Aspis* includes a description of a
> battlefield. And the image that has imprinted itself most firmly upon
> my mind from this year's Menander is that of the three-day corpses
> bloated unrecognizable under the Mediterranean sun, and a bent and
> buckled shield.
>
> (Arnott 1970, 17–18)

Lloyd-Jones (1971, 193) disputes this point, claiming that to make such a
remark "is to concentrate on a trivial part and to ignore the whole," because
Menander's "audience knew that Kleostratos was safe, and could enjoy an
entertainment whose whole tone was kept distinct from that of tragedy." In
response, Arnott (1975, 153) points out that we cannot know how many
of Menander's viewers had fought, and he wonders how those men might
have reacted to the description of "bloated corpses and a buckled shield."
I would add that when the viewers first hear about the swollen bodies,
they do not know that Kleostratos is safe—that information comes later, in
Tyche's speech that repeats the grim detail even as it provides reassurance
that he is alive.

I agree with Arnott that Menander's viewers (far better acquainted with
his theater than we can hope to be) could well have been haunted by those
bodies. In *Aspis*, combat veterans and their families saw their own experiences

and fears played out on stage. If the fantastical resolution of that horror must have been impossible for most of them, they could still have found comfort in witnessing their fears and traumas acknowledged as real and reasonable. Discussing Menander and Athenian society more than 50 years ago, Claire Préaux (1957) suggested that comedy's work is not to reflect reality precisely but to allow viewers to take revenge on our inability to make life as we would like it (88–9), a point supported by Gil (1974, 173–4), who adds that in Menander's drama, both topical allusions and "tacit implications of plot or situation can provide us with a considerable heritage of facts for understanding Athenian life in the fourth century." One of those facts is the traumatic effects of war on individuals and families, a daily reality little witnessed in our sources. In staging this reality, *Aspis* creates a space for trauma, for grief, for healing, and for family drama centered on something far more grave than an impetuous youth in love.[48] In this play, war trauma—personal, familial, a near-constant Athenian social reality—takes center stage.

Notes

*This chapter owes much to the generous assistance of others, and I am glad to thank them here. Corey Brennan provided invaluable historical resources; Bill Race and David Konstan read drafts with great care and patience. I am grateful to them all.

1. For a brief review of Athenian war and politics in Menander's time, see Webster (1974, 2–11). For a different view of war in *Aspis*, see Sommerstein in this volume.
2. *Aspis* has been popular in Menandrean studies, most of which focus on legal issues (chiefly the epiklērate), metatheater, and engagement with tragedy. The scholarship on these issues is too large to list, so I provide only a very few citations. On metatheater, see particularly Gutzwiller (2000); Goldberg (1980) gives a fine discussion of tragic and comic modes in *Aspis*. Cusset (2003), among many others, discusses technical elements of Menander's play with tragedy. Ciesko (2010) has the most recent analysis of characterization. The publication of three commentaries in the last eight years (Beroutsos, Ireland, Ingrosso) suggests that *Aspis* may become even more popular in the future.
3. I use the term "metatheater" loosely: the play-within-a-play that Daos proposes, in which he will pretend that Chairestratos has died, formally duplicates the plot of *Aspis*, and will remind viewers of the mechanisms of theater. By the time Daos invents his plot, the viewers already know that Kleostratos is not dead, so they are watching a theatrical pretense allow a family to protect itself and begin healing. The healing process itself, I suggest, is part of the play as a whole.
4. Scholars take Daos to mean that he could either buy his freedom or stop having to work.
5. An *epiklēros* is an heiress in the absence of a male heir; she is required to marry and provide, retroactively, a son for the dead man. Legally, she will be giving birth to her own brother. The preferred husband for the *epiklēros* is her late father's brother, as he is considered genetically closest to the father.
6. Discussions of Menander's depiction of, and attitude toward the epiklērate in this play are numerous; see, among many others, Brown's response (1983) to MacDowell (1982).
7. Groton (1982, 14) and Krieter-Spiro (1997, 235–6), among others, note his expertise in literature and drama.

8. On PTSD and survivor guilt arising from natural disasters, see, e.g., Cowell (1988), as well as Wilson, Smith, and Johnson (1985); from illness, Alter et al. (1996); from emergency response work, see McCammon et al. (1988) and Ward, Lombard, and Gwebushe (2006); from journalism, see Browne, Evangeli, and Greenberg (2012); from nursing, see Kerasiotis and Motta (2004). The scholarship on various aspects of trauma and PTSD, in these fields and others (such as sexual abuse, domestic violence, rape, among many others) is enormous and enormously varied; I draw on examples chosen not quite at random. On combat trauma in ancient Greece and Greek literature, see most prominently Shay (1994 and 2002); Tritle (2000); Meineck (2012), as well as the other chapters in this volume.

9. In his account of treating a Vietnam War veteran still significantly traumatized 25 years after the war, Kubany (1997) gives a model of how to distinguish between multiple simultaneous causes of guilt in PTSD. The guilt-based trauma of the veteran who lost a buddy in war is brilliantly depicted in Dave Alvin's song "1968."

10. Combined with shame, it may also lead them to avoid those families; see Shay (2002, 81–2).

11. Inside the house—if any viewers stopped to think about that domain—all three women (the sister of Kleostratos; the daughter and wife of Chairestratos) would have been utterly stricken. Chairestratos' wife would have seen her son Chaireas brokenhearted and horrified at losing his bride to Smikrines; the two girls shattered at the destruction of their anticipated marriages; her husband's niece in shock at the prospect of marriage to her elder uncle; and her husband sinking into a melancholic fit.

12. On the likelihood that most Greek citizen men (and many male slaves) would have experienced combat personally, and that therefore their families would have experienced family trauma and anxiety relating to combat, see Tritle (2000, 28).

13. Zagagi (1990, 67) remarks that Menander structures the play, through Tyche, to make "the comic situation more credible to his audience, urging them to regard Smikrines' frustration—the plot's main objective—in relation to their own daily experiences." My reading foregrounds the other characters and their tragic situation, as even knowing that all will end well, viewers could have empathized deeply with those suffering their own realities of trauma and bereavement.

14. I have witnessed this response to death—the desire to be useful—on numerous occasions. Its practical contributions notwithstanding, it is a delaying action, a way of postponing full recognition of what the bereavement means. The same is true for the shenanigans in *Aspis*.

15. I disagree with Lloyd-Jones (1971, 178, 191), who thinks that the audience would view in calm relaxation all the distress and sorrow enacted on stage. He considers *Aspis* "light comedy" (191; see also Konet [1976, 92], on *Aspis* as "a light-hearted play of fortune"), but in my view the play goes back and forth between comedy and tragedy, between comfort and trauma. Viewers whose lives had been touched by personal tragedies caused through warfare would not consider the tragic elements of *Aspis* to be distant from their own experiences.

16. On this point, see Schaps (1982), particularly 206–7. Ciesko (2010, 164) points out that Greek audiences "viewed comedy as something πιθανόν, true to life."

17. Selective use from the speeches of the duchess is a quotational nightmare, as she herself uses ellipses almost constantly. My ellipses are marked in square brackets; unmarked ellipses are original. Bunter's other services in the period of Lord Peter's recovery included finding a flat in London and moving him there.

18. In these respects, he is not too far from the supervisory aspect of Daos' functions as *paidagogos* to Kleostratos (and particularly in his management of Wimsey's domestic possessions).

19. In *Whose Body?* Lord Peter suffers a relapse of PTSD, in which Bunter takes care of him, while he hallucinates that they are back in the war. During this episode, they revert to being Sergeant Bunter and Major Wimsey. The next day, his mother the duchess takes him to the family's country estate for some rest. In this episode, too, the close bond of the two veterans is evident.

20. I use Arnott's Loeb text and translation. Many scholars have noted that this speech shares common points with Attic tragedy. Cusset (2003, 132), after discussing the technically (i.e., metrically) tragic elements, notes that two facts keep the audience from seeing the speech as purely tragic: first, Kleostratos' death is announced too early—in a tragedy it would come after—and, second, Daos' comic mask would have reminded viewers that the play is a comedy.

21. Lombard (1971, 140–2) remarks upon the resemblance of Daos to the loyal *paidagogos* of tragedy. On the closeness of the *paidagogos* to his charges, during the classical period, see Golden (1990, 147–9). There is no reason to think that this relationship had undergone changes by Menander's time.

22. Beroutsos (2005) cites Dickey (1996, 77) on this line. Dickey classifies the word as an "Age Term," and points out that it is not found in prose. It is clear that Daos is integrated into all aspects of his master's life and business: Smikrines expects him to manage much of his own interactions with Kleostratos' estate (163), and rebukes him for not having focused on the proper, legal approach to the situation, precisely because Daos is involved (187–9). Daos asserts that he knows all Kleostratos' business arrangements (197–200), but he draws the line at matters of marriage and the *epiklērate* (200–4).

23. Accompaniment of a slave on campaign was standard practice for Athenians: the slaves were both weapons-bearers and fellow combatants. See Hunt (1998, esp. 165–70) and Fisher (2006, 333). Merely carrying weapons onto the field means taking a share in the risks of combat.

24. Fontana, Rosenheck, and Horvath (1997); cite Milgram and Hobfoll (1986), whose research showed that unit "cohesiveness is…a double-edged sword that cuts in two directions" (349) because it improves combat performance and lowers stress during combat, but increases postcombat stress and trauma because "survivors assess the toll enacted and experience a greater sense of loss and survivor guilt about the death of personal friends than of strangers" (350).

25. And indeed, the waiter's proud boasting that only his tribe, the Thracian Getae, are men and are therefore often sent to the mills (i.e., for punishment) would both invoke disdain in Daos and underscore his loyalty to his master. Krieter-Spiro (1997, 191) and Gaiser (1971, 19), among others, note that Daos' behavior disproves the waiter's charge that Phrygians are cowardly.

26. See MacDonald et al. (1997): "there is a significant association between level of PTSD and race among Vietnam combat veterans" (122). Ward, Lombard, and Gwebushe (2006) found that in South Africa "prehospital emergency services personnel" (226) suffer higher rates of both exposure to "critical incidents" (events that can precipitate PTSD) and manifestations of "general psychopathology" than are found in "similar studies in the developed world" (228–9). They cite generally higher rates of violence in the developing world as an important reason that emergency service PTSD in the developing world should be studied (226).

27. See also Penk and Allen (1991), with their citations. For examples of culturally specific forms of trauma and therapy, see, among others, Cross (1998); Durán et al. (1998); and Shalhoub-Kevorkian (1999, 2001); these studies relate not to combat trauma and PTSD caused by war, but to other forms of trauma.

28. An adjective or metaphor indicating sadness would presumably have modified the word ἡμέραν in line 1.

29. Ingrosso (2010, ad loc) describes this opening speech as an "orazione funebre" that ends with praise for the virtue of the dead man. She cites its similarity to military epitaphs.

30. Menander spares his audience the further horror of the unpreventable destruction of the bodies by birds and wild dogs; in this respect, he soft-pedals even in his most gruesomely realistic detail, by presenting the bodies as damaged only by heat and exposure. On Menander's "realismo soft," with regards to interpersonal violence in the polis, see Gigante Lanzara (1998).

31. Ingrosso (2010, 77) reads otherwise, seeing Daos as praising the commander with the adjective χρηστός. Most readers have taken Daos here as being ironic, at the very least. On this commander, see, most recently, Lamagna (2014).

32. A pit cremation seems more likely than an open-air cremation, as it requires much less firewood, and the remains need not be moved again after the cremation is completed. Would Menander have expected many in his audience to know further gruesome details about cremations? Some of them must have. See Lamagna (2014, 69) on this point.

33. Ireland (2010, ad loc) says much the same. Groton (1982, 88) notes that return of burned remains to the family was customary, but rightly notes that an urn on stage would have been "a grim, out-of-place reminder of the death of Kleostratos' comrade-in-arms."

34. The captives on stage might have been standing quietly in a huddle or (more likely) moving a bit and showing confusion; such staging would provide dramatic texture, as well as some irony: they too are suffering war trauma.

35. See Groton (1982, 9–10) on Tyche and her moral judgment.

36. Krieter-Spiro (1997, 14) notes Daos' degree of authority over the family, in urging Chairestratos to be active rather than sink into depression.

37. It seems very likely that the missing parts of the lines would have mentioned the loot that was to serve as dowry for his sister.

38. Sisti (1971, ad loc) cites *Mis.* 214, in which the elderly Demeas embraces his long-lost daughter Krateia, saying ἔχω σε. Such a parallel underscores the intensity of emotion in this scene. Ingrosso, (2010, ad loc) notes the same parallel and refers to scenes of *anagnorisis* in tragedy, cited also by Ferrari (2001, 944n. 2). *Anagnorisis* normally reunites families, but here it joins two men who have had a long-standing familial relationship intensified by the special bonding formed during shared combat.

39. These two do not appear to need therapy other than restoring order in their home together. The scene also shows "the familial affection" that is seen in all the characters of *Aspis*, other than Smikrines (Hunter 1985, 131–2).

40. Chairestratos' daughter, too, loses her planned marriage, as she had been expecting to be wed to Kleostratos.

41. That is, under these circumstances, a man might well say to himself, "if only I had given her the dowry and kept him here; if only I had managed the wedding sooner." The sister too would have felt tremendous guilt, knowing she was the cause of her brother's military expedition. Scholarship has tended to treat Chairestratos as overreacting; for example, Halliwell (1983, 32): "Chairestratos' collapse …on any interpretation seems an extreme reaction to the state of affairs." But no standard has ever been established for response to the catastrophic loss of a close relative, and the additional distress caused by Smikrines' selfishness exacerbates the situation. Chairestratos is established as generally melancholy, but he is not senseless.

42. Lloyd-Jones (1971, 193–4) criticizes Chairestratos and Chaireas for not appearing "tremendously intelligent," particularly in contrast with Daos. Such criticism does not take into account the simple fact that Daos has known about Kleostratos' death for

considerably longer; the two citizen men are staged in the immediate aftermath of bereavement, when intellect tends not to be at the forefront of response. Daos is certainly impatient with them, as Lloyd-Jones says, but he can take that attitude because he has been preparing to do service to his master's family, and at the very least he is motivated not to wind up as one of Smikrines' possessions.

43. As Ingrosso (2010, ad loc) notes, Chaerea's lament does not advance the plot, but it forms a counterpart to Daos' opening monologue. The viewers watching Chaerea know that Kleostratos is alive, so they can enjoy the comic elements of the speech, while still sympathizing with the unhappy young man, whose laments have a rather deeper foundation than do those of the average nervous lover in New Comedy.

44. Webster (1974, 66–7) rightly observes that "much would depend on the acting" and that between the extremes of obvious comedy or seriousness there is much room for an actor's interpretation. In this play there is an unusual amount of room for a viewer's interpretation as well.

45. See Arnott (1979, 89–92) on issues in attempting to speculate about the final act of the play. This double wedding affirms life even more joyously than does the usual wedding-finale of Menandrean comedy, as those nuptials generally solve a social problem of pregnancy or lost identity, rather than resolving a literal life-and-death situation, as in *Aspis*.

46. Most scholars presume that the fifth act would have involved a comic scene of Smikrines' punishment and humiliation. He is often called the worst villain in extant Menander, but a case could be made that he is the only villain in extant Menander: the other blocking characters (such as Knemon in *Dyskolos*) may be self-centered, callow, or irate, but they do not display Smikrines' callous selfishness. His degree of villainy allows, as noted above, distraction from grief and trauma. Further, it requires punishment (presumably in the missing fifth act). He serves as scapegoat for the entire community—audience as well as the characters—a means of letting off the steam that the half-tragic plot had built up. Cf., Konstan (1983, 70–3) on the similar cathartic function, in Plautus' *Captivi*, of the punishment of the evil Stalagmus.

47. We might note that if the corpse with the shield was not Kleostratos, it was still another dead Athenian; his family can rejoice in his homecoming, but another family would be left to grieve.

48. As Del Corno (1970, 71) notes, the sorrow in this play is owed not to an unhappy lover or a person whose faults damaged his own life (e.g., Knemon in *Dyskolos*) but to the physical reality of death.

Bibliography

Akrigg, Ben, and Rob Tordoff. 2013. *Slaves and Slavery in Ancient Greek Comic Drama*. Cambridge: Cambridge University Press.

Alter, Carol L., David Pelcovitz, Alan Axelrod, Barbara Goldenberg, Helene Harris, Barbara Meyers, Brian Groboos, Francine Mandel, Aliza Septimus, and Sandra Kaplan. 1996. "Identification of PTSD in Cancer Survivors." *Pychosomatics* 37: 137–43.

Arnott, W. G. 1970. "Young Lovers and Confidence Tricksters: The Rebirth of Menander." *The University of Leeds Review* 13: 1–18.

———. 1975. "The Modernity of Menander." *Greece & Rome* 22: 140–55.

———. 1979. *Menander, Vol. I:* Aspis *to* Epitrepontes. Cambridge, MA. Harvard University Press.

Beroutsos, Demetrios C. 2005. *A Commentary on the* Aspis *of Menander. Part One: Lines 1–298.* Göttingen: Vandenhoeck & Ruprecht.

Breslau, Naomi, and Glenn C. Davis. 1987. "Posttraumatic Stress Disorder: The Etiologic Specificity of Wartime Stressors." *American Journal of Psychiatry* 144: 578–83.

Brown, P. G. McC. 1983. "Menander's Dramatic Technique and the Law of Athens." *Classical Quarterly* 33: 412–20.

Brown, Tessa, Michael Evangeli, and Neil Greenberg. 2012. "Trauma-Related Guilt and Posttraumatic Stress Among Journalists." *Journal of Traumatic Stress* 25: 207–10.

Ciesko, Martin. 2010. "Techniques of Foreshadowing and Character Presentation in Menander's *Aspis* in the Light of Greek Dramatic Tradition." *Journal of Classical Studies* 22: 163–215.

Cowell, Alexander McFarlane. 1988. "The Phenomenology of posttraumatic Stress Disorders following a Natural Disaster." *Journal of Nervous and Mental Disease* 176: 22–9.

Cox, Cheryl. 2013. "Coping with Punishment: The Social Networking of Slaves in Menander." In Akrigg and Tordoff 2013, 159–72.

Cross, William E., Jr. 1998. "Black Psychological Functioning and the Legacy of Slavery: Myths and Realities." In Danieli 1998, 387–400.

Cusset, Christophe. 2003. *Menandre ou la comédie tragique.* Paris: CNRS Editions.

Danieli, Yael. 1998. *International Handbook of Multigenerational Legacies of Trauma.* New York: Plenum Press.

Del Corno, Dario. 1970. "Il nuovo Menandro: *Lo Scudo* e *La Donna di Samo.*" *Atene e Roma* 15: 65–79.

Dickey, Eleanor. 1996. *Greek Forms of Address, From Herodotus to Lucian.* Oxford: Clarendon Press.

Durán, Eduardo, Bonnie Durán, Maria Yellow Horse Brave Heart, and Susan Yellow Horse-Davis. 1998. "Healing the American Indian Soul Wound." In Danieli 1998, 341–54.

Ferrari, Franco. 2001. *Menandro e la commedia nuova. Edizione con testo greco a fronte.* Torino: Einaudi.

Fisher, Nick. 2006. "Citizens, Foreigners and Slaves in Greek Society." In *A Companion to the Classical Greek World,* edited by Konrad H. Kinzl, 327–48. Malden, MA: Wiley-Blackwell.

Fontana, Alan, Robert Rosenheck, and Thomas Horvath. 1997. "Social Support and Psychopathology in the War Zone." *The Journal of Nervous & Mental Disease* 185: 675–81.

Gaiser, Konrad. 1971. *Menander Der Schild oder Die Erbtochter.* Zurich: Verlag.

———. 1973. "Menanders Komödie 'Der Schild.'" *Gräzer Beitrage* 1: 111–36a.

Gigante Lanzara, Valeria. 1998. "Il teatro di Menandro: il realismo *soft* e la città dei buoni." *Atene e Roma* 43: 127–32.

Gil, Luis. 1974. "Comedia ática y sociedad ateniense II: tipos del ámbito familiar en la comedia media y nueva." *Estudios clásicos* 18: 151–86.

Goldberg, Sander M. 1980. *The Making of Menander's Comedy.* Berkeley: University of California Press.

Golden, Mark. 1990. *Children and Childhood in Classical Athens.* Baltimore, MD: Johns Hopkins University Press.

Gomme, A. W. and F. H. Sandbach. 1973. *Menander: A Commentary.* Oxford: Oxford University Press.

Groton, Anne. 1982. *A Commentary on Menander's Aspis 1–163.* Dissertation, University of Michigan. Ann Arbor.

Gutzwiller, Kathryn. 2000. "The Tragic Mask of Comedy: Metatheatricality in Menander." *Classical Antiquity* 19: 102–37.

Halliwell, Stephen. 1983. "The Staging of Menander, *Aspis* 299ff." *Liverpool Classical Monthly* 8: 31–2.

Herman, Judith. 1992. *Trauma and Recovery.* New York: Basic Books.

Hunt, Peter. 1998. *Slaves, Warfare and Ideology in the Greek Historians.* Cambridge: Cambridge University Press.

Hunter, R. L. 1985. *The New Comedy of Greece and Rome.* Cambridge: Cambridge University Press.

Ingrosso, Paola. 2010. *Menandro, Lo scudo. Introduzione, testo, traduzione e commento.* Lece: Pensa multimedia.

Ireland, Stanley. 2010. *Menander, The Shield and The Arbitration.* Oxford: Aris & Phillips.

Kerasiotis, Bernadina, and Robert W. Motta. 2004. "Assessment of PTSD Symptoms in Emergency Room, Intensive Care, and General Floor Nurses." *International Journal of Emergency Mental Health* 6: 121–33.

Konet, Richard J. 1976. "The Role of *Tuche* in Menander's *Aspis.*" *Classical Bulletin* 52: 90–2.

Konstan, David. 1983. *Roman Comedy.* Ithaca: Cornell University Press.

———. 1995. *Greek Comedy and Ideology.* Oxford: Oxford University Press.

———. 2013. "Menander's Slaves: The Banality of Violence." In Akrigg and Tordoff 2013, 144–58.

Krieter-Spiro. Martha. 1997. *Sklaven, Köche und Hetären: Das Dienstpersonal bei Menander.* Stuttgart: Teubner.

Kubany, Edward S. 1997. "Application of Cognitive Therapy for Trauma-Related Guilt (CT-TRG) With a Vietnam Veteran Troubled by Multiple Sources of Guilt." *Cognitive and Behavioral Practice* 4: 213–44.

Lamagna, Mario. 2014. "Military Culture and Menander." In *Menander in Contexts*, edited by Alan H. Sommerstein, 58–71. London: Routledge.

Lape, Susan. 2004. *Reproducing Athens: Menander's Comedy, Democratic Culture, and the Hellenistic City.* Princeton, NJ: Princeton University Press.

Lee, Deborah, Peter Scragg, and Stuart Turner. 2001. "The Role of Shame and Guilt in Traumatic Events: A Clinical Model of Shame-Based and Guilt-Based PTSD." *British Journal of Medical Psychology* 74: 451–66.

Lloyd-Jones, Hugh. 1971. "Menander's *Aspis*." *Greek, Roman, and Byzantine Studies* 12: 175–95.

Lombard, D. B. 1971. "New Values in Traditional Forms: A Study in Menander's 'Aspis.'" *Acta Classica* 14: 123–45.

MacDonald, Carol, Kerry Chamberlain, and Nigel Long. 1997. "Race, Combat, and PTSD in a Community Sample of New Zealand Vietnam War Veterans." *Journal of Traumatic Stress* 10.1: 117–124.

MacDowell, Douglas M. 1982. "Love versus the Law: An Essay on Menander's 'Aspis.'" *Greece & Rome* 29: 42–52.

McCammon, Susan, Thomas W. Durham, E. Jackson Allison Jr., and Joseph E. Williamson. 1988. "Emergency Workers' Cognitive Appraisal and Coping with Traumatic Events." *Journal of Traumatic Stress* 1: 353–72.

McFarlane, Alexander C. 1988. "The Phenomenology of Posttraumatic Stress Disorders Following a Natural Disaster." *Journal of Nervous & Mental Disease* 176: 22–9.

Meineck, Peter. 2012. "Combat Trauma and the Tragic Stage: 'Restoration' by Cultural Catharsis." *Intertexts* 16: 7–24.

Milgram, Norman A., and Stevan Hobfoll. 1986. "Generalizations from Theory and Practice in War-Related Stress." In *Stress and Coping in Time of War: Generalizations from the Israeli Experience,* edited by Norman A. Milgram, 316–52. New York: Brunner/Mazel.

Mitchem, Jamie D. 2011. "Survivor Guilt." In *The Encyclopedia of Disaster Relief*, edited by K. Bradley Penuel and Matt Statler, 662–65. Thousand Oaks, CA: Sage Publications.

Penk, Walter E., and Irving M. Allen. 1991. "Clinical Assessment of Post-Traumatic Stress Disorder (PTSD) Among American Minorities Who Served in Vietnam." *Journal of Traumatic Stress* 4: 41–66.

Préaux, Claire. 1957. "Ménandre et la société Athénienne." *Chronique d'Égypte* 32: 86–100.

Sandbach, F. H. 1990. *Menandri Reliquiae Selectae.* Oxford: Oxford University Press.

Sayers, Dorothy. 1923. *Whose Body?* New York: Harper & Row.

———. 1935. *Gaudy Night.* London: Victor Gollancz.

———. 1937. *Busman's Honeymoon.* New York: Harcourt Brace.

Schaps, David. 1982. "The Women of Greece in Wartime." *Classical Philology* 77: 193–213.

Shalhoub-Kevorkian, Nadera. 1999. "Towards a Cultural Definition of Rape: Dilemmas in Dealing with Rape Victims in Palestinian Society." *Women's Studies International Forum* 22.2: 157–73.

———. 2001. "Using the Dialogue Tent to Break Mental Chains: Listening and Being Heard." *Social Service Review* 75: 135–50.

Shay, Jonathan. 1994. *Achilles in Vietnam: Combat Trauma and the Undoing of Character.* New York: Scribner.

———. 2002. *Odysseus in America: Combat Trauma and the Trials of Homecoming.* New York: Scribner.

Sherk, Robert. 1970. "Daos and Spinther in Menander's *Aspis*." *American Journal of Philology* 91: 341–43.

Sisti, Francesco. 1971. *Menandro Aspis.* Rome: Edizioni dell'Ateneo.

Tritle, Lawrence A. 2000. *From Melos to My Lai: War and Survival.* London: Routledge.

Walton, J. Michael, and Peter D. Arnott. 1996. *Menander and the Making of Comedy.* Westport, CT: Praeger.

Ward, C. L., C. J. Lombard, and N. Gwebushe. 2006. "Critical Incient Exposure in South African Emergency Services Personnel: Prevalence and Associated Mental Health Issues." *Emergency Medicine Journal* 22: 226–31.

Webster, T. B. L. 1974. *An Introduction to Menander.* Manchester: Manchester University Press.

Wilson, John P., W. Ken Smith, and Suzanne Johnson. 1985. "A Comparative Analysis of PTSD among Various Survivor Groups." In *Trauma and Its Wake: The Study and Treatment of Post-Traumatic Stress Disorder,* edited by Charles Figley, 147–72. New York: Brunner/Mazel.

Zagagi, Netta. 1990. "Divine Interactions and Human Agents in Menander." In *Recherches et Rencontres 2: Relire Ménandre,* edited by Eric Handley and André Hurst, 63–91. Geneva: Droz.

CHAPTER TWELVE

When War Is Performed, What Do Soldiers and Veterans Want to Hear and See and Why?

Thomas G. Palaima*

For the typical American soldier, despite the perverted film sermons, it wasn't "getting another Jap" or "getting another Nazi" that impelled him up front. "The reason why you storm the beaches is not patriotism or bravery," reflects the tall rifleman. "It's that special sense of not wanting to fail your buddies. There's sort of a special kinship."

An explanation is offered by an old-time folk singer who'd been with an antiaircraft battery in the Sixty-second Artillery: "You had fifteen guys who for the first time in their lives were not living in a competitive society. We were in a tribal sort of situation, where we could help each other without fear. I realized it was the absence of phony standards that created the thing I loved about the army."[1]

Ancient Greek and modern Western societies have in common the creation of works of artistic expression in response to the effects of wars and other forms of social violence. These include masterworks like the Homeric epics (the mythical war against Troy that the Greeks placed *in illo tempore* in the very late Bronze Age, our thirteenth to twelfth centuries BCE), Euripides' *Trojan Women* (performed ca. 415 BCE during the Peloponnesian War, 431–404 BCE), Thucydides' history of the Peloponnesian War, and Studs Terkel's oral history of World War II. We also have poems and stories about war, for example, by Walt Whitman (American Civil War), Wilfred Owen (World War I), Ernest Hemingway (World War I), W. H. Auden (World War II), Yehuda Amichai (mainly post–World War II), Charles Patterson (Vietnam War), Kurt Vonnegut's *Slaughterhouse Five* (World War II), Nick Arvin's *Articles of War* (World War II), and the American short stories of Larry Brown (World War II), Tobias Wolff (Vietnam War), and Tim O'Brien (Vietnam War), as well as songs from Blind Willie Johnson (World War I) to Steve Earle (Iraq War). I cite these as authors and works that stand out as essential and enduring creative responses to the realities of war and war trauma in their given periods of human history. All of these works, including also modern memoirs, essays, and films, live beyond the times in which they were originally composed, heard, viewed, or read.

These masterworks survive not by chance, but because they contain, preserve, and present truths about war and violence that human beings want and need to take in and hold onto. These truths can be pleasing or displeasing depending on who is taking them in or refusing to take them in. The things that happen in times of war are disturbing to experience even secondhand—or for those who went through them, for a second time—and are also threatening to the higher values upon which our lives as members of what we call "civilized societies" are based. Therefore, truths about war have to be spoken, sung, and shown in ways that make it possible for those who have experienced war and violence in different ways, or not at all, to accept them.

How do soldiers who have been at war experience presentations of war? How do the messages of such works change as they survive beyond their original contexts? Are there distinctive or timeless characteristics of what we might generally call the "performances of war"? What is it about the modern experience of war that makes those who know war appreciate ancient Greek epic, tragedy, and history? What qualities appeal to them in positive and negative ways?

These are big questions. Here we will consider the last question, but we should be thinking about all of them as we do so. These questions are important, because war is important and it is not going away.[2] War is with us today, as it was yesterday and as it will be tomorrow. This is a truth that stretches back to the fifteenth century BCE in the Western tradition, the period to which we can assign linguistically some of the earliest lines in the *Iliad* of Homer.[3] It is a truth embedded, embodied, and communicated in the *Iliad* and *Odyssey*, the two oral songs that made sure the ancient Greeks, for generation after generation, would never forget what happens to soldiers who are sent off to war; to soldiers who fight in defense of cities under siege; to men, women, and children waiting anxiously in besieged communities, or waiting back home long separated from their sons, fathers, brothers, uncles, cousins, and nephews fighting in far-off campaigns; and finally to soldiers who try to make it back home and to soldiers who actually do make it back.

It is a truth attested by the themes taken up in Greek tragedies. The surviving tragedies were written in a roughly 60-year period during which the ancient city-state of Athens, in which they were performed, was at war nearly constantly as it aggressively pursued the course of becoming an imperial power. Athens eventually found itself at war and under attack for much longer than the city of Troy. The tragic playwrights Aeschylus and Sophocles were themselves veterans of war. Aeschylus was a Μαραθωνομάχης (*Marathōnomakhēs*), a "Marathon-fighter," the Athenian equivalent of an American veteran of the D-Day landings. He proudly and simply declares this fact in the epitaph he is said to have written for the marker of his tomb in the Sicilian community of Gela, where he died. The inscription makes no mention of his great achievements as a tragedian. His claim to fame is that he fought in the Athenian victory over the Persians in 490 BCE.

Αἴσχυλον Εὐφορίωνος Ἀθηναῖον τόδε κεύθει
μνῆμα καταφθίμενον πυροφόροιο Γέλας·
Ἀλκὴν δ' εὐδόκιμον Μαραθώνιον ἄλσος ἂν εἴποι
καὶ βαθυχαιτήεις Μῆδος ἐπιστάμενος.

Page (1975, 42)

This monument conceals an Athenian, Aeschylus, son of Euphorion, who passed away in wheat-bearing Gela [a city in Sicily].
The grove at Marathon could recount his well-regarded soldier prowess as could the long-haired Persian who knows it.

In historical times, the Greeks believed that the normal—not to be confused with the desired or preferred—state of existence was war. Peace intruded upon war periodically, and it did so in this way. Greek city-states effectively suspended formal military conflicts by truces that they set at anywhere from 10 days to 30 years. They expected that war would eventually reassert itself. In 421 BCE, the Spartans and Athenians were so worn out by war that they contracted an unheard of 50-year truce.[4] They stipulated that both sides renew the truce every year. They were on opposite sides of the battlefield again within 3 years.

By contrast, consider what H. G. Wells wrote about World War I in his 1914 essay, "Why Britain Went to War": "For this is now a war for peace. It aims at a settlement that shall stop this sort of thing for ever…This, the greatest of all wars, is not just another war—it is the last war!"[5] Call to mind two place names, Ypres and Somme.[6] Think of two British poets, Wilfred Owen and Siegfried Sassoon. Hold in your thoughts the contents of one novel, Erich Maria Remarque's *Im Westen nichts Neues*. Then you will understand why, when we remember Wells' remarks now, we do so with irony.

But his ideas were not laughable. Wells was no fool. He was a man who thought sound thoughts. Wells had the wisdom that comes from the stern and hard experience of being apprenticed to a draper at the age of 13. He saw the world clearly and reasoned well. As a novelist and an observer of life, he knew that individual human beings and whole societies were capable of doing monstrous evils. Wells' *The Island of Dr. Moreau* (1896) is a profound, simple, and clear parable about the good and evil elements in our human natures, our animal impulses, and how and why we succeed or fail at controlling them, and how our loftiest thoughts and best scientific methods can be corrupted. It is on a par with Jack Schaefer's American classic *Shane* (1946). Schaefer, just after the end of World War II, examines how and when violent force can, must, or should be applied to resolve conflicting ways of life and disputes arising from competing desires and competing claims to resources. His parable is told through the eyes of a young boy witnessing violent adult events for the first time.

Contemporary luminaries shared Wells' views. In 1918, after four years of senseless slaughter, President Woodrow Wilson and David Lloyd George, the British prime minister, joined Wells in optimistically predicting that World War I would be the last. Wilson called it "the culminating and final war for human liberty."[7]

It took men who knew war firsthand to size things up correctly. French Field Marshall Ferdinand Foch commented on the Treaty of Versailles, as he declined to attend its signing ceremony, "This is not peace, it is an Armistice for twenty years."[8] Foch was not far off in his calculations. Douglas MacArthur, too, came away from World War I with hard-earned knowledge, supported by his own fuller study of human history. He had led troops bravely in combat in World War I. In his famous Rainbow (Forty-second) Infantry Division reunion speech of July 14, 1935, he calculated that "in the last 3,400 years only 268—less than 1 in 13—have been free from wars."[9] MacArthur's estimate of 268 years of peace was optimistically generous.

One substitute for the practical wisdom of the battlefield is philosophical speculation. Just after the armistice that ended World War I, George Santayana visited a coffee house near Somerville College, Oxford, where wounded officers were recuperating. They were singing "Tipperary" in high spirits, as he noted, because they would not be going back to the trenches. Santayana looked at them and thought sadly, "Yet the poor fellows think they are safe! They think that the war—perhaps the last of all wars—is over! Only the dead are safe; only the dead have seen the end of war."[10]

But men like Foch, Santayana, and MacArthur, whether we call them "realists" or "pessimists," were then and still are in the minority. Most human beings do not want to look at war as it is and what it tells us about who we are as members of a society that engages in warfare and what we are willing to let men and now women, mostly young, go through in wars that are fought under the authorization of our governmental leaders and representatives. Here is one small indicator of our reluctance to see war as it is. Wilfred Owen's stark and honest poems about what men go through in times of war were published, after his death, in a first edition of two impressions in 1920 and 1921. By 1929 fewer than 1,500 copies had been sold.[11]

It took until late 1928 early 1929 for Erich Maria Remarque's classic indictment of the Great War to appear. We shall see that this time lag of ten years for a participant to see and to make some sense of a war is not unparalleled. Remarque's literal German title, *Nothing New in the West*, speaks poignantly to the futility of static trench warfare with gas, barbed wire, machine guns, artillery, and tanks. Its English title, *All Quiet on the Western Front*, by inviting us to believe that times of tranquility were real, is characteristic of our refusal to see things in war for what they are.

Take, for example, high-command decisions about troop movements and tactics, despite the terrifying technological changes in weaponry in World War I. "Even when the machine-gun had obviously gained a dominance of the battlefield, General Headquarters in France resisted its growth from the puny prewar scale of two in each battalion. One Army commander, Haig, declared that it was 'a much overrated weapon' and that this scale was 'more than sufficient'."

On the first day of the Battle of the Somme "July 1, 1916, thirteen British divisions marched towards the enemy like ceremonial troops down Whitehall, led by subalterns blowing whistles and clutching one-shot revolvers. At the end of the day 19,000 lay dead."[12] Notice the disconnect in Haig's report on the slaughter: "Very successful attack this morning...All went like clockwork...The battle is going very well for us...Our troops are in wonderful spirits and full of confidence."[13]

After initial ill-conceived attacks were unsuccessful, according to Liddell Hart, "Haig reverted to the method of nibbling, now to be exalted as a definite and masterly strategy of attrition, and to be defended by optimistic miscalculations of the German losses." On the left flank, Australian units suffered horrific losses (23,000 men) "for the ultimate gain, after six weeks, of a tiny tongue of ground just over a mile deep."[14]

The Australian official history of the impact upon the soldiers in these units echoes all the way back through history to the *Iliad*'s account of the soldiers under Agamemnon and other Greek regional commanders at Troy[15]:

> Although most Australian soldiers were optimists, and many were opposed on principle to voicing—or even harbouring—grievances, it is not surprising if the effect on some intelligent men was a bitter conviction that they were being uselessly sacrificed. "For Christ's sake, write a book on the life of an infantryman (said one of them...), and by doing so you will quickly prevent these shocking tragedies." That an officer who had fought as nobly as Lieutenant J. A. Raws should, in the last letter before his death, speak of the "murder" of many of his friends, "through the incompetence, callousness, and personal vanity of those high in authority," is evidence not indeed of the literal truth of his words but of something much amiss in the higher leadership..."We have just come out of a place so terrible (wrote—, one of the most level-headed officers in the force) that...a raving lunatic could never imagine the horror of the last thirteen days."

The unsound sizing up of events, and the ignorance of what soldiers in the field were put through—Lieutenant Raws flatly states, "Hell must be a home to it"—in executing the strategies of commanders back at head-quarters, as exemplified by Wells, Wilson, and Haig, is rivaled recently by the two-word phrase "Mission Accomplished" that marked the end of the so-called combat phase of Operation Iraqi Freedom. Imagine being a soldier or someone who knows what soldiers are going through and hearing such naïve predictions, assessments, and declarations. It would make you, like the two Australian field officers just quoted, desperate for some corroboration of what had actually happened, or what was actually happening, or what was likely to happen. Greek citizens and most of their state leaders shared the views rather of Foch, MacArthur, and Santayana.

If we want a reason, then, for why soldiers and veterans of modern wars respond to recitations of Homer and performances of Greek tragedies, it is because they sing forth a certain kind of "truth" and reflect what is real. They speak truth as the Greeks defined it. The Greek adjective for what is true, *a-lēthēs*, describes something that cannot escape our notice or is unforgettable.

Homer's *Iliad* is 15,000 lines of song distilled from songs sung about war for people who fought and lived through wars for at least seven hundred years. Homer, or the process of construction of the grand epic that is represented by his name, was a kind of Alan Lomax, an ethnomusicologist, with original, creative talents of his own. Imagine piecing together an enormous folk song from, say, the ballads and variants collected by Francis J. Child, *The English and Scottish Popular Ballads* (ten volumes from 1882 to 1898). The *Iliad* has the same folk realism. It does not shy away from depicting the hard facts that folk songs sing to people who are leading hard lives.

For example, the *Iliad* is full of gruesome combat deaths. One is a ghastly decapitation in which the beheaded body of a soldier momentarily stands spurting blood and spinal fluid upward like a water fountain. It occurs in book 20, when Achilles has descended into what Jonathan Shay rightly terms "berserker degradation."[16] It is an apocalyptic vision of violence of the sort too many soldiers have witnessed:

> In almost the same motion, Achilles struck
> Agenor's son Echeclus full on the head
> With his hilted sword. Echeclus' blood
> Warmed the whole blade, and death came
> In an overpowering violet haze.
> Deucalion was next, Achilles' spear-point
> Piercing his elbow just where the sinews join.
> His arm hung uselessly as he stood there
> Staring death in the face. Achilles closed in
> And sliced into his neck, sending the head,
> Helmet and all, flying through the air.
> Marrow spurted up through his spinal cord,
> And then the corpse was lengthwise on the ground.
>
> (*Iliad* 20. 491–503)

Compare this pathos-infused report of the death of Army Specialist Joshua Reeves, a 26-year-old soldier in the Second Battalion, Sixteenth Infantry Regiment of the Fourth Infantry Brigade Combat Team, First Infantry Division, on September 22, 2007, during what was called "the surge" in Iraq. The Humvee he was driving was hit by an EFP, or Explosively Formed Penetrator, a particularly deadly kind of IED (Improvised Explosive Device) that drives a copper plate that has melted into the form of a projectile through the protective armor of armored vehicles:[17]

> He'd been in the right front seat when the EFP exploded…He wasn't breathing, his eyes weren't moving, his left foot was gone, his back side was ripped open, his face had turned gray, his stomach was filling with blood, and he was naked, with the exception of one bloodied sock— and as if all that weren't enough with which to consider Joshua Reeves in these failing moments of his life, now came word from some of the soldiers gathered in the lobby that he'd begun this day with a message from his wife that she had just given birth to their first child.

The truly cruel irony of a young man's losing his life to gruesome injuries from an enemy assault in Iraq while his loving wife is giving birth to their son back home has a parallel at the beginning of *Iliad* book 6.13–20. The Greek warrior Diomedes, on a killing spree, ruthlessly cuts down Axylus, who is described as being in peacetime a paradigm of a generous host and friend to all human beings who passed his way. Yet none of those whom Axylus hosted and befriended could protect him from his grim fate later on the battlefields around Troy.

The *Iliad* also shows us soldiers and gods behaving ruthlessly. Slightly later in book 6 than the episode that describes the killing of Axylus, Agamemnon angrily rebukes his brother Menelaus for even thinking of holding the defeated Trojan Adrastus captive for ransom, although Menelaus would be following an honorable and civilized practice, of which there are numerous examples in the *Iliad*:[18]

> "Going soft, Menelaus? What does this man
> Mean to you? Have the Trojans ever shown you
> Any hospitality? Not one of them
> Escapes sheer death at our hands, not even
> The boy who is still in his mother's womb.
> Every Trojan dies, unmourned and unmarked."
>
> (6.55–60)

In the *Iliad*, religion provides no solace to mortals in the grips of war. The gods themselves are cavalierly merciless even toward their most devoted worshipers. Hera says to Zeus in book 4:

> There are three cities especially dear to me:
> Argos, Sparta, and broad Mycenae.
> Waste these if they ever annoy you.
> I won't stand in your way or take it too hard.
>
> (4.62–5)

The *Iliad* sang to the Greeks and still sings to us about things that human beings should not forget about war, even if many of us do not want to learn about them in the first place. The *Iliad* gives an honest picture of what goes on during times of war. In war what we know is right will be betrayed or ignored. Commanders away from the action will issue orders in disregard for the suffering of the rank-and-file soldiers who do the fighting. The effects of Agamemnon's decisions in books 1 and 2 of the *Iliad* put us in mind of what we have seen of the effects of Field Marshall Douglas Haig's decisions at the Battles of the Somme and Third Ypres. Agamemnon shows little regard for the well-being of his troops in general and little under-standing of their morale at this point in the fighting of what has become a protracted war.

Nonetheless, soldiers will experience what the Greeks called the *kharmē* of war, an exhilarating kind of pleasure that can be remembered and reig-nited, as when an addict takes another dose of a drug. Whether men die or live, stay whole or are maimed, will depend on blind luck or chance. The bravest and strongest and most battle-hardened soldiers will experi-ence intense personal feelings of humiliation and fear—even the noble Hector admits that he is finally facing Achilles because he has been driven by his feelings of public shame (*aidōs*) for having squandered his army. When Hector does come face-to-face with Achilles, he immediately runs like hell trying to escape.[19] The *Iliad* teaches us that in war very few strategic plans will be drawn up well. Most goals will not be well set. Few will be reached efficiently.

As for war having a purpose worth losing one's own life, Achilles, the best field commander among the Greek military leaders at Troy, states clearly in two prominent passages that the war that the massed Greek army has been fighting into the tenth year has no valid casus belli and is tantamount to a personal vendetta on the part of Agamemnon, the ineffective commander-in-chief, and his brother Menelaus, king of Sparta:

> *I* don't have any quarrel with the Trojans
> They didn't do anything to *me* to make me
> Come over here and fight, didn't run off with *my* cattle or horses
> Or ruin *my* farmland back home in Phthia, not with all
> The shadowy mountains and moaning seas between.
> It's for *you* [Agamemnon], dogface, for your precious pleasure—
> And Menelaus' honor—that we came here.
>
> (*Iliad* 1.162–8)

Achilles later rejects Agamemnon's poorly conceived offer of reconciliation by stressing that what men do in battle does not matter, in the big or small picture, and that their longing for the human comforts of their women and families means little compared to the vain and petty desires of the highest ranking officers:

> It doesn't matter if you stay in camp or fight—
> In the end, everybody comes out the same.

Coward and hero get the same reward:
You die whether you slack off or work.
And what do I have for all my suffering,
Constantly putting my life on the line?
....

I've raided twelve cities with our ships
And eleven on foot in the fertile Troad,
Looted them all, brought back heirlooms
By the ton, and handed all over
to Atreus' son, who hung back in camp
Raking it in and distributing damn little.

....
Why do the Greeks have to fight the Trojans?
Why did Agamemnon lead the army to Troy
If not for the sake of fair-haired Helen?
Do you have to be descended from Atreus
To love your mate? Every decent, sane man
Loves his woman and cares for her.

                          (*Iliad* 9.324–9, 335–40, and 345–50)

It is noteworthy here that, even though Achilles feels strongly that the campaign to take Troy has become futile and purposeless, he does not pull out
and head home with his troops. He seems to find the kind of meaning in
the special kinship of men at war that Terkel's World War II veterans (cited
above) found.

Is it any wonder that the *Iliad* still speaks to soldiers who know from
deeply felt experience the insanity of what they are called upon to do when
at war? The cover of Lombardo's translation of the *Iliad* uses, courtesy of the
US Coast Guard, the famous photograph, *Into the Jaws of Death*, showing
the backs of soldiers who have plunged into the waters off the opened front
hatch of a landing craft on D-Day. Homer's *Iliad* plunges us into those same
jaws immediately at the start of his song. In its opening lines, the *Iliad*, the
national epic of a culture that knew what war was in practical and honest
terms, gives us countless sufferings, rotting corpses fed upon by roaming dogs
and vultures, a commander-in-chief committing sacrilege against a priest, a
sudden plague killing horses and men, and dreaded discordance among chief
officers in the high command. The *Iliad* keeps us in those jaws relentlessly and
makes us feel, in describing a few days during the siege of Troy, the realities
of human beings harming and killing other human beings on a grand scale
for years. In our modern period only one creative work rivals the length and
intensity of the *Iliad* in portraying and making us feel what Robert Burns
called "man's inhumanity to man"[20]: Claude Lanzmann's nine-and-one-half
hour documentary film (distilled from 350 hours of rough film) about the
holocaust, *Shoah* (1985, filming begun in 1974).

It is not easy to find examples of soldiers reacting to "performances" of
war. But two such examples help explain why the take on war in Greek

song poems and song drama holds a strong appeal even now. We approach this topic in a necessarily roundabout way by using one song about Vietnam War veterans. It stands for many other such songs that get at the real experiences of soldiers.

"Drive On"
Written and sung by Johnny Cash 1994[21]

Well, I got a friend named Whiskey Sam.
He was my boonie rat buddy for a year in Nam.
He said, "I think my country got a little off track.
Took 'em twenty-five years to welcome me back."

But it's better than not comin' back at all.
Many a good man I saw fall.
And even now every time I dream
I hear the men and the monkeys and the jungle scream.

Drive on.
It don't mean nothin'.
My children love me, but they don't understand.
And I got a woman who knows her man.
Drive on.

It don't mean nothin'.
It don't mean nothin'.
Drive on.

Well, I remember one night Tex and me
Rappelled in on a hot LZ.
We had our 16's on rock and roll
And with all of that fire I was scared and cold.

I was crazy, and I was wild.
And I have seen the tiger smile.
I've spit in a bamboo viper's face.
And I'd be dead, but by God's grace.

Drive on.
It don't mean nothin'.
My children love me, but they don't understand.
And I got a woman who knows her man.
Drive on.
It don't mean nothin'.
It don't mean nothin'.
Drive on.

It was a slow walk in a sad rain
and nobody tried to be John Wayne.
I came home, but Tex did not.
And I can't talk about the hit he got.

But I gotta little limp now when I walk.
And I gotta little tremolo when I talk.
But my letter read from Whiskey Sam,
"You're a walkin' talkin' miracle from Vietnam."

Drive on.
It don't mean nothin'.
My children love me, but they don't understand.
And I got a woman who knows her man.

Drive on.
It don't mean nothin'.
It don't mean nothin'.
Drive on.

Although there are exceptions, phrases like "don't mean nothin'" and "there it is" are used in songs and writing to focus attention on concrete meaning or what would be incomprehensible except for soldiers having been there and having seen what they saw or thought they saw, as in the deaths of Echeclus and Deucalion in the *Iliad* cited above.[22] The narrator in Cash's song sings about things that Hemingway and Orwell and doubtless Lieutenant Raws would have understood and appreciated. "Drive On" is simple and direct and has real punch. There are no abstract thoughts. There is no sentimentality. The veteran's wife "knows" her man through long experience of the posttraumatic stress he clearly suffers. Sentimental love is not part of the human equation here. Even the kind of "old lie," in Wilfred Owen's famous phrase, that society inculcates into its young men to get them to go and fight, to kill and/or die, is expressed here forcefully by using with irony the image of John Wayne.

Cash's song uses common words of one or two syllables. Besides the proper noun that Cash emphatically pronounces Vi-et-naaam, with a lengthened open "a" sound, the only three-syllable words have real force: the unattainable "understand" in the repeated refrain; "remember" in stanza two for the still vivid memory of hitting a landing zone under intensive fire from the enemy, "a hot LZ"; "nobody" to express the universal feeling among the soldiers that stereotypical John Wayne heroics are senseless; "tremolo" for the lasting psychological after effects, here almost a medical diagnosis; and "miracle" for what the narrator-soldier is, in the eyes of his fellow soldier, as a veteran who survived the horrific violence and dangers that he faced in Vietnam and can still function and communicate with others.

We may think here of the straight punch of the lines in Bruce Springsteen's song "Born in the U.S.A."[23]:

Come back home to the refinery
Hiring man said "Son if it was up to me"
Went down to see my V.A. man,
He said "Son, don't you understand"

I had a brother at Khe Sahn fighting off the Viet Cong
They're still there, he's all gone

Here the only three-syllable word is again what soldier veterans want to get from others, but rarely get: "understand." It takes real storytelling genius to sum up the futility of the war and the deep sense of the unjustifiable personal loss of a soldier brother-in-arms flatly in this way: "They're still there, he's all gone."

Compare the similar qualities and tone and messages in these two gems of poems by Ernest Hemingway.[24] These are words that soldier veterans can hear and take into their souls.

"Champs d'Honneur" ©1979. Printed with permission of the Ernest Hemingway Foundation.

Soldiers never do die well;
Crosses mark the places,
Wooden crosses where they fell;
Stuck above their faces.
Soldiers pitch and cough and twitch;
All the world roars red and black,
Soldiers smother in a ditch;
Choking through the whole attack.

"Poem" ©1979. Printed with permission of the Ernest Hemingway Foundation.

The only man I ever loved
Said good bye
And went away
He was killed in Picardy
On a sunny day.

In war stories told, sung, or written by soldiers or by those who can get inside their experiences, what gets told about socially and culturally sanctioned violence? The samples we have so far discussed from Homer to modern times get across unprocessed and unfiltered what violent acts do to those who use violence and those who are its victims.

What does the violence of war do? It destroys, and when it does its job well, it keeps destroying. It destroys human bodies, human hearts, human minds, human psyches, and human souls. It destroys what humans build, physically, spiritually, emotionally, socially, culturally, historically. That is why in Orwell's *Nineteen Eighty-Four*, O'Brien tells Winston Smith during his torture session that Smith "will be lifted clean out of the stream of history."[25] Violence destroys existence, present and past. It destroys belief in God, belief in love, belief in virtue. It "disappears" human beings, a verbal usage made familiar to us from politically motivated atrocities in Latin America.

What does this mean about performance literature dealing with the violence of war that really does its job? It too destroys man-made artifice. It is no surprise then that George Orwell, after his firsthand experiences with violence in the Spanish Civil War, despised Latinate, abstract writing and metaphors that did not speak what was real about the subjects to which they were attached. Great stories about human violence, as we have seen in our samples, are simple and direct and strip away illusions. A true war story can therefore look like it is debasing us. The Homeric poems do much the same thing in a different way. Although they use polysyllabic words and even artificial dialect forms of words that were never used in common speech, these are used in phrases, lines, and whole sections of the songs formulaically again and again. Thus the listeners absorb the many commonplace realities of war as familiar actions and experiences not unlike how Roman Catholics who knew no Latin took in the meaning and feeling of the *Gloria in excelsis deo*; *Kyrie, eleison*; *Pater noster*; and *Credo* when the mass was performed in Latin.

Those who write about war by reaching down into their own souls and speaking directly to their experiences can be accused of dishonoring the sacrifice that soldiers have made, even the horrors they have seen and felt. They can be accused of self-indulgence for violating the code of "not voicing grievances" that World War I soldiers followed even when being maimed (physically and psychologically) and slaughtered on an almost incomprehensible scale. Those who write honestly about war can be condemned by those who would hide the realities of war from us and even from themselves. But the soldiers who lived through what the stories tell us affirm their accounts. Those who want to hide what war is speak of IEDs and VBIEDs (Vehicle Based Improvised Explosive Devices). Yehuda Amichai, a veteran of the Jewish Brigade of the British Army in North Africa during World War II and the Arab-Israeli Wars of 1948 and 1956, speaks about a plain old bomb, in a poetic war story so masterful that it was chosen for a collection of recordings commemorating the first-year anniversary of 9/11.[26] Amichai's poem consists of four sentences. The narrative voice tells us one thing after another in plain language using simple grammar. There are no vivid or emotionally charged words.

"The Diameter of the Bomb"[27] © 1996 by Chana Bloch and Stephen Mitchell. Reprinted by permission of the University of California Press and Chana Bloch.

The diameter of the bomb was thirty centimeters
and the diameter of its effective range about seven meters,
with four dead and eleven wounded.
And around these, in a larger circle
of pain and time, two hospitals are scattered
and one graveyard. But the young woman
who was buried in the city she came from,
at a distance of more than a hundred kilometers,
enlarges the circle considerably,
and the solitary man mourning her death

at the distant shores of a country far across the sea
includes the entire world in the circle.
And I won't even mention the howl[28] of orphans
that reaches up to the throne of God and
beyond, making
a circle with no end and no God.

There it is. Don't mean nothin'.

In 16 short lines, we are told matter-of-factly that a bomb no wider than the length of a young schoolboy's cheap wooden ruler can kill or wound 15 people. A 12-inch bomb can cause the pain of loss to be felt throughout the world. It can even bring the existence of God, or of a God who cares about innocent human beings, into question. Loss and pain without remedy radiate outward from the bomb's single, quick, and relatively small explosion. Its blast destroys love and families. Its blast sucks hope, faith, and belief in divine providence right out of the universe.

Notice here, too, the preponderance of one- and two-syllable words, the absence of any abstractions, and the concrete terms that convey to us the idea that the detonation of one small bomb can cause sorrow around our world and beyond. As in the two Hemingway poems cited above, no time or specific setting is given.[29] Amichai tells us what happens anywhere, any time, any place a bomb explodes and people are killed and wounded.

Homer, Owen, Hemingway, Springsteen, Cash, Amichai, and Australian soldiers of World War I, like Lieutenant Raws, teach us how to tell the truth about war and how to tell when the truth is being hidden. So, for example, official US Department of Defense reports speak of casualties, while O'Brien, in a chapter from his first novel *If I Die in a Combat Zone*, speaks of severed legs, shredded feet, heels ripped off by various forms of mines, and booby traps.[30]

True war stories make clear that soldiers are, in a real sense, prisoners, or, in more modern terms, forced laborers. That is why in my opinion O'Brien uses a quotation from John Ransom's *Andersonville Diary*, an account by a Union soldier of his life-threatening incarceration as a prisoner of war in arguably the worst of Confederate prison camps, as an epigraph for his collection of short stories:[31]

> This book is essentially different from any other that has been published concerning the "late war" or any of its incidents. Those who have had any such experience as the author will see its truthfulness at once, and to all other readers it is commended as a statement of actual things by one who experienced them to the fullest.

What was true in the American Civil War and in Vietnam, was also true in the "good war." Yossarian and his fellow pilots in Joseph Heller's *Catch-22* fight back against their feelings of being compelled to risk their lives senselessly against their wills with phrases like, "Who is Spain?," "Why is Hitler?,"

"When is Right?"[32] They have to break down the false system of logic and language, of regulations and orders, that keeps them in prison.

Knowing what to say and how to speak clearly about war and its many forms of trauma is not easy. It takes a long time to figure out what went on in a war. It requires reaching way down into hearts and souls and often forgetting what enters the mind as explanations from other sources. Producing good "performance art" about war then understandably is a long, hard process. I have already mentioned the ten-year time lag for Remarque's World War I classic. Think of the 16 years for Heller's *Iliad*-steeped *Catch-22* (first published in 1961), or the 24 years for Vonnegut's *Slaughterhouse Five* (first published in 1969). Think of the fact that all classic Hollywood movies about the Vietnam War, except for the jingoistic melodramatic *The Green Berets* (July 1968), starring, naturally, John Wayne, were made after the fall of Saigon. A similar time lag occurs between the end of the Persian Wars (479 BCE) and Aeschylus' play *The Persians* (dated to 472 BCE).

Samuel Hynes, a United States Marine Corps bomber pilot in World War II, takes a serious look at war memoirs in his *The Soldiers' Tale: Bearing Witness to a Modern War*. Like Aristotle analyzing Greek city-states in the *Politics* or Greek song poems in the *Poetics*, Hynes aims at describing the characteristic qualities of the works that soldiers write about the wars they are fighting or have fought: "Generally, the telling of war stories is direct and undecorated, which is the way soldiers seem to prefer it."[33] Hynes is right about style, wrong about it being a preference. Soldiers and veterans do not choose war language like choosing ties off a rack, or preferring to go to *this* restaurant or *that* one, *this* movie or *that*. They tell their stories the way they tell them because that is how they have to tell them. Soldiers and veterans have no choice. The stories cannot be told any other way.

Hynes quotes T. E. Lawrence's appraisal of the famous anonymous *A Soldier's Diary of the Great War*: it is "sane, low-toned and natural."[34] Being sane and low-toned about the abominable madness of trench warfare is quite a feat. An author using such a voice is in effect saying, "There it is."

James Holoka reminds us that Matthew Arnold described the style of the Homeric poems as "rapid, plain, direct and noble." We can also apply to Homer what Holoka and other critics have noted about Simone Weil, who used Homer and Greek tragedy to get across her ideas about what war in the twentieth century should teach us. The hallmark features are sincerity, urgency, an incomparably humane accent, and depth of feeling. [35]

Write or speak or sing or act in a style that is direct, blunt, matter-of-fact, clear of vision, sincere, urgent, deep of feeling, and humane, and you will have a good chance of being heard by soldiers and veterans. This has been true for over three thousand years. This proves, as if proof were needed, what Vietnam veteran and now Hollywood screenwriter Bill Broyles tells us in his classic 1984 *Esquire* essay, "Why Men Love War,"[36] namely that stories about war exclude those readers or listeners who do not hold the truths of war sacred, who cannot take in the truth.[37]

I think it is fair to say then that war stories, songs, and performances try to tell us something about what war really is. Read enough war stories and you will know four things. War is not pretty. War is not good. Only the human agents caught up in war can try to be noble or moral—war itself is neither. And war is ultimately unknowable.[38]

Soldiers are virtual prisoners. They cannot escape their circumstances, even being ordered to face virtually certain death, without suffering serious consequences. We have already mentioned the epigraph for *The Things They Carried*. The same sentiment is found in the World War II oral histories put together by Studs Terkel in his *"The Good War."* Think also of Yossarian in *Catch-22*, Fife in James Jones' *The Thin Red Line* (1962), or O'Brien's entire platoon under Captain Smith in *If I Die in a Combat Zone*.[39] Soldiers have the feeling of being virtual prisoners of war, even when they have not been captured and incarcerated by the enemy.

Replay in your mind Greek tragedies, most notably the *Trojan Women*, any random scene from the *Iliad,* and the wartime comedies of Aristophanes like *Peace, Acharnians,* and *Lysistrata*. Then think of why Johnny Cash's Vietnam vet narrator and Vietnam veterans like O'Brien use the John Wayne movie portrayal of what war is as the prime example of the seductive illusion-making that gave young men false opinions about what fighting for their country would entail. The Greeks, of course, had texts that exhorted young men to fight and die bravely for their communities, their families, and their own lasting honor. The "old lie" that Wilfred Owen, Ezra Pound, and Tim O'Brien do their best to persuade us and all their readers not to tell our own and future children in fact was told first by the Greek poet Callinus (seventh century BCE) and passed down to Owen, Pound, O'Brien and the rest of us through the Roman poet Horace. And ancient Greek political speeches on public occasions, like Pericles' Funeral Oration for the fallen Athenian war dead, emphasized the gains and rewards of fighting and dying in a successful cause. But these essential texts that the ancient Greeks used to inculcate military virtues like courage, honor, discipline, obedience, endurance, and supreme self-sacrifice did not falsify or hide war's brutality and dehumanizing effects. Greek tragedies and comedies about war and its effects were not suppressed, censored, or seriously discouraged during times of war.

In writing a review for the *Times Higher Education Supplement* of a collection of scholarly essays on the *Anabasis* of Xenophon, a firsthand account of an expedition by a mercenary force into the heart of the Persian Empire and back (401–399 BCE), I realized that the Greeks for centuries had no use for war memoirs.[40] War was so omnipresent that no one was interested in being told about its particulars. Few, if any, extended clan groups in fifth-century Athens were without relatively direct experience of the human, social, and economic (there was no deficit spending) costs of warfare and what was at risk for soldiers and their communities when armies of their men took to the field.

Let us try to transport ourselves to ancient Athens midway through the 27 years of the Peloponnesian War. It is late spring 415 BCE. According to modern revised estimates, 3,700 to 6,000 (perhaps more)[41] adult male Athenian citizens, all of them veterans of war, some of them of the campaign in summer 416 through winter 416/415 against the island of Melos, sat viewing Euripides' play *Trojan Women*. They were participating in their city's Greater Dionysia festival. They sat in the open air in daylight in the Theater of Dionysos built against the south slope of the Athenian acropolis. In the open air, they could look around and see one another as the play was performed.

The Melian matter, whether or not it had all played out by the time Euripides had to submit a proposal (or even fairly finished drafts) for the plays he was intending to have produced at the Greater Dionysia in 415 BCE, certainly was being discussed among Athenian leaders and citizen soldiers, in the same way that what to do about city-states on the island of Lesbos that were in revolt had been hotly debated a dozen or so years earlier.[42]

Euripides had ample grounds to think that a play dealing with what happens to a besieged city, according to the conditions of what is called "Homeric warfare practice," once it is taken by the besieging army, would provoke lots of interest. The Melian incident is considered by some the first act of genocide in Western culture.[43] It probably does not fit the technical definition, but, using modern moral judgment, it was a large-scale atrocity and surely wasn't the first. All the adult male citizens of the island of Melos, which preferred to remain neutral in the conflict between Athens and Sparta, were killed and the women and children were sold into slavery. With our modern moral sensibilities, we may find another fact deeply disturbing. The ruling oligarchy of this island community had purposefully not permitted the Athenian negotiators to speak directly to the "people," for fear that the pro-democratic element among the people at large would cut a deal with the Athenians whereby only the recalcitrant ruling party and their close allies would be put to death. The party in control effectively denied the citizens at large an opportunity to save their own lives.

Once the negotiations between Athenian representatives and the Melian leaders broke down, the Athenians, to their discredit, did not differentiate among those who made the decision and those who did not even have a say in it. They killed all the adult males and sold all the women and children into slavery. Peter Green, in a fine, if not wholly persuasive, article on ancient and modern moral concepts and their relationship to the Melian affair and the *Trojan Women*, speaks of "the jungle mentality governing [Athens'] conduct."[44]

The *Trojan Women* gives us an intense and close-up look at how captive women feel when this Homeric form of warfare is practiced. But the very men who duly voted in the Athenian assembly to commit such brutal acts of terror, many of whom then went out and committed them, watched Euripides' tragedy in the theater. The play served in my opinion at some level as the ancient equivalent of the phrase we have already quoted several times regarding what happens in times of war: "There it is."

The Athenians may not have taken in the play as a comment on their lack of morality in acting as they did in the Melian affair. They may have used the play as a way of accepting the miserable consequences of what citizen soldiers had to do in times of all-out war. They may have received Euripides' tableaux of suffering among captive women and unsympathetic conduct among most of the Greek leaders in the same way modern veterans take in Johnny Cash's "Drive On" or Bruce Springsteen's "Born in the U.S.A."

Let us now look at the promised two examples of how modern soldiers have reacted to performances of war, in this case two modern motion pictures. Both films depict war in other than "direct and undecorated" or "sane, low-toned and natural" terms.

The first is a reaction to Francis Ford Coppola's *Apocalypse Now* (1979, with narration drawn from Michael Herr's *Dispatches*,[45] a fine capturing of the atmosphere and feel of the Vietnam War) by Private First Class Reginald Edwards in Wallace Terry's *Bloods*, an oral history of 20 African-American soldiers in Vietnam. [46] Here is Edwards' reaction to the film:

> I went to see *Apocalypse Now*, because a friend paid my way. I don't like movies about Vietnam 'cause I don't think they are prepared to tell the truth. *Apocalypse Now* didn't tell the truth. It wasn't real. I guess it was a great thing for the country to get off on, but it didn't remind me of anything I saw. I can't understand how you would have a bridge lit up like a Christmas tree. A USO show at night? Guys attacking women on stage. That made no sense. I never saw us reach the point where nobody is in charge in a unit. That's out of the question. If you don't know anything, you know the chain of command. And the helicopter attack on the village? Fuckin' ridiculous (13).
>
> I'm in the Amtrac with Morley Safer, right? The whole thing is getting ready to go down. At Cam Ne. The whole bit that all America will see on *CBS Evening News*, right? Marines burning down some huts. Brought to you by Morley Safer. Your man on the scene. August 5, 1965 (1).
>
> Safer didn't tell them to burn down the huts with they lighters. He just photographed it. He could have got a picture of me burning a hut, too. It was just the way they did it. When you say level a village, you don't use torches. It's not like in the 1800s. You use a Zippo (3).

Edwards was worried when the "My Lai" story broke, that what had happened at Cam Ne had been caught on film. "You can get away with murder. And the beautiful thing about the military is there's always somebody that can serve up [*sic*] as a scapegoat" (14).

The second is World War II veteran Paul Fussell's reaction to Steven Spielberg's *Saving Private Ryan*, a widely acclaimed motion picture (1998)[47] that made into icons World War II veterans about whom Tom Brokaw would soon thereafter write an immensely popular hagiography.[48] In Fussell's honest and angry account about what rank–and–file soldiers went through in Europe after the hell of D-Day, he writes[49]:

> I'd like to recommend the retention of and familiarity with the first few minutes of Steven Spielberg's *Saving Private Ryan* depicting the landing horrors. Then I'd suggest separating them to constitute a short subject, titled *Omaha Beach: Aren't You Glad You Weren't There?* Which could mean, "Aren't you glad you weren't a conscripted working–class or high school boy in 1944?" The rest of the Spielberg film I'd consign to the purgatory where boys' bad adventure films end up.

Both Edwards and Fussell take movie representations of war that are now considered classics and find fault with them for not getting across what war really is. For Edwards, the problems lie in the overheating of Coppola's mythic images that tap into both Joseph Conrad's *Heart of Darkness* and Sir James George Frazer's *The Golden Bough*. For Edwards, Coppola's surrealism sacrifices too much military realism. For Fussell, too, after the opening minutes of terror and death on Omaha Beach, the rest of the Spielberg's movie unfolds as a typical Hollywood melodrama, an adventure film for boys of very low quality, effectively a John Wayne movie.

Christine Leche, who has recently taught creative writing to soldiers deployed to a forward operating base (FOB) in Afghanistan, tells us that "it is much more than just the writing that heals—it is *being heard*." She continues, "For veterans, it is knowing their pain is felt vicariously by those who possess the strength to listen, by those with courage enough to tilt a human ear toward wartime stories and to risk being changed by the tremor in their voices. PTSD is, after all, a shared experience: when one family member is affected, the entire family suffers, and thus the community suffers."[50]

It is clear that Johnny Cash's and Bruce Springsteen's songs, Yehuda Amichai's and Ernest Hemingway's poems, Homer's *Iliad*, the short stories of Tim O'Brien, and Euripides' *Trojan Women* pass the litmus test of communicating the real experiences of war in ways that can be seen, heard, felt, and understood by veterans of war and by civilian nonveterans who try hard to absorb what is being said, sung, recited, or performed. Fussell and Edwards show us the negative reactions that veterans have when what happens in war is represented in phony ways, when we take in an account and cannot say, "There it is."

The realities of war need to be taken in with all five senses and understood not only with the mind, but with the heart and the soul. Soldiers and veterans have confronted things that most civilians will never have to face.[51]

World War II veteran Dr. Alex Shulman puts it this way:[52]

> Americans have never known what war really is. No matter how much they saw it on television or pictures or magazines. Because there is one feature they never appreciated: the smell. When you go through a

village and you suddenly get this horrible smell. Everybody's walking around with masks on their faces, 'cause it's just intolerable. You look out and see those bloated bodies. You no longer see humans, because they've been pretty well cleaned up by now. You see bloated horses and cows and the smell of death. Maybe if Americans had known even that, they'd be more concerned about peace.

Shulman, in recounting his experiences to Terkel, mixes his sense memories together by using what is known rhetorically as "zeugma": "you *see*...the *smell* of death" (italics mine). Yet I think that what he went through in war had such a harrowing impact that he came close to *seeing* the smell of death both at that time and later in tapping into his visual and sense memories while talking with Terkel. On such occasions sight, sound, smell, taste, and touch must combine in truly grotesque ways. We can get partway there if we use our imaginations and our capacities for empathy.

Charles Patterson, who served as a US Marine at Khe Sanh, has a poem that complements Shulman's thoughts where our emotions are concerned. His poem about the loss of one of his brothers-in-arms, Marion Henry Norman, at Khe Sanh, comes in two parts, one written in 1968 in Vietnam, the other written in 1983, when he had processed as best he could, and come to terms with, the grief of loss and the absurdity of war.

"Marion Henry Norman Khe Sanh, 1968"[53] Reprinted by permission of Charles E. Patterson from the Signal Tree Publications edition.

They took your life
As if it belonged to them.
If only they had told me
They needed a life,
I would have given them mine.

I wonder
What they did with your life?
Perhaps,
If they don't need it now,
They'd give it back.
                    —Ca Lu, March 1968

I saw you dead
But never buried.
In my heart you've lived,
Laughing, smiling Hank.
I would keep you there forever,
In a memorial more perfect
Than hands could build.

Finding an end to my war
I can mourn you now.
And, in sadness, leave

This loving, painful,
Magic caretaking,
So I may live
At peace.

To celebrate your death,
To elevate your life,
And its conclusion,
Which was neither sweet,
Nor fitting,
Duty's harshest price
For which the consideration
Should have been honor.
                    —*The World, 1983*

What should the consideration have been for the soldiers whom the Athenians sent off to Melos to do their dirty work? How did the citizen soldiers feel en masse and individually as they were leaving the Theater of Dionysus at the end of the set of plays that included the *Trojan Women*? Did the performance of the play help them to see the radiating circles of pain and time, to use Amichai's metaphor, that their actions caused? Were their gods as deaf to the cries of the Melian women and children being carried off into slavery as Amichai's Judeo-Christian God is to the cries of orphaned infants? Could the veterans of Melos see the smell of the exposed bodies of the men they killed? Were the Melian men who died defending their city accorded honor, even begrudgingly, by the Athenian soldiers? Many of the same questions could be posed about soldiers sent off to wars any time and anywhere.

There it is. The truth is all there in true war stories. But it takes real effort to take it all into our hearts, minds, and souls. And, as Patterson reminds us, echoing Wilfred Owen and Horace and Callinus long before him, the truths of war are neither sweet nor fitting.

Notes

*Translations from the *Iliad* are here from Lombardo (1997). Line numbering refers to Lombardo's line numbers. I thank the editors for their very helpful comments and suggestions. I thank Colin Yarbrough for closely reading my final draft and making several key observations that improved how I here convey a few key thoughts and ideas. I dedicate this chapter to the late Joel Cryer, PJ and friend, and to Michael T. Palaima, combat controller, brother and friend, for their stories told and untold.

1. Terkel (1984, 5). The old-time folk singer is Win Stracke. His full account is on pp. 159–62.
2. According to Carter (2011, x), Barack Obama, a president who received the Nobel Peace Prize in December 2009, has "expanded the battlefield, both geographically and technologically, and is prosecuting America's wars with a stunning ferocity."
3. Palaima and Tritle (2013, 727 and n. 1).

4. Tritle (2010, 114–16).

5. Wells (1914, 14).

6. The Battle of the Somme, July 1–November 13, 1916, caused 420,000 British, 195,000 French, and 650,000 German casualties—9,300 per day. The Third Battle of Ypres, otherwise known as Passchendaele, July 31–November 6, 1917, resulted in 585,000 Allied and German casualties, 5,900 per day. For capsule commentaries on the futility of each battle, see http://www.bbc.co.uk/history/worldwars/wwone/battle_somme.shtml and http://www.bbc.co.uk/history/worldwars/wwone/battle_passchendaele.shtml (both last accessed November 12, 2013).

7. Woodrow Wilson, "Address to a Joint Session of Congress, 8 January 1918." In Link (1984, 539).

8. Sempa (2007) (last accessed May 16, 2013).

9. Imparato (2000, 111).

10. Santayana (1922, 102). The passage occurs in Soliloquy 25. On the problem of tracing the true origin of this quotation and its widespread attribution to Plato, see Palaima and Tritle (2013, 734–5).

11. Goldensohn (2003, 117).

12. Andrew Grimes from the *Manchester Evening News* November 1998, accessible online at *Retrospectives on People and Places,* "Douglass Haig (and Lloyd George) by Andrew Grimes: Blood on Their Hands," http://www.aftermathww1.co.uk/grimes.asp (last accessed May 20, 2013).

13. http://www.gcsehistory.org.uk/modernworld/britishsociety/Haigandthe battleofthesomme.htm (last accessed May 20, 2013).

14. Liddell Hart (1935, 326).

15. Liddell Hart (1935, 326–7). For vivid images directly from the letters home of Lieutenant John Alexander Raws, see http://www.australiansatwar.gov.au/stories/stories_war=W1_id=130.html (last accessed November 12, 2013). In a letter dated August 4, 1916, Raws wrote, "For the horrors one sees and the never-ending shock of the shells is more than can be borne. Hell must be a home to it."

16. Shay (1994, 75–99). Shay (1994, 77, 238), in fact refers to Achilles as the "prototype" of the soldier traumatized into a "berserk" state.

17. Finkel (2009), 143. For fuller impact, go to http://nrcdata.ap.org/casualties (last accessed May 21, 2013). Then search for Reeves, Joshua; and read his biography.

18. Achilles' berserker state is marked by the fact that, while in this state, he kills mercilessly and savagely, as he is gloating and boasting, Lycaon, a young son of Priam, depicted as an unlucky innocent, whom Achilles had, on an earlier mission, captured alive and set free for a ransom payment (*Iliad* [book 21.140–5]).

19. *Iliad* 22.150–285. The whole of Arvin (2005), based on the memories his father and grandfather had of their combat experiences, is a meditation upon a soldier in post D-Day fighting who recognizes that he is a coward. See here, too, Hue (1954). On courage and fear, see O'Brien (1990, 39–61, 137–54), and generally Palaima (2000).

20. Robert Burns, "Man Was Made to Mourn: A Dirge" (1784). For the full text of Burns' song poem, background information, the tune to which it was set, and an audio file of a recitation, see www.bbc.co.uk/arts/robertburns/works/man_was_made_to_mourn/ (last accessed June 3, 2014).

21. "Drive On." Words and Music by John R. Cash. © 1993 SONG OF CASH, INC. (ASCAP). All rights administered by BMG RIGHTS MANAGEMENT (US) LLC. All Rights Reserved. Used by Permission of Hal Leonard Corporation.

22. O'Brien (1990, 78): "True war stories do not generalize. They do not indulge in abstraction or analysis. For example: War is hell. As a moral declaration the old truism

seems perfectly true, and yet because it abstracts, because it generalizes, I can't believe it with my stomach. Nothing turns inside. It comes down to gut instinct. A true war story, if truly told, makes the stomach believe."

23. "Born in the U.S.A." by Bruce Springsteen. Copyright © Bruce Springsteen (ASCAP). Reprinted by permission. International copyright secured. All rights reserved.

24. Hemingway (1979, 27 and 61; photo image of working drafts of "Poem" on p. 60).

25. Orwell (1949, 257).

26. http://audiopoetry.wordpress.com/2006/07/13/the-diameter-of-the-bomb/ and http://www.clal.org/911_clal_cd.html (both last accessed May 20, 2013) from the National Jewish Center for Learning and Leadership, recording of 09/11/02 *A Ritual for Beginning to Remember.* Amichai's "bomb" is placed and detonated among civilians. Although the time and place are not given or even hinted at, we deduce that this is what we would call a "terrorist act" of war.

27. Amichai (1996, 118). See also http://www.chanabloch.com/amichai.html for text and Chana Bloch reading and commenting on details of the poem.

28. Amichai (1986, 118), reads "crying."

29. In "Poem," Hemingway refers to the general region of Picardy in northern France; but, like Amichai, he leaves the particular place, time and circumstances of the death—and even the very identity of the main victim—unknown.

30. O'Brien (1979, 125–30).

31. O'Brien (1990, no page number, after table of contents).

32. Heller (1996, 43–4).

33. Hynes (1997, xv).

34. Ibid.

35. Holoka (2003, x).

36. Broyles (1984).

37. Graves (1995, 467), speaks of those who went through trench warfare as "bound to one another by a suicidal sacrament." Those who did not experience the horrors of the Great War were then uninitiated outsiders.

38. It should be understood that I strongly disagree with MacArthur's claim in his Sylvanus Thayer Award address (May 12, 1962): "However horrible the incidents of war may be, the soldier who is called upon to offer and to give his life for his country, is the noblest development of mankind." This is Owen's "old lie" and it still lives and thrives. For the full speech, see http://www.americanrhetoric.com/speeches/douglasmacarthurthayer award.html (last accessed November 13, 2013). Also Whan (1965, 355–6).

39. O'Brien (1979, 148–61).

40. Palaima (2005) (last accessed May 20, 2013).

41. Roselli (2011, 65 and n. 5). There were also theaters in the towns in the territory of Athens that had seating capacities as high as 2,000–2,500 people (Roselli 2011, 68–9).

42. Because the chief city-state fomenting the revolt was Mytilene, the section of Thucydides that tells us of the deliberations of the Athenians is called the Mytilenean debate, in contrast with the Melian dialogue. See Tritle (2010, 67–71, 133–6).

43. See succinctly Palaima (2001).

44. Green (1999, 107).

45. Herr (1977).

46. Terry (1984, 1–15).

47. *Saving Private Ryan* won five Oscar awards, including best cinematography, best sound, and best director, and was nominated for six other awards. The focus on editing, sound, and visual effects makes clear that the opening of the film gave people a strong vicarious sense of the horrors of the landing on Omaha Beach.

48. Brokaw (1999).
49. Fussell (2003, 34–5).
50. Leche (2013, 134–5).
51. For the horrific sense memories that veterans may carry inside them, see the blunt, honest and graphic story told by Kenneth Ashworth's father in Palaima (2012, 37).
52. Terkel (1984, 287).
53. Patterson (2002, 24–5).

Works Cited

Amichai, Yehuda. 1986. *The Selected Poetry of Yehuda Amichai*. Edited and newly translated by Chana Bloch and Stephen Mitchell. New York: Harper and Row, Publishers.

———.1996. *The Selected Poetry of Yehuda Amichai*. Edited and translated by Chana Bloch and Stephen Mitchell. Berkeley: University of California Press.

Arvin, Nick. 2005. *Articles of War*. New York: Doubleday.

Brokaw, Tom. 1999. *The Greatest Generation*. New York: Random House.

Broyles, William Jr. 1984. "Why Men Love War." *Esquire*, November: 55–65.

Carter, Stephen L. 2011. *The Violence of Peace: America's Wars in the Age of Obama*. New York: Beat Books.

Finkel, David. 2009. *The Good Soldiers*. New York: Sarah Crichton Books.

Fussell, Paul. 2003. *The Boys' Crusade*. New York: Modern Library.

Goldensohn, Lorrie. 2003. *Dismantling Glory: Twentieth-Century Soldier Poetry*. New York: Columbia University Press.

Graves, Robert. 1995. *Collected Writings on Poetry*. Edited by Paul O'Prey. Manchester: Carcanet Press Ltd.

Green, Peter. 1999. "War and Morality in Fifth-Century Athens: The Case of Euripides' *Trojan Women*." *The Ancient History Bulletin* 13.3: 97–110.

Heller, Joseph. 1996. *Catch-22*. New York: Scribner Paperback Fiction / Simon & Schuster.

Hemingway, Ernest. 1979. *88 Poems*. Edited by Nicholas Gerogiannis. New York: Harcourt Brace Jovanovich.

Herr, Michael. 1977. *Dispatches*. New York: Knopf.

Holoka, James P. 2003. *Simone Weil's* The Iliad *Or The Poem of Force: A Critical Edition*. New York: Peter Lang.

Hue, William Bradford. 1954. *The Execution of Private Slovak*. Boston, MA: Little Brown and Company.

Hynes, Samuel 1997. *The Soldiers' Tale: Bearing Witness to a Modern War*. New York: Penguin.

Imparato, Edward T. 2000. *General MacArthur: Speeches and Reports 1908–1964*. Paducah, KY: Turner Publishing Company.

Leche, Christine D. 2013. *Outside the Wire: American Soldiers' Voices from Afghanistan*. Charlottesville: University of Virginia Press.

Liddell Hart, Basil H. 1935. *A History of the World War 1914–1918*. Boston, MA: Little, Brown, and Company.

Link, Arthur S., ed. 1984. *The Papers of Woodrow Wilson, Volume 45, November 11, 1917–January 15, 1918*. Princeton, NJ: Princeton University Press.

Lombardo, Stanley, trans. 1997. *Homer. Iliad*. Indianapolis, IN and Cambridge, MA: Hackett.

O'Brien, Tim. 1979. *If I Die in a Combat Zone Box Me Up and Ship Me Home*. New York: Dell.

———. 1990. *The Things They Carried*. Boston, MA: Houghton Mifflin.

Orwell, George. 1949. *Nineteen Eighty-Four*. New York: Harcourt, Brace & World, Inc.

Page, Denys L., ed. 1975. *Epigrammata Graeca*. Oxford: Clarendon Press.

Palaima, Thomas G. 2000. "Courage and Prowess Afoot in Homer and the Vietnam of Tim O'Brien." *Classical and Modern Literature* 20.3: 1–22.

———. 2001. "Apocalypse Now and Atrocity Then." Review of *From Melos to Mylai: War and Survival* by Larry Tritle, and *Kennedy's Wars: Berlin, Cuba, Laos, Vietnam* by Lawrence Freedman. *Times*

Higher Education Supplement, February 16, 30. http://www.timeshighereducation.co.uk/books/apocalypse-now-and-atrocity-then/157508.article (last accessed June 7, 2014).

———. 2005. "Greek Gang Leader With Just the Right Connections." Review of *The Long March: Xenophon and the Ten Thousand*, edited by Robin Lane Fox. *Times Higher Education Supplement*, June 10, 28. http://www.timeshighereducation.co.uk/books/greek-gang-leader-with-just-the-right-connections/196644.article (last accessed June 7, 2014).

———. 2012. "The First Casualty." *Times Higher Education*, December 20/27, 32–7. http://www.timeshighereducation.co.uk/the-first-casualty/422152.article (last accessed June 7, 2014).

Palaima, Thomas, and Lawrence A. Tritle. 2013. "Epilogue: The Legacy of War in the Classical World." In *The Oxford Handbook of Warfare in the Classical World*, edited by Brian Campbell and Lawrence A. Tritle, 726–42. New York: Oxford University Press.

Patterson, Charles E. 2002. *The Petrified Heart: The Vietnam War Poetry of Charles E. Patterson*. Livermore, ME and Rockbridge, VA: Signal Tree Publications.

Roselli, David Kawalko. 2011. *Theater of the People: Spectators and Society in Classical Athens*. Austin: University of Texas Press.

Santayana, George. 1922. *Soliloquies in England and Later Soliloquies*. New York: Charles Scribner's Sons.

Sempa, Francis P. 2007. Review of *The War of the World: Twentieth-Century Conflict and the Descent of the West*, by Niall Ferguson. *American Diplomacy Foreign Service Despatches [sic] and Periodic Reports on U.S. Foreign Policy Reviews*, January. http://www.unc.edu/depts/diplomat/item/2007/0103/book/book_sempa.html (last accessed June 7, 2014).

Shay, Jonathan. 1994. *Achilles in Vietnam: Combat Trauma and the Undoing of Character*. New York: Athenaeum.

Terkel, Studs. 1984. *"The Good War": An Oral History of World War II*. New York: The New Press.

Terry, Wallace. 1984. *Bloods*. New York: Ballantine Books.

Tritle, Lawrence A. 2010. *A New History of the Peloponnesian War*. Chichester, West Sussex, UK and Malden, MA: Wiley-Blackwell.

Wells, Herbert G. 1914. *The War That Will End War*. New York: Duffield and Company.

Whan, Vorin E., Jr., ed. 1965. *A Soldier Speaks: Public Papers and Speeches of General of the Army Douglas MacArthur*. New York and London: Frederick A. Praeger, Publishers.

CHAPTER THIRTEEN

Performing Memory: In the Mind and on the Public Stage*

PAUL WOODRUFF

The dead walk in the minds of those who have survived traumatic losses. They confront us with questions: that is why we cannot forget them, and, at the same time, that is why we cannot bear to remember them. We cannot, at least, until we have taken action about the questions. Some of us cling to the memories that wound us, and in doing that we have to put up with relentless pain, even though memory may have healing power.[1] Others try to obliterate the wounding memories—and fail, of course. Lose memory, and you lose yourself:

> You have to begin to lose your memory, if only in bits and pieces, to realize that memory is what makes our lives...Our memory is our coherence, our reason, our feeling, even our action. Without it, we are nothing.[2]

Between clinging to painful memories and obliterating them, however, lies a third option. And that is for us to perform a remembered past.

Writers are often energized by memories, by the need to give them expression. If you are a writer, you need to move the dead who walk in your mind out of your mind (at least for the moment—they always come back[3]) and onto the page. The poet John Clare (1793–1864) was sustained by remembering the love of his life, a woman named Mary, whom he was not permitted to wed, and who died young:

> I sleep with thee and wake with thee
> And yet thou art not there:
> I fill my arms with thoughts of thee
> And press the common air.
>
> (From "To Mary," by John Clare)

For Clare, the memory that he awakened and then settled into his poems was both comforting and agonizing. Many people who write after trauma find this to be true, but I will give reasons why theatrical performance is especially powerful. By theater I do not mean literature and I do not mean film. I mean living performance in a dynamic interchange with a living audience.

In this chapter, I discuss briefly two plays that deal with traumatic memory, an ancient classic and then a modern one, and then, after that, a third play, which I wrote in 1974 as part of my effort to deal with my memories of the Vietnam War and its aftermath.

Electra—The Woman Who Refuses to Forget

Sophocles' *Electra* feeds on the pain of the memory of her father's death. She seethes with grief and anger, still, after at least ten years have passed. She rises early every morning to scream out her grief and anger into the rising dawn, beating her breast, morning after morning, with enough violence to draw blood.

Needless to say, this does not go down well with her mother and her mother's lover, who would offer her a fairly normal life if she would only forget and live at peace with her family. But this she will not do. As she says:

> My mother and her playmate in bed,
> Aegisthus, like a pair of lumberjacks
> At an oak tree, took a bloody ax and split his skull.
>
> (98–100)[4]

Her mother and Aegisthus, the lover, killed her father; she will never forget, never forgive, never cease raging for revenge.[5]

Needless to say, her habit of screaming for revenge every morning does not endear her to the neighbors, although they sympathize with her cause. The chorus of Sophocles' play is made up of women who sincerely believe that Electra will be better off if she allows herself to forget:

> *Chorus*
> You were right to grieve at first,
> But now it's absurd, this endless wailing.
> You'll cry yourself to death. Tell me,
> Why are you so devoted to your pain?
>
> *Electra*
> Could anyone forget
> The horror of a parent's death?
>
> (145)

Or learn to be as silent as a baby?
My mind is stamped in the image of a crying bird.

(140–7)

…

Chorus
Be hopeful, child, be hopeful.
Even now, in heaven, great Zeus
Sees all, rules all.

(175)

Let *him* bear your grief. It is too much for you.
And as for those you hate, do not forget,
But do not hate too much.
Time is a soft and gentle god.
And still the lord of the cow-grazed height of Krisa,
Apollo, turns this over and over in his mind.

(180)

So does Agamemnon's son.
And so does the godlike king himself, by Acheron.

Electra
But what about me? What hope can I have?

(185)

My life drains away, my strength is gone.
I am some childless woman
With no man to depend on.
I am no better than a foreign servant, a worthless woman,
Brought to tend my father's room,

(190)

Dressed in these rags, laying food on a table
That has no place for me.

(173–92)

Electra's name suggests "unmarried woman," implying that she is denied a traditional role in society. Her mother will not permit her to marry, because a husband or son of Electra would be obliged by custom to kill those who killed Electra's father, that is, Clytemnestra and her new husband. Now the chorus remember the homecoming of Agamemnon—*a homecoming that can seem oddly familiar to veterans today.* Although few veterans of our own time come home to be murdered, many come home to find their lives in ruins, their lovers and their jobs taken by others who stayed at home. The trauma that haunts Electra's memory is a murder that arises as an effect of war on her family, and so, at only one remove, is part of the trauma of war:[6]

Strophe C
Chorus (Remembering the killing of Agamemnon)
Agony to hear, a scream at homecoming,

Agony, in the lap of ancestors,
When he faced the bronze jaws,

(195)

Startled by their assault.
Deception spoke then, lust had its way,
And what they conceived was horrible, horribly given shape,
Whether it was a human—or a god—
Who made it be.

(200)

Electra
The day I hate beyond all others
The day of my worst enemies!
The night, festival of anguish,
Unspeakable, when my father saw

(205)

His own death, his murder at their hands.
When they caught up my life
And threw it away, ruined.
(Praying to Apollo, whose statue is on stage.)
Great god on Olympus,
Make them pay the full price in pain!

(210)

Never let them taste the joy of triumph,
Because they did this thing.

Antistrophe C

Chorus
Tell yourself: "Do not raise your voice again."
Have you any idea where this leads?
You are so far out of line, you'll fall

(215)

Blindly into ruin, your own blindness.
You'll get more than your share of trouble
If the sick spirit in your soul
Is pregnant with battle, if it always hatches war.
Never launch a quarrel against the powers that be!

(193–220)

But Electra speaks with the voice of those who remember hatred for centuries. Think how many parts of the world are riven by remembered hatred, carefully preserved and maintained, like Electra's at the boiling point of rage:

Electra
But I have to be dreadful in dreadful times. Necessity!
I understand my passions. They are no mystery to me.

But in dreadful times, how could I hold back?
This blind fury seethes
Until I die.

(225)

Dear friends, noble as you are, no one now
Can tell me anything that helps.
No one with good sense would think otherwise.
Please go away, spare me your comfort.
My pain is beyond cure

(230)

And I will never let it go.
I will weep without end.

(221–32)

And so she condemns herself to pain. Electra's murdered father is always present in her mind, asking why he has not been avenged. She allows herself to imagine only one way to bury this memory—by killing her mother and her stepfather. Nothing but blood will do. It is a terrifying memory in her, terrifying to me, as powerful as the memories that drive bloodshed in many parts of the world today. Centuries pass, but the dead still walk in the minds of survivors, and blood still flows.

Mrs. Alving Invests in Amnesia—and Loses Everything

Mrs. Alving, in Ibsen's *Ghosts,* is the opposite of Electra. She has been terribly wronged by her husband, but she wishes only to forget, largely for the sake of her son. She does not want him to know how bad a man his father was, and she does not want anyone else to know either. Her son, she believes, must inherit the legacy of a clean reputation. And so she has sunk her husband's entire estate into a charitable project, an orphanage that is to bear his name and glorify his reputation.

But Captain Alving comes back to haunt his wife, although she has done everything she can to put the dead man out of her mind and away from the consciousness of the boy. To her shock and dismay, the old Captain's vice survives in the person of their son. When he makes a pass at the serving girl in the dining room, and a tray crashes to the ground, she hears the ghosts of the play's title. That scene has been played before, when the boy's father seduced a serving maid and impregnated her with none other than this girl who is serving today in the same dining room. To keep the half brother from running away with his half sister, she will have to tell him the truth. But there is an even more horrifying truth coming to the surface in spite of anything Mrs. Alving can do to prevent it: the boy is sick with the syphilis he inherited from his father at birth, but he fears that he has somehow contracted the disease on his own, by living among artists in Paris. Of that burden, at least, she can relieve him.

She will tell him the truth at last and try to heal—not the nagging ghost—but the living boy. She will fail, of course. This ghost is voracious. The orphanage she built with the old man's money burns to the ground, uninsured. And the boy in her arms loses his mind to the dread disease. She is left, horribly, in the grip of a memory that will haunt her until she dies.

The Memory of Veterans

Veterans, typically, combine Electra and Mrs. Alving. They cling to some memories and try to shed others, but may be tortured by both. Performance helps.

In real life, the dead in a veteran's mind ask him why he did not save them (if they were his friends) or why he participated in their deaths (if they were his enemies). Medics, I believe, carry a heavy burden, remembering people on their own side whom they could not save. But even veterans of the so-called good war, World War II, have told me that they agonize over memories of German boys they have killed. A Jewish veteran has told me this, too.

The memories rise, like a road long covered by the risen waters of a lake, when the turbulence of a strong current makes the roughness underneath come to light. There are two ways that the true contours below the surface of water can become evident: one by draining the water, the other, the more interesting way, is by a flood that reveals the shape of the bottom in the turbulent forms of the current at the surface.

That is the image I used in the following poem. This is one of a series of poems I wrote in 1991, 21 years after my return, when the new war in the Persian Gulf awakened old thoughts. At the time, I named the series "Memories in Time of War":

Dreams, Rain

The old road rises, look—
like a dream of rockets.

White water stands in waves
at each pier, breaking high.

In dry days, I recall,
the river was relaxed,

its pools hid everything.
But the rain comes at night;
the river turns torrent.
Now all deep contours show,

especially the old road,
against the swift current.

True, startling as mortars,
impassable, the road

rises. Listen. The dead
stand, unhidden. They call.

(Paul Woodruff)[7]

Perhaps the truth will help—not merely telling it or writing it or acknowledging it, but giving it a temporary life through performance of war or its aftermath. Performance leads to a kind of human wisdom: Living a role as villain or victim or something in between gives one an understanding of the sources of human action. Allowing yourself to play your own role—or a role very like your own—gives you an opportunity to express things you would not dare to say among the people with whom you now live in peace. Violent things, frightened things.

Theater, I believe, is an ideal venue for the sort of performance that releases memory. I see two reasons for the success of theater in doing this. Both flow from the definition of the art of theater that I develop in my book on theater: the art of making human action worth watching in a measured space and for a measured time.[8]

The first reason theater helps is that theater is performed aside from the real world in a sanctified space that is insulated from our own lives, and therefore safer. What happens on stage, we feel, does not have to cross the line into our own lives. The action in a theatrical performance takes place in a space that has been marked off as sacred; the performers' action does not spill directly into our lives, and we in the audience may not normally enter the space of their action.[9]

The second reason for the success of theater in releasing memory is that what happens in theater can happen only for a defined period of time. In theater, as Aristotle famously noted, there is a beginning and an end. We give theater as much attention as we do partly because we know we will not be called upon to watch or listen forever. When the performance reaches closure—when the plot resolves its conflict—we are free to go home and resume our lives. When I as a veteran am involved in a performance that releases memories of war, I know that I will be safe in the long run. I can go back, after the curtain, to being who I am in peacetime.

The final applause will release me from memory into life—at least for now.

Staging My Own Memories: "Ithaca in Black and White"

After I returned from Vietnam I was soon troubled by the changes in me, in my home, and in the woman I loved. I read the *Odyssey* of Homer three times. When Odysseus returns but is unable to recognize his island, and when his wife Penelope is unable to recognize him, I understood. That is how I felt about my coming home, and how it did not feel like coming home at all: the place where I arrived was not home, the girl who welcomed me was not the same girl, and the boy she welcomed was not the same boy.

In 1974, three years after my return from Vietnam, I was still haunted by two men who had died while looking for me to bring help from the sky. They had been in a compound that came under attack in the small hours of the morning, and I was mission commander for a group of helicopters that was supposed to help them out and failed. They had been shattered by a VC rocket-propelled grenade fired at close range, one of them so badly that when I escorted his remains to Graves Registration I had to tell them that we did not have all of his bits and pieces. (The other lived on for a few days but could not be saved.) These two men kept presenting themselves in my mind, calling for help. As time went on I saw them more often, sometimes standing by the side of the road, looking for me to come to their rescue.

I wanted to get all of this out of my mind, so I could start my new life. And so I wrote a play, *Ithaca in Black and White*. I was 31, just 3 years away from separation from the army. In this play, I imagine a modern Ulysses coming home to his island and finding it completely alien, black and white after the exciting Technicolor of war. A black-and-white island, which cheats the memory of the brightly colored home he had left behind.

On his way home, Ulysses encounters his younger self, a boy who is reluctantly going off to engage in the endless war from which the older man has just now escaped. Ulysses takes the boy under his protection, and they arrive by ferryboat on the island. There they find that everyone has believed Ulysses to be dead. They visit the lavish tomb that the islanders have erected to Ulysses, who is represented as a hero in the war. Our Ulysses is in agony: he has lost all his soldiers, and he knows he is not a hero. He feels he is the scum of the earth. (As for me, I was horrified to receive an Air Medal with V for Valor after the event that took my two friends, but I had no words to protest. I threw it away, I think. Even now, 42 years later, this memory seems to plunge me into a black pit.)

The real Ulysses looks like a tramp, a hobo, a homeless vagrant, desperate and dangerous (as we veterans too often do), and the islanders treat him badly when he emerges from the tomb. The younger version, however, is recognized as Ulysses and given a hero's welcome, in spite of his protests. During the celebration, the old tramp strings the famous bow, but no one notices, and it makes no difference.

Penelope has taken on the role of a social worker with veterans and deserters from the war. In her great house on the island, she has provided shelter for many troubled young men. Their presence has sparked a rumor that they are competing for her hand in marriage, but she has never wavered. She helps them because they remind her of Ulysses, and she listens avidly to their stories in hope of hearing about him, or at least of coming to understand his experience. These are not the wealthy suitors of Homer's epic; they are merely the flotsam and jetsam of war, men who would otherwise be homeless. When they hear that Ulysses is home, they flee for fear of their lives.

Penelope accepts the young Ulysses (whose name is Jack) as her husband, but she does not like him at all. She decides to return to the mainland, perhaps to commence her own travels. At the ferry landing, she connects for the first time with the old tramp, whom she has heard about but seen only in passing.

The final scene of the play begins with her speaking to the unresponsive tramp, trying to explain her decision to leave her husband and the island. In a few minutes we will see this scene read by actors, but first I need to prepare you for what is coming, as the two principals struggle with their memories.

Here, two kinds of memory cross—the kind of memory that keeps escaping, and the kind of memory that will not go away. Penelope's memory of Ulysses has become a dream, and an unsatisfactory one at that:

> I did it all for him, well, not for him, exactly, how could I? It was a dream of him, a stupid dream, that was all I had, and I was lucky to have that. You know some nights I'd try to dream him up and he wouldn't come. I'd try and I'd try and I'd scrunch up my mind into knots and he wouldn't come.

Ulysses' memory of her is not much clearer. Now that he is on Ithaca, he can see that this is not the home he remembers, but when he is asked about the home he does remember, he becomes evasive. Its memory is not so vivid to him as that of the war he carries with him, and may carry with him his whole life. Penelope—still not recognizing him—asks him about his home. "Tell me about it," she says:

> *Ulysses:* Tell you what?
> *Penelope:* Your home, you idiot. You told me you were going home.
>   Tell me about it. (*Prompting him*) It must be someplace special.
> *Ulysses: (Evasively)* Yeah, I suppose so.
> *Penelope:* Well, what about it?
> *Ulysses:* Leave me alone! Where else would I go? Jesus!

And soon the memory he is trying to suppress bursts in on the one he cannot bring back. He tells her he fought with only one object, to come home, and while telling her this he brings up the friends he has lost in combat:

> *Ulysses:* Can you believe I had friends with me—in the war—I loved them. (*Interrupting himself*) You could get hurt over there. It was dangerous.
> *Penelope:* What were their names?
> *Ulysses:* Don't remind me. I'll kill you if you remind me. They…died or something. I had to leave them behind; I wanted to come *home*. It wasn't safe. Later, I did try…to find them. I wanted to come home so much.
> *Penelope:* Did you find them?
> *Ulysses:* Home was everything. I had to come home.

Penelope: You didn't find them.

Ulysses: I didn't find any pieces that were big enough, really. I'm telling you about my home, don't you understand?

And so in this one line, the sought-for memories of home clash with the dreaded memories of the dead, and here I slipped out onto the stage the slightest hint of the memory I kept under wraps.

Ulysses and Penelope see that they have had a common experience with memory, and they sit in silence at the end of this scene, beginning to share an understanding. They will cross to the mainland, leaving the island, and we feel they have the potential not to restore an old relationship, but to start something new.

Here is the scene, without commentary:

Penultimate Scene from "Ithaca in Black and White"[10]

ANNOUNCER (offstage radio voice) This story has a moral: Persevere, be patient, do not despair. After the years of waiting, after the trials and the search, after Scylla and the Sirens, Polyphemus and Circe, after the temptations of lonely princesses on magic islands; after the necessary lies and bloody retributions—here, at the end of everything, lies Ithaca, her beaches strewn with magic treasure.

(A bare stage. We hear sounds of the sea, gulls, and a bell buoy. ULYSSES sits, center, on his barracks bag, head down, dejected. PENELOPE hurries across from left to right balancing a huge suitcase. Moments later she returns without it. We see she is dressed to travel. She observes ULYSSES for a while. He does not move.)

PENELOPE You're here. That's good.

(ULYSSES does not respond.)

Don't say a thing. You don't need to.

(He still does not respond.)

I'm trying to say, I don't need your help anymore, I mean, with Ulysses.

(In a bright, quick voice.)

I've given up on him. I feel wonderful. It's a great weight off my shoulders. I haven't felt this good since, well, since…Well, it was before he left. You can't imagine how awful it was. You don't ever want to be left like that. I had to slave for him, night in and day out, night and day. I kept his farm together, I ran after his crazy father, I even listened to his old Sarah. Have you heard Sarah, I mean *heard* her? It could kill an ox, listening to her. Then, later, I had the old soldiers, you know, all my young men. They were so beautiful and sad and angry it tore my heart up. That was it, years of it, day in and night out and I did it all for him, well, not for *him,* exactly, how could I, it was a dream of him, a stupid dream, that was all I had, and I was lucky to have that. You know, some nights I'd try to dream him up, and he wouldn't come.

(ULYSSES looks up now; he is listening.)

I'd try and I'd try and I'd scrunch up my mind into knots and he wouldn't come. I was so stupid, I did all that for him, *all that,* for him, for a stupid dream. He's a gorgeous chunk of a man and I love him, of course, as Sarah would say, of course I love him. But, you know, when a dream comes true it can give you the creeps. I don't know why.

(Deep breath.)

Anyway, I'm leaving the island. Don't ask me what's wrong with him. There isn't anything wrong with him. He's a dreamboat. He was fine, in his place.

(ULYSSES continues to look questions at her.)

I'm sorry, I'm awful. I've been tracking you down for days, I said I wanted to hear your story, and now I finally have you to myself, and I don't give you a chance to say *anything.* I'll try to be calm.

(Beat)

Where will you go now?

ULYSSES I don't know. Home.

PENELOPE Why?

ULYSSES It's a habit with me. I'm good at it. I could go on forever like this, I guess.

PENELOPE Will you…Will you tell me about it?

ULYSSES *(Standing, moving away from her, left)*

About what?

PENELOPE Your home, you idiot. You said you were going home. Tell me about it. It must be someplace special.

ULYSSES *(Evasively)*

Yeah, I suppose so.

PENELOPE Well, what about it?

ULYSSES *(Turns, angry)*

Leave me alone. Where else would I go? Jesus.

PENELOPE Is it beautiful?

ULYSSES I don't remember. Leave me alone.

(But ULYSSES continues to look questions at her. PENELOPE looks at her watch, then anxiously out to sea, right. She paces.)

It was *important.* I remember, it's important.

(PENELOPE stops to listen.)

It means something. What you do makes a difference there. Look, I'm talking about my *life,* my *life* was there. I had to leave it all there, even my mind I think, I left my mind behind. I was an idiot, I left everything on that island. I didn't exist, I wasn't anything at all.

PENELOPE You were a soldier.

ULYSSES Listen, you don't know how I wanted to come home. I killed for it, I did everything for it. Real soldiers, I guess they fight to win, or something, whatever that is. *I* did it to come home. Can you believe I had friends with me—in the war—I loved them. You could get hurt over there, it was dangerous.

PENELOPE What were their names?

ULYSSES *(Angry)*

Don't remind me! I'll kill you if you remind me; they…died or something. I had to leave them behind, I wanted to come *home,* it wasn't safe. Later I did try…to find them. I wanted to come home so much.

PENELOPE Did you find them?

ULYSSES Home was everything. I had to come home.

PENELOPE You didn't find them.

ULYSSES I didn't find any pieces that were big enough, really.
(Interrupting himself)

I'm telling you about my home, don't you understand?

PENELOPE So it *was* beautiful?

ULYSSES What?

PENELOPE Your home. It was beautiful as friendship.

ULYSSES It had to be.

(ULYSSES sits again as at the start of the scene.)

It had to be, all that. And I tried to dream about it sometimes. It wasn't easy.

PENELOPE I know.

(She sits next him, but not romantically, on the barracks bag. They are silent for some time, connected for the first time through their experience of memory.)

Notes

*This is a lightly edited transcript of a talk given at the conference at New York University on December 4, 2011, ending with a performance by actors from the Aquila Theater Company, Nathan Flower and Michelle Vasquez.

1. A memory-enhancing drug may improve the speed and effectiveness of prolonged exposure therapy for posttraumatic stress disorder (PTSD) patients, according to a new pilot study by psychologists at The University of Texas at Austin, the University of Washington and the University of Pennsylvania. (University of Texas Press Release, November 2, 2011. <http://homepage.psy.utexas.edu/homepage/group/telchlab/home.htm>)
2. Luis Bunuel, *My Last Sigh*, quoted in Doerr (2010, iii).
3. See O'Brien (1990).
4. Translation is my own, published in Meineck and Woodruff (2007).
5. In ancient Greece the prevailing view was that grief should have a time limit. But anger over a murder must burn on until justice has been done. See Konstan (2006, 248–53). Controversy flared in classical times, however, over what the limits to grief should be. One reason Plato rejected Homer and tragic poets was their tendency to celebrate grief.

6. Sophocles' audience may have connected the plot of *Electra* to civil war—to the events in 411 that suspended democracy for a time, and then restored freedom. Note the unusual word *eleutheria* (freedom) in the final speech of the chorus (Konstan [2008, 77–80]).

7. Published in *Rattle: Poetry for the 21st Century* Volume 6 (2000), 119.

8. Woodruff (2008).

9. See Woodruff, (2008 [108–22]).

10. I wrote the play in the summer of 1974 and edited it thereafter. It was produced by an ad hoc group in 1983 under the direction of Sandra Fountain, in Austin, where it won a local award.

Works Cited

Doerr, Anthony. 2010. *The Memory Wall*. New York: Scribner.

Konstan, David. 2006. *The Emotions of the Ancient Greeks: Studies in Aristotle and Classical Literature*. Toronto: University of Toronto Press.

———. 2008. "Sophocles' *Electra* as Political Allegory: A Suggestion." *Classical Philology* 103: 77–80.

Meineck, Peter, and Paul Woodruff. 2007. *Sophocles: Four Tragedies*. Indianapolis, IN: Hackett Publishing Company.

O'Brien, Tim. 1990. "The Lives of the Dead." In *The Things They Carried*. Franklin Center, PA: Franklin Library, 255–73.

Woodruff, Paul. 2008. *The Necessity of Theater*. New York: Oxford University Press.

CONTRIBUTORS

Jason Crowley studied at the University of Manchester, and after a brief period of (happy) exile at the University of Nottingham, he now lectures, mere yards from his first intellectual home, at the Manchester Metropolitan University. His main research interest is the human experience of war and conflict, a topic explored in his first monograph, *The Psychology of the Athenian Hoplite: The Culture of Combat at Classical Athens* (Cambridge, 2012).

Juan Sebastian De Vivo received his PhD in Classical Archaeology and an MA in Cultural and Social Anthropology from Stanford University. His research centers upon warfare and material culture in the Greece, with particular interest on the late archaic and early classical period. He served as assistant professor/faculty fellow in the Department of Classics at NYU. He was also fellow at the Humanities Initiative at NYU and a Fellow at the Getty Research Institute.

Sharon L. James is associate professor of Classics at the University of North Carolina, Chapel Hill. She earned her BA degrees in Classics and Spanish Literature at the University of California, Santa Cruz, and her graduate degrees in Comparative Literature at the University of California, Berkeley. Her primary fields of research are Latin poetry, Roman comedy, and women in antiquity. She is the author of *Learned Girls and Male Persuasion: Gender and Reading in Roman Love Elegy* (2003), and is completing a book on women in Greek and Roman New Comedy. In 2012 she co-directed the NEH Summer Institute, "Roman Comedy in Performance."

David Konstan is Professor of Classics at New York University and Professor Emeritus of Classics and Comparative Literature at Brown University. He has published books on friendship in the classical world, pity, the emotions of the ancient Greeks, and forgiveness, and has recently completed a manuscript on the ancient Greek conception of beauty. He is a fellow of the American Academy of Arts and Sciences.

Peter Meineck is an associate professor of Classics at New York University and Honorary Professor of Classics at the University of Nottingham. He was educated at University College London, the University of Nottingham, and by the Royal Marines. He is the founding director of New York's Aquila Theatre and has directed and/or produced over 60 professional stage productions. He was director of the *Ancient Greeks / Modern Lives* and *YouStories* humanities veteran programs. He has published numerous translations of ancient drama and has published widely on ancient performance and the application of cognitive studies to theater in antiquity. He is also a Firefighter with the Bedford Fire Department in New York and a New York State Emergency Medical Technician

S. Sara Monoson is Professor of Political Science and Classics at Northwestern University. She is the author of *Plato's Democratic Entanglements: Athenian Politics and the Practice of Philosophy* (Princeton, 2000) and a wide range of essays on ancient political theory, including, "Dionysius I and Sicilian Theatrical Traditions in Plato's *Republic*" in *Theater Outside Athens*, edited by Kathryn Bosher (Cambridge, 2012). Her current projects include *Socrates in the Vernacular*, a study of the reception of the story of Socrates in contemporary American culture.

Corinne Pache is associate professor of Classical Studies at Trinity University. Her interests include Greek archaic poetry and the modern reception of ancient epic. She is currently working on a book project, *Remembering Penelope*, on the reception of Penelope in recent literature and film. Publications include "'So Say We All'—Reimagining Empire and the *Aeneid*." *Classical Outlook* 87 (2010); "*A Moment's Ornament:*" *The Poetics of Nympholepsy in Ancient Greece* (Oxford University Press, 2011); and "Woman Trouble: True Love and Homecoming in Almodóvar's *Volver*," in *Screening Love and Sex in the Ancient World*, edited by Monica S. Cyrino (Palgrave Macmillan, 2013).

Thomas G. Palaima is the Robert M. Armstrong Centennial Professor of Classics and Director of the Program in Aegean Scripts and Prehistory at the University of Texas at Austin. The recipient of a MacArthur Fellowship (1985–1990) and three Fulbright awards (1979–1980, 1992–1993, and 2007), he has written and lectured widely on human creative responses to war and violence and on music and songs as social commentary. Since 1999, he has been a regular contributor of opinion pieces to the *Austin American-Statesman* and of book reviews and feature pieces to the *Times Higher Education*.

Kurt A. Raaflaub is David Herlihy University Professor and Professor of Classics and History emeritus at Brown University. His work has focused on Greek and Roman political, social, and intellectual history, war and society, and the comparative history of ancient civilizations. His publications include *The Discovery of Freedom in Ancient Greece* (2004), *Origins of Democracy in Ancient Greece* (co-authored, 2007), and edited volumes on *War and Society in the Ancient World* (1999) and *War and Peace in the Ancient World* (2007).

Nancy Sorkin Rabinowitz is Professor of Comparative Literature at Hamilton College. She is the author of *Anxiety Veiled: Euripides and the Traffic in Women* (1993) and *Greek Tragedy* (2008), and coeditor of *Feminist Theory and the Classics* (with Amy Richlin, 1993), and *Among Women: From the Homosocial to the Homoerotic in the Ancient World* (with Lisa Auanger, 2002), *Sex in Antiquity: Essays on Gender and Sexuality in the Ancient World* (with James Robson and Mark Masterson, 2014), and *From Abortion to Pederasty: Addressing Difficult Topics in the Classics Classroom* (2014).

William H. Race, George L. Paddison Professor of Classics at the University of North Carolina at Chapel Hill, is the author of books on Pindar, Apollonius Rhodius, and the Classical Poetic Tradition; and numerous articles on Homer, Sappho, Pindar, Sophocles, and Horace. He served in Vietnam as a 1st Lieutenant, Army Artillery, 1966–1967.

Nancy Sherman is a University Professor and Professor of Philosophy at Georgetown University. In 1997–1999, she served as the inaugural holder of the distinguished chair in Ethics at the United States Naval Academy. She is the author of *The Untold War: Inside the Hearts, Minds, and Souls of our Soldiers* (W. W. Norton 2010); *Stoic Warriors: The Ancient Philosophy Behind the Military Mind* (Oxford 2005); *Making A Necessity of Virtue: Aristotle and Kant on Virtue* (Cambridge 1997); and *The Fabric of Character: Aristotle's Theory of Virtue* (Oxford 1989). She is also the editor of *Critical Essays on the Classics: Aristotle's Ethics* (Rowman and Littlefield 1999). In October of 2005, Sherman was part of a small team invited by the assistant secretary of Defense for Health Affairs to visit Guantanamo Bay Detention Center to observe and advise on medical and psychological conditions of detainees and matters of medical ethics. In 2011, she was invited as an observer to the Vice Chief of the Army's Suicide Review Board. Sherman's father served in World War II as an Army medic. When he died at the age of 89, Sherman found his dog tags in his trouser pockets. He had carried them with him for over 60 years.

Alan H. Sommerstein is Emeritus Professor of Greek at the University of Nottingham. He has worked mainly on Greek tragedy (editing the Loeb *Aeschylus,* 2008; coediting Sophocles: Selected Fragmentary Plays, 2006–2012; *The Tangled Ways of Zeus,* 2010), Old Comedy (*The Comedies of Aristophanes,* 1980–2002; *Talking About Laughter,* 2009), and ancient oaths (*Oath and State in Ancient Greece,* with Andrew Bayliss and others, 2012; *Oaths and Swearing in Ancient Greece,* with Isabelle Torrance and others, 2014); his edition of Menander's *Samia* appeared in late 2013. He is editor of the *Encyclopedia of Greek Comedy* (in preparation). His father, Theophil (Teddy) Sommerstein (1909–1990), a refugee from Nazi Vienna, became one of what were known as the "King's Own Enemy Aliens," serving with the Royal Engineers from Normandy to central Germany.

Lawrence A. Tritle is Daum Research Professor of History (2012) at Loyola Marymount University. Trained in the field of ancient history (PhD, Chicago, 1978), Tritle has published widely in the field of classical Greece, including *From Melos to My Lai. War and Survival* (2000) and *A New History of the Peloponnesian War* (2010). *The Oxford Handbook of Warfare in the Classical World*, edited with Brian Campbell (Belfast), appeared in January 2013. A combat veteran of the Vietnam War (1970, 1LT, Infantry, US Army), Tritle's research interests focus on comparative war and violence, on those who fight as well as the broader impact on culture and society.

Paul Woodruff has been teaching Philosophy and Classics at the University of Texas at Austin since 1973. His books include *Reverence: Renewing a Forgotten Virtue* (2001), *First Democracy: The Challenge of an Ancient Idea* (2005), *The Necessity of Theater* (2008), and (most recently) *The Ajax Dilemma* (2011), which concerns justice and the disparity of rewards. He has also written plays, poetry, short fiction, and opera libretti, as well as translations from the Greek of Plato, Sophocles, and Thucydides. His play *Ithaca in Black and White* (written 1974, revised 1982) won a B. Iden Payne Award for best new script produced in Austin in 1983. He was born in New Jersey, raised in western Pennsylvania, and educated at Princeton and Oxford Universities. He served as a junior officer in the United States Army with MACV at Chau Doc in the Delta of Vietnam from June 1969 to June 1970. Since 1988 he was involved in administration at the University of Texas as department chair (1988–1991), director of the University's Plan II Honors Program (1991–2006), and Dean of the School of Undergraduate Studies (2006–2012).

INDEX

Printed in the United States of America